HUMAN RESOURCE DEVELOPMENT

DAVID McGUIRE

HUMAN RESOURCE DEVELOPMENT

SECOND EDITION

Los Angeles | London | New Delhi
Singapore | Washington DC

Los Angeles | London | New Delhi
Singapore | Washington DC

SAGE Publications Ltd
1 Oliver's Yard
55 City Road
London EC1Y 1SP

SAGE Publications Inc.
2455 Teller Road
Thousand Oaks, California 91320

SAGE Publications India Pvt Ltd
B 1/I 1 Mohan Cooperative Industrial Area
Mathura Road
New Delhi 110 044

SAGE Publications Asia-Pacific Pte Ltd
3 Church Street
#10-04 Samsung Hub
Singapore 049483

Editor: Kirsty Smy
Assistant editor: Nina Smith
Production editor: Sarah Cooke
Copyeditor: Jane Fricker
Proofreader: Neil Dowden
Indexer: Silvia Benvenuto
Marketing manager: Alison Borg
Cover design: Francis Kenney
Typeset by: C&M Digitals (P) Ltd, Chennai, India
Printed and bound in Great Britain by Ashford
Colour Press Ltd

Library of Congress Control Number: 2013951816

British Library Cataloguing in Publication data

A catalogue record for this book is available from
the British Library

ISBN 978-1-4462-5661-9
ISBN 978-1-4462-5662-6 (pbk)

MIX
Paper from
responsible sources
FSC
www.fsc.org   FSC® C011748

Contents

Figures

Tables

About the Author

David McGuire, PhD, is senior lecturer in human resource development at Edinburgh Napier University. A graduate of the University of Limerick and National University of Ireland, Galway, David teaches undergraduate and postgraduate classes in the areas of HRD, leadership and managing diversity. A former Fulbright and Government of Ireland scholar, David is Associate Editor of *Advances in Developing Human Resources*. He sits on four editorial boards (*Human Resource Development Quarterly*, *Advances in Developing Human Resources*, *Journal of Change Management* and *European Journal of Training and Development*). In 2008, David received the Early Career Scholar award from the Academy of Human Resource Development. He is Chief External Examiner at Staffordshire University. His e-mail address is: d.mcguire@napier.ac.uk.

Preface

Human resource development (HRD) is an evolving, dynamic, ever-changing field. It is shaped by the global environment and the people and organisations that work within it. To comprehensively capture the field of HRD within the confines of one book is an impossible task – so herewith is a snapshot of the field, opening up to you, the reader, opportunities and possibilities for further investigation and research.

This textbook seeks to introduce readers to the key debates and challenges within the field of HRD. It aims to cover the key aspects of the field and provide a useful synthesis of research across 15 disciplinary areas. While the textbook is principally oriented towards research and a critical viewpoint, there is much within the text to satisfy the interests of practitioners. To this end, the textbook should inform evidence-based practice and open up a menu of possibilities for advancing organisational practice.

From a pedagogical point of view, each of the chapters includes a set of learning objectives, two 'talking points' (which are brief case vignettes, designed to show HRD in action and provoke dialogue and discussion), an end-of-chapter case study (which in most cases provides an organisational application of the concepts discussed in the chapter) and a set of discussion questions, whereby readers can test their knowledge of the contents discussed in the chapter.

Chapter 1 sets out to unearth the foundations of human resource development. It traces the origins of HRD and looks at the early struggles to clearly define and demarcate the field. In doing so, it explores the multidisciplinary nature of the field and examines differences in emphasis between the US and Europe. It identifies the practical challenges facing the field and identifies the need for HRD to develop its empirical base as well as providing practitioners with useful tools to strengthen the competitiveness of organisations. Finally, the chapter discusses critical dimensions of HRD – a theme that is followed up in subsequent chapters.

The remainder of the textbook is organised into three sections recognising that HRD operates at the individual, organisational and community/societal level of analysis.

Part 1 of the textbook explores the value and application of HRD at the individual level. It recognises that people lie at the heart of HRD's effectiveness and that people are an organisation's most important resource.

Chapter 2 explores how adults learn. It provides a synopsis of the three key schools of learning, namely cognitivism, behaviourism and humanism. It reviews the key tenets underpinning each of the three schools, examining the learning and development implications that emerge. The final section examines critical theory approaches to learning and critiques the role of individuals, educationalists and professional bodies in the learning process.

Chapter 3 recognises the importance of creativity in human resource development. It examines barriers to employee creativity in the workplace and outlines a framework for fostering creativity around the three dimensions of positionality, perspective and perception. Positionality considers the situatedness of creativity and its connectedness to individual identity and historic and cultural context. Perspective acknowledges that creativity is an outcome of one's cognitive style, experiences and risk-taking disposition, while perception sees creativity as being influenced by the work environment, level of leader support and employee motivation. The chapter concludes that further research needs to focus on how to empower employee creativity and investigate group and team creativity in more depth.

Chapter 4 examines the concept of careers and how the notion of career has changed in the last three decades. It looks at how careers are defined and outlines the key principles underpinning five career concepts, namely boundaryless career, protean career, authentic career, kaleidoscope career and the portfolio career. The chapter then goes on to look at the importance of career counselling, focusing in particular on two well-known and widely used instruments – Schein's Career Anchors Inventory and Holland's Vocational Preference Inventory. The chapter concludes with a brief exploration of the benefits of continuing professional development.

Chapter 5 investigates the importance of identity and diversity issues in HRD. For too long, the field of HRD has neglected employee difference and this chapter provides a useful commentary on the role that HRD can adopt as a diversity champion in the workplace. The chapter examines the spread of diversity training in the workplace, exploring the objectives, rationale and social and organisational goals underpinning such training. In particular, the chapter explores the obstacles faced by employees arising from their gender, race or sexuality and identifies interventions that can be used to promote openness to diversity in the workplace.

Part 2 of the textbook examines how HRD operates at the organisational level. It seeks to build an understanding of how HRD can help employees interact with organisational systems, structures and processes more effectively. It recognises that learning and growth lies at the heart of HRD and that investment in employees is critical if organisations are to attain competitive advantages in the marketplace.

Chapter 6 examines one of the core aspects of human resource development – namely training and development. Rather than review a range of training interventions in isolation, this chapter seeks to compare a selection of commonly used interventions across eight separate training dimensions: learning theory; knowledge–skills mix; training transferability; degree of learner involvement; locus of initiation; degree of reflection; individual/social interaction; and cost. This approach is designed to help practitioners make a more informed choice in their selection of training interventions.

Chapter 7 reviews the literature on training evaluation. It assesses the core function of evaluation as one of understanding cause-and-effect in making more effective organisational decisions. It briefly considers evaluation from ontological and epistemological perspectives and moves on to look at Kirkpatrick's Four Levels typology and other commonly used evaluation models in the literature. The final two sections of the chapter examine the concepts of benchmarking and the balanced scorecard and highlight the value of these approaches to practitioners.

Chapter 8 embarks upon an analysis of the role of HRD in performance management. It investigates the adoption of competency-based approaches to managing learning and development in organisations. It then looks at the role of line managers and assesses the range of responsibilities falling upon line-manager shoulders in downsized and devolved organisations. The chapter then briefly examines the three concepts of coaching, mentoring and employee counselling before exploring talent development and how leaders can positively affect the performance management process.

Chapter 9 focuses attention on the area of strategic HRD. It first examines the global setting for HRD and the factors affecting how organisations are operating and structuring themselves in today's uncertain economic environment. A synthesis is provided of six of the key strategic HRD models that have been developed over the last two decades. This is followed by a discussion of the barriers affecting the successful implementation of strategic HRD approaches in organisations.

Chapter 10 discusses the literature on organisational learning. It focuses on the significance of organisational learning, highlighting in particular the contribution of Argyris and Schon and examining single-, double- and triple-loop learning. The chapter moves on to look at the learning organisation concept, taking as its starting point Senge's Five Disciplines. It then explores other perspectives on the learning organisation and steps that organisations can take to embed learning at the heart of their processes.

Chapter 11 provides an overview of the theory and practice in the area of knowledge management. It explores the emergence of the knowledge economy and the central role played by knowledge workers. It examines the significance of knowledge in organisations and defines the concept of the 'ba'. It then considers knowledge creation and knowledge conversion processes before identifying four forms of knowledge that exist in organisations. The role of HRD in knowledge management is then considered.

Chapter 12 produces a synthesis of the literature on leadership development. The chapter reviews research on four prominent leadership approaches (trait, behavioural, contingency, transformational), looking specifically at the developmental implications flowing from each leadership approach. The chapter argues that to date, much discussion on leadership theories has clearly distinguished various traits and characteristics that effective leaders need to have, but has provided little detail on how such traits and characteristics should be developed. The chapter concludes that leadership remains an elusive concept, being shaped and affected by a range of forces. In turn, leadership development is thus a complex process necessitating leadership development consultants to work across all four leadership approaches in developing and delivering well-rounded and effective interventions.

Part 3 of the textbook acknowledges the role of HRD at the community/societal level. In recent times, it is increasingly recognised that HRD has an important role to play in building and developing communities and operating on a cross-national and international basis.

Chapter 13 focuses on the emerging field of international HRD. It examines the cross-cultural applicability of HRD concepts and how HRD interventions can be usefully exported across national boundaries. It presents a framework for examining international HRD, identifying four separate phases in the internationalisation process (multi-domestic, international, multinational and transnational). For each phase, the framework examines the characteristics of the organisation under the headings of structural issues, cultural issues and HRD issues. The chapter concludes that HRD has an important role to play in the internationalisation process and in ensuring the maximisation of organisational efficiencies.

Chapter 14 looks at the role that HRD can play in advancing awareness and understanding of the challenges posed by climate change. It presents a framework though which HRD tools and interventions can be deployed to further organisational sustainability goals and advances the notion of 'Green HRD' – namely a mechanism for transforming self, others and the organisation as prudent users of natural and human-made resources for the benefit of present and future generations.

Chapter 15 considers the role of HRD at the community and societal level. It looks at the increasing levels of attention being given to the issue of corporate social responsibility in organisations, before moving on to examine ethics in HRD. The transformative role of HRD at the national and international level is then examined, with particular emphasis given to the tools that HRD possesses which can be applied effectively at the societal level.

Conclusion and appendix

The conclusion to the textbook presents some thoughts on the state of the field of HRD. It reviews the proposition that HRD exists at the individual, organisational and societal level, and advances a vision for the future of HRD. It argues that HRD is in a constant state of evolution, responding to organisational and environmental change. It identifies a need for the field to develop its empirical base and to continue to foster dynamism and promote diversity of thought.

An appendix to the textbook provides advice and guidance to students undertaking HRD examinations. It showcases examples of examination answers to two HRD questions – these examples are graded at a high, medium and bare-pass level. In presenting these examples along with examiner feedback, it is hoped that students will be able to identify the hallmarks of effective examination answers.

In wrapping up this preface, it is important to recognise that human resource development is a powerful tool empowering individuals, organisations and societies to compete effectively in a global marketplace. It harnesses the latent capabilities of individuals helping them achieve real progress in the organisations, communities and societies where they live. In so doing, HRD practitioners through the application of their skills and talents can make a real difference to the lives of people across the world.

Acknowledgements

I wish to thank my gorgeous wife Fiona and beautiful daughter Amie for their constant love and support during the writing of this book. I am also grateful to the McGuire and Baxter families for their kindness, support and friendship. I would like to acknowledge the advice and insights provided by colleagues at Edinburgh Napier University and former colleagues at Queen Margaret University and Oakland University, Michigan. I would like to thank Dr Thomas Garavan (Edinburgh Napier University), David O'Donnell (Intellectual Capital Institute of Ireland) and Prof. Maria Cseh (George Washington University) for being mentors to me and introducing me to the field of HRD. I would like to acknowledge with appreciation the contributions of Kenneth Mølbjerg Jørgensen and colleagues for their valuable inputs to the first edition of the textbook. Thanks to Robin Grenier for her help and support in writing the creativity chapter. I am grateful for the support and encouragement of Kirsty Smy and Nina Smith (Sage Publishing) and Jane Fricker (copyeditor), who all did a wonderful job. Finally, a word of gratitude to my friends and colleagues within the AHRD and UFHRD for the hand of friendship offered to me over the last 15 years. You are a great bunch of people!

Dr David McGuire
Edinburgh Napier University

Guided Tour

Chapter Objectives Bulleted lists of objectives at the start of each chapter outline what you can expect to learn.

Talking Points Case vignettes highlight HRD in action and provoke critical analysis and discussion.

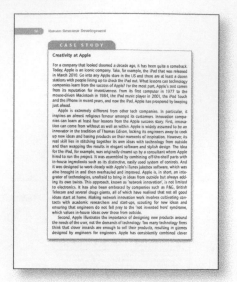

End of Chapter Case Studies with Questions Case studies of high profile organisations will help you to relate theory and real-world practice.

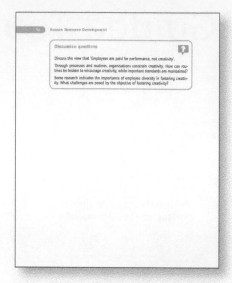

Discussion Questions Test your understanding of the chapter and are ideal for revision.

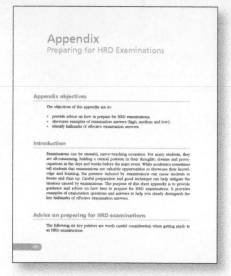

Appendix Provides advice and guidance to students undertaking HRD examinations, including examples of examination answers graded at a high, medium and bare-pass level, along with examiner feedback.

About the Companion Website

Human Resource Development, second edition, by David McGuire is supported by a companion website.

Visit **www.sagepub.co.uk/Mcguire** to access the following resources:

For Lecturers

Instructor's Manual: containing tutor notes for each chapter to support your teaching.

PowerPoint Slides: including key points from each chapter.

For Students

Additional Case Studies: Engaging and relevant case studies to help illustrate the main concepts in each chapter.

Web Links: Explore topics further with a selection of useful websites and videos.

SAGE Online Journals: Deepen your understanding by engaging with relevant SAGE journal articles.

Foundations of Human Resource Development

The objectives of this chapter are to:

- investigate the historical origins of human resource development and its interdisciplinary roots;
- explore the various ways in which HRD has been defined;
- consider a range of metaphors used to describe the field of HRD;
- review the criticisms levelled at the theory and practice of HRD;
- examine the emergence of critical HRD.

Introduction

Human resource development (HRD) is in a state of becoming. With these words, Lee (2001) describes the emerging field of HRD. From its origins (Harbison and Myers, 1964; Nadler, 1970), HRD has evolved as a field of theory and practice with a distinctive tripartite agenda of human betterment, organisational enhancement and societal development. The transformative power of HRD lies in its capacity to empower the creation of innovative and radical solutions to real-world problems.

HRD has evolved to meet the changing individual, organisational and societal environment it inhabits. Its historical development has mirrored changes in the nature of work and reflects the diverse cultures and values it occupies. Alagaraja and Dooley (2003) trace the development of HRD to the work of the toolmaker in constructing human axes leading to the development of agriculture and animal husbandry in the era 5 million to 3000 BC. Swanson and Holton (2001) trace the roots of HRD back to the legacy of the Greeks and Romans (100 BC–300 AD), while Ruona (2001a) identifies the Training Within Industry (TWI) agency in the 1940s as being pivotal to the emergence of contemporary HRD. McGuire and Cseh (2006) highlight some of the more recent key milestones in the development of the field as the publication of Malcolm Knowles' *The Modern Practice of Adult Education: From Pedagogy to Andragogy*, the publication of Nadler's *Developing Human Resources* and the foundation of the Academy of Human Resource Development.

Founded upon the long-established fields of training, education and development, HRD has grown to encompass new emerging fields of knowledge including social capital, knowledge management and the learning organisation (McGoldrick et al., 2002a). By embracing new thinking and focusing on activities and processes intended to improve individual and organisational learning, HRD will inform, shape and remain relevant to professional practice. Notwithstanding these benefits, HRD currently suffers from a limited empirical base and much HRD research has focused on particular organisational contexts (Hamlin, 2002).

This opening chapter explores how HRD is defined and how the shape and nature of HRD have changed over time. It examines the disciplinary origins of the field and explores briefly the role played by HRD practitioners. An examination of criticisms levelled at the field is undertaken and this is followed by an exploration of critical approaches to HRD. The chapter concludes by summarising the key points and assessing the overall potential of the field to add value to individuals and organisations.

Defining HRD

Despite numerous attempts to define the field of HRD, consensus does not yet exist on a specific definition for what HRD is and includes. Attempts to define HRD have preoccupied HRD academics for many years and have led to much debate in journal writings (McGuire and Cseh, 2006; McLean and McLean, 2001; Ruona, 2000; Weinberger, 1998). This led Ruona (2000) to suggest that a major barrier to HRD is that the work of HRD academics and professionals and what HRD stands for are not yet well understood by others. She maintains that the HRD community have not done a good job of working to identify who we are, what we stand for and what we can do for those we serve. It is arguable that the lack of clarity regarding definitional boundaries and conceptual underpinnings may be due to the multidisciplinary and omnivorous nature of the field. In support of this view, Lincoln and Lynham (2007) maintain that HRD calls upon and integrates existing theories to create its unique disciplinary theory and that good theory is imperative to sound, informed practice and the continued development and maturity of a discipline.

The multidisciplinary nature of the field of HRD has been long established. Chalofsky (2004) argues that HRD has been long considered to have a interdisciplinary foundation and maintains that human and organisation studies may describe more accurately the content and substance of HRD. Similarly, Hatcher (2006) maintains that we cannot become complacent about defining such a complex, multidisciplinary field as HRD. He argues that the strength of the field of HRD lies in its multidimensional nature and that while one-dimensional approaches may solve immediate problems, they exacerbate long-term needs. Meanwhile, Swanson and Holton (2001: 145–146) articulate what they see as the core foundational tenets of HRD, namely 'a strong belief in learning and development as avenues to individual growth; a belief that organisations can be improved through learning and development activities; a commitment to people and human potential; a deep desire to see people grow as individuals and a passion for learning'.

Several authors have refused to define HRD. Blake (1995) argues that the field of HRD defies definition and boundaries. He maintains that it has become difficult to put in a box and has become so large, extensive and inclusive that it now has wide, global-reaching boundaries. Lee (2001) refuses to define HRD as she argues that to proffer definitions of HRD is to misrepresent it as a thing of *being* rather than a process of *becoming*. She also argues that defining the field runs the risk of disengaging from the moral dimension of HRD. McGoldrick et al. (2002b) posit that attempts to define HRD have proved frustrating, confusing and elusive. Specifically, they state that the process of defining HRD is frustrated by the apparent lack of boundaries and parameters, elusiveness is created through the lack of depth of empirical evidence of some conceptual aspect of HRD and confusion arises over the philosophy, purpose, location and language of HRD. An earlier contribution by Stewart and McGoldrick (1996) maintains that while no definitive consensus has been reached on the composition of HRD, it comprises strategic and practical components. In addition, they propose that HRD is implicit in organising and managing, and concerns itself with leadership, culture, organisational learning and development and change. Moreover, McLean and Wang (2007) suggest that for some commentators HRD appears to be inwardly directed and without substantial impact. They question whether the lack of definitional consensus is harmful to the field and could potentially lead to the collapse of the field itself.

An examination of the literature also reveals that HRD has been developed from different traditions in Europe and the US. Woodall (2003) argues that in a UK context, there tends to be a close alignment of HRD with human resource management (HRM) programmes, which contrasts strongly with the close association of HRD with adult education within the US. Such differences invariably lead to variation in the focus, direction and overall purpose and goals of HRD. Similarly, Hilton and McLean (1997) maintain that the definition of HRD varies from one country to another and national differences are a crucial factor in determining the way in which HRD professionals work.

Table 1.1 presents a collection of definitions of HRD found in the literature. Examining these definitions provides an insight into the development of the field over time and the interests served by HRD. The earliest definition by Harbison and Myers acknowledges the role HRD plays at an economic and societal level. It views HRD as a vehicle for the modernisation and advancement of society as a whole. This definition contrasts with the emphasis placed by later definitions which tend to focus on the interests of individuals or organisations. There is some evidence of recent expansion of the boundaries of HRD (McLean and Wang, 2007). For their part, Donovan and Marsick (2000) maintain that HRD now includes organisational leadership, organisational values, workforce development and labour economics. Dilworth (2003) includes strategic change management, knowledge management, insourcing and outsourcing of training, team-building and leadership development within the boundaries of HRD.

Table 1.1   Definitions of human resource development found in literature

Author	Definition
Harbison and Myers (1964)	HRD is the process of increasing the knowledge, the skills and the capacities of all the people in a society. In economic terms, it could be described as the accumulation of human capital and its effective investment in the development of an economy. In political terms, HRD prepares people for adult participation in political processes, particularly as citizens in a democracy. From the social and cultural points of view, the development of human resources helps people to lead fuller and richer lives, less bound by tradition. In short, the processes of HRD unlock the door to modernization.
Nadler (1970)	HRD is a series of organised activities conducted within a specific time and designed to produce behavioural change.
Craig (1976)	HRD focuses on the central goal of developing human potential in every aspect of lifelong learning.
Jones (1981)	HRD is a systematic expansion of people's work-related abilities, focused on the attainment of both organisation and personal goals.
Chalofsky and Lincoln (1983)	The discipline of HRD is the study of how individuals and groups in organisations change through learning.
Smith (1988)	HRD consists of programmes and activities, direct and indirect, instructional and/or individual that possibly affect the development of the individual and the productivity and profit of the organisation.
Gilley and Eggland (1989)	HRD is organised learning activities arranged within an organisation to improve performance and/or personal growth for the purpose of improving the job, the individual and/or the organisation.
McLagan (1989)	HRD is the integrated use of training and development, career development and organisational development to improve individual and organisational effectiveness.

Author	Definition
Bergenhenegouwen (1990)	HRD can be described as training members of an organisation in such a way that they have the knowledge and skills needed within the context of the (changing) objectives of the organisation.
Garavan (1991)	HRD is the strategic management of training, development and management/ professional education intervention, so as to achieve the objectives of the organisation while at the same time ensuring the full utilisation of the knowledge in detail and skills of the individual employees.
Chalofsky (1992)	HRD is the study and practice of increasing the learning capacity of individuals, groups, collectives and organisations through the development and application of learning-based interventions with the purpose of optimising human and organisational growth and effectiveness.
ITD (1992)	HRD is the process whereby people develop their full potential in life and work.
Megginson et al. (1993)	HRD is an integrated and holistic approach to changing work-related behaviour using a range of learning techniques.
Horwitz et al. (1996)	HRD is concerned with the processes whereby the citizens of a nation acquire the knowledge and skills necessary to perform both specific occupational tasks and other social, cultural, intellectual and political roles in a society.
Stead and Lee (1996)	HRD is a holistic societal process of learning, drawing upon a range of disciplines.
Stewart and McGoldrick (1996)	HRD encompasses activities and processes, which are intended to have impact on organisational and individual learning. It assumes that organisations can be constructively conceived of as learning entities and that the learning processes of both organisations and individuals are capable of influence and direction through deliberate and planned interventions.
Watkins and Marsick (1997)	HRD is the field of study and practice responsible for the fostering of a long-term, work-related learning capacity at the individual, group and organisational levels. As such, it includes – but is not limited to – training, career development and organisational development.
Armstrong (1999)	HRD is concerned with the provision of learning, development and training opportunities in order to improve individual, team and organisational performance. It is essentially a business-led approach to developing people with a strategic framework.
Gourlay (2000)	HRD focuses on theory and practice related to training, development and learning within organisations, both for individuals and in the context of business strategy and organisational competence formation.
McCracken and Wallace (2000a)	HRD is the creation of a learning culture, within which a range of training, development and learning strategies both respond to corporate strategy and also help to shape and influence it.
McLean and McLean (2001)	HRD is any process or activity that, either initially or over the long term, has the potential to develop adults' work-based knowledge, expertise, productivity and satisfaction, whether for personal or group/team gain, or for the benefit of an organisational community, nation, or ultimately, the whole of humanity.
Nyhan (2002)	HRD refers to educational training and development activities related to working life. It relates to development and learning activities for those who are at work and have completed their basic professional or vocational education and training.

(Continued)

Table 1.1   (Continued)

Author	Definition
Toulouse (2002)	HRD encompasses adult learning at the workplace, training and development, organisational development and change, organisational learning, knowledge management, management development, coaching, performance improvement, competence development and strategic human resource development. Instead of being a subdiscipline of HRM, HRD is becoming a 'multi-disciplinary' or 'trans-disciplinary' field in its own right.
Vince (2003)	HRD should be conceptualised as an approach that supports the impact that people can have on organising. The focus of HRD is on action, on developing the capacity to act, on generating credibility through action and on influencing and working with others in situations loaded with emotion and politics. The HRD function should be about discovering how an organisation has managed to become set in its ways, how to organise opportunities for change that can challenge a tendency to resist change and how to imagine and deliver processes that can underpin organisational development and transformation.
Slotte et al. (2004)	HRD covers functions related primarily to training, career development, organisational development and research and development in addition to other organisational HR functions where these are intended to foster learning capacity at all levels of the organisation, to integrate learning culture into its overall business strategy and to promote the organisation's efforts to achieve high quality performance.

Adapted from: Weinberger (1998).

Several criticisms have been directed at the manner in which HRD has been defined. Nair et al. (2007) argue that current definitions of HRD are limited in scope, solely focused on organisations to the exclusion of individuals and society. Swanson and Arnold (1997) highlight the overemphasis placed on the organisational perspective and suggest that it is difficult to find an article on HRD that does not make some reference to the relationship between HRD and organisational strategy. A second criticism levelled at how HRD is defined is the predominance of UK and US definitions of HRD. McLean and McLean (2001) argue that this trend is unsurprising simply because many students of HRD receive their education in the US. They maintain that there is a need to broaden the debate about HRD to consider how it is viewed in other countries, specifically in Asia and Continental Europe.

Disciplinary origins of HRD

As a discipline, HRD has been shaped by a wide number of disparate forces. In the 1970s and 1980s, Gilley and Eggland (1989) argue, management began to realise the importance of human resources in face of increased competition. Their work coincided with the publication of McLagan's HR wheel (Figure 1.1). McLagan (1989) maintains that

HRD comprises training and development, organisation development and career development. Consequently, HRD is focused on the three elements that contribute to individual performance improvement. For their part, Woodall et al. (2002) see the key contribution of McLagan's HR wheel as distinguishing HRD from other HR functions.

The publication of Hamel and Prahalad's (1994) *Competing for the Future* brought with it the realisation that the competitiveness of firms is closely linked to the possession of core competencies. They postulated that organisations can possess unique clusters of factors that allow the firm to be competitive and the skills possessed by employees is one of those factors. Likewise, Cappelli and Singh (1992) maintain that employees can potentially create competitive advantage, where competencies attained

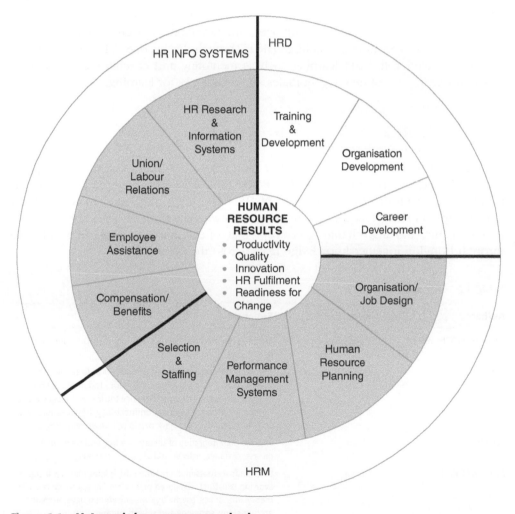

Figure 1.1   **McLagan's human resource wheel**

are firm specific and difficult to imitate. This led to greater emphasis on the resource-based view where an organisation is identified as a collection of competencies and issues such as learning, knowledge management and experience take priority.

For his part, Van der Veen (2006) identifies two distinct stages in the development of HRD. First, he views the emphasis on facilitation and learning of communication as being critical to the increasing level of specialisation of employees within organisations and the need to engender greater levels of collaboration amongst such specialists. Aligned with the development of expertise has been a focus on reflection and transformative learning. The fostering of reflection involved attempts to engage employees in learning the mistakes of the past and moving beyond purely task achievement to systems improvement and enhancement. In this environment, increasing organisational effectiveness became a priority enabling organisations to compete effectively and on a global scale. Second, he highlights the greater autonomy of employees and development of creative thinking skills as furthering the growth of the field of HRD. Through this avenue, HRD embraces elements associated with adult learning such as mentoring and coaching and widens its scope in making use of new technologies and techniques for learning.

Metaphors of HRD

Over the last two decades, several authors and researchers have employed metaphors to describe the disciplinary basis of HRD (see Table 1.2). Such metaphors offer a useful means of capturing the complexity of HRD and the multifaceted nature of HRD. The metaphors show that there is no single conceptualisation of HRD and that HRD is a dynamic, moving, changing concept that offers practical workplace solutions through bringing together knowledge from across the organisation.

Table 1.2   Metaphors of HRD

Authors	Metaphor	Rationale
Swanson (1995, 1999)	Three-legged stool	Each leg represents a main foundation of HRD (economics, psychology, systems theory).
Willis (1997)	Downstream river	The 'HRD river' has evolved so completely as to be distinct from its contributing upstream tributaries (adult education, instructional design and performance technology, business and economics, sociology, cultural anthropology, organisation theory, communications, philosophy, axiology, human relations).
Lee (1998)	Clover	HRD as the integration of theory, practice and being in a diverse, dynamic, eclectic and vibrant community.
McLean (1998)	Octopus	HRD finds its roots in many varied disciplines and is a living, evolving construct, composed of, but not limited to, systems theory, economics, psychology, organisational development, anthropology, sociology and speech communications.

Authors	Metaphor	Rationale
Grieves and Redman (1999)	Wagon train	HRD as a linear journey through time and space, yet experiencing periods of uncertainty, struggle and confusion.
Lee (2001)	Heraclitus	HRD is a changeable, emergent construct.
McGoldrick et al. (2001)	Hologram	HRD has a multilayered context that is subject to constant flux – simultaneously multidimensional, multi-causal, mutually dependent and constantly changing.
Walton (2003)	Theatre	Performance as part of a coherent drama-based Gestalt for HRD.

Adapted from: McGuire and Cseh (2006).

Talking point   The emergence of HRD

Galagan (1986: 4) describes the emergence of HRD in the following terms:

> An omnivorous discipline, incorporating over the years almost any theory or practice that would serve the goal of learning in the context of work. Like an amoeba, it has ingested and taken nourishment from whatever it deemed expedient in the social and behavioural sciences, in learning theory and business.

Galagan seems to suggest that learning lies at the heart of HRD. Do you agree?

Does the lack of a clear uniform definition mean that HRD lacks credibility?

Practical aspects

The relationship between theory and practice is of particular relevance to the field of HRD. At its heart, HRD is an applied discipline and seeks to solve real-world problems through adopting a multidisciplinary approach. Owing to its origins and the fact that its development has primarily been driven by the Academy of Human Resource Development (AHRD) and the University Forum for Human Resource Development (UFHRD), bodies populated primarily by academics, much work remains in bridging the gap between academics and practitioners. Kuchinke (2004) acknowledges this fact and argues that HRD seeks particular proximity between theory and practice, but recognises that much remains to be done to achieve this proximity. Sambrook and Stewart (2002) describe the reality in organisations that the term HRD is rarely encountered in the workplace and even when the term is used, the function described corresponds to little more than training activity. In agreement, Harrison and Kessels (2004) assert that in real life, stakeholders have little patience with HRD professionals who are confused about the function, yet claim it to be crucial to their organisation's success. They posit that there needs to be greater clarity regarding the field's organisational purpose and that this clarity matters more than agreement about whether the field should be called 'human resource development' or 'learning and development' or any number of other associated terms.

The value-added role of HRD has attracted much attention in the literature. Ruona et al. (2003) argue that one of the core challenges facing HRD has been and continues to be that HRD professionals must better demonstrate strategic and bottom-line impact. In a survey of CEOs and senior management at a future of HRD conference, Bing et al. (2003) report that those assembled agreed that the most effective way for HRD practitioners to establish themselves as key players in the development of organisational strategy is to demonstrate how what they do correlates with the productivity and welfare of the company. However, the challenge of demonstrating the utility and value-added nature of HRD is a significant one. Ty (2007) argues that in many organisations HRD is practised indirectly, unintentionally and intuitively. He maintains that there is a lack of systematic application of strategic planning and decision-making throughout the organisation, resulting in organisational learning for lower echelon employees becoming incidental and anecdotal.

There exists some evidence to suggest that the role of the HRD practitioner is becoming more clearly defined. Mavin et al. (2007) ascribes three critical roles to HRD practitioners: first, they act as problem makers who identify and name the development challenges facing an organisation; second, they may be agents of organisational change, internal consultants or experts in uncertainty; and finally, they work in partnership with managers to support business operations. Likewise, Swart et al. (2005) argue that the role of HRD practitioners in the twenty-first century is shifting from training to learning and must be more heavily involved in managing and disseminating knowledge across the organisation more effectively.

Criticisms levelled at the field of HRD

It is clear that for a young field there is significant discussion regarding the direction and ambitions of the field. Some of this discourse can be labelled criticisms – however, it can be argued that it is through valid critique and constructive argument that the foundations of the field become solidified and more widely accepted. Indeed, HRD stakeholders are more likely to take ownership of the field if they are involved and participate in such debates. A moderate position in line with this view is taken by Kuchinke (2007) when he states that the apparent dilemma between maximal inclusiveness (Lee, 2001) and need for definition (McLean and McLean, 2001) may be better understood as a creative tension where the two positions are not mutually exclusive, but are constitutive of each other.

In terms of criticisms related to the very nature of the field, these have focused on the underdeveloped empirical and theoretical base and its relationship to HRM. The underdeveloped empirical and theoretical base of HRD has been acknowledged by several commentators. Stewart (2007) argues that one of the key weaknesses inhibiting the growth of HRD as a field of research and practice is the willingness to engage in esoteric argument and debate over theoretical concepts. He also identifies a high degree of insularity, both geographic and conceptual, that exists in the HRD research community. An older study by Lowyck (1995; cited in Kessels, 2007) argues that HRD research suffers from two major weaknesses: first, he suggests that a lack of rigour is exhibited in carefully building a coherent cycle of empirical research in HRD, and second, he argues that HRD research jumps clumsily from descriptive studies to pre-scription. A broader criticism of HRD which appraises the poor development of the field is forwarded by Vince (2003), who states:

> HRD is based on people development and rational planning; it is rooted in standard-ised products and services; driven by competencies, defined by professional bodies and focused on predictability and consistency. There are too many organisations whose approaches require staff members to learn mechanistically, and only a very small number of models of development that are used (the top three are the training cycle, Kirkpatrick's evaluation ladder and Kolb's learning cycle). HRD has been weak strategically, placing the emphasis on individuals to learn and change, and largely ignoring the wider politics of organising in which HRD exists and can have an impact. (Vince, 2003: 560)

The relationship of HRD with HRM has attracted some comment – although a consensus is emerging regarding the separate and distinct identity of HRD. Traditionally, both fields concentrated on the 'human resource' and organisations often did not appreciate the need for separate departments. As Mankin (2001) argued, HRD roles were often subsumed within the HRM or personnel department where the individuals involved often had very little background or training in HRD. He maintained that this situation resulted from the ambiguous and problematic nature of the concept of HRD, where the relationship between HRM and HRD was not clearly defined. However, he argued that while both concepts have their own identities, they depend upon each other for mutual success and the maximisation of human resource potential within organisations.

It would be foolish to deny that there are not links between HRM and HRD. However, current trends in globalisation and the importance placed on technological advances, knowledge management and value-added creativity have established the critical need for HRD interventions. For his part, Friedman (2005) argues that organisations are emphasising individual customer relationships and product customisation in order to differentiate themselves from their competitors. As he so eloquently puts it, 'There is no money in vanilla' – meaning that standardised products are so easy to replicate that they will no longer form a viable business model. The challenge for HRD then is to find ways to promote creativity thinking and risk-taking amongst employees as well as fostering individual autonomy and self-management and development.

Talking point   HRD activities

While the benefits of HRD have become increasingly recognised by HR professionals, a plethora of job titles exists in organisations for individuals who engage in HRD activities. These include:

- Employee development advisor
- Learning and development manager
- Training and development specialist
- Human capital developer
- Performance improvement consultant
- Organisational development specialist
- Instructional designer
- Talent developer
- Career advisor/counsellor
- Change agent

Questions

What distinct HRD activities do some of these individuals engage in?

Do job titles and labels matter in organisations?

Arriving at a critical understanding of HRD

Critical approaches to HRD render as problematic the 'resource' aspect of HRD as suppressing employee voice. Only in recent years have critical approaches begun to be applied to HRD. Callahan (2007) argues that HRD contains very little critique of the workplace and even less critique of society. She maintains that the non-critical orientation of the field emphasises performativity which serves to subordinate knowledge and truth to the production of efficiency. She posits that those who would work in the interests of workers must make a Faustian bargain when they try to appeal to both worker and employer as the very structures within which we work are controlled by those in power and historically, those in power are not wont to share it. Likewise, Fournier and Grey (2000: 17) argue that a non-critical orientation focuses primarily on 'the principle of performativity which serves to subordinate knowledge and truth to the production of efficiency'. They maintain that critical and non-critical works may be differentiated along three dimensions: performativity, deneutralisation and reflexivity.

For her part, Fenwick (2004) shares some of the aforementioned concerns and is critical of the prevailing performance paradigm within HRD as it focuses little on social justice.

Sambrook (2004) views the emergence of critical HRD as a means of challenging traditional approaches to HRD. She argues that the shortcomings of traditional HRD approaches include a neglect of political factors, a reluctance to explore the views of those marginalised or oppressed and an unwavering adherence to conventional research methodologies. Critical HRD is therefore viewed as embracing a broad agenda taken to include examinations of power, politics, ideology and status (Fenwick, 2004; Githens, 2007; Trehan, 2004). Ty (2007) argues that critical HRD explores the foundation and structure of power relations within an institution and examines questions of social justice and equality. He suggests that critical HRD does not look towards maintaining power relations, but seeks to build power from the bottom and empower workers. Consequently, he provides the following definition of HRD from a critical theory perspective:

> As a product of clashing social forces and ideologies, human resource development (HRD) is a pro-active, forward-looking process that responds to social forces as well as overhauls organisational and social structures. It taps inter-individual human potentials and talents as well as takes into consideration gender, ethnicity, class, environment and other critical issues, thereby paving the way for a new transformed organisational and social order that promotes social justice and lasting peace. Critical HRD takes into account social justice, where all persons in an organisation are engaged in participatory collaboration, are treated fairly, receive just share in the benefits of the organisation, and are equally recognized for all their contributions to the development of the organisation. (Ty, 2007: 132)

Critical approaches to HRD need to be conscious of the need to provide practical, workable solutions to identified problems. As Valentin (2006) points out, critical theory seeks to 'problematise' rather than solve problems and can therefore be justifiably censured for its lack of practical application. Similarly, Fenwick (2004) argues that without due attention to the practical application of critical theory, the movement may become isolated, lack impact and may become considered as elitist. Therefore, in recognising the relativity of employees in relation to their level of economic wealth, political power and cultural dominance, critical approaches should identify clear pathways for guiding employees towards emancipation.

In summary, critical approaches to HRD offer an important vehicle for questioning taken-for-granted assumptions and prevailing methodologies for generating and disseminating knowledge. As Ty (2007) argues, critical HRD does not accept the universality of virtues and ethics but realises the subjectivity and constantly shifting nature of employees' relationship with the organisation. Certainly HRD professionals need to face the reality that they serve two masters and must in some way reconcile the inherent duality and conflict that may exist within their positions (Callahan and Dunne de

Davila, 2004). Indeed as Short et al. (2003) point out, organisations in general need to demonstrate greater corporate accountability beyond shareholders to communities and societies.

Conclusion

The development of the field of HRD charts an interesting and exciting course. As a discipline, HRD has evolved and changed over time to maintain its relevance to individuals and organisations. From its earliest inception by Harbison and Myers, HRD has been connected to the concepts of skill acquisition, self-actualisation and modernisation. Though the emphasis of various definitions have differed, the core of HRD has centred upon improving individuals, organisations and society through a developmental process seeking to maximise individual potential.

From a disciplinary perspective, there remains broad support for McLagan's conceptualisation of HRD as encompassing three separate foci, namely training and development, career development and organisational development. HRD can be viewed as the synergetic combination of all three foci, bringing about greater organisational efficiencies and effectiveness through more fully engaged and skilled employees whose performance and work outputs are congruently linked to the goals of the organisation. In so doing, commitment to learning and development becomes the vehicle through which the dual ambitions of the individual and organisation become realised.

Several criticisms have been levelled at the HRD concept. For starters, the relationship of HRD to HRM has come under much scrutiny. While both concepts acknowledge the importance of human resources, it is clear that a strong case can be made for the contribution of HRD to individuals and institutions. Current trends in globalisation, technological advances and the need for creative innovative employees who can add value to organisations underscore the need for developing employee knowledge and skills. Indeed, there is a clear need to develop the underlying theoretical and empirical foundations of the field to demonstrate the real contribution HRD can make to individuals and organisations.

The emergence of critical approaches to HRD has focused attention on the perceived shortcomings of HRD. It is argued that HRD has uncritically accepted the performance agenda without questioning the consequences for employee subordination and oppression. The lack of attention in traditional HRD discourse to political and power dimensions and an unwillingness to engage with minority or suppressed viewpoints have led to suggestions that HRD has aligned itself closely with capitalist imperatives. Indeed, critical HRD questions how HRD practitioners may be simultaneously agents for both employees and management and posits that employees should be involved more fairly and equitably in the organisational system. However, to date, critical HRD has been criticised for its lack of practical application with the associated implication that it is 'all talk and no action'.

Lloyds Pharmacy

As one of the largest pharmacy chains in the UK, with 1650 pharmacies and employing over 17,000 staff, Lloyds need to ensure that their staff are trained and developed to the highest standards. Located largely in communities and close to health centres, Lloyds staff are committed to the company's vision of 'healthcare for life' and want to meet customers' health needs through proper prevention, management and treatment of illnesses and ailments.

As the new managing director appointed in 2011, Tony Page took charge of the pharmacy chain at a time of rapid change and stiff competition. Tony identified a significant business threat coming from large supermarkets that had begun offering a one-stop shop service, where customers could meet grocery, banking, insurance and healthcare needs under one roof. To compete with these supermarkets, Tony realised that Lloyds needed to improve levels of customer service as well as staff product knowledge and sales expertise.

Beginning with store supervisors, he placed emphasis on ensuring that staff spent more time building relationships with customers to better understand their needs and requirements. He also started spending time on the road, listening to staff about their concerns and better understanding the business and customer views of the brand. Soon afterwards, Tony established the +One training programme – Lloyds' largest ever training programme. A series of two-day workshops were established to convey to supervisors the core customer service standards they were expected to deliver as well as helping supervisors improve their listening and communication skills allowing them to provide a more individualised, personal service to customers. The workshops were complemented with the provision of coaching sessions delivered by operational support managers, thus helping to reinforce and re-emphasise important lessons learned.

To promote the programme across the retail chain, Lloyds collected and shared success stories from supervisors who participated in the workshops and coaching interventions. In addition, a 'best-in-class' competition was run to identify leading pharmacies and further promote supervisors. Training is also provided by Lloyds through an open learning centre where staff can access online training, as well as CDs, books and DVDs. Staff can also work on projects and secondments to broaden their knowledge, skills and experience. To date, Lloyds has reported improved levels of customer loyalty as a result of the training as well as higher levels of confidence amongst supervisory staff.

(Continued)

(Continued)

(Adapted from: Sutherland, B. (2012) Lloydspharmacy's +One Training Programme. *People Management*, 29 February.)

Questions

Assess the key benefits arising to supervisors from participating in the workshops and coaching interventions.

How does the provision of training help in the recruitment and retention of staff?

How does investment in staff training and development help Lloyds become a dynamic progressive organisation?

Discussion questions

From the 25 definitions of HRD listed in Table 1.1, what do you consider to be the key components of HRD?

How does HRD balance the needs of employees, organisations and society?

Discuss how HRD fulfils an important function in the workplace?

What are the challenges facing the field of HRD?

Part 1

HRD at the Individual Level

Adult Learning Theories

Chapter objectives

The objectives of this chapter are to:

- identify the contributions made by cognitivism, behaviourism, social learning and critical learning approaches to understanding how employees learn;
- examine the principles associated with andragogy or adult learning;
- consider the importance of critical reflection in questioning taken-for-granted assumptions;
- look at the roles of individuals, educationalists and professional bodies in the learning process.

Introduction

Understanding how people learn is of crucial importance to furthering their development and potential. Without knowledge, comprehension and appreciation of the myriad ways in which people learn, individual growth is blunted, organisational advancement stunted and community and society possibilities for advancement are diminished. As Gold and Smith (2003) argue, learning is the key factor for survival, sustainability and competitive advantage at the level of the individual, organisation and nation. Given the importance ascribed to learning, it is also worth noting that learning is not a singular process. Merriam (2001: 5) has acknowledged, 'We have no single answer, no one theory or model of learning that explains all that we know about adult learners, the various contexts where learning takes place and the process of learning itself.' She argues that the knowledge base of learning comprises a mosaic of theories, models, sets of principles and explanations.

In recent years, much attention has focused upon expanding conceptions of the learning process. Marsick and Watkins (1999) argue that there has been a shift away from a compartmentalised, almost assembly-line approach to learning towards a holistic, integrated vision of learning connected to individual, organisational and societal development. Various forms of experiential learning, such as lifelong learning, workplace learning and self-directed learning, are becoming increasingly prominent in the literature. Clarke (2005) argues that workplace learning is increasingly recognised as key to developing types of knowledge and skills important for operating effectively in modern organisations. Likewise, Smith (2000) point to the growing trend towards self-directed learning and the autonomous learner, indicating that greater responsibility is being placed on the individual for their own growth. Concomitantly, there has also been a recognition that learning is not purely an individual process, but also a social collaborative one (Slotte et al., 2004). The learning process has been transformed from a trainer/instructor led event to a learner-centred one.

Learning is often viewed as an overarching concept within which human resource development finds its place. Gold and Smith (2003) argue that the terms training, development, education and HRD seems to have become incorporated into the generic term learning. In agreement, Yang (2003) argues that learning is one of the key concepts in HRD and facilitating learning for individuals and organisations is one of the key roles for HRD professionals. Indicative of the importance of learning to HRD was a debate in the literature over whether the learning paradigm or performance paradigm was the dominant focus for HRD research and practice (Barrie and Pace, 1998; Kuchinke, 1998).

While the focus of this chapter deals with theories of learning, it is worth noting that learning does not occur solely in a formal setting. A great deal of learning takes place informally, unintentionally and incidentally (Eraut et al., 1998; Marsick and Watkins, 1990; Slotte et al., 2004). Indeed, a study by Marsick and Watkins (1990) showed that only 20 per cent of learning comes from formal structured training. Informal learning is defined as predominantly experimental and non-institutional, while incidental learning is regarded as unintentional, or a byproduct of a different activity (Conlon, 2004; Cseh et al., 1999). Watkins and Marsick (1994) maintain that informal and incidental learning are critical to organisational growth and effectiveness as it is through these forms of learning that learning flows readily from peer to peer, within and between teams, up and down the organisation, and between the organisation and the external environment.

The structure of this chapter draws upon Lee's (1996) schools of learning theory where she identifies cognitivism, behaviourism and humanism as three key learning theories. She argues that cognitive learning can be equated with education and concentrates upon learning at the head level; behavioural learning can be equated with training and concentrates at the hands level; and humanistic learning can be equated with development and concentrates at the heart level. To this structure, we add a fourth theory: critical approaches to learning. While critical approaches do not describe mechanisms and processes by which people learn, they perform a valuable role in surfacing motives and the underpinning rationale for learning.

Cognitivist theories of learning

An emphasis on the processes involved in learning, rather than the products or outcomes of learning, distinguishes cognitivism from other theories of learning. Both Harrison (2000) and Von Krogh et al. (1994) argue that traditional cognitivist approaches adopted a rationalist stance viewing cognition as the processing of information and the rule-manipulation of symbols. In agreement, Good and Brophy (1990) argue that cognitivists view learning as a reorganisation of the cognitive structure in which individuals store information.

In contrast to the reductionist stance of behaviourism, cognitive theories of learning embrace Gestalt principles, namely, that we experience the world in meaningful wholes. Blanton (1998) argues that our perception is broken up into organised wholes through our ability to organise data so that it makes sense. Aik and Tway (2003) argue that when an individual receives new information, it may attach itself to a pre-existing cognitive structure, change an existing structure or go into a new structure. This accumulation and organisation of experiences encourage new insights and facilitate breakthrough moments and the development of new knowledge and skills.

Cognitive processes represent an important mechanism by which individuals adapt to their environment. In order to deal with and process the large volume of information and arrive at meaningful decisions, individuals develop highly structured cognitive schemas. The association of various concepts through the creation of cognitive schemas (or mental maps) has been long established as central to the functioning of individuals and society. Daniels et al. (1995) argue that schemas act as simplifications, helping managers to overcome the limitations of short-term memory, when they search long-term memory for relevant information. Similarly, Sparrow (2000) maintains that cognitive schemas serve as top-down or theory-driven aids, generated from experience and affecting a manager's ability to attend to, encode and make intelligent inferences from collected information.

Piaget (1952) differentiates two critically important dialectics in the learning process: assimilation and accommodation. This corresponds to the internal and external aspects of the learning process itself. As Piaget (1952: 7–8) states: 'The accord of thought with things and the accord of thought with itself express the dual functional invariant of adaption and organisation. These two aspects of thought are indissociable: it is by adapting to things that thought organises itself and it is by organising itself that it structures things.' In certain cases, an individual may reject new information where it does not fit with the existing structure or would cause substantial changes, which the individual is not willing to accept. Piaget's dialectic of assimilation and accommodation has been applied to areas of routine and non-routine problem-solving (Anderson, 1993; Billet, 1999; Shuell, 1990). In this context, it is argued that routine problem-solving reinforces and refines existing knowledge. Repetition of the activity serves to enhance understanding and embed knowledge more firmly within the individual's cognitive framework. In contrast, non-routine knowledge forces individuals to engage in the development of new knowledge or the extension of existing knowledge. Leont'ev (1981) describes the process of internalisation of new knowledge as not the transferral of an external activity to a pre-existing internal plane of consciousness, but the process by which the internal plane is transformed.

The cognitive preferences of individuals have important implications for the way in which individuals learn. Messick (1984: 5) defines cognitive styles as 'consistent individual differences in preferred ways of organising and processing information and experience'. Evidence has emerged that cognitive styles will influence the choice of learning style and method (Hayes and Allinson, 1996). Consequently, Smith (2005) advocates the use of instruments such as the Myers Briggs Type Indicator (MBTI) as a means of assessing the learning styles of individuals and adapting learning methods to suit these styles. Common dimensions measured by such instruments include sensing vs intuition and thinking vs feeling.

Critics of cognitivist approaches to learning have pointed to their inaccessibility and the difficulty in testing cognitive theories of learning. Wiltsher (2005) maintains that cognitivist theories of learning are biased towards learning that involves intentional rational thought. Robotham (2003) denounces the style approach to learning (i.e. fitting people into pre-ordinated learning categories). He maintains that while this may allow a degree of programme tailoring, dangers exist in encouraging the wholesale adoption of a particular learning style which may subsequently limit individual development.

Behaviourist theories of learning

The view that learning can best be understood through observable behaviour rather than private consciousness forms the basis for behaviourist theories of learning. Stewart (2002) argues that behaviourist theories of learning have two defining characteristics: the general rejection of the internal workings of the mind as an area of study and investigation; and that human behaviour is the product of experience of and within physical and social environments.

As behaviourism is regularly defined in opposition to cognitivism, it is worth examining the objections behaviourists raise against the validity of cognitivism. Zuriff (1985) advances four key arguments against cognitivism:

- Cognitivism, with its focus on introspection is internally flawed and prone to error and distortion.
- Consciousness is private and subjective and consequently should be precluded from objective scientific examination on the basis that experiences are non-verifiable.
- Intersubjective agreement is not possible within a cognitive frame of reference. Therefore, communication and agreement on basic observations are not possible.
- Cognitivism is unreliable. The connection between a private event (introspection) and public verbal report of that event may not be always accurate.

The concept of association involving the connection between sense impressions called stimuli and activities or impulses to action called responses underpins research by Pavlov and Thorndike into how people learn. Howe (1980) maintains that the strength of the connection between the stimuli and response will be influenced by the degree of reward or punishment that results. Similarly, Skinner (1953) proposes that the degree of reinforcement through reward or punishment will influence recurrence of the behaviour.

The notion of conditioning is central to theories of behaviourism. Classical (Pavlovian) conditioning suggests that by virtue of our previous worldly experiences, we produce more accurate and efficient decision-making in those areas routinely experienced due to the associated nature of experience. It posits that much behaviour produces an instinctive response to the presence of a stimulus. Through a series of famous experiments, Pavlov showed that dogs would respond to the stimulus of a bell by salivating in anticipation of receiving food. A second form of conditioning known as operant or instrumental conditioning seeks to explain responses that are emitted from the individual, rather than elicited as a consequence of a stimulus. In this manner, Skinner recognises that some behaviour may not necessarily be caused by sensory stimulation, but by virtue of emission of a discriminated operant (Zuriff, 1985). Skinner (1953: 9) states: 'The environment affects the organism in many ways which are not conveniently classed as "stimuli" and even in the field of stimulation, only a small part of the forces acting upon the organism elicit responses in the invariable manner of reflex action.'

Modern approaches to behaviourism have increasingly recognised the contextual nature of behaviour and the difficulty in reducing behaviour to a simple stimulus – response equation. Social learning theory acknowledges that environmental factors play an important role in learning and behaviour.

Social learning theory

A prominent theory within behaviourism is social learning theory with its emphasis on the contextual nature of experience. Bandura (1977) argues that learning phenomena result from direct experience that can occur on a vicarious basis through observation of other people's behaviour and its consequences. Ormond (1999) identifies four core assumptions of social learning theory:

- Learning can occur without a change in behaviour.
- The consequences of behaviour play a role in learning.
- People learn by observing the behaviour of others and its consequences.
- Cognition plays an important role in learning.

The theory situates learning at the interaction nexus between the individual and the environment. However, as Gibson (2004) points out, social learning theory emphasises the cognitive processes involved in observation. Through observation, Bandura (1977) argues that individuals could visualise the consequences of actions and regulate their own behaviour.

Social learning theory (and socio-cognitive theory in its later form) addresses the behaviour of individuals in society from an agency perspective. The theory distinguishes three modes of agency: direct personal agency, proxy agency and collective agency as directing an individual's functioning and life circumstances. However, it acknowledges that in many spheres of life, individuals do not have control over the social conditions and institutional practices that affect their everyday lives (Bandura, 2002). In this respect, the theory proposes a socially mediated form of agency embracing notions of agency in individual and collective forms. Bandura (2002) also highlights the centrality and pervasiveness of personal efficacy beliefs as the core mechanism driving human agency. He advances two sets of expectations: expectations related to self-efficacy and expectations related to outcomes as the major cognitive forces guiding behaviour. In the former case, he argues that self-efficacy beliefs regulate human functioning through a series of cognitive, motivational, affective and decisional processes. He also points to the importance of collective efficacy beliefs in influencing the functioning of groups and the shaping of societal outcomes. In the latter case, the theory posits that individuals are more likely to undertake behaviours they believe will result in valued outcomes than those that they do not see as having favourable consequences.

Socialisation plays an important role in social learning theory by defining commonly acceptable social norms and boundaries. Brim and Wheeler (1966) view the function of socialisation as one of transforming the human raw material of society into good, able citizens. In this regard, socialisation processes are loosely based around Cooley's theory of introspective mentalism (1909, 1922), which describes the process of how an individual is moulded by the primary group of face-to-face associations in family, friends and neighbours to develop a social self.

Durkheim (1954: 236) describes the influence of society on individual learning as follows:

> The ways of action to which society is strongly enough attached to impose them upon its members are by that very fact marked by a distinctive sign, provocative of respect.

Since they are elaborated in common, the rigour with which they have been thought of, by each particular mind is retained in all the other minds and reciprocally. The representations, which express them within each of us, have an intensity, which no purely private states of consciousness could ever attain; for they have the strength of the innumerable individual representations, which have served to form each of them. The very violence with which society reacts, by way of blame or material repression, against every attempted dissidence contributes to strengthening its empire by manifesting the common conviction through this burst of ardour.

In summary, social learning theory emphasises the reciprocal interaction of environment, behaviour and the person – with each influencing and being influenced by the other (Gibson, 2004). As Lefrancois (1999) comments, social learning theory is both a behaviourist theory that assumes that a great deal of learning involves observation and imitation of models and a cognitive theory that recognises our ability to think, to symbolise and to figure out cause-and-effect relationships and to anticipate the outcomes of behaviour.

Talking point   Social learning for business

According to Harold Jarche (2011), the importance of social learning to contemporary businesses can be summarised in the following 10 statements:

1   The increasing complexity of our work is a result of our global interconnectedness.
2   Today, simple work is being automated (e.g. bank tellers).
3   Complicated work (e.g. accounting) is getting outsourced.
4   Complex and creative work is what gives companies unique business advantages.
5   Complex and creative work is difficult to replicate, constantly changes and requires greater tacit knowledge.
6   Tacit knowledge is best developed through conversations and social relationships.
7   Training courses are artefacts of a time when information was scarce and connections were few; that time has passed.
8   Social learning networks enable better and faster knowledge feedback loops.
9   Hierarchies constrain social interactions so traditional management models must change.
10 Learning amongst ourselves is the real work in social businesses and management's role is to support social learning.

(Continued)

(Continued)

(Adapted from: Jarche, H. (2011) Social Learning for Business. *Sense-making for the Connected Workplace*. http://www.jarche.com/2011/01/social-learning-for-business.)

Questions

Do you agree with each of these statements? If not, why?

How do these statements capture the changing reality of modern business?

Humanist theories of learning

Humanistic approaches to learning trace their roots to the field of humanistic psychology and the work of Carl Rogers emphasising the importance of self-esteem, motivation and self-development (Addesso, 1996; Knowles, 1998; McGuire et al., 2005). Kramlinger and Huberty (1990) argue that the core assumption underpinning the humanistic approach is that learning occurs primarily through reflection on personal experience.

An appreciation of individualism and otherness is central to humanistic learning approaches. Humanist approaches to learning place the learner at the centre of all educational endeavours. Dewey (1916) maintains that the most important learning goals relate to the development of the individual and the development of citizenship. Lee and Smith (2004) argue that humanists stress perception, arguing that each individual creates their own version of reality, with the overall humanistic goal being one of support for the individual in their search for self-definition. Motivation therefore plays a critical role in driving individuals in their endeavours. McFadzean (2001) follows Maslow's writings in positing that individual self-actualisation is a driver of individual learning. Mele (2003) argues that self-actualisation can have two different meanings: developing personal idiosyncrasy, whatever that can be, and developing the noblest potentialities of each human being.

Perhaps the greatest advocate of humanist approaches is Malcolm Knowles (1998), who developed principles for guiding and directing adult learning:

- **Learning motivation:** Adults should know the rationale for learning something prior to instruction.
- **Self-direction:** Adults are independent and are both responsible for their own decisions and capable of guiding their own learning.

- **Role of experience:** The experience of adults should be acknowledged and should form an integral part of the learning process.
- **Preparedness to learn:** Adults will come to learning when they are ready to acquire new knowledge and skills.
- **Learning focus:** Adults view learning as a vehicle to assist them in performing tasks and solving real-life situations.

Humanist approaches to learning have attracted certain criticisms. Purdy (1997) maintains that the individualist focus of humanist learning theories limits its ability to account for change and overemphasises the potency of individuals without due consideration for the effects of structure and collective action. Furthermore, he argues that humanist perspectives do not confront or challenge existing conditions, but help individuals adapt to the demands of the system. A similar argument is advanced by McGuire et al. (2005) who argue that the rhetoric of humanistic approaches, which espouses developmental ideals and a focus on employee self-actualisation, is not matched by organisational actions of compressed career progression pathways, tight budgetary constraints and a market-driven economic philosophy.

A core component of humanism is the emphasis placed on experience in learning. McFadzean (2001) argues that humanist theories of learning are concerned with experiences and feelings, which lead to individual fulfilment and personal growth. Experiential learning theory explores the role that experience plays in shaping both action and reflection.

Experiential learning theory

Experiential learning concerns itself with the cognitive processing of experience involving in particular the elements of action, reflection and transfer. Experiential approaches are based on the premise that learning can be made more meaningful if it is grounded in the experience and context of the learner and that individuals learn more easily when engaged in active problem-solving (Holman, 2000). Similarly, Wilson and Beard (2003) argue that experience is the integrated process by which action and thought are brought together. In this way, they argue that experience creates an organic whole of continuity, process and situation.

The experiential learning and learning styles model is presented in Figure 2.1. The experiential learning cycle involves four learning stages: concrete experience, reflective observation, abstract conceptualisation and active experimentation. Concrete experience involves the individual partaking in a new activity from which learning can occur. Reflective observation entails watching or observing others and/or reflecting on one's own experiences of the activity. Abstract conceptualisation engages the individual in developing a theory to explain the observations and/or activity experienced.

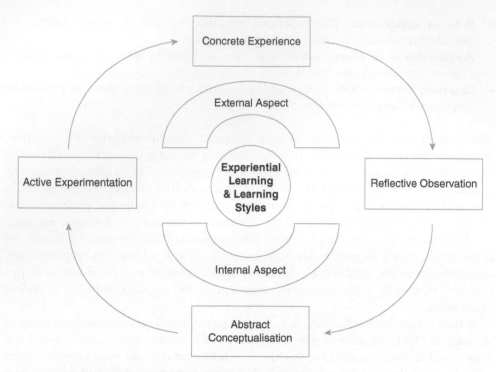

Figure 2.1   Experiential learning and learning styles model

Finally, active experimentation involves the testing of such theories in a new situation. The model also acknowledges the important role played by different types of learning styles. Sadler-Smith et al. (2000) notes that Honey and Mumford's learning styles questionnaire arose directly from Kolb's experiential learning cycle. The four learning styles identified are: activist, reflector, theorist and pragmatist. Activists are individuals who like to engage in new learning experiences and try things out. Reflectors enjoy examining situations from a variety of perspectives and observing and thinking about events. Theorists prefer problem-solving and developing concepts and frameworks within which to predict and explain events, while pragmatists are practical by nature and keen to try new theories or ideas.

Several criticisms have been levelled at experiential learning theory. Reynolds (1998) argues that it promotes an individualised perspective, neglecting the sometimes collectivist nature of learning. Wilson and Beard (2002) argue that by locating itself within the cognitive psychology tradition, experiential learning overlooks or mechanically explains and thus divorces people from the social, historical and cultural aspects of self, thinking and action. A third criticism, by Thagard (1996), maintains that cognitive and experiential approaches neglect the role of emotion in human consciousness, reducing learning to a calculating, functional process.

Talking point   The validity and relevance of VAK theory

How often have we heard individuals describe themselves as 'visual learners' or 'auditory learners' or 'kinaesthetic learners'? What they are referring to is one of the commonly used theories in education known as VAK theory. Arising out of neuro-linguistic programming in the 1970s, VAK theory argues that we process information through the senses, through sight, sound, smell, taste and touch. It argues that as individuals, we possess a preference in terms of the way in which we absorb and process information, leading to three distinct categories of learners, namely:

- **Visual learners:** These individuals think in pictures and develop mental images to represent concepts and ideas.
- **Auditory learners:** These individuals process information through sound – i.e. noises and voices.
- **Kinaesthetic learners:** These individuals absorb information through the sense of physical touch (taste and smell are also included in this category).

Despite its prominent use in education, researchers at Newcastle University have found little evidence to substantiate the main claims of VAK theory. Indeed, it is suggested that individuals use as many senses as possible to absorb and process information. The research also indicates that using visuals helps everyone to learn, irrespective of a high or low preference for visual imagery. It is argued that labelling individuals under VAK theory may actually do more harm than good – leading individuals to having a limited view of themselves and their capabilities.

(Adapted from: Smith, I. (2005) *Different in Similar Ways: Making Sense of Learning Styles.* Paisley: Learning Unlimited.)

Questions

How can we validly assess the learning styles of individuals?

How helpful are learning theories in assisting instructors design training interventions?

Critical theory approaches to learning

Issues of power, domination and control underpin critical approaches to understanding the role of learning within organisations. Within a critical theory paradigm, learning is conceived as a subtle process for engendering commitment to existing systems of production and control. It recognises the existence of powerful interest groups and considers learning as an important socialisation mechanism for advocating specific values and ideals in furtherance of economic exploitation. Students are encouraged to subscribe to current ideas and thinking, while difference of views from the prevailing orthodoxy is discouraged and suppressed. As Poell and Van der Krogt (2003) point out, learning is relevant to the degree that it is related to the primary process of the organisation (i.e. the manufacturing of products or provision of services). Lahteenmaki et al. (2001) argue that learning is still frequently interpreted as a vehicle for manipulating employees and persuading them to achieve organisational aims, which is a far from ideal conception of learning and its implementation in the workplace. The role of critical theory in advancing learning is therefore threefold:

- To challenge the centrality and necessity of the dominant role elites in defining reality and impeding emancipatory change (Alvesson and Wilmott, 1992).
- To render visible the ways in which social inequality reflects inclusive existing public spheres (Fraser, 1994).
- To promote approaches in which differences are resisted in the interests of developing more equal relations (Reynolds and Trehan, 2003).

In pursuit of these objectives, critical reflection processes play a crucial role.

Critical reflection

An important aspect of critical approaches to learning is the individual's capacity to reflect upon both the learning content and process. While critical reflection is often considered soft and irrelevant to the results-oriented and bottom-line world of business (Marsick, 1988; Van Woerkom, 2004), Reynolds (1998) maintains that critical reflection is the cornerstone of emancipatory approaches to education encouraging students to confront the social and political forces which provide the context of their work and question claims of 'common sense' or the 'way things should be'. Similarly, Giroux (1997) contends that critical reflection is essential in evaluating and understanding the epistemological underpinnings of so-called 'taken-for-granted' knowledge. Alvesson and Skoldberg (2000) argue that this involves the two processes of careful interpretation and inner reflection. In the first instance, they posit that careful interpretation calls for utmost awareness of the theoretical assumptions underpinning learning, the importance of language and the necessity of pre-learning.

Linstead et al. (2004) argue that theories provide a useful means of carefully interrogating ideas and worldviews in order to understand their impact and effect on others. Van Woerkom (2004) maintains that learning is often embedded in norms that also impact on an individual's identity, so that this identity may become submerged to some degree within a broader organisational or societal identity. Thinking outside the box can be a difficult endeavour as, Douglas (1986) maintains, all the classifications that we have for thinking with are provided ready-made and consequently, for thinking about society, we have at hand the categories we use as members of society speaking to each other about ourselves.

An appreciation of the potency and pervasiveness of language is crucial to critical approaches to learning. Weick and Westley (1996) argue that language is the critical tool for reflection, both at the inter- and intra-personal level. Weick and Westley (1996) state that discourses, particularly those situated within organisations, are never politically neutral and are sedimented with asymmetrical power relations, reproducing structures in which there is differential access to valued and symbolic goods. Likewise, Habermas (1987) argues that communicative processes are undermined and distorted by structurally based inequities hindering opportunities for dialogue and learning.

The necessity for pre-understanding acknowledges the socially constructed nature of knowledge and learning. Social constructionism subscribes to the notion that knowledge and representations of reality are interactionally constructed, socially transmitted, historically sedimented, institutionally congealed and communicatively reproduced (Gunnarsson, 1997). It is oriented towards action and function and assumes that people use language to describe, explain or construct versions of the social world in which they live (Chimombo and Roseberry, 1998; Donnellon, 1986; Elliot, 1996; Gergen, 1985; Pettigrew, 1979; Pondy et al., 1983). It therefore follows that knowledge and learning cannot be easily separated from context, and context, according to Henderson (2001), affects learning by constraining communication and inhibiting relationships for discourse. Likewise, Fenwick (2003) argues that an individual's learning is complex and multilayered and linked closely with personal history and aspiration as well as organisational activities, vision and culture. Both Fenwick (2003) and Weick (1995) argue that professional development policies need to honour the diverse processes of individuals' continuous sense-making within organisations.

Inner reflection involves directing attention towards the individual, exposing the effect of community and society as well as intellectual and cultural traditions. Alvesson and Deetz (1996) recognise that inner reflection allows an individual to identify if and how certain ways of organising, reasoning and representing the world constrain imagination, thought and decision-making. Van Woerkom (2004) maintains that learning is often embedded in norms that also impact on an individual's identity so that this identity may become submerged to some degree within a broader organisational and societal identity. Giroux (1997) recognises that culture is a terrain of competing knowledge and practice, where some sub-universes are culturally preferred over others. Similarly, Rusaw (2000) argues that individual domination is rooted in organisational and societal ideology, a set of systematic norms, beliefs, values and attitudes that people accept unquestioningly as guides to everyday thinking and behaviour.

A summary of cognitivist, behaviourist, experiential and critical approaches to learning can be found in Table 2.1.

Table 2.1 Summary of learning theories

	Cognitivism	Behaviourism	Humanism	Critical theory
Objectives of theory	• To explore the central cognitive processes involved in learning • To examine how knowledge is acquired, stored, constructed and transferred • To develop more effective tools to assist the individual in storing and recalling knowledge • To facilitate an awareness of the perceptual nature of knowledge and the development of insight	• To establish processes of learning through the observation of behaviour • To examine the relationship between stimuli and responses and how these impact on learning • To identify the influence that environmental factors have on learning • To explore the effects of conditioning on the learning process	• To examine individual drivers of learning • To explore the influence of experience and reflection in driving action and behaviour • To identify the underlying principles of adult learning • To examine the learning of the individual as a whole person	• To challenge the centrality and necessity of the dominant role elites in defining reality and impeding emancipatory change • To render visible the ways in which social inequality reflects inclusive existing public spheres • To promote approaches in which differences are resisted in the interests of developing more equal relations
Core assumptions	• Operates according to Gestalt principles – experience as meaningful wholes • Adopts a rationalist stance rejecting the reductionism of behaviourism	• General rejection of the internal workings of the mind as an area of study • Human behaviour is the product of experience of and within physical and social environments	• Individuals lie at the centre of learning and educational endeavours • Self-actualisation and self-definition is the goal of individual learners	• Asymmetry of power relations exists • Access to developmental opportunities controlled and restricted
Learning perspective	• Information should be structured to facilitate storage and mindmapping • Individual is active in learning process	• Responsibility for learning rests with the teacher • Individual is passive in learning process	• Individuals have responsibility for their own learning in response to perceived needs • Individual is active in learning process	• Individuals should engage in critical reflection • Individual is actively engaged in examining underlying motives
Locus of learning	• Head	• Behaviour	• Interaction with society	• Cognitive and behavioural awareness
Views of development	• Education	• Training	• Development	• Critical insight resulting in emancipatory change
Underpinning theories	• Schema theory • Mindmapping	• Social learning theory • Reinforcement theory • Theory of connectionism	• Andragogy • Experiential learning	• Critical realist theory • Marxist theory
Leading theorists	Piaget, Kolb, Honey, Mumford	Pavlov, Skinner, Thorndike	Dewey, Rogers, Knowles	Freire, Habermas, Alvesson

In the following subsections, we examine the role of individuals, educationalists and professional bodies in learning from a critical theory perspective.

Role of individuals

As recipients and participants in the learning process, individuals are in a key position to question, challenge and critique the principles and assumptions underpinning learning. That many individuals do not engage in this process is testament to the existence of power and control mechanisms protecting and preventing awareness of dominant groups and hierarchies of knowledge. McIntosh (1988) argues that individuals who are members of the dominant group need to recognise their privileged position (of which they are meant to be oblivious) and realise that this unearned privilege has not been good for the individual's development as a human being and society's development as a whole. Understood as a matter of perpetual struggle between contending forces, hegemony, according to Rojek (2003), provides the means for controlling culturally or socially divergent groups within organisations. Brookfield (2003) argues that the concept of ideological hegemony suggests that ideas and actions of leaders gradually become internalised by followers as if they were their own and when, in fact, they are constructed and transmitted by a powerful minority interest to protect the status quo.

The concept of hegemony provides an explanation for the lack of opportunity experienced by particular organisational and societal groups. Morrison (2009) is critical of the pervasiveness of the term 'equal opportunities' and how frequently organisations use this terms to create positive impressions of equality and good corporate citizenship. He argues that even the broadest definition often mistakenly conflates equality of access with equality of outcomes, and ignores the complex social construction of education, its institutional arrangements and the external influences upon both (Morrison, 2009).

Role of educationalists

The role of educationalists and course providers in the learning process is also subjected to scrutiny. While acknowledging that learning is ultimately the responsibility of the student, Dehler et al. (2001) argue that the task of the educator is to create a space in which learning can occur. Freire (1970) maintains that education is politically charged and either teaches the values of the dominant group or helps learners to reflect critically and take action to create a more equitable society. Similarly, Elliott (2003) argues that education, particularly management education, has a utilitarian conception of education born of new right politics. She suggests that this is an ideological terrain whose contours encompass education as a socially valuable enterprise contributing to national economic prosperity as well as a consumer good obtained by individuals to further their careers. To this end, Giroux (1997) maintains that educational courses reproduce the values, social practices and skills needed for perpetuating the dominant social order. Horkheimer (1972) posits that the increasing centrality of economic forces and the diminishing resistance of cultural spheres is exerting control over individuals, societal norms and educational processes and outputs. In this regard, Dehler et al. (2001) maintain that textbooks treat knowledge as a storehouse of artefacts constituted as canon, where knowledge appears beyond the reach of critical interrogation.

Differences also appear in relation to the content of many of the courses provided. Commentators are pointing to an ever-increasing number of courses that are devoid of elements of critique. Grey and Mitev (1995) argue that students are resisting learning anything which they perceive as theoretical, impractical or irrelevant, preferring to learn specific techniques which they see as useful, and mainstream management readily serves up a diet of such techniques. Both Linstead et al. (2004) and Salaman and Butler (1994) contend that many management schools have tended to propagate a view that managers most value practical techniques or methods that have direct or immediate application, leading to a dumbing down of management theory to suit practitioners. Likewise, Elliott (2003) highlights the conflict between giving practitioners what they want, while simultaneously providing practitioners with what educationalists perceive that they need. Such conflicts result in what King (1995) sees as the dissonance between what students said they had gained from the educational programme and their performance back in the workplace. Dehler et al. (2001) argue that management education has become overly reductionistic and simplistic in holding to notions of management as a set of content areas to be learned. Likewise, Cavanagh (2004) acerbically views the role of modern management education as to fill the mind of the student, without altering it, and to arm them with a portfolio of self-help theories and prescriptive management guides. This decline in standards affirms for Gibson (1986) the importance of critical theory approaches in arguing for constant vigilance towards attempts to pass off sectional viewpoints as universal, natural, classless and timeless.

Role of professional bodies

Adopting the role of gate-keepers, professional bodies embrace the language of standards and best practice to control entry to exclusive occupational clubs. This furthers the economic interests of the profession's members by ensuring a substantial premium is required to acquire the skills of the profession through training and education and to access those skills and services subsequently. Professional bodies promote homogeneity amongst their members. By requiring members to satisfy a number of preconditions, they effectively employ pre-selection procedures, engaging those who fit into the dominant culture of the profession. Sirotnik (1983) argues that the products of our created learning culture teach dependence upon authority, linear thinking, social apathy and passive involvement. This promotes stasis among professions and a lack of impetus towards changing the status quo.

Critical reflection is an important skill in moving towards professional self-awareness and professional development. Fenwick (2003) argues that Schon's (1983) notion of the 'reflective practitioner' encompassing both critical reflection on action and reflection on uncertain, volatile and unpredictable situations continues to enjoy popular acclaim in professional development circles. Watkins (1989) ascribes to professional HRD bodies the task of assisting individuals and organisations in critically reflecting on what is oppressing them and how their organisations can free them to create new worlds and to design organisations not for control, but for adaptability. However, Kipp et al. (2003) argue that critical reflection is problematic as it tends to be treated as an isolated skill, does not often take account of power issues and is often not warmly received by practitioners where it is resisted.

Beyer (2001) supports the adoption of normative value-laden approaches and argues that practitioners should be guided by 'the practice of possibility'. He argues that a sharper focus on values and ideals may reveal connections and purposes that are hidden or consciously submerged. In this way, Kipp et al. (2003) argue that practitioners may avoid having their work become nothing more than the dissemination of rhetoric.

The notion of critical discourse communities as a vehicle for emancipation has been advanced by several commentators (Kipp et al., 2003; O'Donnell et al., 2003). The mobilisation of members and an examination of the personal narratives of oppressed members may open potentially rewarding avenues for effecting individual and organisational change. Kondrat (1999) recognises that professional bodies are human constructions and have no existence apart from the human actions that constitute and reconstitute their form and substance. Consequently, critical discourse communities may engage the 'dialectic of enlightenment' (Horkheimer and Adorno, 1979) and liberate individuals from ideologically constrained ways of both thinking and acting (Bokeno, 2003).

Conclusion

The range of learning theories presents a variety of perspectives through which learning can be examined. Cognitivist perspectives emphasise the psychological aspects of learning. Behaviourist perspectives give priority to the contextualised nature of individual action and the range of environmental factors influencing such action. Humanist perspectives seek to explain learning in terms of individual self-definition and self-actualisation, while critical perspectives draw attention to such conflicts and surface underlying assumptions in endeavouring to achieve emancipatory change.

Understanding individual learning is critical to the effective delivery of successful HRD practices. An appreciation of learning theories can lead to changes in the structure of learning interventions, the content of such interventions and how these are facilitated. Differences in learning theories reflect opposing axiological assumptions about human behaviour and also the conception of individuals as solitary or social beings.

Research on learning attests to the growing recognition of the individuality of learning processes. This uniqueness is explained by the perceptual nature of learning and a variety of social and environmental factors. Preserving individual distinctiveness and encouraging creativity ought to be the goal of learning events. However, the drive for standardisation and market forces often produce suboptimal outcomes.

CASE STUDY

MOOCs and learning in the twenty-first century

In recent times, there has been an explosion of interest in MOOCs as a new and exciting vehicle for learning. MOOCs were initially developed in 2008 and the term MOOCs stands for **M**assive (as they are capable of enrolling thousands of learners), **O**pen (as they are free and accessible to all over the internet), **O**nline (as interaction takes place through web-based discussion and noticeboards or through video-based lectures and seminars, and **C**ourses (as they have a definite start and end date, clear assessment strategy and can result in certification). Although MIT, Harvard and Standard run open-learning MOOCs educational sites, the MOOCs model of offering modules and programmes is currently posing a serious threat to traditional education models, and universities and colleges are anxiously debating how they should effectively deal with this new medium of learning.

At a recent TED talk, Professor Anant Agarwal gave an insight into running a MOOC for his course on circuits and electronics. In total, 155,000 students from 162 countries have participated in the module, more he says than he would instruct in 40 years of face-to-face teaching. He argues that this new way of learning is appropriate to reach the millennial generation who have been shown to be more technologically savvy than their predecessors.

The following principles are central to the successful operation of MOOCs:

- **Flipping the classroom:** In contrast to the conventional model of lecturers and professors delivering classes directly to students, the MOOCs model provides students with access to course materials and gets them to discuss, debate and reflect upon these materials with other students as well as the course instructor.

In this way, students gain greater ownership of the material and the instructor becomes an active participant in the learning.

- **Semi-synchronicity:** MOOCs encourage students to participate in a module or course with a distinct cohort of learners. In other words, students are provided with material (assignments, lectures, course notes, case studies) on a weekly basis and will interact with each other based on their materials. However, learners can log into the MOOCs at a location and time most suited to them.
- **Credentials:** Many of the larger educational institutions are now providing credits to students if they successfully complete the assessments associated with the course. This allows students to legitimise and formalise their learning. They also form a useful way of encouraging companies to allow their employees to engage in MOOCs.
- **Gamification:** Students participating in an MOOCs format are exposed to more active forms of learning and the use of technology enables them to have a positive interactive experience.
- **Peer learning:** Through participation on discussion boards and online chatrooms, students are provided with an opportunity to dialogue and converse with other students in relation to the content and materials of the course.
- **Instant feedback:** With the integration of online tests and self-assessments, students are given immediate formative feedback on their progress within a module. This can provide encouragement and motivation to students to advance with their learning.
- **Self-pacing:** As all the materials are available in the virtual learning environment, students can progress with the learning at their own pace. Indeed, they can even pause, rewind and fast-forward through video clips and lectures to suit their own purposes.

(Adapted from: Meister, J. (2013) How MOOCs will Revolutionise Corporate Learning and Development. Forbes. http://www.forbes.com/sites/jeannemeister/2013/08/13/how-moocs-will-revolutionize-corporate-learning-development/; Walters, H. (2013) Reinventing Education for Millennials: Anant Agarwal at TEDGlobal 2013. http://blog.ted.com/2013/06/14/reinventing-education-for-millennials-anant-agarwal-at-tedglobal-2013/.)

Questions

What are the advantages of using MOOCs in workplace learning and executive education?

In what ways do MOOCs incorporate Knowles' adult learning principles more effectively than traditional classroom, instructor-led training?

Discussion questions

With its internal psychological focus, cognitivism has little relevance for HRD practitioners in organising and developing learning interventions. Discuss.

Behaviour is too random to be explained by learning. Discuss.

Humanist approaches are naïve in underestimating the power of market forces on individual learning. Is this true?

Which are the strongest environmental influences on learning?

What changes could be introduced into the learning environment in order to redefine reality and introduce emancipatory change?

Creativity and HRD

3

David McGuire

Robin S. Grenier

The objectives of this chapter are to:

- consider the importance of creativity to the knowledge economy;
- identify the barriers inhibiting employee creativity in the workplace;
- explore the role of perspective, perception and positionality in the creativity process;
- examine how creativity is affected by the work environment and leadership support.

Introduction

In 1975, Steven Kerr wrote a seminal piece entitled 'On the Folly of Rewarding A, while Hoping for B' examining the disconnect between expected organisational behaviour and rewarded organisational behaviour, and identified a series of systems failures leading to individual underachievement and poor organisational outcomes. He demonstrated how many reward systems were compensating employees for sub-standard and poorly aligned performance leading to organisational stasis and showed how such systems were incapable of producing the discontinuous ground-breaking change so desired by their organisations. In today's fast-paced market-driven economy, creativity has been identified as a key driver of competitive advantage, enabling organisations to keep apace of changes in the external environment (Rajan and Martin, 2001). Creative ideas allow organisations to adjust to shifting market demand (Shalley et al., 2004) and significantly add to levels of innovation, effectiveness and productivity in organisations (Amabile and Conti, 1999; Nonaka, 1991). As McLean (2005) points out, organisations depend upon employees feeding their creative ideas into the innovation pipeline to sustain growth and deliver upon rising customer expectations. Nonaka and Takeuchi (1995) define the 'knowledge creating company' as one whose sole business is continuous improvement through developing the intellectual capital of employees and creating new knowledge, products, processes and systems. Indeed, Matheson (2006) sees the emphasis on creativity as indicative of a broader movement among western nations away from the production of goods and services to the production of ideas and knowledge. In spite of its importance, levels of creativity in many organisations remain low. As Taggar (2002) points out, companies have tried numerous strategies to foster creativity, including restructuring work, selecting people on the basis of their attributes and behavioural training, finding to their cost that these strategies are often unsuccessful.

With an acknowledgement of the role creativity plays in the innovation, success and long-term sustainability of organisations, this chapter examines how creativity is recognised and fostered in the workplace through organisational and cultural strategies that encourage creative risk-taking amongst employees. The chapter is structured around three facets affecting the creative process: perception, perspective and positionality.

Definitional issues

Creativity is defined as 'coming up with fresh ideas for changing products, services, and processes so as to better achieve the organization's goals' (Amabile et al., 2005: 367). Madjar (2005) maintains that definitions of creativity all include concepts of appropriateness and usefulness alongside notions of novelty and originality. Such views are echoed by Nickerson (1999), who argues that creativity must not only embrace novelty, but also a measure of utility, such as usefulness, appropriateness or social value. To this end, creativity needs to satisfy notions of commercial or cultural value and be built upon existing foundations and principles (Ward, 1995). In this regard, creativity is not a complete divergence from the past, but often takes the form of small incremental improvements that advance knowledge and understanding.

As a research topic, creativity has been underrepresented in the fields of social and organisational psychology. Sternberg and Lubart (1999) identify six historical barriers to the study of creativity including its origins in a tradition of mysticism and spirituality; problems with the definition and criteria for creativity rendering it elusive and trivial; and the impression from commercial approaches to creativity that the field lacks a strong theoretical and psychological basis. To date, approaches to the study of creativity have been either cognitive, behavioural or personality based. Cognitive approaches have explored the superstructure of the mind and considered how cognitive processes lead to the production of innovative ideas and processes (Gardner, 1993). Behavioural approaches have examined the role of both intrinsic and extrinsic motivation and how reward systems affect levels of employee creativity (Baer et al., 2003). Meanwhile, personality-based approaches have sought to identify individual traits which lead employees to be more creative in their work (Amabile, 1983; Barron and Harrington, 1981). More recent work has explored the social basis of creativity building upon the theories of social creativity (Watson, 2007) and social capital and recognising the importance of communication and interaction in the creative process (Amabile, 1996; Perry-Smith, 2006).

Talking point   Attributes of creative people

Roffe (1999) identifies several key attributes of creative people, including:

- **Need orientation:** Creative individuals have a strong urge for expression and wish to develop new products and designs.
- **Ambivert:** Creative individuals are a mixture of introvert and extrovert.
- **Curiosity:** Creative individuals have strong observation, listening and abstract thinking skills.
- **General interests:** Creative individuals have a wide range of interests.
- **Imaginative:** Creative individuals have a capacity to see things differently or in new ways.
- **Problem-solving:** Creative individuals tend to possess high levels of problem-solving skills.
- **Independence:** Creative individuals have a high level of autonomy and can be non-conformist in nature.
- **Intelligence:** Creative individuals have a capacity to store interesting and unusual information for future use.
- **Conscientiousness:** Creative individuals tend to be highly focused and committed to their creative endeavours.

Questions

What implications does the list of attributes have for talent management in organisations?

How can organisations develop some of the attributes listed above in its employees?

(Continued)

(Continued)

(Adapted from: Roffe, I. (1999) Innovation and Creativity in Organisations: A Review of the Implications for Training and Development. *Journal of European Industrial Training*, 23(4/5), 224–241.)

A multi-factorial approach to examining creativity

Feldman (1999) recognises that approaches to creativity have been unidimensional and this tendency to isolate a single dimension of creativity has had the effect of distorting the research findings. Consequently, multi-factorial research designs will encourage a more weighted holistic approach to the study of creativity, its antecedents and effects. Research using conceptual models like the one presented in this chapter (see Figure 3.1), which emphasises the role of creativity in organisations, requires dynamic thinking utilising broad and complex processes of how individuals and organisations manage positionality, perspective and perceptions in order to strengthen organisational effectiveness.

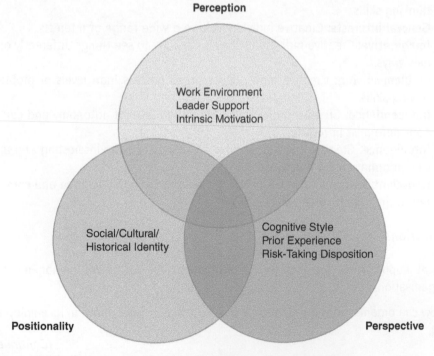

Figure 3.1   The intersection of perception, perspective and positionality

Perception

Much like problem-solving, perception is based on data from rather inadequate information furnished by the senses resulting in a 'best guess' based on the visual stimuli, prior experience and non-sensory information (Coren, 2003). There exists considerable research evidence demonstrating the power of perception in affecting organisational realities (Analoui and Karami, 2002; Parker-Gore, 1996). Perception affects how an employee makes sense of their work environment, the relationships with their supervisor and colleagues and their own level of self-efficacy and self-competence. Perception is socially constructed and influenced by the manner in which events are interpreted. Consequently, Power (1973) argues to behave is to control perception and that we know nothing of our own behaviour but the feedback effects of our own outputs. In this subsection, we examine the effects of environmental conditions, supervisory support and intrinsic motivation on employee perception and creativity.

The work environment exerts a powerful influence on the creativity of employees. Scott and Bruce (1994) maintain that employees may attempt to be creative when they perceive that creativity is valued and supported by the organisation. Amabile et al. (1996) argue that the social environment can affect both the level and frequency of creative behaviour. Majaro (1988) maintains that a suitable creative environment needs to emphasise flexibility and group involvement; respect for diversity; open expression of ideas; the promotion of creative thinking; and the setting of clear objectives. To this list, Shalley and Gilson (2004) add the importance of individual autonomy as they propose that individuals need to feel independent in the level of time they can devote to their work and the means by which the work should be completed. Emphasising the importance of environmental conditions, Csikszentmihalyi (1996) argues that it is easier to enhance creativity by changing the environmental conditions than by trying to get people to think more creatively. However, the reality as expressed by Amabile (1998) is that creativity is often undermined unintentionally in work environments that are established to maximise business imperatives of coordination, productivity and control. Likewise, McLean (2005) maintains that a culture that supports and encourages control will result in diminished creativity and innovation as control negatively affects levels of intrinsic motivation.

Leader support is a critical factor affecting an employee's self-confidence and their motivation to engage in creative behaviour. Amabile et al. (2004) argue that individuals are likely to experience both perceptual and affective reactions to leader behaviours. An individual's perception of the instrumental and socio-emotional support of their team leaders will affect their level of creativity (Oldham and Cummings, 1996; Scott and Bruce, 1994). Tierney and Farmer (2002) found that where supervisors supported an employee's self-confidence, this resulted in greater creative self-efficacy resulting in improved creative performance. Research by Andrews and Farris (1967) established that employees experienced higher levels of creativity when a more participative and engaging style was adopted by management. Similarly, a study by Zhou

(2003) found that informational feedback to employees led to higher creativity than when feedback was delivered in a controlling or punitive manner. Finally, Jaussi and Dionne (2003) maintain that role-modelling behaviour by supervisors is more likely to increase creative behaviour amongst followers – hence it is critical for supervisors to demonstrate creativity themselves and foster a climate which supports creativity.

While the literature on extrinsic motivation (i.e. monetary rewards and recognition) reveals a mixed picture regarding the effectiveness of such practices (Baer et al., 2003), research on intrinsic motivation shows a direct link to creativity (Amabile, 1996; Oldham and Cummings, 1996). It shows that intrinsically motivated individuals are more likely to be curious, take risks, be cognitively flexible and experience positive emotions such as excitement and enthusiasm (Amabile et al., 1990; Deci and Ryan, 1985; Utman, 1997; Zhou, 2003). Isen (1999) maintains that when individuals experience positive moods, they are likely to draw greater connections between divergent stimuli materials, use broader categories and identify more interrelatedness between stimuli. Similarly Amabile et al. (2005) maintain that creativity can be an agent for change where complex cognitive processes are influenced and shaped by, and simultaneously occur with, emotional experience.

As this section points out, perception is critical to how employees relate to and with the work environment and peers, and as such is central in nurturing creativity in the workplace. The perception of the environment in which an employee works affects both motivation and the overall ability to generate creative and innovative ideas.

Talking point   Creativity locks

In 1990, Roger Von Oech wrote a very influential book on creativity and the 'mental locks' that prevent and inhibit creativity in individuals. He first created a list of creativity obstacles and then went on to provide suggestions as to how these obstacles could be overcome. To generate new ideas, he suggests that we need to suspend our evaluative capacity and encourage the free flow of ideas. Below are two lists of creativity mental locks:

Mental locks on creativity

- The right answer
- That's not logical
- Follow the rules
- Be practical
- Play is frivolous

Educational locks on creativity

- Back to basics
- Cover the content
- Knowledge in boxes
- It's all in the head
- Planning makes perfect

- That's not my area
- Avoid ambiguity
- Don't be foolish
- I am not creative

- Every minute is important
- Fun is frivolous
- Testing, testing, testing
- Control above all

Questions

How can we help individuals to overcome barriers to creativity?

What support can organisations put in place to foster creativity?

(Adapted from: Von Oech, R. (1990) *A Whack on the Side of the Head.* New York: Business Plus Imports; Learning Unlimited (2006) *Fostering Creativity: A Hard Look at Soft Thinking.* Edinburgh: The Stationery Office.)

Perspective

Embracing multiple perspectives is critical to the creative process. Garavan et al. (2007) highlight the change of focus, composition and emphasis that occurs when individuals adopt a different perspective. They argue that perspectives empower innovative and creative thinking through opening the possibility of renewing and reinventing relationships between different factors and events. Similarly, Parker and Axtell (2001) argue that understanding frameworks different from your own and empathising with others is fundamental to collaborative working. They maintain that perspective-taking may involve a high degree of cognitive complexity and results in greater levels of empathy and positive attributions. Being open to new perspectives involves adopting an interpretivist epistemological viewpoint and can provide individuals with a rich way of envisioning new realities. Consequently, it follows that individuals do not passively interpret organisational practices, but seek to understand them by applying meanings, terms and concepts, derived from our stock of knowledge, language and the ongoing interpretation of others with whom we interact. It is this prior knowledge that acts as a basis for establishing a particular perspective and for testing new ideas, principles and arguments. An individual's prior experiences will influence what they work on, the approach to the work, the methods judged most adequate for this purpose, the outcomes and products considered most appropriate, and the framing and communication of those outcomes. Thus, opportunities within organisations for experiential learning can result in more creative and 'efficient' work requiring far less effort to isolate and solve problems and better preparation to handle complex problems (Bibby and Payne, 1996).

There is agreement that creativity requires a cognitive-perceptual style involving the ability to suspend judgement, collect and apply diverse material, the use of heuristics and an ability to concentrate over long periods of time, in a setting where response options are open as long as possible (Amabile, 1998; Shalley and Gilson, 2004). Baer et al. (2003) examine Kirton's Adaption–Innovation theory and found that individuals with an adaptive cognitive style tend to operate within particular paradigms and procedures, while those with an innovative style are more likely to take risks and develop new approaches to solving problems. Familiarity with these characteristics and organisational supports to encourage adaptive and innovative styles is essential given the likelihood of strong external pressures of task completion in organisations. Given these pressures, individuals are less likely to explore new pathways or suspend judgement and instead search for solutions that are adequate for the given task – resulting in increased productivity at the cost of creative, new solutions (Forbes and Domm, 2004).

Engaging in creative behaviour requires participants to take risks. Newall et al. (1979) suggest that creativity is an unconventional act which requires individuals to reject or modify previously accepted ideas. Tesluk et al. (1997) argue that an individual's level of creativity depends upon their predisposition towards risk and their willingness to contemplate and accept failure if it occurs. However, research indicates that individuals are more likely to prefer certain outcomes and engage in actions designed to limit their exposure to risk (Bazerman, 1994). Farmer et al. (2003) coin the term 'ego-investment' to delineate the level of risk an individual is prepared to commit to when being creative. They argue that the perceived risk in being creative goes beyond the loss of tangible rewards and entails a potential loss of self or a loss of the sense of identity. Two factors that affect creativity in groups are social loafing and conformity. Thompson (2003) describes social loafing as the tendency of individuals not to work as hard in a group as they would alone. She argues that individuals will typically filter their contributions and only participate where they feel their comments are particularly valuable, potentially denying the group access to other useful information. In the case of conformity, she maintains that individuals will engage in bizarre behaviour to ensure their acceptance in the group and will be cautious about presenting ideas for fear of negative evaluation.

In summary, perspective emphasises the need for drawing from multiple viewpoints based on tacit knowledge and prior experience. By recognising the role of perspective in fostering creative processes, infusing experiential learning opportunities and incorporating structures that allow for thinking time in the creative process, organisations are better able to combat conformity and indolence, and encourage calculated risk-taking.

Positionality

In order to understand and partake in the creative process, we need to acknowledge our own positionality. Maher and Tetreault (2001) define the notion of positionality as one where individuals do not possess fixed identities, but are located within shifting networks of relationships, which can be analysed and changed. These networks are based on cultures and subcultures and distinguished by internal variation (Aguilar, 1981). For his part, Takacs (2002) considers the notion of positionality as the multiple unique experiences that situate each of us in relation to each other. Positionality therefore encourages the identification of individual uniqueness as a reference point for differentiation from others. As Merriam et al. (2001) argue, if the perspective of the individual is limited by positionality then it is important to recognise that in order to understand another, one must first understand oneself. Helping employees to recognise their own positionality and subjectivity and incorporating reflexivity encourage operation on multiple levels, thus promoting creativity in organisations (Etherington, 2004).

Acknowledging the historical, cultural and socially bounded nature of positionality requires an in-depth analysis of how social factors have affected our individual identity. Sheppard (2002) argues that positionality challenges the proposition that there is objective knowledge and sensitises individuals to the reality that their analysis is shaped by their social situatedness in terms of gender, race, class, sexuality and other axes of social difference. Similarly, McIntosh (1998) argues that in many instances, individuals need to acknowledge unearned advantage and conferred dominance in order to create better communication among groups and further higher levels of creativity. In an educational context, Fenwick (2007) maintains that the learner is not an object separable from the educator and, consequently, the educator needs to acknowledge their own positionality through examining social identity markers as these will affect the creativity of learners.

Blake and Hanson (2005) contend that innovations are not simply products of place, but of the people embedded in particular places. By recognising the role of positionality in the creative process and encouraging employees to approach learning, work and collaboration from different historical and societal positions, organisations can maintain an openness to diverse ideas leading to individual and organisational health (Weick, 1995). To do this requires individuals to acknowledge their own positionality, and organisations to understand their role in maintaining or challenging existing positions. Such considerations for the development of creativity have been explored by Robinson and Stern (1997), who consider five features that organisations can support in developing and sustaining creativity. The first is alignment. Here Robinson and Stern focus on the notion that creative ideas must be directed towards organisation goals in order for employees to recognise and respond positively to useful ideas. The second feature is self-initiated activity. This means that intrinsic motivation is necessary for employees to feel empowered to determine the problem they are interested in and feel capable of solving that problem. Unofficial activity is the third feature. Ideas need to be given a chance to develop and informal meetings provide a safe context for that incubation, until they are ready for judgemental resistance. Fourth, is serendipitous discoveries made through fortunate accident; and the last feature is diverse stimuli. In this feature new settings or situations may offer new insight and motivate people to react differently or experiment.

Positionality can also serve as a lens for evaluating creativity. Shalley and Gilson (2004) recognise that an evaluation of creative work requires agreement from those considered knowledgeable within the field. In this regard, Egan (2005) advocates Amabile's (1996) consensual assessment technique as an appropriate method for accurately evaluating the level of creativity associated with a product, service, process or procedure. For their part, Elsbach and Kramer (2003) suggest that judging others' creativity is made easier by the existence of objective evidence. They posit that judgements about individual creativity can sometimes be rendered on the basis of tangible products, such as actual product designs, written reports or innovative programmes. Alternatively, they remark that an individual's creative potential may be inferred on the basis of their role status or reputation in the organisation. However, they conclude that there exists little agreement on universally accepted or empirically established standards for evaluating creativity and creative potential.

An examination of positionality brings to light the individual's place in developing creativity within the forces of the social institution, the cultural domain responsible for the transmittal of new ideas, and those responsible for bringing about change in the domain (Csikszentmihalyi, 1988). Reality is socially, culturally and historically constructed and underlines the importance of acknowledging one's own subjectivities and positions of power. Thus, it is only through acknowledging our own positionality that we can accurately evaluate and support creativity in the workplace.

Conclusion

Cultivating creativity is a difficult and complex process. Whilst Perry-Smith (2006) identifies individual creativity in organisations as desirable, she recognises that it is often difficult to stimulate and may be stifled by a range of organisational practices, particularly during turbulent and uncertain times. Despite having some knowledge of the factors enabling creativity, limited research has been conducted to identify the organisational practices that inhibit creativity. Without a clear understanding of the practices that block creativity and the process by which this occurs, investment in initiatives designed to foster creativity may produce suboptimal results.

Future work is also needed to examine the social dimension of creativity. For too long, creativity has been viewed as a singular endeavour; an act of greatness or a spark of genius. In recent times, creativity in groups and teams is becoming increasingly important as work becomes internationalised to a greater degree and organisations place a stronger emphasis on communication, social capital and social networks. Creative work is contextualised (Mumford et al., 2002) and dependent on the capabilities, pressures, resources and socio-technical system in which employees work (Csikszentmihalyi, 1999); as such, an incorporation of social creativity (Watson, 2007) that includes the dimensions of perspective, perception and positionality is key.

Empowering employees to be creative in the development and analysis of new ideas demands that HRD professionals create opportunities for employees to understand how they see themselves and help them engage in creative thinking and adopt multiple perspectives in their work. This can been achieved through the creation of participative safe environments (De Dreu and West, 2001), encouraging ongoing contact with those outside the organisation or in different areas of the organisation (Anacona and Caldwell, 1992; Dougherty and Hardy, 1996) while limiting the tendency of employees to choose to work with others similar to themselves (Tajfel, 1982). Moreover, HRD interventions need to embrace experiential learning and constructivist principles in order to create a learning environment supportive of creativity. Thompson (2003) argues that this may (initially) involve organisational support for seemingly purposeless and senseless things such as striving for quantity at the expense of quality, suggesting unrealistic ideas and creating space for individual thinking.

If, as researchers have suggested, some level of creativity is required in almost any job (Shalley et al., 2000; Unsworth, 2001), then creating the right environment for creativity is crucial. The degree of support will affect the value placed on creativity by employees. Supervisors and managers should receive training in how to appropriate support, encourage and manage risk-taking and creativity amongst employees. Top management support for creative endeavours will send a strong message to employees that the organisational culture welcomes, embraces and supports creativity. In addition, supervisors and managers should act as role models to employees in both encouraging and engaging in creative behaviours.

The concept of alignment will ensure consistency between actual behaviour and rewarded behaviour. A clear, transparent and accountable process for evaluating and rewarding creativity is required within organisations. Individuals need to be commended for taking appropriate risks, even where doing so occasionally leads to failure. Risk-taking is an important element in creativity and will ensure that an organisation remains innovative in its approach and direction and responsive to market changes. The use of extrinsic rewards needs to be carefully managed and matched by supervisory/managerial acknowledgement of employee efforts.

CASE STUDY

Creativity at Apple

For a company that looked doomed a decade ago, it has been quite a comeback. Today, Apple is an iconic company. Take, for example, the iPad that was released in March 2010. Go into any Apple store in the US and there are at least a dozen stations with people lining up to check the iPad out. What lessons can technology companies learn from the success of Apple? For the most part, Apple's zest comes from its reputation for inventiveness. From its first computer in 1977 to the mouse-driven Macintosh in 1984, the iPod music player in 2001, the iPod Touch and the iPhone in recent years, and now the iPad, Apple has prospered by keeping just ahead.

Apple is extremely different from other tech companies. In particular, it inspires an almost religious fervour amongst its customers. Innovation companies can learn at least four lessons from the Apple success story. First, innovation can come from without as well as within. Apple is widely assumed to be an innovator in the tradition of Thomas Edison, locking its engineers away to cook up new ideas and basing products on their moments of inspiration. However, its real skill lies in stitching together its own ideas with technology from outside and then wrapping the results in elegant software and stylish design. The idea for the iPod, for example, was originally dreamt up by a consultant whom Apple hired to run the project. It was assembled by combining off-the-shelf parts with in-house ingredients such as its distinctive, easily used system of controls. And it was designed to work closely with Apple's iTunes jukebox software, which was also brought in and then overhauled and improved. Apple is, in short, an integrator of technologies, unafraid to bring in ideas from outside but always adding its own twists. This approach, known as 'network innovation', is not limited to electronics. It has also been embraced by companies such as P&G, British Telecom and several drugs giants, all of which have realised that not all good ideas start at home. Making network innovation work involves cultivating contacts with academic researchers and start-ups, scouting for new ideas and ensuring that engineers do not fall prey to the 'not invented here' syndrome, which values in-house ideas over those from outside.

Second, Apple illustrates the importance of designing new products around the needs of the user, not the demands of technology. Too many technology firms think that clever innards are enough to sell their products, resulting in gizmos designed by engineers for engineers. Apple has consistently combined clever technology with simplicity and ease of use. The iPod was not the first digital music player, but it was the first to make transferring and organising music, and buying it online, easy enough for almost anyone to have a go. Similarly, the iPhone is not the first mobile phone to incorporate a music player, web browser or e-mail software. But most existing 'smartphones' before the iPhone required one to be pretty smart to use them. In other words, most technology firms do not view 'ease of use' as an end in itself.

A third lesson from Apple is that innovating companies should sometimes ignore what the market says it wants today. Listening to customers is generally a good idea, but it is not the whole story. For example, the iPod was ridiculed when it was launched in 2001, but Steve Jobs stuck by his instinct. Nintendo has done something similar with its popular motion-controlled videogame console, the Wii.

The fourth lesson from Apple is to 'fail wisely'. The Macintosh was born from the wreckage of the Lisa, an earlier product that flopped; the iPhone is a response to the failure of Apple's original music phone, produced in conjunction with Motorola. Both times, Apple learnt from its mistakes and tried again. Its recent computers have been based on technology developed at NeXT, a company Jobs set up in the 1980s that appeared to have failed and was then acquired by Apple.

The wider fourth lesson is not to stigmatise failure but to tolerate it and learn from it. Europe's inability to create a rival to Silicon Valley owes much to its tougher bankruptcy laws. In fact, in my research work, I find that tougher national bankruptcy laws discourage innovation in a country. Thus, from the policymaker's perspective while bankruptcy laws must be tightened for the brick-and-mortar industries, bankruptcy laws should be lenient in the technology sector. Since innovation involves considerable risk-taking, firms will be averse to taking risk if tough bankruptcy laws rob them of a second chance.

(Adapted from: *Financial Express* (2010) What Apple Says about Innovation. *Financial Express*, 22 April 2010.)

Questions

What key creativity lessons can we learn from the experiences at Apple?

From the case study, assess the validity of the statement that 'the creative process arises from a bolt from the blue'?

Discussion questions

Discuss the view that 'Employees are paid for performance, not creativity'.

Through processes and routines, organisations constrain creativity. How can routines be broken to encourage creativity, while important standards are maintained?

Some research indicates the importance of employee diversity in fostering creativity. What challenges are posed by the objective of fostering creativity?

Career Development

4

Chapter objectives

The objectives of this chapter are to:

- examine how the notion of career has been defined;
- explore a range of contemporary career concepts;
- investigate the field of career counselling through looking at Schein's Career Anchors Inventory and Holland's Vocational Preference Inventory;
- analyse the importance of continuing professional development.

Introduction

In an ever-changing, fast-paced, globalised world, career development and career planning have become increasingly important aspects of human resource development. Managing one's own career and having the right tools to enhance one's own employability are critical skills that employees must possess in uncertain economic times. With increased mobility of people and internationalisation of firms, a wide set of opportunities exist for individuals to develop their careers in new and exciting directions. Employees are increasing faced with myriad choices: whether to prioritise work or family concerns; whether to work in the office or remotely; whether to become a global business traveller or stay closer to home; or whether to become a specialist or remain as a generalist. Such decisions attest to the growing complexity of individual careers where the traditional safeguards of a 'job for life' and 'job security' no longer exist and where employees must be alert to changing market conditions and new workforce and technological trends.

For their part, organisations now view career development as an important aspect of identifying, developing and retaining talent in organisations. Far from seeing career development initiatives as an unnecessary cost and a luxury organisations can ill-afford in recessionary times, the quest to become an 'employer of choice' has led many organisations to invest heavily in initiatives that promote learning and the dissemination and sharing of knowledge. Organisations more and more are seeing value in the notion of careers as vehicles for offering employees a range of learning opportunities and the prospect of gaining valuable experience. Moreover, some studies have shown that job applicants in making career decisions favour organisations who possess a track record in developing and upskilling employees (Winterton, 2004).

However, in spite of research data illustrating the importance of careers, there is also evidence that some organisations fail to take career development seriously, viewing it as a 'nice to have', rather than an essential aspect of their HRD strategy (Sturges et al., 2002). In such cases, organisations often see responsibility for career development resting on employees' shoulders, with limited or no input required from the organisation. Often, such employers adopt a transactional view of employment contracts seeing employee inputs as a monetary exchange, rather than important stages in the development of a career. This chapter explores how careers have been defined and how such definitions have evolved over time. It goes on to examine five prominent career concepts, which shed light on the changing career expectations of both employees and employers. Finally, the chapter looks at the importance of career counselling, focusing specifically on Schein's Career Anchors theory and Holland's Vocational Preference as instruments designed to help employees understand better their career values, needs and work and life priorities.

Defining career

Many definitions of careers have been proposed over the last 30 years (see Table 4.1 for examples), each capturing important aspects of how work activities help fashion a pattern of experiences which shape how individuals define themselves and how they come to be regarded by others. Whilst in the past careers were largely defined in terms of an upward linear sequence or progression of higher status jobs, it is increasingly recognised that careers no longer follow universal or normative stages, but are increasingly individual, fragmented, multidirectional and iterative (Gerstman, 1998). Indeed, Sullivan and Mainiero (2007) describe a growing trend amongst individuals of defining one's career in terms of a patchwork of experiences that enables individuals to achieve a balance between work and family concerns. That said, it is possible to argue that learning lies at the heart of careers and contemporary notions of careers have embraced the centrality of learning and experience to the individual over time. However, it should be noted that, as yet, there is no agreement among academics on a common definition of career (Greenhaus et al., 2008).

As Sullivan and Baruch (2009) report, not only have increased global competition, economic circumstances and technology altered our conceptions of careers, but social norms and new systems of work have also played an important role. With growing levels of workforce diversity, including greater representation of women across all levels of organisations and the expanding use of outsourcing and part-time and temporary workers, careers are being defined in broad terms, with career experiences now encompassing activities and life roles such as volunteering work, periods of entrepreneurial activity and career breaks to engage with family and caring responsibilities. For his part, Chen (1998) provides three broad conceptualisations of career: career as a life process, career as individual agency and career as meaning-making. First, looking at the notion of career as a life process sees careers as a developmental process that accompanies a person's entire life. Chen argues that careers can help individuals achieve growth, self-satisfaction and life goals, and suggests that careers allow individuals to adopt a variety of roles within the domains of family, school, community and workplace. Second, seeing careers as individual agency emphasises the role of careers in building self-awareness and the self-concept. Chen argues that the self-concept helps individuals see their place in society and understand the constellation of situations and circumstances surrounding the individual. This person–environment interaction allows individuals to build self-efficacy and confidence in

Table 4.1 Definitions of career

Wilensky (1964): 'A succession of related jobs arranged in a hierarchy of prestige, through which persons moved in an ordered (more or less) predictable sequence'

Hall (1975): 'A perceived sequence of attitudes and behaviours associated with work related experiences and activities over the span of a person's life'

Arthur et al. (1989): 'The evolving sequence of a person's work experience over time'

Arnold (1997): 'The sequence of employment-related positions, roles, activities and experiences encountered by a person'

Cummings and Worley (2001): 'A career consists of a sequence of work-related positions occupied by a person for the course of a lifetime'

Baruch (2004): 'A process of progress and development of individuals, which is sometimes described as the life stories of people'

Sullivan and Baruch (2009): 'An individual's work-related and other relevant experiences, both inside and outside of organizations, that form a unique pattern over the individual's life span'

Greenhaus et al. (2010): 'The pattern of work-related experiences that span the course of a person's life' their own abilities and contribution to society. Finally, the notion of career as meaning-making considers an individual's subjective perspective of career and how context and life experiences can shape and mould a person's career and life trajectory.

The notion of career is almost exclusively defined in individualistic terms and largely neglects the role of organisations in shaping and moulding that career. Despite the decline of paternalistic approaches based upon notions of long-term job security and 'a job for life', many organisations are now recognising the value of adopting a partnership approach to managing employee careers. Such an approach acknowledges that both employees and organisations have needs which can best be met through collaboration and discussion. According to Hirsh and Jackson (2004), such a career deal requires employers to communicate realistic and positive career messages regarding the organisational commitment to career development, the accessibility of lateral career moves, the leveraging and maximising of employee skills, and the provision of engaging and challenging work. Sturges et al. (2005) argue that central to the concept of the career deal is that employees need to see themselves as assets in which they and their employers must invest. Such activity requires employees to proactively manage their careers and influence key gate-keepers to provide important career outcomes.

Talking point   Visualising your career

One of the goals of career counselling is to help employees gain insight into their careers and how their own personal and work values influence and are affected by their careers. Thinking about your own career and work experiences, answer and reflect upon the following questions:

How do I see my career?

How does my boss see my career?

Where do I want to be in career terms in three years' time?

What things do I need to do to achieve my three-year career goals?

Career concepts

A variety of career concepts have been developed to describe key characteristics of modern careers. With traditional career notions of defined career pathways, promotion based upon seniority, singular employer loyalty and organisational job security becoming increasingly irrelevant in organisational environments characterised by uncertainty and less clearly defined job roles, career concepts have sought to reflect the increasingly number of non-linear, atraditional careers that now exist. This section profiles five career concepts (boundaryless career, protean career, authentic career, kaleidoscope career and the portfolio career), looking at the implications of the career concept for both individuals and organisations.

Boundaryless career

One of the earliest career concepts was developed by Arthur and Rousseau (1996) and labelled the boundaryless career to describe the notion that careers transcend the scope and boundaries of a single employer. This career concept advances the proposition that individuals are independent of their employers and need to adopt greater control over their careers. It proposes that an individual's career gains meaning through participation in external networks and professional associations and that the individual becomes known for their expertise, independent of their employer. Hytti (2010) maintains that core to the notion of the boundaryless career is that the individual develops a personal reputation for being a key resource and building a repository of experience through paid, unpaid and voluntary work. Consequently, she maintains that skills, employability and marketability constitute important attributes of the boundaryless career. For his part, Weick (1996) sees the boundaryless career as a collection of stories of shifting identities, where the individual zigzags across organisational boundaries in developing a portfolio of skills and expertise. Sommerlund and Boutaiba (2007) posit that boundaryless careers require individuals to possess both alertness to opportunities that arise and speedy decision-making to grasp such opportunities. In summary, it can be argued that this career concept fits with the increased organisational change focus, where greater levels of flexibility are demanded from employees and where employees must increasingly stake out opportunities and proactively manage their own careers.

Protean career

The protean career is defined as 'a process which the person, not the organization is managing. It consists of all the person's varied experiences in education, training, work in several organizations, changes in occupational field, etc' (Hall and Mirvis, 1995: 20). As Hall (2002) argues, the protean career is characterised by the core values of freedom and growth and the core attitudes of work satisfaction and professional commitment. As Manikoth and Cseh (2011) point out, the protean career involves individuals proactively responding to change and involves both a values-directed attitude and self-directed attitude towards career management. As such, the protean career requires individuals to be highly self-directed and focused in determining their own career trajectory. The notion of the protean career is thus highly subjective and requires an understanding of the personal narrative and changing circumstances of the individual. Sullivan and Baruch (2009) see one of the positive attributes of the protean careerist as their ability to repackage and reshape their skills and identity to fit the changing work environment and remain marketable. This ability to be adaptive and take responsibility for their own careers as well as adopting a whole-life perspective accentuates the highly personalised, subjective and sometimes contradictory nature of the protean career. Arthur et al. (2005) argue that protean careerists are likely to engage in high levels of internal reflection to determine whether current employment offers sufficient personal fulfilment and satisfaction. The implications of the protean career mean that managers need to individually meet the values of subordinates and ensure that good job-alignment and working conditions enable employees to satisfy their internal values and needs.

Authentic career

The authentic career is one based upon concepts of self-efficacy, self-confidence and the drive and motivation to pursue one's own life goals and path. According to Svejenova (2005), individuals embracing an authentic career path are truthful to themselves, acknowledge their strengths and weaknesses, seek congruence between feelings and communication, and work to achieve continuity between the past and present. For her part, Craddock (2004) defines an authentic career as one where an individual through their work seeks to truthfully reflect their genuinely held values and beliefs. She argues that individuals must pass through four stages – awareness stage, emotional ownership stage, interaction stage and integration stage – to achieve the necessary insights to build a career that responds best to their deeply held values and convictions.

Kaleidoscope career

The kaleidoscope career concept adopts the metaphor of the kaleidoscope to describe the ever-shifting, changeable nature of careers. It argues that such careers are created by individuals who exercise control over their unique circumstances and fashion a particular career path to suit life choices, interests and personal values. Mainiero and Sullivan (2006) maintain that the kaleidoscope career concept embraces the notion of authenticity in that they argue that individuals will seek to be genuine and pursue opportunities that align and fit with their own self-concept, identity and self-worth. Cabrera (2009) argues that the parameters of balance and challenge can affect the career decisions individuals make. She suggests that individuals through their careers will seek to achieve balance between their work and non-work lives and search for autonomy and responsibility in the jobs that they take. Cabrera reports that the kaleidoscope model has been used to make important distinctions between the careers of men and women. She posits that men follow an *alpha* career pattern, where they seek challenge in their early career, authenticity in mid-career and balance in their late career. In contrast, she proposes that women follow a *beta* career pattern in that they seek challenge in early career, balance in mid-career and authenticity in their late career. To this end, she argues that women's careers appear to be more relational in character and craft unique career paths to fit their own values and lifestyle choices. In this way, it can be argued that the kaleidoscope career concept attributes little control to organisations over employee careers and assigns organisations a more supportive role in helping employees achieve balance and fulfilment in their careers.

Portfolio career

With increasing focus within organisations and society on employability and more flexible forms of working, it is clear that many individuals are grasping the opportunity to design their own careers to suit both their interests and individual circumstances. The notion of career becomes viewed as a collection of valuable experiences from which the individual builds expertise and networks. The concept of the 'portfolio career' was coined by Charles Handy (1994), who describes the portfolio career in the following terms:

> more and more individuals are behaving as professionals always have, charging fees not wages. They find they are 'going portfolio' or 'going plural'. 'Going portfolio' … means exchanging full-time employment for independence. The portfolio is a collection of different bits and pieces of work for different clients. The word 'job' now means a client. (p. 175)

Within the concept of the portfolio career comes from individuals a lifelong commitment to self-employment, whereby individuals do not become employees as such, but contract their skills to organisations for a specific period of time in order to achieve particular tasks (Templar and Cawsey, 1999). Platman (2003) views this form of career management as offering many advantages to workers including choice, opportunity, liberation from organisations and self-control, so long as individuals have the experience, wisdom and skills to manage this form of employment relationship. She suggests that the portfolio career concept may be especially attractive to older workers who have accumulated a long period of expertise, knowledge and skills. For organisations, she maintains that portfolio-based working arrangements allow firms to keep in touch with reliable, knowledgeable and experienced workers, whilst retaining talent and institutional memory.

Talking point   Career approaches at Michelin

A 'paternalistic' model of career management where staff have limited control over their next job move continues to be a successful strategy at the Michelin Group. The unconventional approach to career management was outlined by Alan Duke and Daniel Boulanger, retired international career managers at the tyre company, who both spent 35 years at the group in a variety of different countries and business units.

Their own career paths were indicative of a strategy where 'priority is given to personal development rather than a manager's need to fill a vacancy'. This approach meant that managers and their staff often only worked together for a maximum of two to three years, and 'managers had no right to retain people' – even if they did not want to lose a talented member of their team.

Duke – who was also the company's first diversity director – explained that the company 'based management on a long-term view and a respect for its people', adding that most of Michelin's personnel team had come from the line. The firm was founded by the Michelin family in France in 1898, and while it had grown from 50 staff to 115,000 employees worldwide, the firm still approached career management from the perspective of recruiting 'a personality for a career, rather than competencies for a job'.

It was the responsibility of career managers to identify staff's individual career moves and make them happen, Duke said. Career managers were also tasked with mapping a career path for the company's top 50 performers to reach their full potential, he said, and were appraised on their ability to fulfil these expectations. Career managers were aided by a model known internally as 'the beard', in which employees were spread across job levels from A to K, which helped identify future job moves and talent gaps.

Duke was asked whether staff and managers were receptive to having their career paths decided for them, and finding themselves placed in departments they might have no interest in. But despite the unorthodox approach, Duke said that turnover at the company was very low and that employees remaining at Michelin for the duration of their career was not uncommon. 'That's the real beauty of it – it works', he concluded.

(Adapted from: Stevens, M. (2012) Michelin Succeeds by Managing Employees' Careers. *People Management*, 27 April.)

Questions

What is the incentive for an organisation to help its employees manage their careers?

Do you believe employers have a moral obligation to assist their employees in managing their careers?

What are the benefits to employees and the organisation of a formal career development strategy?

Career counselling

Providing advice and guidance to employees on their career options has become an important function of HRD professionals and career development consultants. In large part, these professionals seek to achieve congruence between an individual's skills, needs and values and their occupational interests. Such work can involve career planning alongside mentoring and coaching interventions to help the employee fulfil their potential. In this section, we examine two well-known and widely used instruments (Schein's Career Anchors Inventory and Holland's Vocational Preference Inventory) designed to bring individuals towards a greater level of career self-awareness.

Schein's Career Anchors Inventory

Since its development in the mid-1970s, Schein's Career Anchors Inventory has become one of the most well-known and utilised instruments in the area of career counselling. In his work, Schein (1996) describes the career anchor as being an individual's self-concept comprising an individual's self-perceived talents and abilities; an individual's values and their career motives and needs. Career anchors keep individuals rooted within particular jobs and roles as they fulfil an individual's inner needs, desires and values as well as making best use of their talents and skills. The Career Anchors Inventory catalogues eight different self-concepts which act as a stabilising force in the lives of managers and employees. For their part, Suutari and Taka (2004) suggest that Schein's work offers valuable insights into the 'internal careers' of individuals, offering an understanding of the career direction employees want to pursue in their working lives. Arthur et al. (1989) suggest that whilst employees may not always have a well-defined career plan, they often examine the pattern of career experiences to date and use this pattern to determine new career options.

Table 4.2 describes each of the eight career anchors developed by Schein (1996). A facilitator can guide individuals to achieving a career anchors profile, or individuals can take the career anchors self-assessment online (available at http:// careeranchorsonline.com).

Table 4.2   Schein's Career Anchors

Technical/functional (TF) competence career anchor

Individuals with this career anchor possess strong feelings of competence in a particular area – not necessarily interested in management per se. It is the area of work that 'turns them on'. Individuals in this group actively disdain and fear general management, viewing it as a 'jungle', 'political arena' and waste of talent and skills. Due to their disdain for general management positions, they tend to leave companies rather than be promoted out of their area of specialism.

General management (GM) competence career anchor

Individuals with this career anchor possess a strong motivation to rise to positions of managerial responsibility and believe they have the skills and values necessary to do so. In the initial stages of their careers, they may take technical/functional jobs, but view these jobs as interim stages to higher general management jobs. They perceive their competence as a combination of three areas: analytical competence; interpersonal competence; emotional competence.

Autonomy and independence (AU) career anchor

Individuals with this career anchor find organisational life to be restrictive, irrational and intrusive into their private lives, and fashion careers which give them independence and autonomy. Individuals with this career anchor may also possess high technical/functional expertise, so outward possession of this career anchor is not always obvious. Individuals with this career anchor experience little conflict over missed promotion opportunities and feel little failure or guilt about not aspiring higher. They often experience a trade-off between status and income versus lifestyle freedom.

Security and stability (SE) career anchor

Individuals with this career anchor look for long-run career security, good benefits, basic job security, decent income and good pension and retirement provision. They 'trust' the organisation to do the right thing and have often become heavily socialised to organisations' norms. They may sometimes be regarded as 'organisation man/woman' and in so doing, they may do little to develop their own careers.

Entrepreneurial creativity (EC) career anchor

Individuals with this career anchor have an overarching need to build or create something which is entirely their own product. They see their creativity as an extension of the self. Sometimes, individuals with this career anchor may end up transitioning to managerial roles through four mechanisms: (1) they get bored and turn the organisation over to others; (2) they have difficulty managing a larger organisation and are forced out; (3) they develop a special role in the organisation to continue to express creativity; (4) they express creativity through a senior management role.

Service/dedication to a cause (SE) career anchor

Individuals with this career anchor seek to pursue work that achieves something of value, such as making the world a better place to live in, solving environmental problems, improving harmony amongst people, helping others, improving people's safety or curing illnesses. They may pursue opportunities even if it means leaving the organisation and may decline promotion opportunities if it takes them away from valued activities.

Pure challenge (CH) career anchor

Individuals with this career anchor enjoy working on seemingly insolvable problems and difficult complex tasks. They look to overcome barriers and obstacles and compete against difficult opponents. For them, novelty, variety and difficulty become ends in themselves. Challenges may take the form of intellectual, strategic, interpersonal or sporting trials amongst others.

Lifestyle (LS) career anchor

Individuals with this career anchor seek to balance personal needs, family needs and career requirements. They want to make all aspects of life work together in harmony and an integrated whole. Success is defined in broader than career terms and in relation to life as a whole. Often family can take overall priority dictating the geographic area where the individual lives, type of work and how life works as a whole.

Adapted from: Schein (2013) http://www.careeranchorsonline.com

Work by Feldman and Bolino (1996) led to the categorisation of these eight career anchors into three distinct groupings: talent-based anchors, needs-based anchors and values-based anchors. The talent-based anchors category includes individuals who hold technical function competence, general management competence and entrepreneurial creativity. While individuals with technical/functional competence are often promoted to managerial positions because of their superior technical skills, Schein (1996) argues that these individuals often recognise that being an effective manager requires a completely different skillset. He argues that effective managers possess technical expertise as well as political awareness, financial and analytical skills, interpersonal and negotiation skills and the emotional intelligence necessary in handling difficult complex decisions. The needs-based category encompasses individuals who hold security and stability, autonomy and independence or lifestyle career anchors. For these individuals, work meets an important internal need, allowing them to pursue a particular lifestyle or providing the long-term stability which they yearn for. In difficult economic times, Schein (1996) argues, the shift from 'employment security' to 'employability' is likely to discomfort individuals with a security and stability career anchor. In some cases, this prompts these individuals to seek employment in the public sector, which is perceived as offering greater security and stability than the private sector. The values-based anchors category includes individuals with a pure challenge or service/dedication to a cause career anchor. For these individuals, life meaning and life purpose is often found through work and such individuals become committed to tackling a range of societal problems. As a result, these individuals are likely to be highly self-motivated and driven to achieve in their goals.

Schein's Career Anchors Inventory is subject to several important limitations. Suutari and Taka (2004) argue that the typology has to date been subject to limited empirical investigations and greater work is needed to address some of the inconsistencies that have surfaced in empirical research. They also question whether individuals possess a single overriding career anchor and suggest that career anchors may change over time dependent upon an individual's life experiences and external influences. For their part, Feldman and Bolino (1996) maintain that there has been little refinement of Schein's original career anchors classification and they argue that the concept could be reframed to reflect changes that have occurred over the last 40 years.

Holland's Vocational Preference Inventory

Holland's Vocational Preference Inventory is a widely used career counselling instrument which seeks to align an individual's personality type to a particular organisational working environment. Holland (1966, 1985, 1997) viewed working environments as falling within six key interest domains (realistic, investigative, artistic, social, enterprising and conventional) and argued that individuals would strive to achieve congruence between the working environment and their own personality type. According to Hogan and Blake (1999), Holland is clear in his belief that vocational interests are an expression of personality. Table 4.3 describes each of the six interest domains.

Table 4.3   Holland's Vocational Preference Inventory

Realistic: Individuals who possess a realistic vocational preference tend to be practical and enjoy physically demanding activities. They may like working with tools and machinery, being outdoors, working with their hands and perhaps working with animals. They approach problems in a practical, problem-solving manner.

Some indicative careers: Surveyor; tree surgeon; engineer; mechanic; electrician

Investigative: Individuals who possess an investigative vocational preference tend to enjoy intellectual and scientific pursuits. They enjoy complex, abstract problems and possess a logical, analytical technical mind. They often like to perform experiments and conduct research.

Some indicative careers: Chemist; geologist; physicist; computer programmer; lawyer

Artistic: Individuals who possess an artistic vocational preference value creativity and self-expression. They view their work in terms of their own identity and rely strongly on their own feelings and intuition. They often like the freedom to dress the way they wish, keep few appointments and keep their own agenda and timetable.

Some indicative careers: Author; artist; journalist; composer; playwright; sculptor/sculptress

Social: Individuals who possess a social vocational preference place a high emphasis on human relationships. They often seek to help others overcome personal and professional problems and adopt a caring, individual approach. They enjoy group and teamwork and value friendship, generosity and kindness.

Some indicative careers: School principal; nurse; counsellor; social worker; teacher

Enterprising: Individuals who possess an enterprising vocational preference enjoy managing and persuading others in their efforts to achieve their goals. They can often be found in economic and financial environments and are often energetic, confident, optimistic and assertive individuals. For many, the accumulation of wealth and power is important.

Some indicative careers: Hotel manager; business executive; salesperson; buyer; trader

Conventional: Individuals who possess a conventional vocational preference enjoy routine, structure, organisation and planning. They enjoy being in control and are highly reliable and dependable. They often gravitate towards office environments and prefer rules and regulations. They are precise, accurate and detail oriented.

Some indicative careers: Auditor; administrative assistant; bank employee; tax expert; pharmacist

Adapted from: Holland (1997).

As Nagy et al. (2010) point out, Holland represented the six key interest domains in a hexagon across a two-dimensional space (see Figure 4.1). Within this space, Holland hypothesised that interest domains would be located next to those to which they were most similar. The presentation of the six interest domains in a hexagon allows

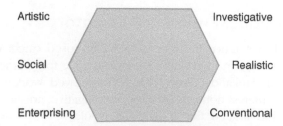

Figure 4.1   Holland's hexagonal model

individuals to gain a more rounded understanding of the types of working environments most suited to their personality.

To date, research indicates strong support for Holland's Vocational Preference Inventory and its ability to link personality traits and key interest domains, particularly in a US context (Day and Rounds, 1998; Sodano, 2011; Tracey and Rounds, 1993), although there are some indications that its reliability may vary somewhat internationally (Rounds and Tracey, 1996).

Continuing professional development

Continuing professional development (CPD) has long been considered a crucial component of career growth and learning. Defined by Madden and Mitchell (1993) as the maintenance and enhancement of the knowledge, expertise and competence of professionals throughout their careers, it looks at the processes and procedures by which professionals stay up-to-date with current knowledge, skills and environmental trends. Lammintakanen and Kivinen (2012) argue that CPD includes both formal interventions as well as informal, individualised activities that may emphasise individual or collective learning. They suggest that formal learning focuses on narrow job-related skills and concentrates on building professional expertise, whilst informal learning promotes portable skills tied to social elements not always linked to a single organisation. For his part, Owen (2004) suggests that CPD is a central element in strategic organisational change that supports growth, maturity and increased prosperity of businesses. He argues that CPD is critical to bridging the skills gap, helping businesses develop in new and innovative ways. He identifies an increase in spending in corporate sponsored senior management development as firms appreciate the need to have strong organisational leadership. Brosnan and Burgess (2003) also witness a significant uptake in the use of the internet to deliver continuing professional development. They argue that web-based CPD offers employees the opportunity to engage in organic learning and build relationships with other employees and learners online.

One of the key benefits to CPD is that it can be delivered in a work setting. Cooper et al. (2010) argue that CPD in the workplace can be facilitated through guided learning, mentoring and coaching. They argue that workplaces provide useful sites for translating knowledge into practice and to engage in active experimentation in relation to new practices and work activities. Reflection lies at the core of CPD and learners are encouraged to mull over their own practices and consider new and more effective ways of working. For many learners, a key aspect of CPD relates to accreditation and the ability to gain professional recognition for engaging in learning activities. In many cases, professional bodies prescribe particular forms of CPD or pathways that learners must follow to achieve certification of knowledge and skills. Similarly, such systems often mandate learners to update their skills at regular intervals to ensure competence is maintained (Murphy et al., 2006).

In recent times, there has been a move to recast CPD within the context of sustainable professional development. As an approach, it acknowledges that both employers and employees have an important role to play in building employee competence and expertise. It recognises that CPD approaches need to move away from being ad hoc and reactive and that the professional development of staff needs to be structured, affordable and linked to longer-term individual and organisational learning. Sustainable professional development approaches have a systemic underpinning with both employers and employees forging a commitment to lifelong learning and viewing CPD as an investment in both the employee's and organisation's future. However, it accepts the reality that organisational resources are finite and that CPD efforts must be in line with what is affordable and linked to organisational priorities.

Conclusion

Career development remains a vibrant and important area within the field of human resource development. The concept of careers has changed significantly in the last two decades in line with economic and technological change. It is clear that careers can no longer be defined in terms of attachment to particular organisations, but rather careers have become more strongly associated to the identity and values of individual employees. Active management of one's own career has become a critical activity for employees in order to retain employability and relevance in the jobs market. Indeed, individuals need to pay close attention to current jobs and career opportunities that arise to ensure an appropriate work–life balance and that their career ambitions and values are satisfied. For their part, Sullivan and Mainiero (2007) attest to the growing pervasiveness of work-creep leading to a blurring of work–family boundaries through the proliferation of wireless and mobile technologies and remote working facilities.

In recent years, a number of career concepts have emerged to describe the changing nature of careers and help explain how environmental and economic conditions and personal values are affecting how individuals think about and conceptualise careers. Such concepts recognise the changing expectations of both employers and employees and how their respective roles have evolved in relation to career management and development. It also attests to more strategic approaches to careers being taken by both employers and employees.

In light of current recessionary pressures and declining levels of job security, there is an increasing focus and emphasis being placed on career counselling. A key focus of career counselling lies in ensuring a good fit between an employee's personality traits and vocational choices. Instruments such as Schein's Career Anchors Inventory and Holland's Vocational Preference Inventory are valuable in guiding employees towards jobs that are particularly suited to them. Moreover, they can offer particular benefits to organisations who engage in succession planning in achieve person–job fit and sourcing development interventions to help employees move upwards to the next level.

Finally, continuing professional development remains an important aspect of career development in that it helps professionals keep their knowledge, skills and competence updated. Labelled as either continuing professional development or continuing professional education, it recognises that formal and informal interventions play an important role in helping both individuals and organisations grow and develop. While there is evidence that participation in CPD is sometimes discouraged by supervisors and managers, CPD can be beneficial to employees in helping them connect with other learners, build their confidence and competence and ensure that learners perform up to certifiable standards.

CASE STUDY

Managing careers and talent at Barclays

Barclays is a financial services company with 75,000 employees worldwide. It has long practised succession planning, but the process was onerous and lacked a group-wide perspective. As a result, the discovery of talent was ad hoc and subjective, and there was little development or movement of high potential people across the organisation.

A central Talent Team was charged with the task of refreshing and improving the end-to-end talent-management processes, including executive resourcing, succession planning, leadership development, middle-management talent identification, and graduate recruitment and development.

The new approach involves senior managers working with HR business partners in a more collaborative way to identify and develop talent. There is less emphasis on paperwork, and more concentration on dialogues between senior managers, HR and high potential individuals. It is corporately managed for the top three organisational levels (roughly the top 500 posts), and more devolved for the 'emerging talent' below this level.

'Talent' is now defined through 20 characteristics Barclays looks for in its future group leaders. These are grouped together under 'the three E's': be Exceptional (e.g. driving for success, stretching the boundaries), Edge (e.g. learns quickly, demonstrates sound judgement) and Energising (e.g. mobilises others, makes things happen).

The refreshed succession planning framework has a strong focus on the distribution of potential so that areas of risk can be identified. It asks leaders what action they are taking to develop and deploy talent in their business area.

Talent Development Forums (TDFs) have been introduced to ensure that high-potential people, identified during group talent conversations, gain access to the key experiences they need to reach group-wide leadership roles. TDFs bring 'talented' individuals into a direct discussion with senior executives (outside their own

(Continued)

(Continued)

line management), plus an input from HR. The process started with selected talent identified in the top three levels, and is now being extended downwards. The outcome is a set of agreed career development actions. The process has also helped senior executives get to know the high-potential population better.

For the 'emerging talent' group of high-potential middle managers, Talent Partners are assigned. These are senior managers who develop individuals towards group leadership roles through an intensive coaching relationship.

(Adapted from: Hirsh, W. and Jackson, C. (2004) *Managing Careers in Large Organisations.* London: The Work Foundation.)

Questions

What is the impact of the recent recession on individuals' careers?

Given the increased emphasis on 'talent', should organisations be committed to developing and promoting existing staff or are they better off 'buying in' talent from external labour markets?

What are the benefits of getting your training and development programmes accredited?

Discussion questions

Platman (2003) argues that portfolio careers offer many advantages so long as individuals have experience, wisdom and skills to manage this form of employment relationship. What are the downsides of portfolio careers?

Debate the usefulness of tools such as Schein's Career Anchors and Holland's Vocational Preference Inventory.

How can employees be encouraged to take a more structured and strategic approach to their continuing professional development?

Identity and Diversity

5

The objectives of this chapter are to:

- explore why HRD has largely neglected diversity issues to date and why diversity should play an important role in HRD;
- investigate the benefits of diversity training in organisations;
- consider the barriers faced by minority groups in the workplace and how these can be overcome;
- examine ways in which organisations can embrace diversity in the workplace.

Introduction

Modern workplaces have become a melting pot of diversity – with employees of different genders, ages, races, abilities, sexual orientations and religious outlooks. In this context, there is an increasing awareness on the part of organisations of the need to understand, accommodate, value and leverage such difference and in doing so realise important competitive advantages. In a globalised market, organisations are seeking to connect with consumers' beliefs and cultural norms and are engaging employees who can bring knowledge of these important attributes to the table. Indeed, organisations have learned the high costs associated with an insufficient understanding of local customs and values and are also realising that regional and national markets are not homogeneous entities, but comprise groups of consumers with particular traits. More generally, the benefits of valuing workplace diversity have been articulated by Cox and Blake (1991) as enhanced creativity and problem-solving; reduced employee turnover; more successful marketing campaigns to underrepresented societal groups; greater flexibility to adapt to changing market conditions; and an increased level of productivity.

With such advantages, why then are some organisations resistant to the notion of diversity? Research has indicated that diversity resistance often takes three forms: the cost argument, the political correctness argument and the cultural preservation argument. In relation to cost, some critics claim that the costs of workplace diversity outweigh the benefits and that diversity advocates engage in 'distant cheerleading', praising workplace diversity at a distance without having to deal with practical concerns on a daily basis (Dick and Cassell, 2002). The political correctness argument sees workplace diversity with its attendant diversity training programmes as a form of political correctness which will invariably lead to needless nervousness and caution on behalf of members of the majority group. Such commentators hold the view that diversity training is a perverse form of 'reprogramming' designed to intimidate and blame members of the majority group for historical segregation (Holladay and Quinones, 2008; Stewart et al., 2008). Finally, proponents of the cultural preservation argument seek to preserve a homogeneous monoculture whereby diversity is ignored and treated as a non-issue. In such environments, new employees are forced to assimilate pre-existing norms and values and cultural challenge is not permitted (Andresen, 2007; Sippola, 2007).

In the field of HRD, diversity concepts have faced a considerable degree of resistance. Bierema (2009) notes that diversity is rarely discussed in HRD textbooks, research and academic programmes. With its foundations in democratic values (Hatcher, 2006), it can be argued however that HRD has an important role to play in examining the ethical and social impact of organisational policies and practices, and liberating organisations from the dominance of privileged interests. However, such progress will be difficult to achieve. As McGuire et al. (2005) point out, humanistic ideals in organisations are often overlooked by an instrumental focus on increasing shareholder returns, profit and market share. Consequently, diversity advocates must present a strong case for making diversity a cornerstone of organisational policy and convince organisational decision-makers that a diversity and equality agenda is complementary to organisational goals, rather than contrary to them.

This chapter explores the need for diversity training in the workplace and looks at the benefits and criticisms that have been levelled at it. It then examines the challenges and obstacles faced by employees because of their gender, race or sexuality and outlines HRD interventions that can be deployed to improve openness to diversity in the workplace. Finally, a series of conclusions are drawn in advancing HRD's role in promoting diversity in the workplace.

Diversity training

As a response to legislative requirements and increasing levels of diversity, many organisations have instigated diversity training programmes as a means of dispelling myths regarding diversity, identifying appropriate behaviours and making managers more aware of their responsibilities towards different groups in the workplace. The social goals of diversity training programmes are usually to significantly reduce the incidence of prejudice, bullying and harassment in the workplace and to foster a positive working environment for all employees. To this end, diversity training has become popular as a means of protecting organisations both against a damaged public reputation and against the actions of errant misguided employees and managers.

Through the use of didactic (lectures, videos, persuasion and education) and interactive (discussions, role-playing, simulations, case studies) approaches (Pendry et al., 2007), diversity training often seeks to identify individual feelings about diversity, distribute information about legal requirements and organisational policies and outline the personal impact of discrimination experiences (Hite and McDonald, 2006). In this regard, Anand and Winters (2008) argue that diversity is increasingly being positioned as a competency in organisations as it often leads to a more open, diverse environment leading to higher levels of creativity and divergent thinking.

Safeguarding employee identity is a core objective of diversity training and diversity initiatives in organisations. As Losert (2008) points out, the increase in working hours experienced across westernised countries has led to difficulties in maintaining a healthy work–life balance, leading to a strong need to be able to assert one's own true identity in the workplace. Through diversity training, employees can therefore positively affirm their own distinctiveness, secure in the knowledge that this distinctiveness will be respected by the organisation. There is increasing awareness that in many cases identity is indeed socially constructed, leading to the acceptability of certain behaviours affecting the culture, symbols and ethos of the organisation itself. This emphasises the importance of embedding values of openness and respect for difference across the organisation.

Several pitfalls have been identified in conducting diversity training programmes. Sanchez and Medkik (2004) argue that focusing on awareness-level training only (where knowledge and insights are provided) without behavioural coaching and diversity skill development poorly equips employees and managers in resolving differences in the workplace. Hite and McDonald (2006) highlight problems associated with poorly devised training which is often of too short duration, ignores the role of power in diversity issues and is a one-off event rather than a sustained systemic process. They also point to inadequacies of diversity training evaluation, where participant reactions become the predominant focus, rather than organisational culture change.

In summary, diversity training has the potential to have a transformative effect on organisational behaviour and culture, provided it is designed correctly and is strategically linked to an organisational commitment to valuing diversity. Where diversity training is postured on blaming members of the dominant group for discrimination and workplace/ societal divisions, it is likely to trigger defensive responses, making individuals resistant to change (Karp and Sutton, 1993; Lindsay, 1994). Furthermore, in cases where diversity training involves overly sensitive material and highly personalised experiences, individuals may become uncomfortable and react unfavourably to the training provided.

Gender and the workplace

The participation of women in the workplace and management positions is not new. As Miles (1998) points out, in pre-industrial times, women balanced household chores alongside aspects of agricultural work such as dairy, milking, butter and cheese-making. Despite long-term participation in the labour market, inequalities still exist with male working-age employment in the UK (79.6 per cent) surpassing female working-age employment (69.1 per cent) (Office for National Statistics, 2009). Pay disparities across the gender divide still persist in the UK, with men currently earning 12.8 per cent more than women (Office for National Statistics, 2008). Consequently, it is worth examining why such structural inequalities still exist in an era defined by employment law regulations and a strong focus on equal opportunities.

Removing the barriers to full female participation in the workplace and creating a level playing field across both genders require both an understanding of the obstacles inhibiting full involvement and the development of comprehensive HRD solutions to address issues of inequity and discrimination. O'Neil and Bilimoria (2005) identify three critical factors distinguishing men's and women's careers, leading to differences in workplace experiences. First, they argue that women are differentially tasked with child-rearing and household responsibilities and this has a much greater impact on women's careers than men's. They posit that women's developmental and promotional opportunities are moulded by family responsibilities and this influences career continuity and advancement in the workplace. Second, O'Neil and Bilimoria maintain that women's careers have a distinct relational emphasis which is markedly different from men's. Indeed, Ackah and Heaton (2004) establish that the burden of finding a sustainable system of coping with household and family responsibilities is a key factor explaining why women's careers have not fitted within a traditional upward advancement model with its assumption of a stay-at-home spouse. For this reason, women's careers are marked by periods away from the workplace and are more fragmented and discontinuous than men's careers. Third, O'Neil and Bilimoria found that women's underrepresentation at higher organisational levels constrains their progress and career advancement. The lack of identifiable role models, the persistence of a dominant masculine culture and continued stereotyping and gendered role behaviours has fostered an environment where a minority female presence at board level is accepted.

Coined by journalists Carol Hymowitz and Timothy Schellhardt in a 1986 *Wall Street Journal* article, the metaphor of the 'glass ceiling' describe both the obstacles to women's career advancement and the scarcity of women in top leadership positions. Described as 'a transparent, but real barrier based on discriminatory attitudes or organisational bias, that impedes or prevents qualified individuals (including but not limited to women) from advancing into management positions' (Gibelman, 2000: 251), the glass ceiling hinders succession planning and development initiatives as well as impeding organisational creativity. Van Vianen and Fischer (2002) identify a masculine organisational culture as leading to the persistence of the glass ceiling. They argue that masculine cultures consist of hidden assumptions, norms and practices that promote communication practices, images of leadership, organisational values and definitions of success which promote the masculine over the feminine.

Since the glass ceiling came to light, three other concepts have emerged that have attempted to describe the difficulties that women have experienced in accessing top leadership positions. The concept of the 'glass escalator' was developed by Christine Williams (1992) to explain the steady acceleration of men through the organisational ranks. She maintains that men are sometimes faced with invisible pressures to move up the career ladder in particular professions. She alludes to a set of gender privileges that men possess which more easily place them on an upward trajectory. The concept of the 'glass cliff' was introduced by Michelle Ryan and Alexander Haslam (2004) to explore a phenomenon whereby women's suitability for promotion rises when the chances of failure increases. In their research, Ryan and Haslam (2007) found that because women were more likely to be appointed to top management positions during crisis periods, the risks to their leadership increase and they are more likely to encounter rising levels of conflict and higher stress levels leading to greater exposure to criticism. Finally, the term 'Lucite ceiling' appears to have been coined by Diana Henriques (1991) in an article written in the *New York Times*. In the article, Henriques describes a transparent glass ceiling made from solid unbreakable Lucite to depict the double-marginalisation experienced by women from minority ethnic backgrounds. She argues that minority ethnic women are even more unlikely than (majority) white women to achieve senior management positions and face even greater obstacles and levels of inequality.

More recently, the re-emergence of the 'Queen Bee' concept has been used to describe the lack of support for women in senior management from other women. Mavin (2008) employs the concept to examine the lack of female solidarity caused by some women's opposition to changes in traditional sex roles. She acknowledges the sexist nature of the term and argues that many women in senior management positions will choose to work with men and separate themselves from other women in the organisation, thus withdrawing opportunities for career advancements and looking after their own self-interests. Rather than being a role model for other women, Mavin argues that queen bee managers are fiercely competitive and aggressively engage in fortress keeping and information withholding behaviour to realise their career ambitions. In summary, she characterises the queen bee as an individual senior woman who accepts and understands organisational power bases and sacrifices her femininity to achieve career success.

Several HRD interventions have been shown to help women overcome gender barriers in the workplace. One such intervention is mentoring. According to Kram (1985), mentoring performs two important roles. First, it provides individuals with valuable career support in the form of sponsorship, increased exposure and visibility and coaching sessions. Second, mentoring performs a psychosocial role whereby individuals benefit from friendship, advice, guidance and feedback. Ehrich (2008) maintains that the mentoring process allows women to build levels of self-confidence, learn new leadership skills and construct powerful networks across the organisation and beyond. In addition, Monserrat et al. (2009) maintain that effective mentoring programmes can help prevent career mistakes, increase levels of job satisfaction, and produce higher levels of affective and continued commitment in the organisation.

Networking is an equally important HRD intervention in women's career development. As the glass/Lucite ceiling and queen bee concepts often resist access to networking, this can result in their underrepresentation at senior levels of organisations. Tonge (2008) asserts that social networks can provide access to important information and further relationships with other connected individuals as well as providing important support and encouragement in an individual's career development. She argues that networking is essential to success in any professional career and that the primary advantage derived by women from networking is that of social support. For their part, Donelan et al. (2009) suggest that social networks may help women overcome feelings of isolation and insecurity and enable greater access to role models.

Talking point   Lehman Brothers' Erin Callan: through the glass ceiling – and off the glass cliff

Smart, sassy, young and charismatic, Callan was briefly the golden girl of Wall Street. In multiple television appearances, Callan adopted a plain-speaking patter in the spring of 2008 to reassure investors over the future of the 158-year-old investment bank. A fashionable figure, she seemed a refreshing change from the middle-aged men around her. The only problem was that she got things desperately, spectacularly wrong.

The daughter of a police detective, Callan, 44, has emerged as one of the most intriguing figures from Lehman's demise. She was one of four former Lehman Brothers executives chastised in a 2,200-page bankruptcy court report, which concluded that the bank used misleading gimmicks to bolster its balance sheet by $50bn (£25bn). The court-appointed examiner found evidence that Callan breached her duties by ignoring 'ample red flags' over contentious deals known as 'repo 105' to mask the bank's financial condition.

While Lehman's chief executive, Dick Fuld, and his lieutenants have been lampooned for greed, arrogance and hubris, Callan's predicament has evoked a more complicated response from the financial media and Wall Street. There is a sense of disappointment in her but also a flickering of sympathy that, partly because of her gender, she may have been shoved into an impossible, no-win position, dubbed 'the glass cliff'.

'The biggest mistake Erin Callan made was to accept that job', says Vicky Ward, author of a new book on Lehman's demise, *The Devil's Casino*. She argues that Callan was the unwitting face of a poorly judged effort by Lehman to boost diversity in its top ranks. 'They promoted somebody who wasn't remotely qualified and they made a big "to do" about it.'

A former tax lawyer, Callan joined Lehman's in 1995 and swiftly became a high-flyer, rising to head the bank's successful division serving hedge funds. She caught the attention of Lehman's president, Joe Gregory, who was leading an aggressive company-wide effort to improve Lehman's representation of women, gay people and ethnic minorities. He handed her the bank's top finance job in December 2007, to widespread surprise.

'She didn't even have a basic accounting degree', says Ward. 'To be chief financial officer, you're going to have to sign off the finances.'

To those fighting for more diversity in the financial industry, Callan's rise and fall has a familiar ring. Michelle Ryan, an associate professor of psychology at Exeter University, says there can be a tendency, which she dubs the 'glass cliff', to promote women as a 'bold move' in moments of crisis, when all else has failed: 'I do see her position as a really classic case of the glass cliff. Women often tend to occupy these dangerous leadership positions in dangerous times, when things are getting hairy. When things are going great, it's usually men who occupy these roles.'

Some argue that if the banking industry contained more women, the reckless risk-taking that contributed to the financial crisis might have been mitigated. However, the evidence suggests that Wall Street's gender imbalance has worsened as a result of the recession.

(Adapted from: Clark, A. (2010) Lehman Brother's Golden Girl, Erin Callan: Through the Glass Ceiling – and Off the Glass Cliff. *Guardian*, 19 March.)

Questions

Research contends that that sexism causes those in power to appoint women to risky leadership positions because they don't want to risk tainting a prominent man with the stink of failure. Was this the case with Erin Callan and Lehman Brothers?

How can the glass cliff effect be counteracted?

Race and the workplace

Racial barriers still persist in the workplace. While Sir Trevor Phillips, chairperson of the UK Equality and Human Rights Commission, reports on research that racial prejudice in the UK has markedly declined, he points out that sharp inequalities persist (Phillips, 2009). He argues that educational success is strongly linked to race, and racial disadvantage in itself is often associated with socioeconomic disadvantage. In this way, individuals from an ethnic minority background may enter the workplace at a disadvantage to the majority white community. Research supporting such linkages can be found in the UK Race to the Top report (published by Business in the Community, 2009), which points out that just 5.6 per cent of ethnic minority individuals reach senior management positions, despite these groups representing over 10 per cent of the UK population. Similar racial inequalities persist in the US. Research indicates that differentials based around pay still exist with black men still paid less than white men (Rodgers, 2006). Weeks et al. (2007) argue that notwithstanding the fact that the US represents a melting pot of diversities, blacks tend to fall into lower socioeconomic groupings than whites and it is often difficult to distinguish judgements made on racial or socioeconomic grounds.

Many of the difficulties encountered by ethnic minorities in the workplace can be traced back to the concept of privilege. McIntosh (1993: 31) describes privilege as 'an invisible container of unearned benefits that operates in such a way as to maintain its invisibility, to keep its beneficiaries ignorant of its presence, and to preserve its existence'. By its nature, privilege works to retain its invisibility as by acknowledging privilege, whites must recognise that race as well as hard work contributed to their achievements (McIntosh, 2002). Consequently, the experience of organisations and the workplace is not uniform for all employees. As Grimes (2001) points out, the power of the privileged races can set limits on what activities can be performed and who can perform them. She maintains that knowledge is political and involves a context and a situation such that objective knowledge mostly coincides with the viewpoint of the majority dominant group and the viewpoint of minority groups is marginalised.

According to Barrett et al. (2004), individuals from a minority racial background must overcome a range of institutional and personal challenges to achieve career success. Such challenges exist to protect the privileged position of the dominant majority and serve to limit and exclude access to career opportunities and development to minority employees. Barrett et al. (2004: 86) describe institutional challenges as 'structural and environmental barriers such as limited access to vocational guidance and assessment, tracking into "appropriate" jobs and discrimination in hiring, promotions and transfers'. They go on to describe personal challenges as pertaining to specific individual problems or issues and provide examples such as low self-confidence, limited career exploration, greater career indecision and an unwillingness to play the political game.

The experience of exclusion and isolation is particularly common for individuals from a minority racial background. Minority racial employees are more prone to stereotyping as a result of lower numerical representation and having to adapt to a majority culture that is inhospitable and alien to them (Browne and Misra, 2003). In relation to organisational culture, Hite (1996, 2007) describes the inescapability and pervasiveness of institutional racism as requiring minority racial employees to develop reserves of resilience, inner strength, confidence and impeccable skills. Faifua (2008) notes increasing moves towards worker mobilisation through trade unions and workplace groups. He argues that this often arises out of the need to combat a sense of isolation, a drive to reassert identity and promote unity in the workplace and an attempt to open new opportunities for individuals and groups. This attempt to re-establish community seeks to bring minority employees together under a banner of common aspirations and reassert democratic ideals at the heart of the workplace.

Alongside networking and worker mobilisation, mentoring also plays an important role in widening opportunities for employees from a minority racial background. A key discussion in the research literature examines whether the mentor to a minority racial employee should come from a white background or minority racial background. Barrett et al. (2004) advocate mentoring by a white male as they tend to have stronger networks and more influence. However, Barrett et al. acknowledge that having someone from the same racial background brings with it more candid communication due to commonalties of experience. While covering many of the same points as Barrett et al. (2004), a different conclusion is reached by Thomas (2001) in relation to mentoring minority racial employees. Thomas (2001) argues that having a mentor of the same racial background leads to closer, fuller developmental relationships. He argues that having a mentor from a minority background is particularly important in an individual's early career where the minority racial employee may need to build confidence, credibility and competence. However, Thomas et al. (2007) caution that, regardless of racial background, mentors need to have the necessary competencies to effectively mentor individuals and training may often be required to develop mentor skills to an appropriate level.

Sexuality and the workplace

Openly expressing one's sexuality in the workplace is still fraught with difficulty. Ward and Winstanley (2005: 447) argue that 'sexuality is an under-researched area of diversity in work organisations as well as being one of the most difficult to research'. Alongside this fact, there is an acknowledged lack of robust statistical data on the proportion of the UK population who self-identify as lesbian, gay, bisexual or transgendered (LGBT) (Colgan et al., 2007). Kirby (2006) maintains that the workplace sometimes represents a hostile environment for LGBT individuals and a place where they may be likely to face discrimination. She argues that such discrimination often results from fear, stereotyping and misunderstanding, indicating that there exists a need to educate workplace managers and supervisors on sexuality in the workplace alongside greater research on the topic.

LGBT people often face a range of discriminatory practices and behaviours in the workplace. Gedro et al. (2004) argues that such practices and behaviours can include being passed over for raises or promotions; having to take on additional responsibilities; being subjected to verbal harassment or property damage and loss of respect from colleagues and co-workers. Likewise, Kirby (2006) argues that individuals who disclose their sexual orientation (other than the majority hetero-sexual orientation) in the workplace are more likely to encounter negative atti-tudes and receive fewer promotions. This often leads to LGBT people closeting their sexuality or alternatively, taking on the persona of a heterosexual while at work.

The suppression of sexuality (and identity) while at work has significant conse-quences for LGBT people in the workplace. Gedro (2010) argues that lesbians face dual pressures emanating from their gender and sexuality. She posits that lesbians also encounter pressures related to gender expression. She explains that gender expression relates to how an individual portrays their gender identity to others through behaviours, dress, hairstyles, voice and other body characteristics. As such, lesbians are often expected to follow traditional female-role norms, yet gender expression does not correlate neatly with sexual orientation. Consequently, the dominance of heterosexual norms often forces LGBT people to act and behave unnaturally in the workplace.

The decision to 'come out of the closet' or disclose one's sexuality in the work-place is a major decision for LGBT people. Research by Schmidt and Nilsson (2006) identifies that the early stages of sexual identity development for LGBT people can be characterised by homonegativity, identity confusion, inner turmoil and feelings of personal alienation. Consequently, it may take some time for individuals to reach a fully integrated gay identity. Nam Cam Trau and Hartel (2004) argue that the deci-sion to come out is often made through balancing identity issues with the priority placed on careers and relationships. Gedro et al. (2004) identify several stages in the process of coming out. First, LGBT people often learn about pre-screening, which involves trying to ascertain what the response of a boss or supervisor will be once their sexuality becomes known. In so doing, an assessment is made on the degree of homosexual tolerance on the basis of music, art, beliefs, films, etc. Second, upon deciding that it may be safe to reveal one's sexuality, individuals carefully select the timing and communication method by which to disclose. Third, LGBT people may engage in a process of educating others about the challenges and issues they face and advocate changing policies and procedures to be more open and respectful of people of all sexual orientations.

Talking point   Coming out in the workplace

In their research, Gedro et al. (2004) document the experiences of lesbians coming out in the workplace. In the following interview extracts, Pam, a marketing director, describes her experiences:

> With an employee that works for me, we were at lunch and I hadn't come out to him and he had been with the company maybe four months or something like that and he was talking about him and his wife and he happened to be talking about the gay area of town. Not calling it the 'gay area of town' but you know that him and his wife like to go to a restaurant down there. I said, 'Oh, we go there a lot too.' And then I just threw in, you know, that's kind of the gay area and I happen to be a lesbian and I like that restaurant cause I feel so comfortable there. From then on, I wasn't having to hold back anything.

> The people who report to me, pretty much every one knows. The people who I've worked with several years, pretty much every one knows. But it's not the kind of thing like when I'm into a new position I don't announce it immediately ... I'd rather for the person to get to know me and to from a work perspective get to know my work before they categorize me.

Questions

How can organisations encourage and foster a more tolerant inclusive culture?

What support can be given to minority groups in the workplace to help them overcome discrimination and prejudice in the workplace?

Human resource development has an important role to play in supporting LGBT people in the workplace. HRD professionals need to ensure that organisational policies are open and inclusive and work with managers and supervisors to make them aware of workplace issues affecting LGBT people. In relation to organisational practices, Barbosa and Cabral-Cardoso (2007) note that selection decisions tend to favour familiar applicants in order to avoid the uncertainty associated with the 'unknown' – consequently, this may disadvantage applicants having a sexual orientation different from the majority. Barbosa and Cabral-Cardoso (2007) also emphasise the importance of developing an open, tolerant organisational culture, as prescribing a particular dress code and look, for example, may reflect the outlook of the dominant majority. Bairstow and Skinner (2007) argue that discriminatory practices may exist in reward practices, with some benefits only available to heterosexual couples such as unequal pensions, healthcare provision, access to bereavement leave, company car use and access to other corporate services.

Conclusion

To date, the field of HRD has devoted only limited attention to diversity issues in the workplace. A study of four years of AHRD proceedings by Bierema and Cseh (2003) concluded that gender and race issues were considerably underrepresented in HRD research and much HRD research neglects diversity issues. To treat organisations as singular entities devoid of diversity is to ignore the richness of employee backgrounds and experiences. If organisations are to prioritise creativity and innovation, then it is imperative that unique perspectives are valued and appreciated. Thus, it is critical that organisational barriers faced by diverse groups are identified and addressed.

A 'cradle to grave' review of organisational practices needs to be adopted to ensure that such practices meet the needs of both the dominant group and diverse group. The direct and indirect effects of organisational practices need to be considered as such practices can often affect the culture that exists within the organisation. Enabling employees to live their identity within the organisation without fear of harassment or reprisal will lead to employees with higher levels of job satisfaction and job commitment. Thus attention needs to be devoted to integrating diversity within an organisation's structural, political and cultural framework.

HRD interventions can be usefully deployed towards embedding diversity as a core objective of the organisation. Mentoring and networking activities will allow minority individuals to forge important relationships and help them develop and advance their own careers. Such interventions can boost an individual's level of self-confidence and can assist individuals link up with important role models. Diversity and awareness training can make supervisors and managers more aware of the challenges facing diverse employees and help them support employees facing instances of workplace discrimination.

CASE STUDY

The significance of Stephen Lawrence

By Ian Blair

The collective failure of an organisation to provide an appropriate and professional service to people because of their colour, culture or ethnic origin. It can be seen or detected in processes, attitudes and behaviour, which amount to discrimination through unwitting prejudice, ignorance, thoughtlessness and racist stereotyping.

Amid the torrent of words spoken and written after the convictions of two men for the murder of Stephen Lawrence in 1993, there has perhaps been too little emphasis on the Macpherson report into the initial investigation of the case and on the 46 words above. These were the heart of the report, a definition of the then little-known concept of institutional racism.

The first reaction to the trial process has been to contemplate the appalling and naked racism not only implicit in the murder, but seen in the surveillance video of the suspects fantasising about torturing and killing black men.

The Met had expected the Macpherson report to be highly critical; after all it had seen some of its own witnesses perform lamentably on the witness stand. It was braced for condemnation. Subsequently its homicide investigation and intelligence systems were transformed. The most important idea the Met had, however, was to create a series of independent advisory groups (IAGs), comprised of many of the force's fiercest critics, to provide feedback on policy as well as individual cases and incidents.

Much merriment has been had at the expense of the Met for its fostering of staff associations based on ethnicity and faith after the Lawrence case. Yet it was the Black Police Association which suggested that it send its Yoruba-speaking members down to Peckham to help solve the murder of Damilola Taylor in 2000. What the IAGs demanded was just that sort of approach: emotional intelligence, an understanding that racial hatred, like misogyny, underlay much serious violence and that only by undertaking investigations with communities rather than doing investigations to them would the Met succeed.

I have no doubt the changes that flowed from Lawrence underpinned the rise in minority recruitment at the Met, which has quadrupled in the past decade. I also have no doubt that if, as is widely agreed, the inner-city riots of last summer [2011] were not racially based, that is due to ten years of change in London's policing.

Sir Robert Mark, commissioner of the Met in the 1970s, suggested that 'the police are the anvil on which society beats out the problems and abrasions of social inequality, racial prejudice, weak laws and ineffective legislation'. Thanks to the energy and passion of the Lawrences, the deserved beating of the police over the inadequate original investigation into their son's death gave the whole country its single greatest opportunity for change in relation to matters of race and diversity.

Yet there is far to go. The Mark Duggan case, which precipitated the riots in August [2011], seems to indicate that the Yard has forgotten at least some of its

(Continued)

(Continued)

training. The *Independent on Sunday* reports that ethnic-minority citizens are twice as likely as their white peers to die under the age of one, three times as likely to be excluded from school and four times as likely to be murdered. We must remember that racism springs from not just thuggery, but the denial of equal opportunity and fair treatment. It would be a betrayal indeed of the progress that has been made since 1993 if we lost sight of the significance of Stephen's legacy.

Ian Blair was commissioner of the Metropolitan Police (2005–2008). (Adapted from: Blair, I. (2012) The Significance of Stephen. *New Statesman*, 16 January.)

Questions

Discuss the importance of managing diversity both internally and externally for the Metropolitan Police Service.

What mechanisms could the Metropolitan Police Service put in place to improve diversity awareness and understanding amongst police officers?

How important is it that police force membership should reflect the communities which they serve?

Discussion questions

Why do organisations resist diversity? How can HRD adopt a more proactive role?

How can the HRD function support minority employees in the workplace?

What is the business case for embracing diversity in the workplace?

Part 2
HRD at the Organisational Level

Training and Development 6

The objectives of this chapter are to:

- examine the learning theories underpinning particular training interventions;
- look at the knowledge/skills mix associated with training interventions;
- review Baldwin and Ford's model in relation to training transferability;
- present a framework for examining training interventions across a number of important dimensions.

Introduction

The provision of training and development programmes in organisations realises a number of important benefits for individual employees, their work departments and the organisation as a whole. Elangovan and Karakowsky (1999) argue that organisations gain from training programmes through the improved performance and increased productivity that accompany employee development, while employees enjoy extrinsic and intrinsic rewards associated with skill development and performance improvement. As an expensive investment in an employee's future (Cheng and Ho, 2001), organisations are constantly seeking to improve on the effectiveness and return on their investment. Consequently, much attention has been devoted towards optimising training design and facilitating greater transfer of training back to the workplace (Holton and Bates, 2000). However, critics have argued that much research on training effectiveness is both atheoretical and faddish (Baldwin and Ford, 1988; Clark et al., 1993). In particular, Clark et al. (1993) state:

> Researchers have frequently attempted to increase the effectiveness of training by focusing on training techniques. Special attention has also been paid to the arrangement of training environments. But without a theoretical basis for studying the techniques and training environments, researchers are often at a loss either to explain why they are effective or to predict their effectiveness in other settings or for other trainees. (p. 294)

In recognising the criticisms levelled at research on training effectiveness, we have decided in this chapter not simply to review a selection of commonly used training interventions, but rather, we examine these training interventions across seven separate training dimensions: learning theory; knowledge–skills mix; training transferability; degree of learner involvement; locus of initiation; degree of reflection; and cost. Employing this approach permits a more detailed analysis of the strengths and weaknesses of each intervention, allowing the reader to make a more considered choice of intervention to fit their particular circumstances. Table 6.1 provides an overview of training interventions across each of these dimensions.

Learning theories

It is widely acknowledged that there has been something of a 'language turn' in contemporary discourse on education, training and development (Holmes, 2004; Honey, 1998). This emphasis on learning asserts that the individual learner should take responsibility for learning and determine the 'what' and 'where' of learning as well as adjudicating the effectiveness of the learning process. Garavan (1997) argues that increasing an individual's capacity to learn and their involvement in the learning process is critical to ensuring its effectiveness. Training provision should therefore be sensitive to the learning needs and styles of participants. Despite arguments by Swieringa and Wierdsma (1992) that training is one of the most important interventions to nurture the learning process, both Robotham (2003) and Berge et al. (2002) maintain that training focuses too much on the trainer, while in learning, the focus is on the learner.

Selecting particular training interventions to fit the learning styles of participants is a common method used by trainers. Hayes and Allinson (1996) suggest that it is unclear whether once having identified an individual's learning style, it is then more effective to match the training style used to that particular learning style or to aim for a deliberate mismatch between training and learning styles. Whichever approach is adopted, it is important to have a detailed understanding of the learning theories underpinning training interventions.

Table 6.1 An examination of the dimensions of commonly used training interventions

Intervention	Learning theory	Knowledge–skills mix	Training transferability	Degree of learner interaction	Locus of initiation	Degree of reflection	Cost
Lecture	Cognitivism (expository teaching)	Predominantly knowledge driven	Low level of similarity between learning and performance context	Large number of participants	Formal, planned and highly structured	Reflection on action	Generally low
Role play	Constructivism (simulation)	Both knowledge and skills based	High level of similarity between learning and performance context	One-to-one exercise with observers	Structured activity	Reflection in action	Medium
Group discussion	Collaborative learning Experiential learning theory	Can be knowledge or skills based	Medium degree of transferability as discussion tends to be specific	Involves a number of participants	Loosely structured activity	Reflection on action	Low
Workshops	Collaborative learning Experiential learning theory	Can be knowledge or skills based	Medium degree of transferability as discussion tends to be specific	Involves facilitator and number of participants	Highly structured activity – facilitator led	Reflection on action	Medium
Case study	Constructivism (simulation)	Can be knowledge or skills based	Medium degree of transferability as discussion tends to be specific	Individual activity	Structured non-directed activity	Reflection on action	Low
Projects	Constructivism	Tends to be knowledge based	High level of applicability to performance context	Individual activity	Self-directed activity which typically follows a set structure	Reflection on action	Low
Distance learning including e-learning	Cognitivism	Predominantly knowledge driven	Low level of similarity between learning and performance context	Individual activity – limited interaction	Structured activity in an informal setting	Reflection on action	Medium – high
Learning logs	Reflective learning	May relate to both knowledge and skills	High level of applicability to performance context	Individual activity	Informal, self-directed activity	Reflection on action	Low
Mentoring/ apprenticeship	Experiential learning theory	May relate to both knowledge and skills	High level of applicability to performance context	Individual activity	Structured activity facilitated by experienced individual	Reflection on action	Medium
Outward bound training	Experiential learning theory	May relate to both knowledge and skills	Medium degree of transferability as discussion tends to be specific	Individual or group activities	Planned and highly structured set of activities	Reflection in action	High

Lectures are the most common form of training intervention and are used by 93 per cent of organisations in training employees (Communications, 2001; Froiland, 1993). Although less common, distance learning also concerns the presentation of material in a structured logical manner. Based upon cognitivist approaches to learning, the use of lectures and distance learning assumes that individuals are capable of structuring and ordering information in order for it to make sense. Anderson (2000) distinguishes three categories of information – procedural, declarative and episodic. He suggests that procedural information relates to routines and sequences, while declarative information involves the accumulation of facts, concepts and principles. Finally, episodic information entails the recall of different events. Cognitivism assumes that individuals are capable of encoding these types of information for future recall and utilisation (Silber, 2002).

The use of role plays, case studies and simulations constitutes useful methods for developing skills through practice, changing employee attitudes and increasing diagnostic and problem-solving skills (Carter, 2002). Based upon a constructivist view of learning, these methods require participants to interact with material in a specified context. Both Hwang (1996) and Bednar et al. (1991) advocate a constructivist view of learning and argue that learners build an internal representation of knowledge as well as a personal and social interpretation of such experiences. Such views ascribe to human knowing as a relational phenomenon (Patriotta, 2003), with Bramming (2004) arguing that individual and organisation are mutually constitutive, meaning that they are always producing each other and at the same time are the products of each other.

The use of group discussions, workshops and outward-bound training engages participants in experiential learning. Following Piaget's (1970) dialectic of cognitive organisation and cognitive adaption, experiential learning theory is viewed as an action-oriented process actively shaping the attitudinal and belief system of individuals through experiencing specific situations. In this regard, Holman et al. (1997) argue that the social relationships that individuals form are of critical importance to learning. The construction of meaning is considered to be both an internal and external activity and collaboration with others can form the basis of learning as much as argument and debate with oneself.

Knowledge–skills mix

Determining the correct mix of knowledge and skills is critically important in determining the content of training programmes. Increasingly, knowledge is becoming a key organisational resource impacting on the competitiveness of firms. Leonard-Barton (1992) argues that managing knowledge is a skill and managers who understand and develop it will dominate competitively. Within the firm, Itami (1987) emphasises the embodied nature of knowledge and its importance in determining an organisation's competitive power. Nelson and Winter (1982) argue that firms constitute a 'repository of knowledge' whose past and present ways of organising and managing stimulate or inhibit knowledge creation. Both Kessels and Harrison (2004) and Russell and Parsons (1996) maintain that research into knowledge-intensive organisations provides support for an emphasis that is less on devising management systems to 'control' learning or to 'manage' knowledge, and more on finding new ways to encourage people to think creatively and feed their thoughts back into the organisation.

Alavi and Denford (2012) identify three important knowledge management processes central to the effective functioning of knowledge in organisations, namely, knowledge creation, knowledge storage and retrieval, and knowledge transfer and sharing. According to Mitchell and Boyle (2010: 69), knowledge creation 'refers to the initiatives and activities undertaken towards the generation of new ideas or objects'. They see the process of knowledge creation as distinguishing 'between what is known and what must be known for project/product success'. To this end, knowledge creation involves tapping into tacitly held insights and experiences, that may be embodied, embraced, embedded or encultured, and through learning and development interventions, making such knowledge explicit for the benefit of the organisation as a whole. While commentators may differ in categorising knowledge as a process, outcome or output, there is consensus that the key role of knowledge creation is the generation and development of new ideas to enhance organisational products and processes.

Knowledge storage and retrieval examine the development of organisational memory and a knowledge management architecture for safely and efficiently storing knowledge and allowing its speedy retrieval when required. To this end, Alavi and Denford (2012) differentiate between internal and external organisational memory. They explain that internal memory includes knowledge that resides within the heads, experiences and insights of individuals and groups of individuals, whereas external memory comprises stored and codified knowledge which may consist of organisational policies, procedures and computer files. Gammelgaard and Ritter (2005) assert that knowledge can be retrieved by four primary mechanisms: reliance on individual memory, recovery from organisational databases, recalling knowledge through social capital and recollecting knowledge through communities of practice. These four mechanisms help organisations maintain a current and relevant supply of knowledge through which they can achieve competitive advantage in the marketplace.

Knowledge transfer and sharing is the third knowledge management process identified by Alavi and Denford (2012). Wilkesmann et al. (2009) argue that knowledge transfer and sharing can occur at the individual, intra-organisational and inter-organisational level. Knowledge transfer is often relational in nature and can rely upon the networks, linkages and trust built up between individuals, business units and organisations. As knowledge transfer and application are often linked to improved performance outcomes, it is critical that the learning and development function offers opportunities for individuals and groups to come together informally to share ideas and build collaborative ventures. Efforts must also be made to ensure that useful knowledge moves around the organisation and does not become entrenched within organisational silos. The dynamic interchange of individuals and networks will ensure that organisational knowledge remains current and aligned to business needs.

In relation to skills, many studies have focused on highlighting the significant gaps between current workforce skills and organisational skill requirements (Saunders et al., 2005). Increasingly, skills have been usurped into the language of competencies, which seeks a stronger linkage to overall organisational strategy. Empirical evidence exists to suggest that the competency movement has taken hold in a number of countries, among them Australia, the US the UK, the Scandinavian countries and Israel (Boyatzis and Kolb, 1995; Garavan and McGuire, 2001). Competencies have been conceptualised in a number of different ways: as characteristics of individuals, as characteristics of organisations and as a mode of discourse between education and the labour market (Garavan and McGuire, 2001). The transition from skills to competencies is marked by recognition of the importance attaching to the knowledge economy and the role of skills in supporting knowledge creation and dissemination.

Dick et al. (2001) distinguish three categories of skills that can form the basis of training programmes, namely, verbal skills, intellectual skills and psychomotor skills. Within the realm of verbal skills, they argue that these skills require learners to provide specific responses to relatively specific questions. These skills do not require symbolic manipulation or application of rules and procedures. The second category, intellectual skills, requires learners to apply their cognitive capabilities towards solving a problem or in manipulating information. The increasing intellectualisation of work arising from modern integrated production systems demands that employees have the capacity to detect, identify and solve problems (Svensson et al., 2004). Finally, psychomotor skills involve the coordination of mental and physical activity (Dick et al., 2001). In a training context, there is evidence to suggest that video-based training is an easier medium for learning psychomotor skills than traditional classroom methods (Marx and Frost, 1998). Indeed, further research by Ginzburg and Dar-El (2000) indicates that forgetting is quicker in relation to intellectual skills and psychomotor skills.

Training transferability

The successful transfer of skills and knowledge from the training room to the workplace is one of the key challenges facing instructors and organisations. A study by Georgenson (1982) suggests that employees transfer less than 10 per cent of training expenditures back to their workplaces. Kelly (1982) argues that one of the reasons for a low rate of training transfer relates to the isolated and peripheral nature of the training function and the fact that training transfer is not 'built into' the training programme. Not only does such research pose problems for investing organisations eager to expand production and increase profits, but it also undermines the reputation of the training profession and its perceived utility. Eraut (2004) maintains that training transfer is particularly difficult because of the differences in context, culture and modes of learning. In this section, we examine the characteristics of trainees, explore similarities in the learning-performance context and consider the work community and support provided to the learner in facilitating transfer of training.

Baldwin and Ford (1988) define training transfer as the application of knowledge, skills and attitudes learned from training on the job and subsequent maintenance of them over a period of time. In their seminal model, they identify trainee characteristics (personality, trainee ability, motivation effects), training design (principles of learning, sequencing and training content) and work environment (support-in-organisation, continuous learning culture, task constraints) as factors affecting the transfer of training process (Figure 6.1).

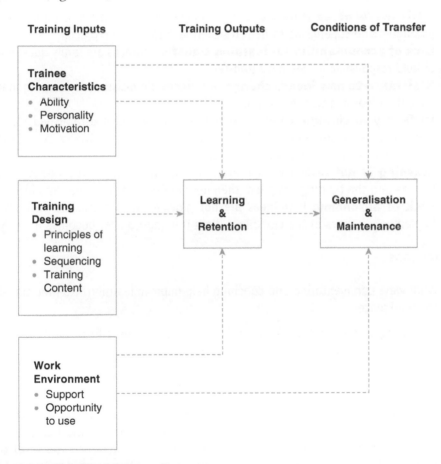

Figure 6.1   Model of training transfer process

Source: Baldwin and Ford (1988).

Talking point   Training transfer in the workplace

Holton et al. (2010) identify eight challenges to effective learning/training transfer in the workplace. Understanding such barriers can help improve the effectiveness of training programmes.

- **Lack of time:** Individuals are faced with very heavy workloads and lots of priorities which can affect their commitment to transfer learning back to the workplace.
- **Learning transfer is not seen as important:** In this case, either the employee or the organisation does not recognise or emphasise the importance of learning transfer in the workplace.
- **A DIY model of learning transfer:** Trainees receive insufficient support from managers and supervisors to help transfer back to the workplace.
- **Lack of accountability for learning transfer:** Trainees are rarely questioned or held responsible for learning transfer.
- **Resistance to new ideas/change:** If trainees are resistant to learning materials, then learning transfer is unlikely.
- **Difficulty in changing behaviour:** Trainees may have established routine inefficient behaviours in the workplace over time and may experience difficulty in changing such inefficient behaviours.
- **Learning is not relevant:** If there is a poor fit between the needs of the trainee and the training provided, then learning transfer becomes less likely.
- **Lack of autonomy:** If trainees are not provided with sufficient freedom to implement changes in the workplace, then training transfer becomes unlikely.

Questions

In what ways can mentoring and coaching help improve learning/training transfer in the workplace?

Should greater consideration be given to 'follow-up' sessions which could be scheduled three and six months after training is delivered?

The personality, ability and motivation of trainees is an important factor in determining the level of training transfer. A study by Oakes et al. (2001) found that personality factors can influence skill acquisition, which in turn can influence the level of job performance. From a Jungian personality perspective, Myers and McCauley (1986) argue that variations in behaviour are actually quite orderly and consistent, being due to differences in the way individuals prefer to use their perception and judgement. In this regard, Smith (2005) argues that the degree to which an individual is sensing or intuitive and thinking or feeling will affect how we perceive and take in information. Humphreys (1979) states that ability is an important factor in determining both the success of training and its effective transfer back to the workplace. Indeed, Schmidt and Hunter (1992) argue that cognitive ability represents the most valid predictor of job learning and performance. As an innate quality of an individual, cognitive ability determines the speed of acquisition of new skills and knowledge. The motivation of individuals plays a key role in the success of the training programme. Thomson et al. (2001) argue that trainees are often very instrumentalist in relation to undertaking training and development activities, and often are preoccupied with the 'exchange' value of qualifications rather than their actual 'use' to the organisation. Furthermore, trainers need to be aware of the anxiety levels of participants as these can affect feelings of self-efficacy and the conviction of individuals that they can master a given task (Wexley and Latham, 1991). Both Brown and Morrissey (2004) and Brown and McCracken (2004) argue that verbal self-guidance, where people learn to overcome negative self-statements that inhibit transfer, can improve transfer in terms of self-efficacy.

The degree of similarity between the learning and performance contexts is critical to effective training transfer. A number of studies on training transfer have concluded that transfer increases with the similarity between the training context and performance context (Bruce, 1933; Gibson, 1941; McKinney, 1933). Stein (2001) argues that effective learning requires the building of an instructional environment sensitive to the tasks trainers must complete to be successful in practice. In this regard, Kim and Lee (2001) distinguish between near transfer, where a high degree of similarity exists between training and task content, and far transfer, where there exists an approximate match between training and task content (Table 6.2).

Both Clark et al. (1997) and Nitsch (1977) argue that it is important that training be demonstrated in varied contexts in order to enhance training transfer, particular far transfer.

Table 6.2 The relationship between training content and design and training transfer

	Near transfer	**Far transfer**
Relationship between the training content and work task	Close match such that the training content and outcomes relate to one work task	Approximate match such that the training content and outcomes relate to a set of related work tasks
Training design	• Specific concepts • Procedures • Problem-solving • Decision-making	• General concepts • Broad principles • Problem-solving rules • Decision-making rules

Source: Kim and Lee (2001).

The degree of support and encouragement offered to trainees will affect the rate of training transfer. Clark et al. (1993) report that the expected training transfer climate will affect the perceived job utility of training. They found that trainees were more motivated to learn when they perceived that their training was related to performance in their current job or would provide them with an opportunity for future advancement. They also found that the level of supervisory support will affect trainee motivation and where supervisory support is low, trainees will place a low utility value on training. MacNeil (2004) argues that there is a need for supervisors to move away from managing in a command and control style, which is inadequate for the facilitator role of enabling trust, to tacit knowledge sharing in teams.

Individuals need to be provided with an opportunity to practise learned skills when they return to the work environment. Relapse prevention strategies, which may involve practice opportunities and assessment strategies, can be used to reinforce learning outcomes. Research has shown that relapse prevention strategies, which help minimise skill erosion among trainees, can positively affect levels of training transfer (Tziner and Haccoun, 1991; Wexley and Nemeroff, 1975). Likewise, Duncan (1984) argues that the amount of training transfer increases with an increasing amount of practice and, second, that variation in training techniques increases the level of training transfer.

Degree of learner interaction

The degree of learner interaction in the learning process is crucial to the success of the training event and ownership of learning. Verdonschot and Kwakman (2004) argue that contact and interaction between people are key ingredients for learning and knowledge construction to take place.

Hillman et al. (1994) distinguish four forms of interaction: learner–teacher, learner–learner, learner–content and learner–technology. With regard to the first two listed forms of interaction (person-to-person contact), Patel (2003) considers the interaction between a trainer and student to be a social act that needs to encompass the personal, professional, social and human needs of the learner. He argues that these needs are not merely to learn knowledge but to be heard, praised and accepted within a community of learners. Person-to-person encounters also present other advantages for ensuring beneficial learning occurs. First, direct interactional relationships encourage bonds of respect and friendship to be formed amongst training participants. Von Krogh (1988) argues that such bonds are manifested in behaviours such as mutual trust, empathy, access to help and cooperation and leniency in judgement. Second, Duncan (1972) argues that with face-to-face conversations, there is a constant back-channelling process, during which participants respond to each other and constantly reinforce each other's contribution with simple gestures, eye contact, nodding of a person's head and short verbal exchanges. Sacks et al. (1974) agree that in face-to-face encounters, there is a turn-taking system in action.

In learner–content situations, learners are required to display greater self-discipline and motivation to learn. In contrast to previous forms of interaction, Thompson and Thompson (2004) describe learner–content methods (e.g. distance education) as instructional delivery in which learners and teachers are separated during the learning process by time and/or space. As a training method, distance learners may suffer from diminished access to social networks and support through shared experience usually found within educational environments, but it may provide learners with the freedom to become self-directed in their learning. Patel (2003) defines self-direction in interaction terms as marked by a situation where the student takes ownership of knowledge and the methods of establishing knowledge and develops responsibility for it. Knowles et al. (2005) describe the difficulties of developing self-directed learners and decry the instructor-dependency culture that arises the minute adults walk into traditional education and revert back to the conditioning of their previous passive school experience. They argue more generally that trainers need to acknowledge and respond to adults' need for self-direction. For their part, Cho and Kwon (2005) maintain that organisations are increasingly looking to self-directed learning to increase flexibility in the delivery of training programmes and reduce training costs.

In learner–technology situations, learners are expected to have an advanced level of technical ability prior to commencing instruction. Benjamin (1994) argues that e-learning frees learners from rigid schedules and physical limitations and passes control for learning back to the learner. The anonymity and security of the internet may also empower certain learners to become more involved than in a traditional face-to-face situation. However, Vrasidas and Zembylas (2003) argue that online interaction suffers from reduced speed of communication and lacks continuity, richness and immediacy when compared to face-to-face interaction. They argue that the absence of non-verbal cues and the often disjointed nature of online communication interrupts the continuity of conversation and can create obstacles to learning for students inexperienced in technology-mediated interaction.

In summary, the degree of learner interaction plays an important role in encouraging learners to become more actively involved and to take on more ownership of their learning. Streibel (1991) comments that a training system should encourage discourse practices involving collaboration and interaction to produce more effective learning. If the goal of such a system is self-directed learners, then Kerka (1999) argues that self-directed learners are neither independent nor dependent, but interdependent, forming new understanding through dialogue, feedback and reflection with others.

Locus of initiation

The degree of formalisation of training courses and the structure attaching to both organisations and programmes can have a significant impact on the effectiveness of the training itself. Merx-Chermin and Nijhof (2004) argue that it is necessary in work organisations to configure work–learning environments to facilitate processes of knowledge retrieval, development of new knowledge combinations and the sharing of knowledge across departmental boundaries. Maxwell et al. (2004) recognise the importance of organisational culture as enabling greater dissemination and dispersal of training throughout the organisation. They argue that learning is a means of transmitting and changing culture as well as a product of it.

Some commentators, however, have suggested that organisations need to re-examine training approaches. Bryans and Smith (2000) argue that there is a need for organisations to move beyond the narrowness of training, while avoiding the decontextualisation of development. They suggest that individuals should form dialectical relationships with organisations which are richer and more responsive to the conditions of a knowledge economy. This involves recognising and removing barriers to knowledge sharing and facilitating inclusion and open communication within the organisation. McCracken (2005) argues that key to the creation of a learning culture is the strategic recognition of training and HRD by top management. Likewise, Sambrook and Stewart (2000) advocate greater involvement of line managers and employees in order to create an open learning culture within the organisation.

Degree of reflection

In line with broader moves within professional associations to develop more reflective practitioners, this section examines the degree of reflection associated with training interventions. Childs (2005) argues that the quest to become a reflective practitioner is marked by means and ways whereby thought–action becomes deliberately and deliberatively linked as an iterative process. She maintains that critical reflection aims to stimulate not thought alone, but reflected actions, whereby the individual examines their behaviour and the lessons to be learned from it. Likewise, Swieringa and Wierdsma (1992) argue that it is through reflection that both individuals and groups can make a 'leap' in their learning process.

In defining critical reflection, Dewey (1933) argues that reflective thinking is characterised by a state of doubt, hesitation, perplexity or mental difficulty in which thinking originates through a process of searching and enquiring to put an end to doubt and uncertainty. Later work by Schon (1983) draws an important distinction between 'reflection in action' and 'reflection on action'. He describes the former concept as 'a reflective conversation with a unique and uncertain situation'. Jones and Kriflik (2005) argue that it represents a spiral integrating elements of appreciation, action and reappreciation allowing managers to think creatively and permit them to reframe problems and experiences. In relation to the latter concept, Schulz (2005) argues that reflection on action allows employees to bridge practical knowing and theoretical knowledge about practice. This encourages a deeper understanding of system and product processes and greater awareness of differences in rhetoric and reality.

Stein (2000) maintains that reflection leads to new understanding through surfacing social, political, professional, economic and ethical assumptions which are influencing a particular course of action. Clearly, an understanding of such assumptions can lead to new thinking and innovation, which has benefits for both the individual and organisation. In this regard, Reynolds (1998) suggests that critical reflection involves an analysis of power and control and an examination of the 'taken-for-granted' world within which the task or problem is situated. However, both Densten and Gray (2001) and Reynolds (1999) argue that engaging in reflection can cause individual discomfort and dissonance. They argue that three attributes are needed for critical reflection: namely, open-mindedness, responsibility and wholeheartedness. Likewise, Robotham (2003) sees an important role for trainers in leading by example and promoting reflective practice. However, he argues that unless trainers are able to engage actively in introspection on their own learning processes, they will be less able to promote such engagement in others.

Cost

The issue of cost is critical to determining commitment to employee training programmes. As a needs-based investment, Wright and Belcourt (1995) argue that training and development has long struggled between those who regarded it as a cost (input-based) and those who viewed it as a benefit (output-based). Training is an expensive activity and, as Palmer and Smith (1999) argue, the majority of training programmes have produced disappointing outcomes in relation to the level of money invested. Underpinning investment in training has been the traditional assumption that organisations support training because it shows concern for employees and there is an assumption that the benefits will exceed the cost (Campbell, 1994). Moreover, the success of training programmes has often relied on subjectively perceived quality as adjudged through happy-sheets from participants.

Research has shown that the most successful SMEs (small and medium sized enterprises) provide much more training than average (Competitiveness, 1996). However, the cost of training is considered to be greater for SMEs due to the absence cost of managers and the fact that training costs are spread over a small group of employees (Loan-Clarke et al., 1999). Moreover the direct financial costs of training include annual registration fees, costs of books and journals, costs of attending events, programme documentation and research. Some less direct costs include time, networking activities, committee membership by legal professionals and other voluntary meetings.

Talking point   Costing training and development

In many organisations, training is delivered through HRD departments that are established as revenue or profit centres and charge participants for taking part in training interventions. In the eyes of some commentators, charging organisational departments for training courses runs contrary to the goal of establishing a learning culture across the organisation. Below are the advantages and disadvantages of structuring HRD departments as revenue/profit centres.

Advantages of a revenue/profit centre approach

- Training interventions are taken more seriously. If participants want training, they need to pay for it.
- Charging for courses gives HRD departments a good idea of what training is most popular and most needed across the organisation.
- It ensures that the HRD department is not taken for granted and is viewed as a professional service.
- Training courses are taken by participants who need the training and who are motivated to attend and participate on the course.
- Gives some level of financial autonomy to the HRD department.

Disadvantages of a revenue/profit centre approach

- Charging for training discourages new skills and new perspectives.
- Training becomes viewed as an expensive luxury.
- Moving to a revenue/profit centre increases the level of administration and paperwork.
- It increases the pressure on HRD practitioners to prove the added-value of training interventions.
- If HRD departments charge for training courses, they may need to devote more energy and resources to marketing training interventions.

Questions

Does charging for training courses run contrary to developing a learning culture across the organisation?

Will a revenue/profit centre approach allow HRD departments to be more independent and self-sufficient?

Conclusion

Exposing training interventions to an underlying set of dimensions illustrates the underlying purpose and structure that can have a critical impact on training outcomes and effectiveness. Training is an expensive activity, hence it is crucial that training expenditure can be soundly justified and fits with the organisational vision and strategy. The dimensions examined in the chapter allow the reader to make an informed choice to fit the overall objectives being pursued. Moreover, by drawing on research findings, the reader will have a clearer understanding of the impact that effective training can have on employee participation, commitment and organisational effectiveness.

Getting the right mix of training intervention is as much an art as a science – however, training practitioners need to carefully consider the overall training objectives and look at a range of dimensions (such as learner interaction, transferability, degree of reflection) in developing an overall training programme. Such attention to detail will invariably improve the effectiveness of training interventions and benefit the organisation as a whole.

CASE STUDY

Walgreens Pharmacy

Walgreens is the largest pharmacy retail chain in the United States. It was founded in 1901 and currently operates 8,061 pharmacy outlets (or drugstores) across all 50 US states. In February 2013, Walgreens announced that it was launching Walgreens University, with a goal to lead the industry in classroom and online programming that engages, educates and develops team members for rewarding long-term careers.

'Walgreens University is not solely a building, but a national program with national access and offerings for team members at every level of the company', Kathleen Wilson-Thompson, chief human resources officer said. 'We hope every one of our 240,000 team members will find ways to grow their careers and improve themselves through the educational opportunities that Walgreens University will expand or introduce.'

With the opening of Walgreens University, the company is doubling its annual investment in employee education and development, and plans to double the number of learning opportunities for team members through expanded online classes, regional training sessions and in Deerfield, Illinois campus classrooms. More than 100 courses will be available through one of the few corporate training

(Continued)

(Continued)

programmes to offer college credit for certain classes, including pharmacy technician training and management and retail fundamentals.

'To meet our company goals, we need a workforce that learns and grows every day through opportunities available when, where and how each individual needs it', said Wilson-Thompson. 'We aim to be the best in our industry for employee education and training, and among the best of all major American corporations. For Walgreens to compete effectively and expand our business, our team members need to continuously grow new skills and capabilities throughout their careers with us.'

Education providers to Walgreens University include Lake Forest Graduate School of Management, offering a customised MBA programme; University of Maryland University College; Webster University; the University of Phoenix; and DeVry University, Keller Graduate School of Management. Tuition discounts of 10–25 per cent will be available to many Walgreens team members, and UMUC's 25 per cent discount will also be available to employee spouses and dependants. Team members will also have access to non-credit management courses offered online from Harvard Business Publishing, a subsidiary of Harvard University.

The Walgreens learning and development team led by Warren Lindley, divisional vice-president, organisational design and effectiveness, built the University curriculum and system of instruction after extensive consultation with Walgreens leadership and external experts. Bruce Bryant, Walgreens senior vice-president and dean of Walgreens University with more than 40 years' experience with the company, said, 'We want Walgreens customers everywhere to find and experience in our stores the products and services they need to get, stay and live well. The launch of Walgreens University is a significant step toward consistent, higher quality training for our entire team at every corner of America. It also makes Walgreens a great place to work and grow professionally.'

'If we are to attract, retain and develop the best talent, if we are to achieve the organizational agility necessary to adapt to changing markets, we need an industry-leading education and development programme', said Wilson-Thompson.

(Adapted from: *Wireless News* (2013) Walgreens Opens Doors to Walgreens University. *Wireless News*, 26 February.)

Questions

How can corporate universities help deliver effective training and development to organisational employees?

How can the effectiveness of corporate universities be assessed?

Discussion questions

Given that the lecture format is used in 93 per cent of training instances, what learning outcomes is a lecture-style classroom format most suited to?

Too often, training interventions are selected because of trainer preferences – rather than learner preferences. How important is learner-focused training? Why?

What factors need to be examined to improve training transferability?

Technology is changing the relationship between trainers and learners. What are the benefits of technology-mediated training?

Evaluating Training Outcomes

7

Chapter objectives

The objectives of this chapter are to:

- briefly examine the evaluation process in ontological and epistemological terms;
- review the Kirkpatrick Four Levels taxonomy and criticisms associated with it;
- explore the usefulness of benchmarking and different forms of benchmarking;
- consider the importance of the balanced scorecard to delivering a complete picture of organisational performance.

Introduction

In an increasingly competitive environment, organisations are looking to HRD pro-grammes to add value and increase employee capability. There is increasing evidence that organisations in a knowledge economy are relying upon and investing large sums of money in HRD programmes and are looking to evaluation to determine the degree of success of such programmes and return on investment (ROI) arising from them. While many organisations continue to invest large sums of money in evaluation inter-ventions, some organisations now take the view that the level of return may not be worth the investment.

The primary purpose of evaluation is to assist organisational decision-making. In essence, it represents a serious attempt to understand the process of cause-and-effect and how training can affect individual behaviour, group and departmental targets and organisational efficiency. Preskill and Torres (1999) maintain that evaluation is a process of enhancing knowledge and decision-making within organisations and communities. They argue that evaluation is a means for understanding the effect of our actions in a work environment and a process for measuring and promoting shared individual, team and organisational learning. For his part, Swanson (2005) identifies one of the functions of evaluation as being that of discrimination: being able to make judgements based upon the information provided and surrounding circumstances.

Too often, however, evaluation has been considered in simplistic terms, thus ignoring the wider implications and factors affecting evaluation processes. It is worth noting that evaluation is inherently a political activity that occurs in a fluid, complex environment. Weiss (1987) argues that politics and evaluation are connected in that training programmes are creatures of political decisions and evaluation itself feeds into the decision-making and resource-allocation model. Likewise Newby (1992) maintains that evaluation data can be used as a source of power and argues that this may account for much of the defensiveness of training practitioners when faced with proposals for evaluation.

Many of the shortcomings of evaluation can be traced back to HRD practitioners themselves. According to Russ-Eft and Preskill (2005), most HRD practitioners lack an in-depth knowledge of evaluation approaches and few HRD evaluations consider their work within the context of organisational learning, performance and change. Indeed, Preskill (2007) argues that the field of HRD has been painfully slow to recognise that there is a rich and relevant set of evaluation theories beyond Kirkpatrick's Four Levels evaluation taxonomy. A further shortcoming arises from a narrow instrumentalist view of evaluation. Michalski and Cousins (2001: 37) argue that training providers often view the purpose of evaluation as 'mostly to highlight training merit and worth and to sustain and expand training budgets'. This restrictive view of evaluation has led to calls that organisations need to move beyond the bottom-line to look at a wider set of evaluation criteria, such as organisational culture change and contribution to community and society (Newby, 1992).

A number of factors have been identified by Lewis and Thornhill (1994) to explain why organisations do not engage in evaluating HRD programmes. First, they identify the 'confounding variables effect' where organisations refuse to evaluate because of the difficulty of disentangling training from other stimuli. Second, they recognise the 'non-quantifiable effect' where the effects of training are difficult to quantify. Third, many organisations do not evaluate training due to the 'cost outweighing the benefits effect'. In this regard, research by Brinkerhoff argues that for many organisations the cost of evaluation is not worth the benefit with the impact from training usually less than 15 per cent (Brinkerhoff, 2006a). Fourth, the 'act of faith effect' occurs when organisations suppose that training must bring about beneficial effects and this negates the need for evaluation. The 'trainer sensitivity' effect discounts evaluation due to the possible negative feedback that could arise and affect the confidence of the trainer. Finally, the 'organisational political *effect'* arises when conducting training evaluation may have adverse political consequences for the HR department or senior management.

Conducting training evaluations can be expensive; consequently, it is important to identify occasions where it is best not to evaluate. It is arguable the occasions not to evaluate HRD programmes include: when the programme is low in cost, compared to the cost of evaluation; when it's a one-off programme; when results won't influence decision-making; and when no one is interested or competent enough to carry out the evaluation. In the following sections, we examine the concept of evaluation in ontological and epistemological terms. We probe Kirkpatrick's Four Levels taxonomy and consider other common evaluation models. We investigate the incidence of benchmarking and how it is conducted. Finally, we analyse the importance of the balanced scorecard and how it assists organisations in strategic planning and priority setting.

Examining evaluation in ontological and epistemological terms

In order to evaluate an HRD programme, a wide range of information is needed. Organisations will seek to establish the number of participants, how well they did, what participants learned, the quality of the trainer and training and the estimated return on investment. An effective evaluation therefore requires both descriptive and judgemental information indicating facts and figures about the HRD programme, but also opinions and beliefs regarding aspects of the programme. Concerns regarding validity and reliability affect both perceptions and approaches towards evaluation. HRD practitioners seek out evaluation instruments and approaches that accurately and fairly measure what they are intended to measure, but also exhibit preciseness in measurement over time. They must understand what is being measured and how it is being measured. While factual knowledge is often easy to collect, assessing the level of learning, the effectiveness and transferability of such learning and attitudes towards the programme itself requires consideration of issues of ontology and epistemology.

The concept of ontology is measured on a continuum from realist to constructivist. A realist ontology views reality as an objective entity independent of the observer, capable of determination through a positivist methodology. According to Morgan and Smircich (1980) realist ontologies take an objectivist view of the social world as an independent concrete structure. They argue that through the adoption of a realist ontology, evaluation attempts to freeze the world into structured immobility where individual actors are influenced by a set of more or less deterministic forces. This allows the clear identification of an HRD programme strengths and weaknesses. The use of a positivist epistemology through quantitative evaluation instruments and approaches such as Likert scale attitudinal measures is indicative of this approach. Indeed, Stewart (1999) contends that most evaluation processes adopt a functionalist realist position supporting a view of evaluation as an objective process. However, he criticises realist approaches to evaluation for their adherence to semblances of objectivity and their reluctance to recognise that knowledge is inherently personal and is constructed by participants in the educational and training environment.

Constructivist ontologies recognise that knowledge is interactionally constructed, socially transmitted, historically sedimented, institutionally congealed and communicatively reproduced (Gunnarsson et al., 1997). It embraces the notion of multiple realities and argues that people use language to describe, explain or construct versions of the world in which they live (Chimombo and Roseberry, 1998; Gergen, 1985; Hill and McGowan, 1999). HRD evaluations recognising constructivist principles place importance on the uniqueness of training for each individual and emphasise that training builds upon prior experiences and distinctive skillsets that each person possesses and therefore training outcomes will differ for each person taking part. The use of a phenomenological epistemology through qualitative approaches such as interviewing and focus groups supports a constructivist ontology. It seeks to understand the progress made by individuals through their participation in training and identify the obstacles and barriers they encountered. Constructivist approaches have been criticised for their lack of generalisability and the openness of the data to bias (halo/horn effects amongst others). Indeed, Ardichvili and Kuchinke (2002) argue that while constructivist researchers pride themselves on their ability to report a more accurate, realistic picture of people's lives, they often fail to do just this.

In summary, knowledge of realist and constructivist ontologies and their associated epistemological approaches will provide HRD practitioners with a valuable insight into the relative merits of each paradigm. It will allow HRD practitioners to identify an evaluation methodology best suited to their needs and the outcomes they wish to achieve. Moreover, a combination of approaches may be selected by HRD practitioners to overcome weaknesses of each paradigm and provide more accurate holistic feedback on the training intervention.

Talking point   The importance of evaluation – CIPD viewpoint

In February 2013, the Chartered Institute of Personnel and Development (CIPD) released the following statement sharing their views on the importance of evaluation in organisations:

Evaluating learning and talent development is crucial to ensuring the effectiveness of an organisation's learning initiatives and programmes. Effective evaluation means going beyond the traditional 'reactions' focus based on a simplistic assessment of learners' levels of satisfaction with the training provision. Rather,

(Continued)

(Continued)

it is important to use simplified yet sophisticated approaches such as CIPD's 'RAM' model (relevance, alignment, measurement) to evaluate learning outcomes and the extent to which learning provision is aligned with business objectives. Such a focus helps to ensure that learning and talent interventions deliver value for both learners and organisations alike. Practitioners should also recognise that whilst levels based evaluation typified in Kirkpatrick and Return on Investment (ROI) dominate our thinking, they are often poorly used. An output, change and improvement focus is much more productive. The promise of 'big data' and its HR counterpart, talent analytics, will present new opportunities for effective evaluation.

(Adapted from: CIPD (2010) Evaluating Learning and Talent Development. CIPD Factsheet. http://www.cipd.co.uk/hr-resources/factsheets/evaluating-learning-talent-development.aspx#link_cipd_view.)

Questions

How can the importance of evaluation be emphasised in organisations?

What do we mean by the word 'value' in the expression 'to ensure learning and talent interventions deliver value for both learners and organisations alike'?

Kirkpatrick's Four Levels taxonomy

Being serious about training evaluation requires more than the allocation of resources to summatively appraising a training programme. Organisations need to recognise that evaluation is more than a closing after-thought or concluding period of a training programme but needs to be systematically integrated into a training programme. As James and Roffe (2000) point out, evaluation should be an ongoing progressive activity, comparing the actual and real to the predicted or promised. They see the real value of evaluation as highlighting good and bad practice, detecting errors and correcting mistakes, assessing risk, maximising investment, and optimising individual and organisational learning. In this regard, Campbell (1998) advocates preparing an evaluation schedule involving a wide range of stakeholders so that lines of responsibility and accountability can be clearly established and potential conflicts can be more easily resolved.

Without doubt, Kirkpatrick's Four Levels taxonomy is currently the most commonly used method for evaluating training interventions. Although developed in 1967, it remains to this day a highly influential model and underpins the UK Investors in People model (Santos and Stuart, 2003). The Kirkpatrick taxonomy proposes evaluation along a hierarchy of learning outcomes (reactions, learning, transfer and results). Russ-Eft and Preskill (2005) characterise Kirkpatrick's taxonomy as a conceptually simple approach to evaluation but nonetheless attest to its standing over time and its apparent straightforward appeal with practitioners. In a critique of Kirkpatrick's work, Holton (1996) argues that despite its dominance as the leading training evaluation taxonomy, the Four Levels approach has received little research and is seldom fully implemented in organisations. Figure 7.1 explains Kirkpatrick's Four Levels taxonomy in greater depth.

Evaluating participant reactions is the most common form of training evaluation. As Lanigan and Bentley (2006) point out, reactionnaires (or so-called 'smile sheets') are effortless to create, simple to administer and easy to store in a cabinet drawer. Reports on the use of reactionnaires show that 2 per cent of companies evaluate at the results level, 11 per cent at the behaviour/transfer level, 29 per cent at the learning level and 89 per cent at the reactions level (Bassi and Van Buren, 1999). However, much research casts doubt on the highly questionable assumption that because trainees were satisfied with the training, that it was effective (Burrow and Berardinelli, 2003; Collins, 2002). Indeed, Preskill and Russ-Eft (2005) argue that at best, reliance on reactionnaires limits the amount and usefulness of information obtained and at worst, inhibits HRD professionals' involvement with the strategic operations of the organisation. To be anyway effective Pershing and Pershing (2001) argue that HRD practitioners designing reactionnaires must pay careful attention to issues of structure and content.

Assessing the overall level of trainee learning is a difficult process and can be affected by a number of factors. Some of these factors include: trainee motivation, training design, prior trainee experiences, training delivery and perceived relevance of the training material. For his part, Dionne (1996) argues that any HRD programme evaluation needs to take account of the relationship between the learning to be acquired, the design of the training and the teaching strategies used. In a similar vein, Holton (1996) maintains that the level of learning will be affected by readiness for training, job attitude, ability level and trainee personality. Too often, HRD practitioners use simple tests to assess the level of learning without taking full account of the range of factors affecting the learning of trainees. Indeed, it can be argued that the level of trainee learning will be affected by whether trainees adopt a surface or deep approach to learning (Biggs, 2003). Surface approaches indicate an intention to get training out of the way with minimum trouble, yet fulfilling course requirements; while deep approaches signal a meaningful engagement with the training in fulfilment of personal need or interest, self-actualisation or professional curiosity. Consequently, deep learning may be affected by the degree to which trainers stimulate learner curiosity and self-interest and build upon the previous experiences of learners.

Determining the level of transfer from the training site back to the workplace is a difficult task. As we have already seen in Chapter 6, transfer is an important element in ensuring the programme adds value to the organisation. Unless transfer is handled

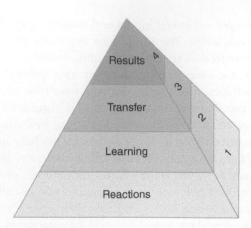

Level 1: *Reactions:* The responses of trainees to the content and methods of the programme are elicited. Feedback sheets (sometimes called reactionnaires or 'happy sheets'), oral discussions and checklists are used. This level constitutes a formative evaluation.

Level 2: *Learning:* The actual learning of trainees is measured and an assessment is made regarding how well trainees have advanced in their level of knowledge and skills. This is achieved through the use of tests, projects, portfolios and learning logs. This level constitutes a formative evaluation.

Level 3: *Transfer:* The effect of the training programme on the behaviour of the trainee in the workplace is measured. Observation, interviews, critical incident technique and post-programme testing are often used to assess the level of training transfer. This level constitutes a summative evaluation.

Level 4: *Results:* The impact of the training on the performance of the employee is examined. Workplace metrics (such as productivity, levels of waste, throughput) and cost–benefit analysis can be used here; however, it is often difficult to establish casual linkages to the improvement resulting from training. This level constitutes a summative evaluation.

Figure 7.1   Kirkpatrick's Four Levels taxonomy

effectively, trainees will gradually lose the information gained on the training programme (Velada and Caetano, 2007). Research by Wexley and Latham (2002) suggests that 40 per cent of training content is transferred immediately and this level of transference falls to 25 per cent within six months and 15 per cent over a year. Two key factors appear highly significant in influencing training transfer: first, the level of training transfer may be increased by improving the connection between the training context and performance context (Vermeulen, 2002) and second, by enhancing the level of social support that employees receive upon returning to the workplace, particularly from their supervisors (Nijman et al., 2006).

Establishing the impact of training is critical to assessing the overall effectiveness of training programmes. Many authors have argued that this element of the process is just too complex and too difficult to be done (Smith, 2004) and the benefits of training are often subjective and difficult to quantify and express in monetary terms (James and Roffe, 2000). Jack Phillips (1991) added a fifth level of return on investment to Kirkpatrick's Four Levels evaluation. As Kline and Harris (2008) point out, establishing the ROI of training promotes justification of current and future budgets; improves training programme selection; impacts positively on the tracking of costs; increases the prediction of revenue based on improved service and product selection; and improves the awareness of the level of accidents, turnover and absenteeism.

Talking point   Level 1 evaluation – myths and reality

The first and initial stage of Kirkpatrick's Four Levels taxonomy is the Reactions stage. It is designed to help organisations assess participant reactions to training invention's and gauge their feedback on issues such as the quality of the setting, instructor, materials and learning activities. In theory, level 1 evaluation is meant to act like the proverbial canary in the coal mine alerting the organisation to problems and difficulties that are being experienced. However, several myths have arisen regarding level 1 evaluation and we will now examine three of these:

Myth: Level 1 evaluation is a simply a 'smile sheet' or 'reactionnaire' and contains little or no useful or actionable information.

Reality: A key and crucial benefit of level 1 evaluation lies in its ability to identify content sequencing problems, training delivery and facilitation issues as well as venue and setting problems. Speedy detection of these issues allows them to be quickly remedied without causing undue long-term damage to the training programme itself.

Myth: As long as learners are happy and content, then the training must have been successful.

Reality: The extent of learner happiness is not a predictor of overall learning. As the stages within Kirkpatrick's Four Levels taxonomy are not correlated, a high rating at one level does not translate to a high rating at a subsequent level – in other words, just because a learner is happy doesn't mean they have learnt anything.

Myth: Learners are well equipped to assess the quality, value and relevance of the training as it relates to their actual job.

Reality: Learners are not always the best individuals to assess the effectiveness of training transfer – they may not know themselves what components of the training will be useful in their day-to-day jobs. Thus, training transfer should be carried out by trained evaluation experts or by line managers supported by the HRD function.

(Continued)

(Continued)

Questions

Despite large sums of money being invested in training, only limited resources are often devoted to evaluation, with level 1 evaluation being the most common form of evaluation. How can the effectiveness of level 1 evaluation be improved?

Sometimes level 1 evaluation is often seen as an exercise conducted by trainers to 'validate their worth'. How can the emphasis of level 1 evaluation be shifted from being perceived as an ego-boosting exercise to one designed to improve the quality of training design and delivery?

Other commonly used evaluation models

Apart from Kirkpatrick's Four Levels taxonomy, a plethora of other evaluation models have appeared in the training literature (see Table 7.1). No single methodology or training evaluation model can satisfy the requirements of every evaluation – thus each of the different frameworks and models presented claim to be effective for particular circumstances and situations. As Bates (2004) argues, the models used during the evaluation of a training programme have a strong impact on the overall determination of the effectiveness of the training. Indeed, Russ-Eft and Preskill (2001) assert that evaluation has arisen out of the need to establish effectiveness and accountability – hence, a need by both contractors and consultants to prove the quality of their work to their paymasters. Moreover, as Bramley (1996: 4) reminds us:

> Evaluation is a process of establishing the worth of something. The 'worth' which means the value, merit or excellence of the thing is actually someone's opinion. This opinion is usually based on information, comparison and experience, and one might expect some consensus in this between informed people. Sometimes there is some disagreement about the worth of something because people are using different criteria to make the evaluation.

Table 7.1   Other common evaluation models and approaches

Hamblin Evaluation Framework (1974)

Reaction level: Measures employee opinions regarding the nature of the training programme. It examines usefulness of training, perceptions in relation to content and trainers.

Learning level: Measures the content of what trainees have learned, particularly in relation to knowledge, skills and attitudes.

Job behaviour level: Measures the impact of the HRD programme on the behaviour of employees in the workplace. It seeks to establish the level of training transfer.

Department level: Measures effect of learning on departmental metrics and examines how changes in job behaviour have impacted upon the department.

Organisation level/ultimate value: Measures how the organisation has benefited from the HRD programme. This will be examined in terms of metrics such as growth, profitability and productivity.

Warr, Bird and Rackham Evaluation Matrix (1976)

Context: Focuses on factors such as identification of training needs and objective-setting in relation to organisation culture and climate.

Input: Examines the design and delivery of the training activity and how individual interventions are framed.

Reaction: Explores the process of acquiring and using the feedback received in relation to individual trainee experiences.

Output: Measures training outcomes along three dimensions: immediate post-intervention changes, training transfer back to the workplace and impact on departmental and organisational performance.

Easterby-Smith Evaluation Framework (1986)

Context: Examines factors surrounding the HRD programme, such as organisational culture, climate, values, provision of support and availability of technology.

Administration: Examines how the HRD programme is marketed and communicated to employees. Looks at pre-programme instructions, location of programme and expectations communicated to trainees.

Inputs: Examines the various elements to comprise the training programme – such as training techniques to be used, topics to be covered, format of training room, etc.

Process: Examines the content of the HRD programme and the means by which the content is delivered. Focuses on how learning is structured and the experiences of participants.

Outputs: Examines the changes that occur as a result of the HRD programme. At the individual level, this focuses on the knowledge, skills and attitude changes.

Kaufman, Keller and Watkins Five Evaluation Levels (1995)

Level 1(a): Input: Assesses the availability and quality of human, financial and physical resources.

Level 1(b): Processes: Measures participant reactions in terms of programme acceptability and efficiency.

Level 2: Micro-level acquisition: Looks to establish participant mastery and competency of the knowledge and skills covered in the training intervention.

Level 3: Micro-level successful application: Seeks to establish how the knowledge and skills covered in the training programme are utilised in the work/organisational setting.

Level 4: Macro-level: Calculates the impact of the training in terms of organisational contribution and pay-offs.

Level 5: Mega-level: Estimates the societal level impact of the training intervention and its overall contribution and pay-offs.

Brinkerhoff Successful Case Method (2003)

This method adopts a qualitative approach and through storytelling and case studies seeks to establish the impact of training and how successful the lessons of the training have been applied to an organisational setting. Interviews (either face-to-face or telephone) and focus groups are the typical method by which information is collected.

Brinkerhoff Human Performance Technology (HPT) Evaluation Model (2006b)

Setting of HPT goals: Clarifying, documenting and establishing the intended outcomes and purposes of the HPT training programme.

(Continued)

Table 7.1   (Continued)

Analysis of performance issues: Explores the performance outcomes of the HPT training intervention in terms of primary, secondary and tertiary performance needs.

Design of the HPT training intervention: Assesses the technical adequacy, cost-effectiveness and overall accuracy of the training design.

Implementation of the HPT training initiative: Tracks the progress, execution and feedback associated with the training intervention and whether key milestones have been met.

Sustaining impact and worthy performance: Assesses the longer-term impact, value and effectiveness of the training intervention and how outcomes can be enhanced.

CIPD Model of Value and Evaluation (2007b)

Evaluation is considered across four dimensions:

Learning function measures: Focuses on the effectiveness and efficiency of the learning function. It examines the provision of training and competence of personnel within the function.

Return on expectation measures: Looks at the anticipated benefits of the training programme and whether these have been achieved. Attempts to establish what changes have occurred as a result of the programme.

Return on investment measures: Examines the benefits resulting from the training programme relative to the costs incurred over a specific period of time. Explores how learning is contributing to the attainment of key performance targets.

Benchmark and capacity measures: Compares the programme to a set of internal and external standards. Seeks to promote good practice and a culture of continuous improvement.

Passmore and Velez SOAP-M Evaluation Model (2012)

Evaluation should be considered across five separate dimensions:

Level 1: Self: Based upon the participants' self-evaluation of the quality, value and effectiveness of the training intervention.

Level 2: Other: This component of evaluation is carried out by line managers, peers or stakeholders to establish the impact of the training and identify any changes that have occurred.

Level 3: Achievements: Looks at the effectiveness of the training in terms of accomplishment of key activities and tasks.

Level 4: Potential: Seeks to identify the degree to which training helps participants fulfil their individual potential.

Level 5: Meta-analysis: Combines a range of studies to assess the effectiveness and significance of the training programme.

CIPD 'RAM' Approach to Evaluation (2013b)

The effectiveness of the learning intervention is evaluated across three dimensions:

Relevance: To determine whether the training intervention will meet new opportunities and challenges for the business.

Alignment: To ensure that the training intervention is aligned with key strategies such as reward, organisational development, engagement and other aspects of HR.

Measurement: To examine the effectiveness of the training intervention through return on investment and broader measures of change and improvement such as return on expectation.

Looking specifically at the models and frameworks that have been developed over the last four decades, many take the Kirkpatrick Four Levels framework as their starting point. Hamblin's (1974) model bear some similarities to that of Kirkpatrick's but places greater emphasis on the results stage – breaking this up to look at the effect at the departmental level and organisational level. Similarly, Kaufman et al. (1995) draw inspiration from Kirkpatrick's work, but seek to integrate a higher societal or mega level. The models by Warr et al. (1976) and Easterby-Smith (1986) trace their roots to systems theory looking at context, inputs and outputs. A process approach is also adopted by Brinkerhoff (2006b) in his five-stage Human Performance Technology (HPT) Evaluation Model.

Some evaluation frameworks have countered the highly quantitative focus of many existing models, arguing that evaluation needs to embrace a more qualitative and holistic emphasis. A key evaluation approach in this regard is Brinkerhoff's (2003) successful case method. This approach documents stories of successful participants by telephone or in person to ascertain the impact of training on individual and organisational performance. More recent evaluation frameworks have been inspired largely by professional bodies and associations. A model by CIPD and developed by Valerie Anderson (2007) identifies internal (learning, ROI) and external aspects to evaluation (benchmarking and capacity indicators). She also recognises the subjective aspects of evaluation through examining return on expectations. A more recent model developed by the CIPD (2013a) emphasises the qualities of relevance, alignment and measurement and advocates a broader, more holistic approach to evaluation.

Benchmarking

Understanding how an organisation is performing in relation to its competitors is critical to an organisation's survival and long-term growth. Aligning an organisation with industry standards is an important method of preserving good practice. In addition, benchmarking identifies strengths and weaknesses and empowers organisations to examine their internal processes and systems and prioritise areas for improvement. Yasin (2002) argues that benchmarking is a multifaceted technique that can be utilised to identify operational and strategic gaps and search for best practices that would eliminate such gaps. It allows an organisation to examine its performance against established standards and can help promote a culture of continuous improvement within the organisation. Kumar and Chandra (2001) argue that benchmarking may be considered a form of backward engineering which encourages organisations to develop customised processes and methods to achieve desirable end goal standards.

The process of emulating successful organisations has fostered high levels of creativity and innovation amongst employees and managers and led to significant change in products, processes and practices. Product benchmarking involves the comparison of an organisation's product against a similar offering by a competitor. The analysis of both products is done with reference to a specific set of criteria, such as product characteristics, functionality, performance and environmental features. As Wever et al.

(2007) point out, effective product benchmarking can contribute to product improvement and lead to significant cost reductions. As such, product benchmarking provides hard data and facts about a product; however, with product life cycles shortening, this information often becomes obsolete quite quickly (Kumar and Chandra, 2001).

Process benchmarking seeks to identify activities where the firm has superior performance or cost advantage relative to competitors, which can be used for building competitive advantage (Anderson, 1999; Ralston et al., 2001). In this regard, Delpachitra and Beal (2002) consider process benchmarking as an indirect measure of operational efficiency as it examines budgets, work systems, administration, technology and human resources. They argue that it is often difficult to get organisations to participate in this form of benchmarking as it often involves divulging commercially sensitive or confidential information.

Best-practice benchmarking involves seeking out organisations regarded as superior performers in specific functional areas and developing benchmarks against these particular areas of expertise. In this regard, best practice cannot simply be copied – it must be adapted to the specific style and context of the organisation (Bhutta and Huq, 1999). Indeed, the organisation must not simply transfer the practice, it needs to understand the drivers for such a practice, the prevailing culture and skillset needed before the practice is integrated into the organisation.

In spite of the obvious benefits to be derived from benchmarking, most organisations do not engage in benchmarking. A study by Davies and Kochhar (2002) identifies several reasons why British companies do not engage in effective benchmarking. First, they identify a preference for company visits among executives (so-called 'industrial tourism'); however, they found that these visits tended to be superficial and did not lead to substantial change. Second, they identified a preoccupation among executives with metrics rather than the practices behind superior performance. Third, many organisations believed their enterprises were unique and would not benefit from benchmarking. Fourth, a lack of planning led to suboptimal benchmarking results for many organisations. Fifth, they found that three-quarters of all companies believed they were better than they actually were and did not need to engage in benchmarking. Finally, some companies reported difficulty in finding benchmarking partners. Hinton et al. (2000) confirm this problem and report that accessing suitable comparable partners was the most common difficulty experienced with benchmarking.

Balanced scorecard

Widely regarded as one of the most important innovations in strategic change management and performance measurement, the balanced scorecard has become the management tool of choice for organisations worldwide (Pangarkar and Kirkwood, 2008). Developed by Robert Kaplan and David Norton in 1992, the balanced scorecard seeks to provide organisations with a range of organisational metrics necessary for effective strategy development and implementation. In essence, the balanced scorecard works as an organisational dashboard and includes a range of real-time measures that give management a quick view of how the organisation is faring across a range of key performance indicators (DeBusk et al., 2003). The appeal of the balanced scorecard lies in the ability to manage a range of metrics rather than focusing on a single measure of performance.

Traditionally, organisations have overemphasised financial measurement at the expense of some of the drivers of financial measures. Maltz et al. (2003) argue that traditional financial measures can give misleading signals for continuous improvement and innovation and are not relevant to the skills, knowledge and competencies required in today's competitive environment. Likewise, Chakravarthy (1985) found that financial measures are incapable of differentiating levels of organisational performance and that such measures only record the history of a firm. For this reason, the balanced scorecard aligns financial and non-financial measures to give a more complete overview of the organisation's performance.

As a holistic, multidimensional performance measurement tool, the balanced scorecard brings together a wide range of financial and non-financial data to create a complete picture of the organisation's status. Kaplan and Norton (1996) argue that the balanced scorecard addresses a serious deficiency in traditional management systems: their inability to link a company's long-term strategy with its short-term actions. In this sense, the balanced scorecard focuses on better understanding the causal relationships and links between inputs and outcomes and the levers that can be used to improve organisational effectiveness (Dye, 2003).

Providing organisational decision-makers with more complete information about the organisation will enable better decision-making and more targeted training and development interventions. For their part, Kaplan and Norton (1996: 26) argue that the balanced scorecard permits 'a balance between short-term and long-term objectives, between outcomes desired and the performance drivers of these outcomes and between hard objective measures and softer subjective measures'. They identify four perspectives through which the organisation's activity can be examined (Table 7.2).

Not only does the balanced scorecard provide accessible information to managers, it represents a useful device for communicating with employees. Mooraj et al. (1999) maintain that the balanced scorecard may be used to define and disperse an organisation's core values, through making employees aware of the mission, vision and major strategic goals. It also enables employees and departmental teams to identify development priorities necessary to fulfil the identified strategic goals.

Despite its widespread appeal, several criticisms have been levelled at the balanced scorecard. Olve et al. (1999) argue that the seeming simplicity of the balanced scorecard leads to an underestimation of the difficulties in implementing it within an organisation. Indeed, recent research has shown that as many as 70 per cent of balanced scorecard

Table 7.2   Balanced scorecard dimensions

Financial perspective: This examines the market share, return on equity, financial results and cash-flow of the organisation. It provides an indication of the financial health of the organisation.

Customer perspective: This explores the target market of the organisation, customer profile, the degree of penetration, performance delivery targets, customer loyalty, satisfaction and retention. It highlights the strength of the relationship between the organisation and its customers and is an important indicator of how well the organisation is doing in the market.

Internal process perspective: This provides data on the operational effectiveness of the organisation. It looks at the level of automation, throughput, quality, cost and order fulfilment. This highlights how well the organisation is functioning internally.

Learning and growth perspective: As the organisation represents a combination of people and processes, it is important to collect data on the skillsets of employees, the training and development opportunities available, employee satisfaction, employee turnover and level of internal promotions. This perspective reflects the priority placed on people issues in the organisation.

Source: Kaplan and Norton (1996).

initiatives fail due to difficulties in implementing certain aspects of the process (Atkinson, 2006; Othman, 2008). The balanced scorecard has also been criticised for failing to take account of key stakeholder interests (Chang, 2007; Neely et al., 1995).

While the theory underpinning the balanced scorecard argues for the need to measure performance and the drivers of performance, the balanced scorecard does not include a casual model depicting cause–effect relationships across the four perspectives, although Kaplan and Norton (1996) do recommend development of this model. Indeed, research studies have shown that many of the popular performance measures used (customer service, productivity, market share) exhibit weak correlativity (Malmi, 2001). Some organisational measures may work in a converse-expectancy manner (for instance profitability and customer service levels may on occasions have an inverse relationship). Finally, with the large volume of data to be collected, Othman (2006) cautions that the balanced scorecard may become an exercise in developing more paperwork than one having any strategic impact.

Conclusion

Evaluation remains an important aspect of the training process. Without evaluation, there is no mechanism for establishing the changes to be made to the training programme, the degree of learning attained by participants and the effectiveness of training along both financial and non-financial metrics. In terms of general observations from the research data, it appears that HRD practitioners are not very knowledgeable about evaluation processes and often employ evaluation in a strategic manner to both satisfy political motives and justify training expenditures. These factors will affect how the evaluation is structured and the results obtained from the implementation of the process.

A knowledge of ontology will provide HRD practitioners with an understanding of the evaluation choices available to them and the methods (qualitative and quantitative) through which the data should be collected. Too often, organisations rely solely on reactionnaires ('smile sheets') to gain instant feedback on participant satisfaction with training. Such practices ignore the rich tapestry of evaluation information that can be collected through a considered and planned evaluation methodology. Employing a variety and combination of evaluation techniques will provide organisations with more accurate and detailed information leading to the more effective selection of participants, tailoring of teaching styles and individualising the learning experience.

The Kirkpatrick Four Levels taxonomy remains the most consistently used method for evaluation training. Its conceptual simplicity makes it attractive to HRD practitioners; however, all four levels are rarely implemented by organisations. The reactions level measures contentedness of participants with training content, training structure, instructor style and assessment type. The learning level examines the knowledge and skill progression of participants arising from the training course. The transfer level assesses how well learning is employed in the workplace. Finally, the results level gauges the impact of training on organisation metrics such as productivity and profitability. A key criticism of the Kirkpatrick Four Levels taxonomy relates to the lack of correlation between each of the levels. Furthermore, HRD practitioners need to be aware of other evaluation models, beyond that of Kirkpatrick, which may be more appropriate to their needs.

As a process, benchmarking enables an organisation to measure its achievements against industry standards and identify strategic gaps in its operations. Three types of benchmarking are commonly in operation: product benchmarking enables organisations to conduct an analysis of their product versus a competitor's offering along a specific set of criteria such as functionality, design, performance and environmental features. Process benchmarking compares the effectiveness of work systems and practices and identifies areas where further improvements can be made. Finally, best-practice benchmarking ascertains centres of excellence across organisations where specific practices are widely admired and propel superior performance. These practices are then adapted and incorporated into the host organisation to improve overall efficiency and effectiveness.

The balanced scorecard offers organisations an opportunity to manage their operations more effectively through examining performance across a range of metrics, rather than solely relying on traditional financial measurements. The balanced scorecard allows organisations to look at outputs and the drivers of those outputs. In so doing, it allows management to set a range of priorities for the short, medium and long term to align the organisation with the external environment. Through the four perspectives of financial, customer, internal process and learning and growth, a more complete picture of the state of the organisation is provided and such an analysis can be easily communicated to employees. Some research on the balanced scorecard questions its overall effectiveness and there is evidence to suggest that weak levels of correlativity exist among some of the metrics used in the balanced scorecard.

CASE STUDY

Evaluation of aviation training

It is well recognised that about 60–80 per cent of all aviation accidents and mishaps occur due to human error. Identifying deficiencies in aviation training and ensuring that training courses are as effective as possible is crucial to airline and passenger safety. Flight deck crew and cabin crew must learn how to coordinate their efforts and function effectively as a team to ensure passenger safety in the air. In almost half of all incidents involving fatalities, the accident cause was attributed to either lack of coordination amongst cockpit crews, captain's failure to assign tasks to flight deck and cabin members and a lack of overall effective crew supervision. Failures in team-work have led to tragic consequences and highly embarrassing publicity in the media. In December 1972, Eastern Airlines Flight 401 crashed into the Florida Everglades because the flight deck crew failed to realise that the altitude hold feature of the autopilot had been accidentally disconnected. In response to such incidents, the concept of crew resource management (CRM) was developed. CRM involves the train-ing of all crew personnel in airline resources including equipment, people and infor-mation to ensure that both flight deck and cabin crew work effectively as a team. As a system for managing inflight crew coordination, CRM focuses on promoting team-work skills in a way that helps error avoidance, encourages early detection of errors and helps minimise consequences resulting from CRM errors.

CRM involves training regarding the effective interaction of flight deck crew and cabin crew as well as the interface of both sets of crew with airline systems. Key aspects of CRM training for flight deck and cabin crew include instruction in the following areas:

- Human error and reliability as well as error detection and correction
- Standard operating procedures and safety culture values
- Stress management fatigue and vigilance
- Information acquisition, processing and decision-making
- Situational awareness and workload management
- Communication, assertiveness and coordination inside and outside the cockpit
- Leadership and team behaviour
- Individual and team roles and responsibilities
- Identification and management of the passenger factors: crowd control, pas-senger stress, conflict management, medical emergencies
- Specifics related to aeroplane types (narrow/wide bodies, single/multi deck)
- Safety incident and accident reporting

CRM training is delivered through a wide variety of training interventions including traditional classroom instruction, case studies, self-study, awareness training, modelling, skills training, simulation and coaching during flying operations. A key premise underpinning CRM training is that knowledge, ability and motivation are all necessary to effect enduring changes in behaviour.

A study by the Civil Aviation Authority (2006) found that the following methods were used to assess the effectiveness of CRM training. Evaluation measures were broadly grouped under the four categories of reactions, learning, behaviour and organisation.

Category 1: Reactions

- Reaction sheet/happy sheet
- Oral feedback and debriefing

Category 2: Learning

- Learning related to attitudes
- Attitude questionnaire
- Cockpit/flight management attitude questionnaire
- Informal oral feedback
- Learning related to knowledge
- Multiple choice tests
- Written exam
- Oral feedback

Category 3: Behaviour

- Behaviour marker system
- Technical checklist
- Informal feedback

Category 4: Organisation

- Company climate survey
- Safety performance
- Incident reporting
- Business performance
- Confidential reporting

(Continued)

(Continued)

- Technical performance
- Training audits
- 360 degree appraisal

Given the importance of passenger and aircraft safety, it is vital that CRM training evaluation is thorough and that the results of the evaluation are used to drive improvements in CRM training delivery. Likewise, it is critical that flight desk and cabin crew undergo regular updating and retraining to ensure that the latest safety standards and measures are adhered to.

(Adapted from: Civil Aviation Authority (2006) CAP 737: Crew Resource Management (CRM) Training; Guidance for Flight Crew, CRM Instructors (CRMIS) and CRM Instructor-Examiners (CRMIES), West Sussex; Salas, E., Burke, C.S., Bowers, C.A. and Wilson, K.A. (2001) Team Training in the Skies: Does Crew Resource Management (CRM) Training Work? *Human Factors*, 43(4), 641–674.)

Questions

Do you agree with the key premise underpinning CRM training that 'knowledge, ability and motivation are all necessary to effect enduring changes in behaviour'?

What lessons can we learn from how CRM training is evaluated that can be applied to other organisations?

Discussion questions

Identify and discuss occasions when evaluation is 'an unnecessary waste of resources'.

Kirkpatrick's Four Levels typology continues to be the most commonly used evaluation model. Why is this the case? What are the merits associated with the Kirkpatrick model?

What are the benefits associated with the proper use of benchmarking?

Does the balanced scorecard involve too much measurement?

Performance Management and HRD

8

Chapter objectives

The objectives of this chapter are to:

- examine how organisations develop core competence;
- consider the role of line managers in performance management in increasingly devolved organisations;
- look at developmental relationships such as coaching, mentoring and employee counselling;
- explore the role of leaders in the management of performance in organisations.

Introduction

Getting employees to achieve optimum level work performance is a long-standing challenge facing HRD professionals. Gradually, organisations are recognising that greater effectiveness can be achieved through strategic HR and performance management initiatives. This slow realisation is moving organisations beyond operational and technological fixes towards greater engagement with employees. Krinks and Stack (2008) report that the three most critical challenges facing organisations are developing and retaining employees; anticipating and managing change; and enhancing operational effectiveness through becoming a learning organisation and transforming HR into a strategic partner. For her part, Bierema (1997: 23) has lamented the 'machine mentality in the workplace which has created a crisis in individual development'. She argues for an expansive development focus for employees that is not restricted to productivity metrics, but which treats employees as more than mere machines and equips them to meet broader workplace and societal challenges. However, Hassan (2007) reports that to date, most organisations do not yet recognise the importance of HR and fail to include HRD personnel in the strategic planning process.

The performance paradigm has for a long time been the driving force behind theory and practice in the field of HRD; concerning itself with how employees can be more effectively developed, how resources utilisation can be optimised, how quality is enhanced and how employees can be more effectively engaged in the organisation (Beaver and Hutchings, 2004; O'Donnell et al., 2006; Rummler and Brache, 1995). In this regard, Holton (2002) views the purpose of HRD as to advance the HRD efforts by improving both individual capabilities and the overall work system. For her part, Holbeche (2008) cites research studies showing that 80 per cent of performance needs are due to factors about the structure and definition of the job, with the remaining 20 per cent of performance improvement needs due to knowledge or skill requirements. Such studies underscore the need for HRD professionals to examine job structures and systems as well as providing skill development programmes.

Differences in approach to HRD's role in performance management are evident in the US and UK literatures. As Simmonds and Pedersen (2006) point out, a clear dichotomy exists between the US performance outcomes paradigm, which is underpinned by coaching, mentoring and leadership development, and the UK learning and development paradigm emphasising training, education and development. Indeed, such differences in emphasis illustrate the tension between learning and performance as the primary outcome of HRD. However, Ruona (2000) argues that both learning and performance should be viewed as central goals of HRD, given the interactive relationship that exists between them. Indeed, she suggests that improved performance may be the ultimate outcome, with learning the crucial motivator towards achieving this outcome. In spite of the differences and tensions that exist there is one overriding imperative: namely that to be viable, HRD must contribute to the attainment of organisational goals and bottom-line performance in a cost-effective manner.

This chapter examines the role of HRD in performance management. It looks at the evolution of competency frameworks and how organisations are deploying such frameworks. With the increasing use of devolvement to line managers, the chapter examines the challenges and difficulties faced by front-line supervisors and managers in combining traditional operational responsibility with new HR tasks. Coaching, mentoring and employee counselling are explored as mechanisms for supporting employees to achieve high-level performance. The role of leadership in performance management is then discussed followed by some tentative conclusions on the role of HRD in performance management.

Developing core competences

The management of learning and knowledge is increasingly regarded as critical to the strategic well-being of organisations. In the knowledge economy, the traditional development model of 'training, education and experience' is being replaced by a contemporary emphasis on learning and development. This highlights an increased recognition of the role of tacit knowledge and skills in the modern economy and a realisation that the exploitation of ideas and creative insights will give organisations a crucial edge in a competitive market. As Rainbird (1995) points out, competitive advantage is secured when organisations have skills and capabilities that are unique, difficult to replicate and imitate by competitors. The goals of out-learning the competition and staying ahead of the game have placed a premium on customised HRD strategies that satisfy the dual goals of structuring and aligning learning to organisational goals, but providing space for learning to move in new and innovative directions.

For the last two decades, competency frameworks have been employed as an effective means of structuring development processes within organisations. As Hafeez and Essmail (2007) point out, much discussion has taken place on the distinction between competences and competencies. They propose that competences refer to the activities that an organisation must excel at to outperform competitors, whereas competencies relate to individual knowledge, skills and attributes necessary to carry out a function effectively. For his part, Post (1997) argues that competences are created when distinctive activities are executed through application of a range of individual competencies. Employee knowledge and skill specialisation and its combination in an organised structured form will generate collective learning and are likely to lead to processes and products that are unique and add value. Understanding how individual competencies feed into organisational core competences is critical, if organisations are to successfully leverage and capitalise upon their own distinctive offering. Mapping employee capabilities and determining the future-relatedness of such competencies in helping the organisation achieve its strategic goals is an essential element in strategic planning and goal-setting. In the mid-1990s as the information age took hold, competency frameworks began to emphasise the importance of knowledge and learning in a more substantial way. There was also a realisation that with more complex roles, effective performance was more likely to be driven by tacit intangible skills than explicit characteristics (Garavan and McGuire, 2001). The recognition of 'tacit' and 'explicit' knowledge by Nonaka and Takeuchi (1995) opened up the field of knowledge management through recognising the importance of highly subjective insights, intuitions and ideals. As Boud and Garrick (1999: 48) put it, the current and future wealth of organisations exists principally in the heads of employees and 'walks out of the office building every day'. Building upon Senge's (1990) work on the learning organisation emphasising the importance of shared mental models and systems thinking, Nonaka and Takeuchi recognised the importance of sharing personal knowledge through frequent interaction and transcending traditional boundaries. Indeed, such has been the widespread adoption of competency frameworks and the premium now placed on knowledge that Garavan (2007) classifies competency-based systems as a traditional HRD activity, citing knowledge management and business partnering solutions as transformational activities.

In today's networked economy, organisations not only need to understand their own core competencies, but also need to evaluate the dynamic capabilities of outsourced partners to ensure they are contributing to organisational success. Perunovic et al. (2012) argue that service vendors need to understand both their own unique capabilities and client expectations in order to secure and maintain existing business. They argue that service vendors need to invest in new skills, technologies and innovations so as to maintain their own distinctiveness and 'edge' as well as help clients produce and develop cutting-edge products and services. Increasingly, as Boulaksil and Fransoo (2010) point out, outsourcing decisions bring with them the issue of cross-organisational interdependencies, necessitating the building of strong relational capital between vendors and clients. A strong vendor–client relationship is crucial to maximising any benefits from outsourcing and harvesting cost and time efficiencies.

The emphasis on core competences arises from the ability of organisations to leverage their unique resources and special assets in a way which adds value to the organisation. Hafeez and Essmail (2007) maintain that organisational core competences represent the collective learning of the organisation, imbuing the organisation with a unique identity and standing, which distinguishes the organisation in the marketplace and helps it compete more effectively. In their article, Gilgeous and Parveen (2001) identify several examples of core competence. They posit that Canon has developed core competences in the fields of optics, imaging and microprocessor controls, allowing it to build leading products in the fields of photocopying, laser printers, scanners and facsimiles. Likewise, they argue that Honda's core competence in engines has enabled the company to capture market share in the car, motorcycle, lawnmower and generator businesses.

The role of line managers in performance management and employee development

With HRD professionals adopting more strategic roles and becoming more fully involved in change and innovation processes, much responsibility for traditional HRD practices has been devolved to line managers. Getting line managers involved in HR follows Guest's (1987: 510) avocation to HR departments that, 'If HR is to be taken seriously, personnel managers must give it away.' For their part, Larsen and Brewster (2003) identify devolution to the line as a growing global trend, but one which has widespread implications for the organisation's capacity to develop, implement and administer HR policies across the entire firm. Indeed, 'giving away HR' has resulted in

HRD professionals encountering a number of problems, including: having less interaction with the line; experiencing difficulties in defining new HR roles; having to overcome resistance to change amongst employees and line managers; and dealing with skills gaps and resource deficiencies amongst line managers (CIPD, 2007a).

One of the most vaunted advantages for devolving HR has been the closeness of line managers to front-line employees and a greater understanding of the difficulties faced at shop-floor level. Indeed, Beattie (2006) argues that in recent years, there has been a resurgence in recognition of the workplace as a site of natural learning and an increasing awareness of the need to consider the developmental responsibilities of line managers. Hales (2005) maintains that the spread of more participative forms of management means that line managers are taking on the roles of 'coach', 'conductor' or 'leader' and that the process of HR devolvement means that line managers are becoming 'mini-general managers'. Budgetary cuts also mean that line managers' responsibilities are being stretched to include traditional HR functions including grievance and discipline handling. As McGuire et al. (2008) argue, such widespread devolvement may represent a lack of appreciation of the workloads, priorities, time pressures and skillsets of line managers, jeopardising HR standards and effective delivery. In this regard, attention should be paid to the findings of the UK National Skills Task Force (2000), who argue that the capability and commitment of line managers are amongst the most important factors in determining the effectiveness of workplace learning.

Getting line managers interested in taking on HR responsibilities has presented an ongoing challenge to HRD practitioners. On the one hand, Harris et al. (2002) argue that providing greater authority to line managers and encouraging initiative-taking may address a long-standing criticism levelled at HR departments: namely, a lack of appreciation of the immediacy of the line manager's problems. However, research indicates that many line managers view HR issues as secondary to more immediate business goals and consequently devote less time to HR issues (Cunningham and Hyman, 1995; Perry and Kulik, 2008). A lack of training for line managers in handling HR issues has also been cited as a key factor in the inconsistent application of HR policies on the shop-floor level with Longenecker and Fink (2006) arguing that management development is not a priority for the top management with reliance placed on the notion of 'trial and error'. Some organisations, however, have recognised the need to equip line managers for their new responsibilities, with O'Connell (2008) reporting that many organisations are accrediting workplace training programmes both to improve line-manager skillsets and in an effort to raise educational levels.

With increasing levels of globalisation, the role and duties of line managers have become more complex, requiring line managers to liaise and work with colleagues cross-culturally. Through technology, e-mail, teleconferencing, special projects and work specialisation, individual expert input is being sought according to core skills and competencies. Line managers are thus required to display high levels of cultural competence, defined by Selvarajah (2006) as a learnt activity about a specific culture and the application of cultural knowledge in sensitive, creative and meaningful ways to individuals from diverse backgrounds. Such mindsets are helping organisations learn and develop capabilities in diverse cultural settings, and tailor products and services to meet specific customer expectations.

As the competition for attracting and retaining talent goes global, line managers are playing an increasingly important role in identifying future leaders and assessing skills gaps and development needs. Many commentators have argued that line managers are in the best position to recognise and bring high-potential employees to the attention of senior managers and the HR function (Fulmer et al., 2009). For his part, Wilson (2012) argues that line managers have a clear role in facilitating the personal growth of employees, thereby positioning talent pipelining as a clear responsibility of line managers. Thus, line managers need to be centrally involved in the design of development plans and career pathways for high-potential employees.

Developmental relationships: Mentoring, coaching and employee counselling

Fostering healthy developmental relationships in the workplace is critical to successful performance management. While little research has been conducted into the relationship between psychosocial support in the workplace and training effectiveness (one exception is Brinkerhoff and Montesino [1995] who found that social support increases training transfer), it has been assumed that the existence of constructive relationships and psychosocial support between managers and their subordinates is critical to effective performance. However, some research exists indicating that where employees feel supported by the organisation where they work, they are more likely to be emotionally attached to the organisation and have trust in their managers (Allen and Meyer, 1990; Tan and Tan, 2000; Wayne et al., 1997). Such findings underscore the social exchange view of commitment, whereby commitment represents a dyadic concept contingent upon the level of engagement by both parties to the relationship (Shore and Wayne, 1993).

With the advent of boundaryless careers, forming developmental relationships is becoming increasingly important for individual career development. D'Abate et al. (2003) highlight the importance of development relationships to enhancing employee skills, improving socialisation within the organisation and in formulating career plans. Rock and Garavan (2006: 330) define 'developmental relationships as either formal or informal relationships where the individual takes an active interest in and initiates actions to advance the development of another'. Central to successful developmental relationships are the three ideals of *assessment, challenge and support* required to help individuals grow and progress (McCauley and Douglas, 1998).

Mentoring

Mentoring provides a variety of benefits to employees at all levels of the organisation. It has long been perceived as a beneficial hierarchical relationship, where the mentee gains from the advice and guidance of a more experienced colleague. An examination of the literature identifies myriad benefits associated with well-structured mentoring processes. Research by Groves (2007) stresses both the psychosocial benefits (integration, motivation, acceptance, affiliation) and career facilitation benefits (career advocate, coach, challenging assignments, exposure) to mentoring interventions in organisations. Likewise, Higgins (2000) reports that having a mentor results in enhanced career development and advancement, speedier career progress, higher salary compensation and higher career satisfaction. In practice, most mentoring programmes are shifting from sponsorship mentoring (where the mentor holds a senior position and performs an advocacy role) to developmental mentoring (which emphasises mutuality of learning and self-direction) (Clutterbuck, 2008). A useful mnemonic is provided by Ross (2007) to describe the activities that mentors engage in:

Manage the relationship
Encourage the learner
Nurture the learner
Teach the learner
Offer support, advice and guidance
Respond to the learner's needs

Despite the fields of mentoring and coaching being in existence for several decades now, confusion often still exists between the two concepts. In an attempt to illustrate the differences between coaching and mentoring, Rosinski (2004: 5) makes the following statement:

> Although leaders can act as coaches, I have found that this role is often confused with mentoring. Coaches act as facilitators. Mentors give advice and expert recommendations. Coaches listen, ask questions and enable coachees to discover for themselves what is right for then. Mentors talk about their own personal experience, assuming this is relevant to mentees.

While the above statement has its merits, it provides a view of mentoring that is largely directive and tends to imply that mentors do not listen, ask questions or enable mentees in the process of self-discovery – all of which are key attributes of a good mentor (Garvey, 2013). For her part, Minton (2010) argues that mentoring is highly structured, where there is mutual negotiation and agreement on the purpose, ground rules, duration and resources involved in the relationship. Clutterbuck (2004) argues that a good mentor tends to be someone who already has a good track record in developing other people; has a genuine interest and passion in seeing people advance and grow; has a good understanding of how the organisation works; combines patience, communication and interpersonal skills; has a wide network of contacts and influence; and has sufficient time to devote to the relationship.

Talking point   The value of mentoring

Read the following description of one employee's experiences of mentoring and answer the questions posed:

> The ground rules of mentoring are simple. You must like your mentor and they must like you. If this is the case, they will spare you some of their valuable time, always the most precious currency.

> You should make it fun and easy for your mentor. It will be fun if you do your preparation, and later act on the advice, and it will be easy if you pick a time and place that suits them.

> I have worked in numerous start-ups and in one I received some fundamental mentoring from our chairman, Sir Campbell Fraser. He had been chairman of Dunlop and director-general of the CBI, and he used this experience to help me simplify the complex software system we were trying to sell into a simple description of what it did and who might be interested. He then picked up the phone to someone in senior management at British Telecom, as BT Group was then known, and was instrumental in us getting our first order. He used his skills to identify the potential flaws in the unique selling points of our product, and, having done so, felt he would not damage his reputation by setting up an initial exploratory meeting. Mentors are understandably protective of their personal networks, and you should always take this into consideration before randomly asking to be connected.

> Mentors will give you the advantage of their experience and hopefully stop you making any simple mistakes. If there is a common failing of the aspiring entrepreneur, it is not being able to see the wood for the trees. But if people do take your advice and have success, then you will have really made a difference, which is a great feeling. I recently heard Kevin Spacey, the actor, speak in his capacity as artistic director of the Old Vic, and he put it very nicely. 'When you have success, then it's great to be able send the elevator down for someone else.'

(Adapted from: Southon, M. (2008) Ups and Downs of Mentoring. *Financial Times*, 5 January.)

> **Questions**
>
> What does it mean to be a mentor in terms of style, time, preparation and benefits? Apart from personal contacts and advice, what other important roles do mentors play?
>
> Successful mentoring relationships often result in direct, no-nonsense feedback. How can conflict be managed in a mentoring relationship?

Coaching

The field of coaching has experienced a strong revival in recent years. The CIPD *Annual Survey Report* (2008a) reports that 71 per cent of UK organisations undertake coaching activities with employees, the main purpose of which is either general personal development or to remedy poor performance. Critically, coaching has been promoted as a tool allowing managers to adapt to change more rapidly and effectively (Jones et al., 2006). For his part, Bluckert (2005) outlines the role of a coach as one who creates enough space for the individual to take risks to learn, develop and change. Stern (2008) sees coaching as an integral component in the development of leader capabilities and equipping leaders for further challenges. Effective coaching programmes recognise the necessity of failure in the leadership growth process and help individuals overcome difficulties through the adoption of an experiential learning approach (Goffee and Jones, 2008).

For the most part, coaching can be viewed as a human development process aimed at bringing about growth and effective change, often through knowledge, skill and experience acquisition. According to Bachkirova et al. (2013) coaching can be used in a variety of contexts and coaches can take on many forms including line managers as coaches; expert coaches who have achieved mastery in a particular field; performance coaches who target specific behavioural change; and developmental coaches who focus on longer-term leadership competence. Tschannen-Moran (2013) identifies the following roles that coaches undertake to help coachees attain their desired goals:

- To cultivate motivation through imparting a clear vision of success.
- To expand awareness and appreciation of the status quo and changes that are required.
- To build self-efficacy through instilling confidence and through persuasion and encouragement.
- To frame opportunities for development and advancement.
- To encourage experimentation to broaden coachees' outlook and field of opportunity.
- To help coachees recognise and celebrate success.

As Bachkirova et al. (2013) point out, the field of coaching finds it roots in the discipline and principles of andragogy, experiential learning and transformative learning. By its nature, coaching is designed to be largely non-directive and driven by the coachee's needs with a view to helping the coachee achieve self-actualisation. Growth is achieved through the powerful use of feedback, reflection, storytelling, experimentation and dialogue. Goal-setting and goal appraisal form an important part of the coaching experience helping the coachee chart progress and framing the coaching experience towards action.

Career counselling

Career counselling is a growing field of research within HRD. In an era marked by downsizing and the end of paternalistic employment relationships, yet an era where employee engagement and increased devolved responsibility is commonplace, Lenaghan and Seirup (2007) insist that open and honest communication channels need to exist between employees and employers. They argue that counselling skills are important in rectifying work problems, particularly performance issues, and that creating a warm welcoming environment is an important step in getting employees to engage with this concept. Likewise, Garvey (2004) sees a distinct therapeutic value in career counselling where the agenda is owned by the individual and the emphasis is on individual development and growth.

Nathan and Hill (2006) outline some of the issues that employees may bring up at a career counselling session:

- Personal relationships affecting work performance
- Lack of career advancement
- Breakdown in employee–supervisor relations
- Performance-related issues
- Job dissatisfaction
- Lack of employee self-confidence
- Job-related stress
- Difficulty in making career decisions

Talking point   Distinguishing key concepts

Bresser and Wilson (2010) outline the differences between the concepts of therapy, counselling, mentoring, consultancy and coaching through employing the metaphor of driving a car:

A therapist will explore what is stopping you driving the car.

A counsellor will listen to your anxieties about the car.

A mentor will share tips from the experience of driving cars.

A consultant will advise you on how to drive the car.

A coach will encourage and support you in driving the car.

Questions

Discuss what the set of statements above tell us about the key differences between therapy, counselling, mentoring, consultancy and coaching?

How can we ensure that mentors and coaches respect appropriate disciplinary boundaries?

(Adapted from: Bresser, F. and Wilson, C. (2010) What is Coaching? In J. Passmore (ed.), *Excellence in Coaching: The Industry Guide.* London: Association of Coaching and Kogan Page.)

Table 8.1 highlights and summarises the differences between mentoring, coaching and career counselling.

Table 8.1   Differences between mentoring, coaching and employee counselling

	Mentoring	Coaching	Career counselling
Definition	Mentoring is defined as a pairing of a more skilled or experienced person with a lesser skilled or experienced one, with the goal (either implicitly or explicitly stated) of having the lesser skilled person grow and develop specific career-related competencies (Godshalk and Sosik, 2003).	Coaching is defined as a process whereby a coach works with clients to achieve speedy, increased and sustainable effectiveness in their lives and careers through focused learning. The coach's sole aim is to work with the client to achieve all of the client's potential – as defined by the client (Rogers, 2008).	A one-to-one interaction between practitioner and client, usually ongoing, involving the application of psychological theory and a recognised set of communication skills. The primary focus is on helping the client make career-related decisions and deal with career-related issues (Kidd, 2006).
Orientation	Past- and future-oriented	Future-oriented	Past-oriented
Focus	Problem- and opportunity-focused	Opportunity-focused	Problem-focused

(Continued)

Table 8.1   **(Continued)**

	Mentoring	**Coaching**	**Career counselling**
Function	The function of mentoring is to provide career and psychosocial support to mentees. Mentors may also engage in advocacy and protection of mentees.	The function of coaching is to enable individuals to develop their potential within specific areas through effective questioning, feedback and problem framing.	The function of counselling is for the client to help themselves; to clarify the difficulties they face and attempt to resolve them.
Key emphasis	Transfer of advice and experience from mentor to mentee.	Facilitating the development, learning and enhanced performance of the coachee.	Non-judgemental listening, typically related to a particular crisis.
Contributing disciplines	A multidisciplinary field comprising amongst others psychology, education, management development, training, organisational development, philosophy and conflict resolution.	A multidisciplinary field comprising amongst others psychology, education, management development, training, organisational development, philosophy and conflict resolution.	Psychology, psychotherapy, cognitive behavioural therapy.
Guided by	Mentor: Individual who is more senior and experienced than the mentee, who may or may not be in the same organisation, but who is knowledgeable about the sector and organisation.	Coach: Individual whose role is to develop the resourcefulness of the coachee through skilful questioning, challenge and support.	Counsellor: Qualified specialist who guides clients through an established process of problem identification, developing new perspectives and goal establishment and commitment.
Form of relationship	Mentor acts as a teacher, role model, host and senior guide to the mentee.	Partnership of equals between coach and coachee.	Counsellor acts as a trained specialist focusing on helping the client resolve problems and concerns.
Forms of intervention	Cross-organisational mentoring Cross-departmental mentoring Virtual mentoring	Leadership and executive coaching Life coaching Sports coaching	Career counselling Relationship counselling Employee assistance programmes (EAPs)

Talent development

With organisations increasingly focusing their attention on identifying, rewarding and retaining talent, the area of talent development has attracted attention within the literature. Gandz (2006) argues that talent development is typically undertaken for three primary purposes: to ensure that there are zero talent outages; to enable a managed succession process to take place; and to boost an organisation's reputation as a leading employer. Garavan et al. (2012) provide the following definition of talent development:

Talent development focuses on the planning, selection and implementation of development strategies for the entire talent pool to ensure that the organisation has both the current and future supply of talent to meet strategic objectives and that development activities are aligned with organisational talent management purposes. (p. 8)

Nilsson and Ellstrom (2012) maintain that talent management is associated with activities that include incorporating new knowledge and doing things more quickly and efficiently. Thus, they argue that it is coupled with a focus on talent pools and processes that enable the supply of employees across all organisational levels with the requisite knowledge, experience and skills to perform effectively. This leads Nilsson and Ellstrom to review the meaning of talent and to consider whether talent is specific and context-bound or relative and portable to new settings; whether talent is associated with inherited predispositions or can be acquired through learning and educational activities; and whether talent is generic or universal. Such discussion is reminiscent of debates on the nature and characteristics of competencies in the last decade and, as such, work remains to clearly delineate both concepts. Indeed, Garavan et al. (2012) assert that 'talent' can be defined as the possession of unique managerial and leadership competencies.

The creation of a talent pipeline architecture and development pathways is becoming a key priority for many organisations. Development pathways are described as 'experiences, exposures and challenges' by Gandz (2006: 2) providing individuals with valuable opportunities to fast-track career advancement and giving organisations a competitive advantage in the marketplace. Indeed, Souder (1983) identifies three components to pathway planning: namely, self-assessment and objective setting; current and future position planning; and identification of development needs. Increasingly, however, it can be argued that development pathways need to consider individual factors including geographic mobility and issues concerning work–life balance. Certification and professional accreditation can also be an important consideration in mapping development pathways as they enhance an individual's mobility and can improve their standing and credibility within the organisation.

Much of the work on talent development has coincided with an emphasis on employer branding. Employer branding is characterised as 'a specific form of managing corporate identities by creating both within and outside the firm, an image of the organisation as a distinct and desirable employer' (Lievens, 2007: 53). Within the context of talent management and development, the appeal of employer branding lies in creating a strong employer appeal in the minds of potential employees. Kucherov and Zavyalova (2012) cite the following advantages of a strong employer brand:

- The creation of a positive image in the labour market.
- Establishing distinctiveness and uniqueness vis-à-vis competitors.
- Building recognition as an employer of choice in the minds of the target audience.
- Marketing and promotion of HR policies and the employee experience.

- Setting out the conditions of the psychological contract with employees.
- Promotion of an organisation's cultural values.

In summary, the provision of talent development through formal programmes, relationship-based developmental experiences, job-based developmental experiences and both informal and formal developmental activities (Garavan et al., 2012) will help organisations adopt a more strategic focus to building a high-performance work culture and securing the next generation of managers and leaders. The construction of developmental pathways allows for the customisation and individualisation of the employee experience helping employees take greater ownership of their own development. It also encourages greater engagement with stronger affective commitment to the organisation's culture and priorities.

The role of leadership in performance management

First-class leaders select first-class followers: second-class leaders select third-class followers.

Much has been written about a supposed 'crisis in leadership' with the need for organisations to develop managers into leaders to achieve high performance. Both Groves (2007) and Rothwell (2002) identify shrinking mid-management layers depriving managers of critical on-the-job experience, depleted resources for employee development and a global war on talent as creating shortfalls in crucial leadership positions. Such trends are forcing organisations to move beyond the short-term succession replacement agenda towards developing a leadership function, rather than developing individual leaders (Kur and Bunning, 2002). To this end, a growing trend relates to the increasing participation of managers in leadership development programmes to develop the leadership function (Groves, 2007).

Increasingly, organisations are recognising the importance of the leadership role played by line managers. As Rappe and Zwink (2007) report, the performance of line managers has an immediate effect on the organisation's bottom-line and on employees. Research has shown that employees who feel supported in the workplace have higher levels of employee commitment (Wayne et al., 1997) and are more likely to have higher levels of performance (Eisenberger et al., 1990). In today's business climate, line managers are particularly expected to have competencies in the areas of communications and interpersonal and soft skills to fulfil the roles allocated through devolvement (Rappe and Zwink, 2007). Moreover, leadership is becoming a shared responsibility across the organisation and recognised as a 'dynamic, interactive influence process among individuals in groups for which the objective is to lead one another to the achievement of group or organisational goals or both' (Pearce and Conger, 2003: 11). In contrast to other leadership forms, shared leadership recognises the lateral influences on leadership as well as upward and downward influences

(Bligh et al., 2006). It recognises the distributed nature of leadership and suggests that leadership is a pluralistic multivariate concept. For their part, Waldersee and Eagleson (2002) view leadership as a series of functions and characterise effective leadership as a balance between task-oriented and relations-oriented styles. This gives rise to the notion that leadership is not individually centred but may exist across groups.

In line with this trend, the focus of much leadership development has shifted from individualised conceptions of leadership to contemporary relational approaches (Boaden, 2006). The mode for delivery for leadership development programmes has also changed. For his part, Mintzberg (2004) argues that there has traditionally been an overdependence on classroom-based teaching in leadership development programmes. Likewise Cohen and Tichy (1997: 70) have stated that:

> Most of what has been done in leadership development falls dramatically short. It has been too rote, too backward and too theoretical. It has rarely been tied to a business's immediate needs, nor has it prepared leaders for the challenges of the future.

Critically, Leskiw and Singh (2007) identify a shift from traditional training (talk and chalk) approaches to programmes based on action learning principles. Likewise, Marcus (2004) signals a transition to customised, interactive learning programmes focused on real business issues combined with developmental relationships and supportive participant feedback. Typical items for discussion on such programmes are indicated by Doh (2003), who maintains that modern leadership development programmes need to focus on strategic and global issues, operations in decentralised environments, community perspectives, contingency planning and dealing with diversity.

More recent research indicates that the key distinction between average and superior performance, particularly at management level, relates to emotional intelligence. It is estimated that emotional intelligence contributes to superior performance as much as 66 per cent for all jobs and 85 per cent for leadership positions (Goleman, 1995; Kunnanatt, 2004). Building upon the work of McClelland (1973) and Sternberg (1997), Goleman (1998) argues that superior performance demands emotional competence as well as technical competence. Likewise, he argues that emotional intelligence is more important to superior performance than a higher IQ. He identifies five dimensions of emotional intelligence, namely self-awareness, self-regulation, motivation, empathy and social skills. Emotionally intelligent managers are more socially skilled, thus exhibiting high levels of interpersonal effectiveness. Thus, they are equipped to show empathy, handle conflict effectively, build influential networks and manage stress.

In light of research findings indicating the desirability of emotional intelligence, much attention has focused on developing emotionally intelligent leaders. An empirical study by Groves et al. (2008) found that it is possible to enhance the emotional intelligence of individuals through deliberate training. Participants to the study partook in a leadership development programme focused on enhancing emotional intelligence and demonstrated higher capability in perceiving emotions, thinking with emotions, understanding emotions and regulating emotions when compared to a control group. A study by A.M. Grant (2007) compared the impact of attendance at a long-term (13 weeks with weekly 2.5 hour workshops) versus short-term (two-day block intensive) coaching skills training intervention on the emotional intelligence levels of participants. He found that participation in the long-term programme led to increases in emotional intelligence, while participation in the short-term programme did not lead to changes in emotional intelligence. He concluded that longer-term interventions are needed to alter the underlying emotional intelligence levels of participants.

Conclusion

HRD performs an important role in improving employee performance. An important task of HRD professionals is to examine the relationship between work structures, employee skills and strategic outlook in determining how overall effectiveness can be improved. It argues for performance improvements to be made employee-centred, such that adjustments to new systems and practices can be made seamlessly. Thus, HRD looks at making the organisational system more effective through making employee contribution more effective.

Line managers are playing an ever-widening role in organisations. Their operational duties are increasingly matched to HR commitments and other devolved responsibilities. Line managers are increasingly working not only within the confines of their own departments, but need to work across the organisation and outside the organisation, liaising with external contractors, outsourcing providers and a range of other stakeholders. In addition, the growth of self-service HR systems is bringing more responsibility for operational HR delivery to bear on overworked line managers. HRD professionals must recognise and bear responsibility for these changes and any impact on the quality of delivery. Failure to do so will invariably damage how HRD provision is perceived in the organisation and the importance attached to it.

Fostering developmental relationships and developing future leaders remain vital to long-term success and sustainability. Recent years have seen a revival in coaching schemes and organisations are recognising the value of mentoring, coaching and employee counselling as important communication and development tools. Such interventions can help building a community of learning in an organisation, encouraging greater interaction, communication and relationship-building.

There is also a realisation that leaders need to be developed throughout the organisation and that leadership responsibility does not solely lie with the CEO. Moreover, leadership research is progressively recognising the key role of emotional intelligence in nurturing closer bonds between employees and the organisation.

Supporting performance at Marriott Hotels

In 1957, John Willard Marriott opened his first hotel in Arlington, Virginia. Little did he realise that some 55 years later, the Marriott chain he founded would include 3,700 properties in 73 countries, counting 53 hotels in the UK alone. Indeed, the J.W. Marriott Marquis hotel in Dubai is officially listed as the world's tallest hotel, comprising 72 floors and 1608 hotel rooms. Such is the reputation of Marriott Hotels in the UK, that for the last six years it has been named in the *Sunday Times* annual list of best companies to work for. Its focus on staff has been driven by the company's guiding principle that 'if you take care of your associates, they will take care of the customer and the customer will keep coming back'.

With a culture that encourages long-term growth and development, it is not surprising that many employees choose to build long-standing careers at Marriott Hotels. One in five employees has been working for Marriott Hotels for more than 10 years and internal staff surveys have reported that 71 per cent of employees are excited about the direction the hotel group is heading in and 76 per cent of employees love working at Marriott Hotels. Marriott's workforce is highly diverse with staff speaking some 80 languages and coming from a wide range of backgrounds and education levels.

To ensure high levels of performance from associates, Marriott Hotels invests heavily in staff training and development. To this end, the company has developed the 'Marriott Ways – First 90 Days' corporate induction programme, whereby staff are introduced to key aspects of customer service. As part of the orientation programme, new staff are invited to spend one night at the hotel as a guest free-of-charge to experience first-hand the high quality of service at the hotel.

Within Marriott Hotels, there exists a strong culture of long-term growth and development. The hotel group prides itself on promoting from within – with Marriott associates receiving 78 hours of training and 34 hours of professional development each year. Such training is critical to ensuring that high levels of customer service are maintained. Marriott prides itself on having an informal culture, with senior managers walking about daily to speak directly with staff. Indeed, this forms part of the Marriott philosophy which states that 'no manager is too busy to talk to an associate'.

At a managerial level, Marriott operates an extensive mentoring and coaching programme to ensure that all managers possess the requisite skills to build strong working relationships with associates. Managers interact regularly with associates

(Continued)

(Continued)

and there is a strong emphasis on communication and involvement. Coaching and career counselling are key aspects of the managers' role – as such activities are clearly linked to talent management and succession planning within the hotel group.

Keeping track of operational performance is also a critical aspect of life at Marriott Hotels. The balanced scorecard approach features prominently as the organisation seeks to maximise profitability, market share, guest satisfaction and associate satisfaction. Sales progress figures are available to managers on a monthly basis and market share details are compiled continuously and displayed on noticeboards located strategically within administrative backrooms of the hotel.

(Adapted from: Marriott Hotel Profile. Sunday Times Best Companies to Work for 2013. http://www.b.co.uk/Lists/ListedCompanies.aspx?Survey=133&Size=352.)

Questions

Management by Walking Around (MBWA) is a commonly used management practice. What are the key advantages of this approach in a hospitality setting?

What are the advantages and disadvantages of a culture of promoting from within?

Discussion questions

Simmonds and Pedersen (2006) distinguish between the US performance outcomes paradigm and the UK learning and development paradigm. Is there a stronger role to be played by mentoring and coaching in the UK?

Do line managers have the skills to operate effectively in devolved organisations?

By devolving HRD issues to line managers, is the HRD function relinquishing control over core activities? Will this decision damage the reputation of the HRD function in the longer term?

What key benefits arise to the employee from developmental relationships such as coaching and mentoring?

Strategic HRD

9

The objectives of this chapter are to:

- examine a range of factors that exist within the global environment affecting the design and delivery of strategic HRD;
- explore key models and frameworks of strategic HRD;
- consider different forms of capital that exist in the organisation;
- identify barriers that exist to implementing strategic HRD approaches.

Introduction

Adopting a strategic approach to the provision of HRD is seen by many organisations as being critical to responding to globalisation and rapid changes in the external environment. The drive to achieve competitive advantage has long affected organisational approaches to HRD with the need to show a positive return on investment cited as a key priority. Thus, HRD professionals are increasingly being tasked with showing how their work adds value to the business and aligns to organisational goals and priorities. As Anderson (2009) points out, HRD professionals are expected to work with senior managers to develop and implement workplace learning practices that fit with organisational systems and contribute to enhancing the bottom-line.

Some commentators, however, dispute the need for strategic HRD (SHRD) to be a separate concept distinct from HRD. Gold et al. (2010) argue that HRD, in and of itself, is strategic and that HRD is designed to have a long-term impact. However, they argue that the intent of a strategic approach to HRD is to concern itself with performance at the organisational as opposed to the individual level and fostering a long-term (as opposed to short-term) impact from HRD interventions. The nomenclature of strategic HRD also makes it clear that SHRD approaches involve discussions and assessments by senior organisational decision-makers regarding the direction being set out by the organisation and aligning HRD strategies directly to the organisational direction of travel.

Garavan (1991: 24) first defined strategic HRD as 'the strategic management of training, development and of management/professional education interventions so as to achieve the objectives of the organization while at the same time ensuring the full utilization of the knowledge in detail and skills of individual employees. It is concerned with the management of employee learning for the long-term keeping in mind the explicit corporate and business strategies.' In so doing, Garavan was emphasising the interdependence between individual and organisational development and the need to move beyond the notion of training for training's sake.

Subsequent definitions of HRD have emphasised the importance of fostering a learning culture and building learning capacity and capability to meet changes in the external environment. In particular, the rapid growth of information and communication technology systems has transformed international business and resulted in an awareness of the interconnected reach of cross-cultural and global teams and the need for HRD to be responsive and adaptive to global challenges. In 1999, Walton defined SHRD as 'concerned with ensuring that there are processes in the organisation which facilitate learning; ensuring the appropriate stewardship is exercised over the learning process; and providing direction to ensure that core competences of organisations are enhanced through learning'; and this was followed by McCracken and Wallace (2000a: 283) who viewed SHRD as 'creation of a learning culture, within which a range of training, development and learning strategies both respond to corporate strategy and also help to shape and influence it'.

In this chapter, we examine the key models and strategic drivers for HRD. We first explore the global context through identifying key factors affecting the shape and delivery of HRD provision. We then examine some of the seminal contributions and frameworks that have shaped SHRD approaches in organisations.

SHRD and the global environment

Garavan (2007) identifies the global environment as being an important factor affecting the shape and nature of SHRD. Within the global environment, he pinpoints economic and political trends, technology change, labour-market characteristics, and national and cross-cultural differences as factors affecting how SHRD is designed and delivered. Arguing that the global environment creates uncertainty for organisations, he advocates constant environmental scanning to ensure that organisations are aware of the most up-to-date trends and changes to market conditions. For his part, Friedman (2006) singles out 10 globalisation forces which he argues are affecting how businesses operate and deliver products and services in today's economy:

- **Creation of single economic blocs:** Through the creation of economic trading areas such as the European Union, businesses have been able to benefit from the free movement of goods, services, people and best practices, unleashing greater levels of creativity and boosting levels of competition.
- **Connectivity:** The development of the internet and low-cost connectivity has enabled businesses to create almost seamless global commercial networks through which business can be transacted quickly and at low cost.
- **Workflow software:** The increasing use of workflow software means that geographically dispersed individuals and teams can work collaboratively across joint projects and across standardised platforms.
- **Communities:** The use of social communities to create innovations and solve problems has greatly impacted upon businesses through processes such as the development of open-source software, blogging, podcasting, vodcasting as well as the growth of community content and community answers across the internet.
- **Outsourcing:** With the rapid growth of globalisation, organisations are distinguishing between core functions and peripheral/support functions within their organisations and in the latter case are reallocating these to organisations who geographically can serve these needs in a more efficient, cost-effective manner.
- **Offshoring:** In an effort to control costs, organisations are often shifting subsidiary operation to low-cost, low-tax, high-productivity environments where such functions can operate in a more cost-effective manner.
- **Supply-chaining:** Anticipating and responding to customer demands quickly and efficiently is a key function of business – and creating more sophisticated supply chains through the use of technology has become a key aspect of maintaining competitiveness in a globalised world.
- **Insourcing:** Through the use of third-party managed logistics, a close relationship is formed between an organisation and third-party supplier to deliver core organisational products and services.
- **Informing:** The increasing use of knowledge networks to update individuals and organisations of changes to the external environment has enabled businesses to operate more rapidly and responsively.
- **Personal digital assistants (PDAs):** The use of mobile and hand-held devices to keep up-to-date and communicate is shaping how, where and when business is delivered and transacted.

In 2009, Friedman effectively added an eleventh force affecting globalisation, namely environmentalism and the green movement. He argued that the push to develop green solutions is changing how markets and products are received and appraised by customers. He argued that delivering green solutions would not only result in improvements to global warming and the worsening environmental crisis, but would also make organisations more efficient and technologically advanced.

Alongside these globalisation factors, Peterson (2008) identifies the effect that political, economic, regulatory and cultural forces can have on the shape of strategic HRD interventions. She argues that while organisations cannot exercise control over these variables, such forces can enable or inhibit an organisation's ability to forge strategic relationships, align systems and process, develop accountability systems and build a high-performance work culture. Underscoring the importance of alignment with the external environment, Semler (1997) argues that organisations must ensure that they are able to proactively adjust to external market conditions, as failure to do so can damage organisational success. He suggests that external alignment is more important than internal alignment and that senior management must exercise control to ensure alignment is achieved.

Talking point   Outsourcing and the future

With the increasing use of outsourcing by firms in order to control costs, consider the following questions:

In 10 years' time, will organisations have a need for HR departments and HRD professionals?

What role will HRD professionals play in such organisations?

As HRD becomes more strategic, how important are the following factors:

- the relationship and support provided by senior management to the HRD function;
- the physical location of the HRD function within the organisation;
- the relationship and support that exist between HR and HRD practitioners;
- the relationships that exist between HRD practitioners and line managers?

Models of strategic HRD

Over the last 20 years, several academics have produced important models mapping out the key characteristics of strategic HRD. Such models have attempted to outline sets of principles by which organisations can align themselves to the external environment and improve the efficiency and effectiveness of their internal processes. Table 9.1 presents a synopsis of the key SHRD models.

Garavan (1991) – Characteristics of SHRD

Garavan's (1991) seminal model for defining strategic HRD was instrumental in shaping thinking about how organisations could improve the strategic basis of their HRD provision. Nine key characteristics were identified to help organisations improve the effectiveness of HRD interventions. The model conceptualised an enhanced role for trainers, arguing that they should act as innovators and internal consultants, rather than simply reactive training facilitators. Garavan identified the need to recognise the importance of culture as an enabler or inhibitor of change – impacting on how HRD is delivered across the organisation. The involvement of line managers as key organisational actors was acknowledged as the support of line managers is crucial in getting employee buy-in to HRD programmes. Similarly, the model identified the need for top management support for SHRD programmes. Top management provide credibility, status and financial support for HRD programmes underlining their significance within the organisation. Evaluation of HRD was included as evaluation offers valuable insights into key areas for future development as well as appraising training effectiveness. Perhaps most importantly, however, Garavan's model acknowledged the need for strategic alignment of HRD provision with overall organisational goals, thus ensuring that HRD delivery is future-focused and designed to build upon the organisation's core competences. Achieving integration or congruence with the organisation's mission ensures that HRD is not reactive, but works in line with key business objectives and helps with the organisation's overall growth and development.

Ulrich (1998, 2007) – A new mandate for human resources

The focus of Ulrich's work has been on reshaping how HR activity is configured and delivered in organisations and, in doing so, Ulrich provides some suggestions on how HRD in particular can be reconstructed and redesigned. Critically, Ulrich argues that HRD professionals must focus on creating value and solving real organisational problems. The work of HRD professionals is framed within Ulrich's Human Capital Developer role, which sits alongside the other four HR roles of HR leader, employee advocate, strategic partner and functional expert. Reorganising the HR function to bring it closer to the business ensures that HRD addresses workplace issues and needs. Especially, Ulrich sees a clear role for HRD professionals in partnering with senior management and line management to build a learning culture and mindset across the organisation. He sees HRD professionals as champions and advocates for employees ensuring that the employment relationship offers reciprocal benefits to both parties. In this regard, HRD professionals act as change agents, ensuring organisations are future-proofed and making certain that employees have the requisite knowledge and skills to meet contemporary business challenges.

Table 9.1 An examination of SHRD characteristics

Garavan (1991) – Characteristics of SHRD	Ulrich (1998, 2007) – New mandate for human resources	McCracken and Wallace (2000a) – Redefining SHRD characteristics	Harrison's (2002) six critical SHRD indicators	Grieves' (2003) strategic HRD characteristics	Garavan (2007) – Strategic perspective on HRD
Integration with organisational mission and goals.	Partner with senior and line management.	Shaping organisational mission and goals.	There is a learning and development vision and strategy that supports the goals of the organisation.	Information from all internal levels in facilitating organisational and individual learning to cope with change.	Alignment must be achieved between the organisational mission, corporate plans and HRD vision.
Top management support • Control of resources • Centrality	Be experts in how work is organised and executed.	Top management leadership.	All learning and development activities support organisational goals.	Devolving responsibility to line managers.	Environmental scanning should be regularly conducted and reflected in the shape of corporate strategy and HRD.
Environmental scanning.	Be a champion for employees.	Environmental scanning by senior management.	Activity supports and is supported by other HR policies.	Employee-centred approach to learning embracing employees and managers.	HRD planning should be formal, systematic and integrated with both corporate and HRM planning.
HRD plans and policies.	Be a champion for continual organisational transformation.	HRD strategies, plans and policies.	Learning and development as an organisational process is 'owned' by managers.	An emphasis on work-based organisational learning.	HRD solutions must to appropriate to the problems faced and must add value.
Line manager commitment and involvement.		Strategic Partnerships with line management.	Learning and development specialists establish effective business partnerships across the organisation.	A focus on organisation's business strategy.	Sharing ownership of HRD is critical to adding value to the organisation.
Existence of complementary HRM activities.		Strategic partnerships with HRM.	The outcomes of learning and development operations help to drive down costs and to increase the value of the organisation's human assets.	Knowledge, skills and competence of SHRD practitioner-facilitation.	
Expanded trainer role.		Trainers as organisational change consultants			
Recognition of culture.		Ability to influence corporate culture.			
Emphasis on evaluation		Emphasis on cost-effectiveness evaluation.			

McCracken and Wallace (2000a) – Redefining SHRD characteristics

McCracken and Wallace's (2000a) model sought to refine and re-examine Garavan's (1991) model of strategic HRD. They identified the need for a stronger leadership role by senior managers in HRD activities, both in terms of directing HRD strategy and monitoring the external environment to identify both threats and opportunities for growth. In several areas, McCracken and Wallace advocated a move beyond the operational to embrace a more strategic outlook. First, they argued that HRD plans and policies should be supplanted by HRD strategies developed in association with top management. In other words, where previously HRD plans and policies flowed from organisational objectives, now HRD strategies are developed in parallel with organisational objectives. Second, the notion of strategic partnership is advanced, both to describe the relationships between HRD specialists and line managers as well as relationships between HRD specialists and the HR function. Strategic partnerships with line managers bring HRD specialists to the organisational coalface, involving HRD specialists in operational problems, whilst sharing with line managers ownership of HRD solutions. Strategic partnership with the HR function helps bring about cohesive thinking about the shape of the overall HR provision as well as achieving congruence between HR and HRD activity. McCracken and Wallace also argue that HRD specialists must not only recognise culture, but must also demonstrate an ability to shape, influence and change culture to fit with organisational priorities. Finally, they argue that HRD interventions should not only be evaluated, but need to show a justifiable cost-effectiveness and return on investment.

Harrison (2002) – Six critical SHRD indicators

Harrison's six critical SHRD indicators encompass much of the thinking about SHRD contained within the Garavan (1991) and McCracken and Wallace (2000b) models of SHRD. In her first two indicators, Harrison discusses the concept of strategic alignment and the need to ensure that learning and development activity supports organisational priorities and goals. She argues that strategic alignment can be facilitated through greater HRD representation at board level. Harrison also identifies the need for functional alignment across the HR division to ensure that HR and HRD processes are mutually supportive. She considers that a mutual interdependency exists between the HR and HRD function and, consequently, staff from both areas need to work closely together to achieve common goals. Like McCracken and Wallace (2000b), Harrison embraces the notion of partnership between HRD specialists and line managers as the key to ensuring HRD interventions produce successful outcomes in the workplace. Such partnerships will invariably result in closer working relationships between both parties, resulting in a deeper understanding of operational problems by HRD specialists and greater ownership of HRD solutions by line managers. Finally, Harrison emphasises the importance of evaluation as a form of maintaining organisational effectiveness and competitiveness. She embraces the notion of pay-forward evaluation, whereby investment in human capital can provide a return in the medium to long term.

Grieves' (2003) strategic HRD characteristics

Grieves' thinking on strategic HRD emanates from his view that middle and line managers are becoming increasingly involved in change management processes and need to be adequately equipped to deal with the complexities of change. He sees SHRD as an enlightened, skills-focused change management tool designed to meet contemporary business challenges and rescue HRD from a narrow focus on designing and providing training programmes and solutions. He sees line managers as performing a critical role in day-to-day delivery of HRD solutions and helping boost levels of organisational learning. Grieves advocates an employee-centred approach to learning that moves to embrace continuous lifelong learning rather than reactive stand-alone training. Most importantly, however, Grieves sees SHRD as offering valuable organisational advantages provided it is inclusive of all staff and that learning is promoted and shared across the organisation and through the facilitation of HRD practitioners.

Talking point   Types of capital

Much of the literature on strategic HRD finds its genesis in the resource-based view of the firm which looks at the distinctiveness and uniqueness of a firm's key assets. As Kelliher and Reinl (2009) point out, the resource-based view posits that the long-term survival of a firm is contingent on a firm's unique business offerings and the development of distinctive core competencies over time. As such, a firm possesses multiple sources of capital which it can deploy in the creation of core competencies. These forms of capital include the following:

- **Human capital:** Defined as 'the sum of the workers' skills, experience, capabilities, and tacit knowledge' (Edvinsson and Malone, 1997: 34–35).
- **Social capital:** Defined as 'encompassing the norms and networks facilitating collective action for mutual benefit' (Woolcock, 1998: 155).
- **Intellectual capital:** Defined as 'applied experience, organizational technology, customer relationships and professional skills that provide a firm with a competitive advantage in the market' (Edvinsson, 1997: 270).

- **Physical capital:** Defined as 'tools used to produce and distribute goods and services ... including equipment, infrastructure, transportation and communication technology' (Schwartz Driver, 2010: 52).
- **Customer capital:** Defined as 'the combined value of the relationships with customers, suppliers, industry associations and markets' (Kannan and Aulbur, 2004: 393).

Combined, these forms of capital represent the net value of an organisation and combine to help an organisation produce products and services that are not easily replicable. An organisation needs to have a strong awareness of which forms of capital are most valuable to it and also most difficult to replace. Underpinning these forms of capital is the need to have both appropriate processes and systems to unleash the potential of such capital and a comprehensive development plan to ensure employees have the skills and knowledge necessary to deliver added value to products and services.

Questions

How can investment in human capital help improve levels of social, intellectual and customer capital?

Given that we can place a monetary value on physical capital, how can we measure the value of human capital, social capital, intellectual capital and customer capital?

Garavan (2007) – A strategic perspective on HRD

In 2007, Garavan produced a critique of the literature on SHRD in which he examined existing models of SHRD and offered some insights into future directions for SHRD. He argues that SHRD is a multi-level concept which enables an organisation to combine different knowledge elements, connect prior and new knowledge and merge internal and external knowledge to ensure sustained competitive advantage. He posits that SHRD creates core capabilities which make an organisation more change-ready and adaptive to change. He maintains that SHRD has moved from a prescriptive set of practices to a more descriptive and holistic approach to achieving internal and external alignment and promoting an organisational learning culture. In so doing, he recommends that HRD professionals connect with customers both internally and externally through formulating solutions that deliver practical and measurable business results. In addition, SHRD must recognise the context, the importance of multiple stakeholders and partnerships and the development of vertical and horizontal linkages across the organisation.

Barriers to the implementation of strategic HRD approaches

A comparison of strategic HRD contributions reveals several commonalities regarding how strategic HRD should be delivered in organisations. First, most commentators agree that HRD professionals need to develop strategic partnerships with line managers in organisations. Far from simply devolving HR responsibilities to line managers, HRD professionals need to be actively involved in operational issues, understanding workplace dynamics and supporting line managers in addressing the challenges they face. Many line managers continue to view HRD professionals with suspicion and believe that devolvement is merely a form of work-shifting from the HRD function to the line, whilst HRD professionals spend increasing levels of time operating at senior management level. Moreover, line managers often feel ill-equipped to deliver HRD interventions and do not feel that they are skilled or qualified enough to facilitate workplace learning effectively. With widening spans of control, they also feel too overburdened with work to deal with additional HRD responsibilities. For their part, Reilly and Williams (2006) argue that there has been resistance to devolution from HRD professionals because of a sense amongst some individuals that the HRD function may be losing power and control as well as fears over job security if line managers became proficient in operational HRD delivery. Consequently, shared ownership of HRD in some organisations remains somewhat aspirational and can be characterised as a work-in-progress.

The changing role and function of HRD professionals have resulted in some confusion and anxiety amongst HRD staff in relation to the activities they are now expected to discharge. Many HRD professionals feel ill-equipped to discharge their new roles and feel a bit lost at sea dealing with operational workplace issues. This is particularly the case in brownfield sites (companies which have been long established) where HRD professionals have been accustomed to particular forms of delivery and are resistant to change. Nevertheless, the proposed changes to the structure of HR and HRD have forced HRD professionals to relearn and reorient themselves to their organisation's portfolio of activity and obliged them to build a repository of hands-on knowledge about how the organisation really works and its internal dynamics.

The advocation to HRD professionals and senior managers to engage in boundary and environmental scanning in order to ensure organisations keep up-to-date with a fast changing global environment is undoubtedly a positive development for the evolution of the HRD function. It places change management and organisational development firmly within the remit of the HRD function and provides HRD professionals with a more strategic role within the organisation. However, many HRD professionals have expressed concern regarding the vague nature of environmental scanning and how such activity should be realised in day-to-day practice. In some cases, Tamkin et al. (2006) report that greater organisational development involvement has been accompanied by a focus on HRD branding, which may require HRD professionals to acquire additional skillsets from the marketing discipline.

While many of the models and frameworks for strategic HRD comment on the need for HRD provision to be cost-effective, the recession of recent years has led to increased levels of outsourcing by organisations. This has inevitably led to some HRD outsourcing, requiring HRD professionals to adopt a networked approach, working alongside senior managers, line managers and contracted HRD facilitators. While it can be argued that this is a realistic and unavoidable consequence of financial pressures, one effect is that it may decrease the visibility of HRD professions and thus undermine their status within the organisation.

Conclusion

Strategic HRD has taken its place as a key mechanism for aligning organisational goals and priorities and ensuring that HRD provision is structured, systematic and future-oriented. Adding value and creating value in a cost-effective manner have become key drivers for HRD activity in organisations. To perform a strategic role, HRD needs to be recognised by senior management as making a valuable contribution and needs to help the organisation face future challenges through environmental scanning and proactive pre-empting of future trends and developments. Such activity pushes strategic HRD firmly within the realms of organisational change and development, whereby HRD helps ensure that organisational structures and systems are fit for purpose and poised to achieve sustainable advantage through leveraging human capital.

Strategic HRD models and frameworks have proposed a readjustment to the activities and responsibilities of HRD professionals. Increasingly, the role of HRD professionals is built around the importance of developing an appropriate learning architecture to support innovation, add value and reduce operational costs. To achieve such goals, HRD professionals operate within a decentralised structure working in partnership with line managers and individual business units to ensure value is delivered locally and to ensure good practice is spread and disseminated across the organisation. Moreover, HRD is no longer located within a distinct HRD function, but dispersed across the business, being co-owned and delivered by line managers.

Finally, HRD professionals are building strategic partnerships with the HR function and senior management. To be seen as performing a significant role, the HRD function needs support and leadership from senior management as well as sufficient resources to discharge HRD activity efficiently and effectively. In addition, the HRD function has realised that it needs to work proactively with the HR function to deliver complementary messages regarding the purpose and direction of the organisation, ensuring that employees, through their work activities, understand and remain aligned to the organisation's vision.

Civil Service Learning

Jerry Arnott could be forgiven for feeling a little lonely nowadays. Only a couple of years ago, the civil service learning and development team was 2,000-strong, and was itself part of a larger HR team of approximately 10,000 people. Now, only 300 L&D staff remain as part of a shrinking HR pool, and Arnott presides over 60 of them, as head of a newly formed internal organisation: Civil Service Learning (CS Learning).

The change process has been swift, but it has – partly by design and partly by necessity – transformed learning within the civil service. 'It's clearly an ambition for the civil service to modernise, to become leaner, more efficient, more flexible and more collaborative with other sectors', says Arnott. 'And all of these pointers have an implication for the capability agenda for the civil service and the skills and knowledge requirements we have of civil servants.'

This journey began in September 2009, during the Labour years, under the banner of Next Generation HR. The credit crunch clearly heralded the approach of a new dawn. 'We knew there would be efficiency demands coming our way, so we thought we'd look at how to better deliver services across the civil service in all areas of HR. It was partly about stripping out duplication and wastage and at the same time looking at how we could enhance the quality of service.'

What they found, says Arnott, was a mess. He was part of a team attempting – for the very first time – to put a figure on the total annual L&D spend in the civil service. The figure they came to was £275 million, and 'that was just what we could get our hands on – there's a good chance it was well above that'. About half of the £275 million went on private contractors, and the other half on internal L&D, some of it delivered at the residential Civil Service College in Sunningdale. Over 70 per cent of delivery was in the classroom and therefore 'out of touch with the rest of the world'.

A decision to centralise generic learning and development across the civil service resulted in the introduction of a 'common curriculum': a new commitment to e-learning and blended learning and, crucially, procurement of market-provided, rather than internal, solutions. 'We knew from day one that having more than 2,000 L&D professionals doing the same thing in different places didn't make sense. It was a fixed cost that didn't necessarily guarantee quality', says Arnott. 'Where we are now is that well over 90 per cent, probably 95 per cent, is delivered through external provision. We've let go of pretty much all of our internal L&D capability.'

The common curriculum is split into three areas – working in the civil service, leadership and management development, and core skills. A menu of 49 broad courses across these areas is then split vertically by a five-tier grade structure, running from administrative level to senior civil servant. All civil servants can register on the CS Learning portal, and see the courses applicable to their level, that of their direct reports or, indeed, the level they aspire to. 'We currently have just over 60 face-to-face offerings, which tend to be one or two-day workshops; about 130 e-learning programmes, many in areas that have never been covered before in an e-format; and 4,500 learning resources – some, for example, available through Ashridge's virtual learning library.'

Despite classroom-based learning falling from 70 per cent to around 5 per cent of the total, Arnott claims it's wrong to think the new approach is all about self-managed learning. 'There will be a very strong, top-down learning requirement within the civil service for the next few years, going right back to civil service reform … that will mean all civil servants will need to be fully equipped and supported in key areas.' He offers the examples of commercial skills, project management and developing an innovative culture – 'themes that will be coming down on top of what we've created here, which is a bottom-up self-driven learning approach.

'The biggest challenge to really embedding this new approach to L&D is to build the commitment and the belief in our line managers, in particular. Because many of them won't have experienced the offer that's now available, they will still have – and do have – the belief that real learning happens only in the classroom. And with that is the belief that e-learning is rubbish', he says. With departments choosing what courses their people do, CS Learning's success or failure will rest largely on line managers. While those line managers who understand the importance of learning will obviously give people the time to learn, Arnott recognises that some will be reluctant to do so. But Arnott is equally clear that the CS Learning model is precisely the one needed to deliver better learning for civil servants: 'We are heading into a different world here and L&D is going to be one of the levers and enablers to get us there – so it makes sense to let go of what we had before and to almost start again.'

(Adapted from: Smedley, T. (2012) Interview with Jerry Arnott, Director, Civil Service Learning, The Civil Service. *People Management*, 26 June.)

Questions

How effective in your view has Civil Service Learning been at delivering more for less?

What steps can Civil Service Learning take to change line managers' views that e-learning is rubbish?

How can a culture of self-managed learning be fostered in the civil service?

Discussion questions

What effect have Friedman's 10 globalisation forces had on strategic HRD provision in organisations?

What steps can HRD professionals take to build trust and status with both line managers and senior managers?

What additional measures can HRD departments take to improve their cost-effectiveness?

Organisational Learning and the Learning Organisation

10

The objectives of this chapter are to:

- examine the importance and significance of organisational learning, distinguishing between single-, double- and triple-loop learning;
- explore Senge's Five Disciplines of the learning organisation;
- consider a range of perspectives from leading commentators on the learning organisation concept.

Introduction

Increasingly, organisations have realised that to bring about effective change, they need to emphasise learning. Learning from your mistakes, learning the lessons of the past and learning how to do things differently are key factors that have been recognised in contributing to organisational sustainability and success. It is clear that organisations as non-physical entities cannot learn on their own, but are reliant on the continuous learning efforts of employees. Learning brings about change through expanding individuals' capacity to think differently and approach problems and challenges in new and innovative ways. Brokering a learning culture also makes it easier for employees to acquire, improve and transfer knowledge as well as empowering employees to question under-lying organisational assumptions and the status quo. Sadly, however, many organisations do not recognise the importance of learning and are doomed to lose market share and core capabilities through lack of investment in the professional development of employ-ees and inadequate recognition of the need to keep abreast of environmental trends.

Faced with uncertain, fast-changing market conditions, organisations have become increasingly reliant on the knowledge, skills and insights of employees as well as the ability of these employees to collaborate, share information and work effectively in cross-disciplinary teams to build and deliver state-of-the-art products and services. Therefore, a core value proposition of many organisations and key to the competitive position that companies hold in the marketplace are the intuitions, tacit understand-ings and teamworking abilities of employees and their ability to learn faster and respond more quickly to market conditions and changing customer demands. Open-ness to new ideas, experimentation and taking initiative are featuring as ever more important attributes required of new employees. Indeed, networks and communities of practice (either real-time or virtual) continue to offer important avenues for helping develop employee expertise, enhancing their professional standing and building awareness of emerging trends and industry transitions. Alongside employee attributes, organisations must also possess facilitating structures and an enabling culture to allow learning to become embedded in organisational norms and routines. Heraty and Morley (2008) emphasise the importance of a supportive culture, shared vision and effective communication as key factors for fostering learning in organisations.

This chapter sets out to examine key theories and contributions related to organisa-tional learning and the learning organisation. It explores the importance of organisational learning and identifies conditions under which single-, double- and triple-loop learning can occur in organisations. It goes on to highlight practical examples of organisational learning, before moving to explore the learning organisation concept.

The significance of organisational learning

Across the research literature, many definitions exist in relation to organisational learning. Dixon (1999: 11) defines organisational learning as 'the intentional use of learning pro-cesses at the individual, group and systems level to continuously transform the organisa-tion in a direction that is increasingly satisfying to its stakeholders', while Gibb (2008) says that organisational learning involves the learning and relearning of complex organisational interactions in order for the system to survive. For their part, both Kroth (2000) and Lundberg (1995) regard organisational learning as denoting processes enhancing the actions of organisations through better knowledge and understanding. What these defini-tions have in common is an emphasis on both reflection and action as key drivers of learning and change. The definitions also acknowledge the social relational context for learning and that interpretation, sense-making and insight are gained through interaction.

For their part, Edmondson and Moingeon (1996) argue that the field of organisational learning is quite fragmented with some researchers focusing on *how organisations learn* – i.e. how systems adapt or change or process incoming stimuli – whilst other researchers focus on *how individuals learn* – i.e. how individuals embedded in organisations grow, develop, adapt and change as a result of learning. In agreement, Garavan and McCarthy (2008) assert that organisational-level explanations of organisational learning emphasise culture and routines, whilst individual-level explanations centre on the behaviours and cognitions of employees. On this issue, Hedberg (1981: 6) makes the following comments:

> Although organisational learning occurs through individuals, it would be a mistake to conclude that organisational learning is nothing but the cumulative result of their members learning. Organisations do not have brains, but they have cognitive systems and memories. As individuals develop their personalities, personal habits and beliefs over time, organisations develop worldviews and ideologies. Members come and go, and leadership changes, but organisational memories preserve certain behaviours, mental maps, norms and values over time.

One of the most significant contributions in the area of organisational learning was the identification of single and double learning by Argyris and Schon (1974, 1978) and triple-loop learning by Hawkins (1991). Single-loop learning relates to habitual operational learning where the focus is on error detection and correction. In this situation, norms and values remain unconscious and unchallenged and individuals are focused on making routine decision-making without questioning underlying policies and motives. Argyris (1999) gives the example of a thermostat to explain single-loop learning, whereby the thermostat is programmed to detect temperatures that are either too hot or too cold and correct the temperature accordingly without questioning whether the appropriate temperature has been set. According to Marsick (1988: 193): 'In single loop learning, a person continues to try out the same strategy or variations on it, and continues to fail, because his or her solutions are based on a set of undiscussable governing values that frustrate success, such as remaining in control and avoiding what are perceived as negative feelings.' Thus, the lack of true reflection and questioning in single-loop learning means that it is unlikely to lead to innovative or radical breakthroughs as individual and organisational routines remain largely intact. That said, single-loop learning is appropriate for routine, repetitive issues as it helps to get everyday jobs done in an efficient manner (Argyris, 1999).

Double-loop learning is a form of systemic learning, whereby individuals are encouraged to question and critically examine taken-for-granted assumptions and theories-in-use. It is relevant for complex, non-programmable issues such as those that fundamentally challenge the ways that structures and systems operate within the organisation. As such, Romme and Van Witteloostuijn (1999) characterise double-loop learning as a transformation process, as through the organisation's knowledge and competency base, new policies, objectives and mental maps are formulated. They argue that double-loop learning takes place through ongoing dialogic and open enquiry processes with the interactions between organisational actors being central to the learning taking place. For many individuals, double-loop learning represents a difficult, unsettling process and organisational defence routines are often deployed to limit or reject changes to organisational goals, norms and values. Argyris (1996) argues that organisational defence routines, which include bypasses, cover-ups and games, refer to any actions, policies or practices that prevent the experience of embarrassment or threat and at the same time limit or prevent the discovery of new learning.

Triple-loop learning is also known as deutero or transformative learning as it represents an attempt by organisations to capture the lessons of learning and the conditions under which learning occurred. Triple-loop learning was never included in Argyris and Schon's writings, but according to Tosey et al. (2011), the first mention of triple-loop learning is made in the writings of Hawkins (1991). A critical aspect of triple-loop learning is reflection, where individuals review the entire learning process and develop insights and understandings into the conditions under which learning occurred. Such reflection according to Tosey et al. (2011) should focus on enquiring into the governing variables, values and norms underlying organisational action in the hope that replication of such conditions can bring about new frame-breaking learning. For their part, Romme and Van Witteloostuijn (1999) argue that triple-loop learning results in 'collective mindfulness', where employees discover how they and their colleagues have facilitated or inhibited learning and produced new strategies and structures for learning.

Overall, it can be argued that the systems thinking focus of organisational learning with its emphasis on feedback loops, action learning and error detection and correction has led to the embedding of learning processes in organisations which have undoubtedly improved productivity and performance. An expansive definition of organisational learning by Fiol and Lyles (1985: 803) sees it as 'a process of improving actions through better knowledge and understanding', highlighting the collective situated nature of learning, in that it builds upon shared insights, experiences and memories to change behaviours and improve outcomes.

Talking point   Organisational learning in the NHS

In few organisational environments is a culture of learning more important than in the health service. Ensuring that doctors and nurses are properly skilled and qualified is not sufficient – it is vital that professionals across the health service work together in teams and share knowledge and experiences to benefit not only patients, but the health service as a whole. In their research, Nutley and Davies (2001) describe efforts to move the health service beyond adaptive (single-loop learning) towards generative (double-loop) as well as meta-learning (triple-loop) approaches. In particular, they highlight the area of obstetrics and gynaecology and give examples of single-, double- and triple-loop learning approaches.

Single-loop learning

A hospital examines its care of obstetric patients. Through clinical audits, it finds various gaps between actual practice and established standards (derived from evidence-based guidelines). Meetings are held to discuss the guidelines, changes are made to working procedures, and reporting and feedback on practice are enhanced. These changes increase the proportion of patients receiving appropriate and timely care (that is, in compliance with the guidelines).

Double-loop learning

When the hospital examines its obstetric care, some patients are interviewed at length. From this it emerges that the issues that are bothering women have more to do with continuity of care, convenience of access, quality of information and the interpersonal aspects of the patient and professional interaction. In the light of this, obstetric care is dramatically reconfigured to a system of midwife-led teams in order to prioritise these issues. The standards as laid down in the evidence-based guidelines are not abandoned but are woven into a new pattern of interactions and values.

Triple-loop learning

The experience of refocusing obstetric services better to meet patient needs and expectations is not lost on the hospital. Through its structure and culture, the organisation encourages the transfer of these valuable lessons. The factors that assisted the reconfiguring (and those that impeded it) are analysed, described and communicated within the organisation. This is not done through formal written reports but through informal communications, temporary work placements, and the development of teams working across services. Thus, the obstetric service is able to share with other hospital services the lessons learned about learning to reconfigure.

Questions

Beyond the benefits to patients, what other advantages do you foresee to the refocusing of obstetric care to better meet patient needs?

How can organisations be encouraged to partake in double- and triple-loop learning?

(Text in italics is taken directly from article)

(Adapted from: Nutley, S.M. and Davies, H.T.O. (2001) Developing Organisational Learning in the NHS. *Medical Education*, 35(1), 35–42.)

The learning organisation

Arising as a product of organisational learning, the learning organisation concept provides practitioners and consultants with a practical roadmap for embedding organisational learning and for clearly depicting the characteristics of organisations which embrace organisational learning. According to Sambrook and Stewart (2005), operationalising organisational learning as the learning organisation is not unproblematic, particularly given the contested nature of organisational learning – yet many commentators use Senge's Five Disciplines framework as a starting point for discussion of the learning organisation. Published in 1990, Senge's *The Fifth Discipline* identified five key components for developing innovative learning organisations. In this section, we will review each of these five constituent parts before looking at other significant contributions to the development of the learning organisation concept.

Systems thinking

In order to make organisations more effective, individuals must first understand how the structures, processes and strategies underpinning the organisation work and the effect that changes to the internal and external environment can have on the system as a whole. Knowing how departments and business units relate and are interconnected to each other and how knowledge, information and data flow through the organisation is crucial to identifying opportunities for improvement. According to Swanson and Holton (2001), systems theory challenges us to carefully consider inputs, processes, outputs and feedback, forcing a more holistic, expansive view on organisational dynamics and possibilities for change. Defined as 'a collection of elements in which the performance of the whole is affected by every one of the parts and the way that any part affects the whole depends upon what at least one other part is doing' (Ruona, 2001b: 117), systems underpin the operation of organisations and force us to consider organisations as dynamic organisms. Seeing organisations as dynamic systems permits a closer examination of both subcultures and substructures and can help leaders determine the degree to which these are properly aligned to the overall organisational mission and vision. It also allows leaders to deal with issues of instability and unpredictability that may arise within the internal and external environment.

Personal mastery

Achieving a high level of expertise or dominance in specific skills can enable individuals to achieve consistently high levels of performance. As Senge (1990) points out, employees with high levels of personal mastery have a continual desire to learn more about their work, clarify and deepen their personal vision and focus their energies on a specific task or activity. Such commitment often stems from career ambition or personal goal to achieve a particular role or position within the organisation. To this end, Lee-Kelley et al. (2007: 211) assert that 'such employees are motivated to understand what is happening across the organisation, how they fit into the organisation and crucially, how their work contributes to the corporate success'. In this regard, individuals committed to personal mastery will often make significant sacrifices to satisfy internal aspirations and in doing so, they may prioritise work over other aspects of life. Operationally, these individuals are likely to take full ownership of their own learning – and the trigger for learning will often originate from the individuals themselves (Blackman and Henderson, 2005).

Mental models

According to Senge (1990), mental models refer to the deeply engrained assumptions and generalisations that we possess, which shape both our perceptions and evaluations of individuals and organisations. They refer to the cognitive schemas through which we create meaning and build a vision of reality. These often tacit mental images evoke powerful feelings and responses, directing particular behaviours and eliminating certain courses of action as off-limits. Howard (2012) argues that mental models sometimes inhibit 'out of box' thinking as individuals often look for data and evidence which confirms a priori understandings of reality. As mental models are largely hidden and unarticulated, they are highly perceptual and variable in nature and strongly linked to the specific context we are operating in. Hill and Levenhagen (1995) describe three forms of mental models: intuitive models, metaphors and formal models which are operationalised and tested through action. In this way, mental models act as important guides for individuals in decision-making processes.

Talking point   Disrupting the status quo – the case of Virgin Money

In January 2012, Sir Richard Branson stood in the cold clear air outside the first high-street bank branch of Virgin Money. Located in Newcastle, in the same building as Northern Rock, the first UK bank casualty of the global recession, Branson vowed to change the world of banking for the better. Above the bank's entrance, a banner loudly proclaimed: 'Our Quest to Make Banking Better Starts Here'. With Virgin Money, Branson aims to bring change to an industry that has never been on the cutting edge.

At Branson's side is Jayne-Anne Gadhia – Virgin Money's chief executive officer since March 2007. Through her leadership, Virgin Money have begun revolutionising the way in which banking is done. With an internal motto of 'EBO – Everyone's Better Off', Virgin Money seeks to achieve benefits for both customers and society,

(Continued)

(Continued)

whilst at the same time making a profit. This motto is underpinned by the values of transparency and simplicity. Organisational practices and product offerings are designed with this motto and values in mind.

Virgin Money's first savings account offered customers 2.85 per cent annual equivalent interest. Whilst not the best rate on the market, the savings account offered two distinct advantages (not offered by competing banks), namely, no minimum balance requirement and no withdrawal limits. Unlike other banks, the interest rate was available regardless of whether customers conducted their banking online, over-the-phone or in-branch.

Virgin Money also unveiled a new design and approach to conducting in-store banking. Inside Virgin's high-street banks, customers sit on sofas and easy chairs sipping complimentary cappuccinos and surfing the web using free Wi-Fi. Staff also explain bank products to customers using iPads and the bank is decorated with Branson memorabilia including a gold-plated Virgin Records chart topper, photographs from Branson's various yachting and ballooning adventures, a model Virgin train and so on. Such an approach to banking follows the pioneering example of Umpqua Bank, based in Roseburg, Oregon, who invited customers to Wii-video game tournaments and live music concerts in branch.

Such an approach to banking is indicative of Branson – and he remains a key selling point and figurehead for Virgin Money. According to Patrick Barwise, emeritus professor of management and marketing at London Business School: 'Customers see a young guy with a beard who doesn't wear suits, who worked in the rock music business and who developed a global airline business.' In promoting and fostering a new approach to banking, Branson and his colleagues at Virgin Money are clearly setting out a new vision of a vibrant, competitive, engaging and fun banking sector.

(Adapted from: Kahn, J. (2012) Branson's Virgin Money Seen Disrupting U.K. Retail Banks. *Bloomberg Business Magazine*. http://www.bloomberg.com/news/2012-03-28/branson-s-virgin-money-seen-disrupting-u-k-retail-banks.html.)

Questions

Whilst customers in the UK often complain about their banks, only 2.5 per cent of customers switched banks in 2012 (BBC News, 16 August 2013). What further steps can Virgin Money take to break the mental models and deeply ingrained images and perceptions that UK customers have in relation to banking?

Is this new approach to banking (cappuccinos, free Wi-Fi, concerts and Wii tournaments) congruent with the mental perception that we may have of banking as staid, conservative and prudent?

Building shared vision

Ensuring that an organisation's goals, values and mission are shared across the organisation is essential to achieving alignment and fostering commitment to a common future. According to Hodgkinson (2002), traditional approaches to vision-setting typically involve senior management engaging in top-down, rational, long-term planning, establishing the direction of the organisation for the next three to five years. In this regard, organisational vision is typically owned by senior management and communicated and cascaded to employees through briefings and strategy documents. However, Jones (1998) argues that all employees need to emotionally connect with the organisational vision for it to be effectively enacted. Famously, Mintzberg (1994: 111) stated that 'the big picture is painted with little strokes', meaning that it is important to recognise that the achievement of an organisational vision can only occur through the daily aligned activities of employees. He argued that a vision should act as an inspirational image of a desired future that is achieved through strategy-making and a long-term proactive commitment to learning.

Team learning

For organisations to be effective, it is critical that workplace teams appreciate the importance of communicating and learning together. Improving organisational processes, products and services is a collective endeavour and regular communication, interaction and dialogue are necessary to ensure that the efforts of team members complement each other. Yeo (2002) argues that team learning often results in double-loop thinking as through dialogue, team members question taken-for-granted assumptions, structures and values and solve complex tasks through the strengths of individual team members. In this way, Yeo (2002) maintains that team learning results in synergies, which results in individual empowerments, helps overcome defensiveness routines and builds shared identity. Indeed Senge (1990) asserts that team learning is foundational to the learning organisation as teams represent the fundamental learning unit in organisations, without which organisational learning cannot take place.

Other perspectives on the learning organisation concept

Alongside Senge's (1990) work, there exist a number of other important contributions to the task of defining the characteristics of the learning organisation concept. Whilst all of these contributions agree that all organisations have the capacity to learn, they recognise that 'learning organisations are characterised by proactive interventions to generate, capture, store, share and use learning at the systems level in order to create innovative products and services' (Marsick and Watkins, 1999: 206). In this section, four further conceptualisations of the learning organisation are reviewed. Table 10.1 provides an overview of each of the learning organisation frameworks explained in the chapter.

Pedler, Burgoyne and Boydell (1991) – Learning organisation

In their work, Pedler et al. (1991: 1) define the learning organisation as one 'that facilitates the learning of all of its members and continuously transforms itself in order to meet its strategic goals'. This definition advocates a commitment to the professional development of employees as well as an emphasis on the development of the company as a whole and a realisation that organisational synergies will flow from the learning of employees. Pedler et al. (1997, 2nd edn) identify three stages in the evolution of the learning organisation. The first stage, labelled 'surviving', is where companies develop basic habits and processes and deal with problems on a fire-fighting basis. The second stage, labelled 'adapting', is where companies adapt in light of accurate understandings and analysis of environmental change. The third stage, labelled 'sustaining', is where companies create a context for learning, enabling them to achieve a sustainable adaptive position in a symbiotic relationship with the external environment. They identify 11 characteristics of the learning organisation as follows:

- A learning approach to strategy
- Participative policy-making
- Informating
- Formative accounting and control
- Internal exchange
- Reward flexibility
- Enabling structures
- Boundary workers as environmental scanners
- Inter-company learning
- A learning climate
- Self-development opportunities for all

Fundamentally, Pedler et al. (1997) argue that the learning organisation involves itself with whole-system thinking as well as emphasising dialogue across the organisation to improve knowledge and information flows and building organisational effectiveness. It recognises that organisations are capable of radical transformation and that sustainability is achieved through a long-term commitment to individual, organisational and contextual learning.

Goh (1998) – Strategic building blocks of the learning organisation

To develop a learning organisation, Goh (1998) asserts that organisations need to understand the strategic internal drivers capable of building learning capabilities. He asserts that an important role needs to be played by organisational leaders in creating

Table 10.1   Overview of learning organisation frameworks

Senge (1990) – The Fifth Discipline	Pedler, Burgoyne, and Boydell (1991) – Characteristics of the learning organisation	Goh (1998) – Strategic building blocks of the learning organisation	Marsick and Watkins (1999) – Integrated model of the learning organisation	Heraty (2004) – Learning structure within organisational-led learning architecture
Systems thinking	A learning approach to strategy	Mission and vision	Create continuous learning opportunities	Experiential learning
Personal mastery	Participative policy-making	Leadership	Promote enquiry and dialogue	Teamwork
Mental models	Informating	Experimentation	Encourage collaboration and team learning	Learning as a work incentive
Building shared vision	Formative accounting and control	Transfer of knowledge	Establish systems to capture and share learning	Learning alliances and networks
Team learning	Internal exchange	Teamwork and cooperation	Empower people towards a collective vision	Formal learning events
	Reward flexibility		Connect the organisation to its environment	Learning certification
	Enabling structures		Use leaders who model and support learning at the individual, team and organisational levels	
	Boundary workers as environmental scanners			
	Inter-company learning			
	A learning climate			
	Self-development opportunities for all			

the conditions within which learning can occur. Learning capability is posited as being derived from five core strategic building blocks:

- **Mission and vision:** Ensuring that employees have a clear understanding of the mission, vision, values and goals of the organisation is crucial if employees are to feel empowered to act and take responsibility for new initiatives.
- **Leadership:** Organisation leaders need to empower and encourage employees in their learning as well as fostering a culture of experimentation. Leadership needs to be shared with managers acting as coaches, facilitating the growth of employees.
- **Experimentation:** For new knowledge to be created, employees must be encouraged to take risks and try out new ideas and approaches. Freedom to question the

status quo and suggest improvements is essential to capitalising on opportunities that arise.

- **Transfer of knowledge:** Leaders must foster a culture of working together across the organisation and work hard to dismantle organisational silos and barriers to information and knowledge sharing.
- **Teamwork and cooperation:** Cross-functional teams and group problem-solving are effective mechanisms for developing new and innovative ideas and approaches.

For his part, Goh (1998) maintains that the learning organisation must be supported by an effective organisational design and the development of employee skills and competencies which support the alignment and facilitation of learning.

Marsick and Watkins (1999) – Integrated model of the learning organisation

Marsick and Watkins (1999: 203) consider learning organisations to be 'ones that are characterised by continuous learning for continuous improvement and by the capacity to transform themselves'. They identify seven action imperatives that characterise organisations on the path to becoming learning organisations:

- Create continuous learning opportunities
- Promote enquiry and dialogue
- Encourage collaboration and team learning
- Establish systems to capture and share learning
- Empower people towards a collective vision
- Connect the organisation to its environment
- Use leaders who model and support learning at the individual, team and organisational levels

In identifying the seven action imperatives, Marsick and Watkins (1999) argue that their conceptualisation of the learning organisation contains three components: a commitment to systems-level, continuous learning; the creation and management of learning outcomes; and a drive to improve the organisation's performance and value through learning. As such, the learning organisation involves the interaction of both people and structure towards the strategic use of learning in the creation of change.

Heraty (2004) – Architecture of organisational-led learning

Whilst Heraty (2004) does not strictly articulate a conceptualisation of the learning organisation, she does propose an architecture for organisation-led learning. Using the architecture metaphor, she argues that structures and frameworks can guide and facilitate or hinder and frustrate the achievement of organisational goals and aspirations. Underpinning organisation-led learning are the activities of HR specialists, the HR function and the organisation itself. These activities represent the foundations upon which all learning within the organisation rests. Sitting atop the foundations is the learning structure, which Heraty (2004) describes as comprising six elements: experiental learning, teamwork, learning as a work incentive, learning alliances and networks, formal learning events and learning certification, all of which are supported by a shared organisational vision and organisational communication mechanisms. This architecture provides a useful guide to help embed organisational learning in practice, acknowledging both the key role to be played by organisational actors (HR specialists, HR function) and the learning structure necessary (teamwork, learning alliances and networks, formal learning events, learning certification) to support organisational-led learning. The learning structure strengthens the possibility of learning taking place and provides employees with the opportunity to participate in learning for both individual and organisational benefit.

Conclusion

Embedding a tradition of learning within organisations can be a difficult and complex task. Learning has the capacity to bring about significant transformational change both for individuals and organisations as a whole. However, learning critically involves the development of insight – the ability to see past taken-for-granted assumptions towards a new vision of possibilities and opportunities. It requires individuals to move beyond the comfortable and familiar status quo to embracing the uncertainties of change and new experiences. For change to happen, managers and leaders need to mitigate against organisational defence mechanisms and routines which limit the potential for unearthing new learning.

For organisational learning to be truly effective, it is necessary to capture information about the conditions and circumstances under which breakthrough learning arises. Replicating the environmental settings in which learning took place can be a successful trigger for further learning and can contribute to meeting present and future organisational knowledge and skills requirements. Organisational learning should not be viewed as the aggregate learning of members of groups, but should be viewed as an organisational improvement process, integrating business processes and developmental approaches.

Increasingly, learning organisations are being regarded as the gold-standard which all organisations should aspire to become. While learning organisations have been described by Ellinger et al. (2002) as market-oriented, having an entrepreneurial culture as well as a flexible organic structure and run through a facilitative leadership style, there is little consensus in the literature on how to become a learning organisation. A wide variety of practices and approaches are advocated; however, most recognise the goal of embedding learning processes as a way of promoting change and in so doing dealing with environmental uncertainty.

In conclusion, building an organisation's learning capacity relies upon establishing trust, dialogue and collaboration amongst organisational members as well as structures which enable the sharing of learning across departmental boundaries. Greater levels of socialisation and experiential learning in organisations will encourage high degrees of creativity and provide organisational culture, systems and technology that are designed to support learning, rather than control it.

CASE STUDY

Netflix – a learning organisation in the making

Established as a small dot-com company in 1997, Netflix has grown quickly to become the industry leader in the movie-rental and entertainment market with over 24 million subscribers. Such growth is not coincidental – rather it is steeped within the company's tradition of innovation and growth. The company was inspired by the experiences of its founder and CEO, Reed Hastings, who was charged a $40 late fee for his late return of a rental of *Apollo 13*. Hastings began to reflect upon a better model for supplying home entertainment. He realised that gym membership allowed members to pay a flat monthly fee and work out as often or as little as they liked – and he wondered whether such a model might work in the movie-rental business. This experience inspired the Netflix business model of an all-you-can-watch monthly subscription service.

Revolutionising the way in which consumers engaged with home entertainment, Netflix entered into a market dominated by the two video giants of Blockbuster and Hollywood Video. Initially, Netflix introduced a mail-order, video-rental experience, whereby customers selected across a library of over 100,000 titles with the DVD delivery by post to the customer's door, but this service has been replaced by instant streaming, whereby customers download movies and TV programmes directly onto their TV, PC, tablet or other enabling devices (including Wii, Xbox 360 and Sony PS3 console). With an expanding presence in over 43 countries, Netflix has harnessed the power of technology to deliver home entertainment services to customers in an easy, accessible, inexpensive way. Thus, the Netflix model has totally altered the governing rules of the video-rental market by changing rental, delivery and access system dynamics and guiding customers towards a new, more convenient model of home entertainment.

Alongside using the internet to allow customers to access the service and stream content, the Netflix offering is also enhanced through content licensing agreements and the Cinewatch service. With deals concluded with the main movie studios (Warner Bros., Universal Studios), Netflix has ensured that its customers have exclusive access to the top movies and TV programming ahead of its rivals. In many cases, this has reduced the inclination of customers to sign up to expensive pay-per-view cable channels and provided a one-stop shop entertainment service.

The Cinewatch service is Netflix's predictive analytics tool – which offers customers with personalised movie recommendations based upon members' ratings and the users' own previous movie-rental behaviour. By rating movies using one to five stars, members are directed to new titles which align with their interests and tastes. The Cinewatch service also offers enormous benefits to Netflix as it allows the company to gain insights into what their customers like and improves its ability to spread targeted marketing information among its subscribers.

Blockbuster's filing for bankruptcy in the US in September 2010 marked a significant transition in the move from bricks-and-mortar towards on-demand, subscription-based online movie and TV services. It also cemented Netflix's arrival as the key dominant player in this new market. Moving to streaming movies eliminated Netflix's need to invest in DVD warehouses and pay hefty postal fees. Building a comprehensive cloud-based infrastructure using Amazon web services allowed Netflix to build a highly resilient, customer-focused website enabling its members to download content faster and onto more devices, improving the customer experience and customer satisfaction.

In September 2013, it was revealed that Netflix actively studies TV and movie piracy sites to help it decide on programming to add to its online streaming service. Netflix's vice-president of content acquisition, Kelly Merryman, disclosed that through examining movies and TV shows that were heavily downloaded on piracy sites, Netflix gained a valuable insight into customer tastes and content likely to have popular appeal.

(Adapted from: Ryan, L. (2013) Leading Change through Creative Destruction: How Netflix's Self-destruction Strategy Created its Own Market. *International Journal of Business Innovation and Research*, 7(4), 429–445.)

Questions

How does systems thinking help us understand the internal dynamics of how Netflix operates?

How important is leadership in the development of learning organisations?

What key differentiators does Netflix possess in the new instant-streaming movie market?

Discussion questions

Some commentators have argued that organisational learning helps build 'collective organisational memory'. Why is 'collective organisational memory' important?

One of the criticisms of Senge's Five Disciplines is that while it clearly describes the five disciplines of a learning organisation, there is little guidance on how to create a learning organisation. What practical steps can an HRD practitioner take to create a learning organisation?

What are the key obstacles facing organisations in becoming a learning organisation?

Should an organisational vision focus on outcomes or aspirations?

Knowledge Management 11

The objectives of this chapter are to:

- examine the importance of knowledge in organisations and consider the process of knowledge creation;
- explore the concept of the 'ba' and look at how knowledge conversion processes operate in organisations;
- identify the four forms of knowledge that exist in organisations;
- articulate the role that HRD can play in the area of knowledge management.

Introduction

Much has been written in recent times about the transition to a knowledge economy. With the increased use of technology across desktop, tablet and mobile platforms and the proliferation of internet-based companies and e-business solutions, it is clear that the age of knowledge working and the knowledge worker is definitely upon us. Increasingly, companies are looking to knowledge workers to add value and use their knowledge, skills, experience and expertise to develop more innovative processes, systems, products and services. As Friedman (2005) memorably stated: 'there is no longer any money in vanilla', signalling the importance of building organisational uniqueness that is not easily replicable.

Allied to the increased interest in knowledge management has been a noticeable shift in emphasis towards resource-based, human capital approaches to human resources as well as the widespread application of talent management initiatives. Organisations now devote considerable sums to attracting, developing, leveraging and retaining employee capital and ensuring a favourable return on investment is achieved. Quantifying employee net worth and contribution has enabled many companies to justify exorbitant net asset values on their corporate balance sheets. Indeed, the IT company Infosys estimates the value of its human resources as 57% of its overall net assets (Infosys, 2012). Assigning a value to human contributions and accounting for it on an organisational balance sheet recognises employees as an asset, rather than a liability accruing wages, pensions and business costs (Kaye, 2012) and requires organisations to rethink how this asset can be best deployed for organisational advantage.

Faced with increasingly complex problems, organisations are realising that there exists a strong, pressing need to build knowledge capabilities and acquire, create, capture and share knowledge to outsmart competitors and achieve sustainable competitive advantage. The importance of knowledge is recognised by Davenport and Prusak (1998: 5) when they state:

> Knowledge is a fluid mix of framed experience, values, contextual information, and expert insight that provides a framework for evaluating and incorporating new experiences and information. It originates and is applied in the minds of knowers. In organisations, it often becomes embedded not only in documents or repositories but also in organisational routines, processes, practices, and norms.

Building an organisation's capacity to learn is critical to effective knowledge management as is the creation of an appropriate knowledge management system and infrastructure. Choo (1996) argues that the creation and use of knowledge critically affects an organisation's capacity to grow and adapt. He maintains that knowledge management also helps an organisation make sense of changes and developments in the external environment.

The chapter first examines the knowledge-creation process looking at the explicit and tacit characteristics of individual and organisational knowledge. It goes on to explore the concept of the 'ba', seeing it as a shared space for advancing individual and collective knowledge. Enablers and barriers to knowledge sharing in organisations are then identified and four forms of organisational knowledge are identified. The chapter concludes by examining the role of HRD in knowledge creation and dissemination within firms.

The process of knowledge creation

In order to understand how knowledge management works at an organisational level, it is first necessary to comprehend how knowledge is created and stored. Nonaka et al.

(2000: 2) define knowledge as 'a dynamic human process of justifying personal belief towards the truth'. To this end, they argue that knowledge is context-specific, relational, dynamic and humanistic. Four types of knowledge are created depending on individual awareness of knowledge processes at work and whether knowledge is created internally or acquired through external sources (see Table 11.1). In proposing this classification, Spender (1996a) acknowledges the fact that individuals possess a high level of knowledge of which they are not consciously aware. Human thought is therefore subject to explicit and implicit processes which direct activity. Individually based knowledge may therefore be either highly conscious or tacit and automatic in nature. In this regard, Reber (1993) suggests that the explicit conscious system will be a 'higher-order' system with characteristics that differentiate it from the lower-level tacit system. He maintains that there should be less difference between individuals in their tacit cognitive capabilities and greater difference between their higher order capabilities. In essence, there will exist greater variability amongst individuals in terms of their technical expertise than their underlying intuitive nature. Furthermore, he suggests that the tacit system should be more robust and less prone to disruption than the higher-order conscious system. The importance of implicit/tacit knowledge lies in the fact that it is a local, informal, subjective form of knowledge, which is automatic, requiring little or no time or thought (Smith, 2001). It is essentially a product of socialisation processes and is embedded in local cultural and organisational value systems. According to Sternberg (1997), cognitive tacit knowledge incorporates implicit mental models and perceptions that are so ingrained they are taken for granted. Spender (1996b) argues that some forms of individually based knowledge may be automatic in nature, such as the recognition process which is almost instantaneous in response and requires little logistic computation.

There exists broad agreement in the literature that knowledge can exist across communities and organisations. This perspective sees knowledge as a shared societal construct deriving its importance from the fact that language and knowledge are the organising and structuring principles of social life (Burkitt, 1991). For his part, Reber (1993) distinguishes between social knowledge that is explicit and social knowledge that is implicit. Where the social knowledge is implicit, knowledge is acquired through the process of socialisation. Baumard (1999) terms this process 'the articulation of tacit knowledge' involving both endogenous methods (imagination, induction, mental elaboration) and exogenous methods (socialisation, non-formalised interaction, observation,

Table 11.1   Matrix of organisational knowledge

	Individual	Organisational
Explicit	Conscious	Objectified
Tacit	Automatic	Collective

Source: Spender (1996a).

sensation). This type of knowledge is characterised as furtive, discretionary and simultaneous. In contrast, social knowledge that is explicit provides the basis for the ordering of societal activities. Objectified social knowledge is regarded as universal, generalisable knowledge and can often take the form of rules, laws and regulations. Such knowledge is inevitably formed from an explication of collective implicit knowledge acquired through socialisation. Objectified social knowledge provides a platform for individual interaction in society through the wide dissemination of socially accepted norms, rules and procedures. In agreement, Habermas (2001) argues that cultural values and motives interpenetrate in social orders, whereby these orders in turn lend reality to normative patterns by specifying values with regard to typical situations. In essence, objectified social knowledge creates an institutionalised social order based on a pre-established consensus on a set of intersubjectively recognised values.

In 1998, Nonaka and Konno introduced the concept of the 'ba'. Defined as 'a shared space for emerging relationship', the idea of the 'ba' is that it can be a physical, virtual or mental space and, in so being, provides a platform for knowledge creation. They argue that through interaction and the transcending of individual knowledge boundaries, new insights and creativity can emerge. They argue that new knowledge is more likely to emerge when there is a concentration and intensification of knowledge resources and intellectualising capabilities. Meaning is created through the dynamic exchange of ideas, thoughts, reflections and insights with creativity often emerging through the synthesis of rationality and intuition. Nonaka and Konno (1998) maintain that a 'ba' can be created through the integration of structural design, resource concentration and reward and recognition. In such situations, the 'ba' can be conceived as an ongoing knowledge conversion spiral, provided adequate boundary scanning takes place, sufficient resources are allocated to the 'ba' and there is a commitment to ongoing investment in the skills of employees. In their research, Nonaka and Konno (1998) identify four specific knowledge conversion processes:

- **Socialisation** (*tacit to tacit*): Through shared experiences, individuals can acquire tacit knowledge and understanding and can build insights and organisational awareness, often without using language. Tacit knowledge is often related to gut instinct and connected to particular emotions, contexts and incidents. The knowledge gained from these encounters (sometimes for example passed from master to apprentice) cannot be fully articulated into words and thus remains tacit in nature. Observation, imitation and practice are often mechanisms through which tacit knowledge is disseminated from one individual to another.
- **Externalisation** (*tacit to explicit*): Described by Nonaka and Takeuchi (1995: 64) as the 'quintessential knowledge creation process', externalisation involves the clear expression of tacit understandings into tangible concepts and models. Reflection and dialogue are critical to the process of externalisation as initial concepts often need further development and refinement. Analogies and metaphors can also be helpful in guiding design teams and concept engineers towards an

approximation of the product or concept to be created. Externalisation can not only lead to new products and services, but can lead to changes in customer expectations and the creation of new product markets. As such, it involves bringing new ideas and concepts 'out of the ether into the open'.

- **Internalisation** (*explicit to tacit*): Internalisation involves individuals taking ownership of knowledge and insights that have been acquired and stored in their own knowledge banks. Through internalisation, individuals become valuable knowledge assets, capable of using the knowledge they have attained to build new concepts, ideas and product designs. Armed with knowledge, technical skills and experience, individuals can envision new possibilities and systems of working. To assist the internalisation of knowledge, guide books, manuals and instructional materials can help build the capabilities of other organisational team members – such that these individuals can build up their own insights and experiences.

- **Combination** (*explicit to explicit*): Combination is described by Nonaka and Takeuchi (1995: 64) as the 'systemisation of concepts and ideas into a knowledge system'. Knowledge can be shared through a variety of mechanisms such as documents, meetings, telephone conversations and virtual communications. University education and formal development programmes are often based upon the sharing and dissemination of explicit information, which practitioners often take and apply within their own organisations.

Talking point   How a beer aided the design of Canon's revolutionary mini-copier

For many years, Canon's product design team struggled with an important problem. In a growing market for home and business photocopying, Canon realised that they needed to produce a machine that was both reliable and affordable to stand apart from competitors such as Xerox and Ricoh. Their research indicated that 90 per cent of maintenance problems with Canon's photocopiers arose from the fixed nature of the photocopying drum used to store ink and imprint images onto paper. Such problems with the photocopying drum could only be resolved through regular expensive repair visits from trained technicians. Whilst conventional approaches to addressing this problem lay in improving the durability of drums and cleaners, Canon designers sought a new solution.

Faced with these problems, the task confronting Canon's design team was clear – to construct a reliable machine with a revolutionary, low-cost, disposable ink drum. The breakthrough for the design team came one day when project leader, Hiroshi Tanaka, ordered a case of beer for his hard-working team members. Sitting in a circle discussing

(Continued)

(Continued)

the design problems facing them, Tanaka realised that from holding a beer can in his hand that a circular aluminium drum for storing ink could be manufactured simply and at a relatively low cost. The idea of producing disposable ink cartridges or drums with a limited life expectancy meant that the core components of the copier would remain essentially maintenance-free. In addition, the concept of a disposable aluminium cartridge helped kick-start the process of component miniaturisation and also led to overall copier weight reduction. These process improvements allowed Canon to upgrade their production processes and take a leadership position in the photocopying market.

(Adapted from: Nonaka, I. and Kenney, M. (1991) Towards a New Theory of Innovation Management: A Case Study Comparing Canon, Inc. and Apple Computer, Inc. *Journal of Engineering and Technology Management*, 8(1), 67–83.)

Questions

How can organisations be encouraged to view all employees as potential 'knowledge creators'?

How can employees be encouraged to speak up and think outside the box?

Knowledge sharing

Getting employees to share knowledge and expertise in organisations often appears like an unnatural process as individuals are often paid for their individual insights and achievements. Gagne (2009) asserts that knowledge sharing in organisations is often affected by individual, organisational and technological factors. She identifies individual inhibitors to knowledge sharing as including: a lack of trust in the other party; fear of a loss of power; and lack of access to social networks. Brown and Duguid (2001) discuss the 'stickiness' associated with knowledge sharing, particularly across organisational departments. They identify an oft reluctance to share knowledge between a firm's research lab and engineering department – often as both divisions have differing motivations and traditions. For their part, Blankenship and Ruona (2009) identify project teams, work groups and strategic communities as HRD mechanisms through which trust can be established across different departmental units. Such social structures can help build trust and relationships through which knowledge sharing becomes more accessible and straightforward.

At the organisational level, barriers to knowledge sharing exist in the form of a lack of leadership, lack of appropriate reward structure and lack of sharing opportunities (Gagne, 2009). The support of top management for knowledge management approaches to succeed is deemed critical by Conley and Zheng (2009). The authors argue that top management act as role models to the remainder of employees within the organisation – thus helping foster a knowledge-sharing culture across the organisation. Likewise, employees must be incentivised to contribute to and participate in knowledge management ventures. Riege (2005) asserts that the meaningful incentivisation of employees can only take place if knowledge-sharing behaviours are integrated into the organisation's performance management system.

Technological factors such as the lack of an appropriate IT system and a lack of training can also affect knowledge-sharing approaches (Gagne, 2009). Whilst technology can undoubtedly assist the flow of knowledge and information, it needs to move beyond acting as a repository for information and take a more active role in knowledge sharing. To this end, Conley and Zheng (2009) assert that technology is enabling the creation of online communities of practice and is becoming central to enabling the development of effective relationships amongst employees who may be geographically dispersed. Technology can thus enhance an organisation's collaborative and communicative capabilities and improve knowledge flow across project and work groups. However, such a positive outlook is contingent on the provision of adequate training and the fostering of trust amongst participants.

Within organisations, knowledge can take four forms:

- **Embedded knowledge:** Successful organisations often recognise that knowledge can be embedded and codified within particular local contexts and situations. Such knowledge can be found in organisational rules, norms and routines. Embedded knowledge can often take the form of tacit knowledge, which is socially constructed and dispersed across different business units and departments.
- **Encultured knowledge:** This category of knowledge refers to the stories, norms, rituals and values that exist within organisations. Blackler (1995) argues that this knowledge is crucial in socialisation and acculturation processes as it helps build shared meaning and understanding. As Schein (2010) points out, culture helps give employees a frame of reference or mindset, through which they can interpret organisational activity.
- **Embodied knowledge:** Embodied knowledge relates to knowledge that has been made formal and explicit through the practical know-how and day-to-day skills of employees. For her part, Lam (2000) points out that embodied knowledge is strongly connected to the problem at hand and is highly applied in its focus. Knowledge can thus be embodied in raw materials, products, services as well as business practices and processes (Demarest, 1997). Embodied knowledge can be considered as knowledge which has been packaged and converted from a tacit to explicit form.
- **Embraced knowledge:** Sometimes referred to as 'embrained knowledge' (Blackler, 1995), this form of knowledge recognises the cognitive skills and capabilities of employees and their contribution to overall organisational success. Understanding complex situations and contexts often requires higher-level intellectual abilities that are perfected over time. Lam (2000) considers embrained knowledge to be formal,

abstract or theoretical knowledge which focuses on universal principles and scientific understanding. She argues that this form of knowledge is often highly privileged in the western world, leading to privileged, status-driven positions.

Talking point   Knowledge spectrums

Knowledge can be characterised across a number of spectrums in an organisation. Some of these spectrums are as follows:

Situated	Abstract
Explicit	Implicit
Individual	Distributed
Physical	Mental
Developing	Static
Verbal	Encoded
Formal	Informal

Questions

What do the spectrums shown above tell us about the accessibility of knowledge?

Where is knowledge creation located in organisations?

Role of HRD in knowledge management

Building organisational knowledge capabilities is a core aspect of HRD. In order for knowledge to be created and shared across the organisation, HRD professionals must ensure sufficient investment in employee development and talent management initiatives as well as the provision of appropriate structures to enable knowledge flows across the organisation. In this section, we will examine how the HRD function supports knowledge workers as well as designing structures for knowledge sharing in organisations.

Supporting knowledge workers in their learning

The work of knowledge champions is becoming increasingly important in organisations. According to Jones et al. (2003), knowledge champions are tasked with keeping innovators focused on organisational goals and the acquisition of knowledge that will be relevant and useful to the organisation. They argue that a key activity of knowledge champions is the assimilation, institutionalisation and dissemination of knowledge, such that new tacit knowledge is transformed to fit with the overall direction and strategy of the organisation. In many cases, knowledge champions form part of a large centralised knowledge management team – whose role is to transmit centrally/globally produced knowledge to local and regional units, ensuring that such knowledge fits and aligns with local cultural norms and modes of behaviour (Sandhawalia and Dalcher, 2011).

An emerging approach to developing knowledge workers pertains to stratified development. Based upon the concept of stratified medicine, this approach acknowledges the limitations of traditional 'sheep-dip' training styles and advocates a personalised, tailored approach to fulfilling training needs based upon participant and role profiling. Such bespoke solutions lower development costs and offer organisations more targeted performance outcomes – as the individuals participating in the training are those who really need it. Stratified approaches may also lead to improved HRD resource allocation at a time when training budgets are stretched.

Creating and supporting a culture and environment for learning is necessary to stimulate interest and commitment to continuing professional development amongst knowledge workers. Garvey and Williamson (2002) assert that the cultural and psychological context for learning can powerfully affect an individual's motivation to learn and set the expectations that either engage or alienate employees from learning. To this end, recognition must be given to the importance of learning by senior management and learning opportunities should, where possible, be linked to career planning goals and initiatives. Moreover, some commentators, such as Garrick (1998), argue for a shift from instrumentalist views of learning to more questioning, critical, knowledge-based approaches. He maintains that 'contemporary work-based learning strategies rarely deal in self-criticism, paradox, irony or doubt, yet it is precisely these qualities that give substance to learning' (p. 79).

Structures for knowledge sharing

According to Blankenship and Ruona (2009), organisations are formed around social structures which help to configure work activity, sustain workplace relationships and provide stability and identity for employees. Building a knowledge community within organisations recognises the importance of both learning and trust in how knowledge is formed, shared and ultimately leveraged for organisational value. In this section, three structures for knowledge sharing are described: learning communities, communities of practice and the role of networks.

Learning communities offer a useful vehicle for individuals to learn and share expertise. Built around the notion of reflection, collaboration and professional development, learning communities are defined as 'those environments that foster mutual cooperation, emotional support, and personal growth as the professional staff work and learn together to achieve what they cannot accomplish alone' (Watts, 2010: 9). For her part, Houseman (2007) identifies five characteristics of effective learning communities, including the need for supportive and shared leadership; shared values and vision; a commitment to collective learning and the application of learning; a positive collegiate atmosphere for learning and a culture of sharing professional practice. Through inclusion, collaboration, reflection and an emphasis on critically examining professional practice, learning communities offer valuable developmental space for learning and knowledge sharing (Stoll et al., 2006).

Communities of practice (CoPs) are central to knowledge generation efforts in many large organisations. Ardichvili et al. (2003) assert that COPs have become the knowledge management tool of choice for companies including Hewlett Packard, British Petroleum, Chevron, Ford, Xerox, Raytheon, IBM and Shell. Defined by Wenger and Synder (2000) as 'groups of people informally bound together by shared expertise and passion for a joint enterprise', they offer organisations six distinct advantages: they help drive strategy; they start new business lines; they quickly solve problems; they help transfer best practice back to the organisation; they improve talent recruitment and retention; and they help develop professional skills and competence. Zboralski (2009) argues that CoPs represent self-emerging and self-organising networks developed by individuals with a common interest or field of application through which members build trusting relationships through communication and interaction. In this way, CoPs help their members engage in boundary/environmental scanning and keep their skills updated through accessing the latest information and developments.

Networks represent an important tool allowing individuals access to professional expertise and connections to influential individuals. On their own, Swan et al. (1999) regard networks as a social communication structure through which information and knowledge can be transferred and shared amongst individuals in the community. Networks allow information to pass through internal organisational boundaries through a series of strong and weak ties based upon the degree of relational capital. Where strong ties exist, due to frequent interaction and intimacy/closeness between the parties, regular two-way communication, the exchange of information and the building of trusting are inevitable (Granovetter, 1973; Kang, 2007). For their part, Seufert et al. (1999) assert that the openness and richness of networks can bring about a fertile environment for the creation of entirely new knowledge through the formation of new collaborations and partnerships either within or outside the organisation.

Conclusion

In today's knowledge economy, organisations are increasingly realising the need to build appropriate structures to foster knowledge creation and sharing in order to remain competitive. While some individuals have dismissed knowledge management as a short-term, passing fad, the reality is that in contemporary business, value is added through the technical expertise, experience, insights and know-how of employees and groups of employees. Knowledge workers have thus become a modern commodity and the war on talent has a lot to do with ensuring the attraction, development, recognition and retention of intellectual capital within the organisation.

Knowledge comes in many different forms. Not only can we describe knowledge as explicit or tacit, but knowledge may also be embedded, encultured, embodied or embraced. Converting tacit to explicit knowledge is key to unlocking the potential of employees and organisations – as making explicit tacit insights and intuitions can lead to breakthroughs in new product, service and process knowledge. Communities and networks offer a useful vehicle for employees to come together, share experiences and build relationships and collaborations that help knowledge creation and generation.

Cultivating a knowledge generation environment requires the development of appropriate HRD practices. As Thite (2004) points out, innovation and creativity cannot flourish under tightly controlled conditions, thus organisational structures need to provide knowledge workers with the space and autonomy to engage in experimentation, to take risks and to envision new possibilities. Knowledge champions can perform a critical role in organisations through ensuring that knowledge and good practice are disseminated quickly and effectively across departmental units and geographic boundaries. In summary, it is clear that in this knowledge era, organisations must invest in and commit to knowledge workers and knowledge structures to survive and remain competitive.

CASE STUDY

Knowledge management at Black & Decker

As the world's largest producer of power tools and related accessories, Black & Decker is a well-established international household brand. Operating under product tradenames such as DeWalt, Mac Tools, Stanley, Bostitch and Emhart, it has over 23,000 employees worldwide with manufacturing centres in 11 different countries. Founded by two young entrepreneurs, S. Duncan Black and Alonzo G. Decker, just outside of Baltimore, Maryland in 1910, the business grew steadily and Black & Decker open its first full-scale manufacturing plant in the small town of Towson, Maryland in 1916. By 1923, Black & Decker made its first attempt to adapt power tools for consumer use.

Core to Black & Decker's business philosophy is a culture of continuous improvement and a drive to develop and bring new inventions to market before their competitors. The creation of a knowledge sharing culture is critical to effecting a culture of continuous improvement. As a global organisation, information needs to move

(Continued)

(Continued)

across both time and geographic boundaries as well as across different departments and business units. To this end, the emergence of communities of practice – informal networks of employees driven by a common set of interests – has helped the transmission and dissemination of information, avoiding the problem of 'reinventing the wheel' in different geographic locations.

Increasingly tacit knowledge is being recognised as an important driver of growth across the business and regular attempts are made by the company to capture tacit knowledge held by knowledge experts and to store and share this knowledge through online repositories and databases. Across the organisation, there is widespread use of video-conferencing and online discussions facilitating knowledge exchange. Environmental scanning is an important activity carried out to ensure that Black & Decker is aware of competitor activities and changes in market demand.

Structurally, Black & Decker has made changes to improve the flow of knowledge within the organisation. The company uses project teams and knowledge experts to maintain internal databases and ensure that sufficient investment in employee skillsets takes place. Managing knowledge is now considered a core activity of an organisation's managers – however, whilst the company identifies subject-matter experts, the use of knowledge champions is as yet absent.

Research has also identified several areas where improvements to knowledge flow and dissemination can take place at Black & Decker. To date, efforts at rewarding individuals and teams for sharing knowledge have been perceived as ineffective and little encouragement is given to individuals to share information with other departments and business units. More work is also needed to improve the interface between human and technological infrastructure to ensure that knowledge stored in repositories can be easily and quickly retrieved. Knowledge, whilst viewed as a driver of performance, is not treated as a crucial organisational resource and management need to take a stronger leadership role in emphasising the value of knowledge to overall business competitiveness.

(Adapted from: Pemberton, J.D., Stonehouse, G.H. and Francis, M.S. (2002) Black and Decker – Towards a Knowledge-Centric Organisation. *Knowledge and Process Management*, 9(3), 178–189.)

Questions

The key conclusion from the case study appears to be 'much done, more to do'. How can Black & Decker effectively measure its progress towards becoming a knowledge-based organisation?

How can the role of knowledge champion be properly integrated into the organisation?

Discussion questions

How can the value of knowledge in organisations be accurately measured and assessed?

Do you agree with Garrick's (1998: 79) view that 'contemporary work-based learning strategies rarely deal in self-criticism, paradox, irony or doubt, yet it is precisely these qualities that give substance to learning'?

What are the key arguments in favour of introducing knowledge champions in organisations?

In what other ways can HRD support the creation of dynamic knowledge capabilities in organisations?

Leadership Development 12

Chapter objectives

The objectives of this chapter are to:

- examine the four key streams of leadership (trait, behavioural, contingency/situational and transformational);
- explore the developmental implications flowing from leadership theories;
- consider the criticisms levelled at leadership theories.

Introduction

Are leaders born or are they made? Such has been the starting point for much discussion about leadership theory and the potential for developing effective leaders. While leadership theories often accurately describe key characteristics of the leadership experience, the ensuing explanation of leadership development interventions is often generic and only rarely connected to a particular leadership theory. To add to the confusion, leadership development is often conflated and confused with management development (Mabey and Finch-Lees, 2008: 33; Sadler-Smith, 2006: 280) necessitating a clear demarcation of boundaries and clarity regarding the purposes and outcomes of leadership development.

Many researchers have expressed concern about the lack of about progress in the field of leadership development. As early as 2000, Lynham noted that:

> There exists a deficiency of real scholarly knowledge about leadership development. The majority of research in the field of leadership development has focused on the what of leadership, rather than the how of leadership development resulting in a lack of knowledge and empirical evidence regarding the subject of leadership development. (p. 12–1)

Further criticisms of leadership theories come from Zaccaro and Klimoski (2001), who argue that leadership theories are largely context-free and do not pay sufficient attention to structural contingencies that can affect and moderate leadership conduct. For his part, Avolio (2007) maintains that leadership theories overlook the role and support of followers and he advocates a more integrated approach to developing leadership theories.

This chapter seeks to provide an integrated framework for linking leadership theories with specific developmental interventions. It provides a synopsis of four prominent leadership theories (trait, behavioural, contingency, transformational) and examines the developmental potential emanating from such leadership theories, identifying specific developmental interventions associated with those theories. The chapter concludes with a discussion of how an integrated framework linking leadership theories and developmental interventions aids our understanding of how we approach and think about leadership development.

An integrated framework for linking leadership theories and developmental interventions

The search for a single leadership theory that is applicable across all contexts and can be used to identify potential leaders has attracted considerable attention in the leadership literature. As different theories investigate various elements of the leadership experience, it is instructive to look across all theories to explore how leaders can be developed most effectively. The rationale for examining leadership development from a contextual perspective is advanced by Olivares et al. (2007: 79), who state:

> Leadership development, as a type of human development, takes place over time; it is incremental in nature, it is accretive; and it is the result of complex reciprocal interactions between the leader, others, and the social environment. Hence, effective leadership development realizes that leaders develop and function within a social context; and, although individual-based leader development is necessary for leadership, it is not sufficient. Leadership requires that individual development is integrated and understood in the context of others, social systems, and organizational strategies, missions, and goals.

To this end, the integrated framework (Table 12.1) aims to present a cross-cutting analysis of the key features of mainstream leadership theories and the developmental implications that flow from them.

Table 12.1 Key features of leadership theories

	Trait theories of leadership	Behavioural theories of leadership	Situational theories of leadership	Transformational theories of leadership
Underpinning philosophy	The possession of particular inherent qualities enabling an individual to distinguish themselves in a leadership role.	The actions and behaviours of leadership will determine their overall effectiveness. Certain leadership actions are likely to lead to more effective outcomes.	The leadership style to be adopted is determined by the level of situational control, the relationship with followers and level of positional power.	The ability of the leader to inspire followers to transcend their own interests and work towards the benefit of all.
Key characteristics	• A large number of different traits have been identified by various authors. • The big five personality traits include: neuroticism; extraversion; openness to experience; agreeableness and conscientiousness	• Within the Ohio studies: consideration and structure • Within the Blake and Mouton (1964) studies: concern for people and concern for production	Under contingency theory, there are two key factors (from Fiedler, 1964): • A leader's task or relationship motivational orientation • A leader's situational control (examined in relation to leader–member relations; task structure and positional control)	The four key characteristics of transformational leadership are: • Inspirational motivation • Intellectual stimulation • Individual consideration • Idealised influence
Key contributors	Stogdill (1948, 1974); Mann (1959); Bass (1990); Kirkpatrick and Locke (1991); Judge et al. (2002); Goleman et al. (2004)	Fleishman et al. (1955); Tannenbaum and Schmidt (1958); Blake and Mouton (1964); Blake and McCanse (1991)	Fiedler (1967); House (1971); Hersey and Blanchard (1988)	Tichy and Devanna (1990); Bass and Avolio (1994)
Relationship with followers	Often assumes a close relationship due to possession of particular leadership traits.	Advocates that the best leaders are concerned with both people and tasks. Encourages greater standards-based employee participation.	The state of the relationship with followers will determine the appropriate leadership action to be taken.	Relies upon a close inspirational relationship between the leader and followers.

	Trait theories of leadership	Behavioural theories of leadership	Situational theories of leadership	Transformational theories of leadership
Developmental rationale	Leader will become more effective if specific traits are more fully developed.	Through training and learning, leaders will be able to determine the appropriate leadership actions to be taken.	Leaders are trained to assess the environmental context and adopt appropriate actions which fit with the specific context.	Leaders are trained to respond effectively to followers' needs and connect with them on a deep individual level.
Developmental interventions	• Use of trait-based inventories to establish degrees of possession of particular traits • Trait-based specific training programmes (such as EI training interventions)	• Self-analysis inventories followed typically by communications and team-building activities • Competency-based development activities (may include empowering, coaching and motivational approaches)	• Self-analysis inventories to determine degree of task or relationship orientation • Environmental analysis inventories to establish degree of situational control	• Follower analysis inventories • Developing of coaching, mentoring and communication skills with followers • Improvement of leaders' listening skills • Counselling and feedback sessions to increase leader effectiveness
Criticisms of theory	• Some difficulties exist in specifically defining particular traits • Most trait theories lack specific weightings for particular traits • Most trait theories view traits as universal, regardless of context	• Behavioural theories seek universal understanding of leadership without taking into account context-specific factors • Assumes that the leader will demonstrate the same set of behaviours across all subordinates	• Requires leaders to have a malleable style and to adopt their leadership approach according to the particular situation. • Does not explain what should happen when there is a mismatch between leader and environment.	• Many transformational theories seek leaders in a 'hero' mode, which can sometimes lead to abuse of power • Encourages followers to go beyond their self-interests and pursue outcomes contrary to their best interests

Trait leadership

Trait leadership views the possession of particular inherent qualities enabling an individual to distinguish themselves in a leadership role (Pierce and Newstrom, 2008: 65). It advances the view that leaders are born and that leadership research can usefully identify key leadership characteristics such that individuals possessing key traits can be promoted to leadership positions within organisations. The key thrust of trait leadership research has therefore been to identify the qualities of effective leaders and produce inventories and questionnaires that test for levels of innate traits within individuals. To this end, trait leadership to some degree has reflected leadership trends more generally. Allio (2005) is critical of the modern inclusion of traits such as humility, credibility and modesty as little more than evidence of a current backlash against charismatic leadership advocates. In agreement, Fiedler (1996) maintains that there is an overemphasis on traits and leaders who have abilities, skills and resources that are useful to the organisation will be selected and accepted as leaders.

One of the earliest theories of trait leadership is that of 'great man theory' (James, 1880; Bernard, 1926). It advocated that individuals would naturally rise to leadership positions through possessing all the necessary skills and traits to make them effective in their role. According to Bass (1990), the great man was believed to be unique and have features that would differentiate him from others. An added dimension to the theory suggested that the progeny of 'great men' would also become effective leaders. Great man theory was common in the 1930s and 1940s with Mostovicz et al. (2009) maintaining that through describing and cataloguing the traits of effective leaders, others could learn about and emulate such traits, making their leadership efforts more effective. However, research evidence on great man theory yielded inconclusive results (Stodgill, 1948), with the added criticism that the theory was elitist, discriminatory towards women, promoted nepotism and lacked attention to situational factors.

Much of the contemporary focus on the trait approach to leadership examines the big five personality traits: extroversion, neuroticism, openness, agreeableness and conscientiousness (Costa and McCrae, 1992; Goldberg, 1990). Briefly defined, extroversion looks at an individuals' outward orientation, sociability and level of assertiveness. Neuroticism explores an individual's levels of anxiety, tension, stress and levels of negative emotions. Openness examines an individual's outlook and perspective, the broadness of their interests, adventure-seeking nature and level of imagination and creativity. Agreeableness looks at an individual's sense of altruism, level of friendship and easy disposition. Finally conscientiousness considers an individual's commitment to a task, their level of self-discipline and sense of duty. Research studies which have examined the relationship between these five factors and leadership effectiveness have found mainly contradictory results. Judge and Bono (2000) identified agreeableness as the strongest predictor of transformational leadership – a finding contradicted by Ployhart et al. (2001), who found that agreeableness was not predictive of transformational leadership. In the latter case, the authors uncovered a strong correlation between openness and transformational leadership. The clear difference in findings between Judge and Bono (2000) and Ployhart et al. (2001) may be accounted for by the difference in organisational settings – Judge and Bono conducted their study in an organisational context, whereas the Ployhart et al. study was carried out in a military context. A later study by Lim and Ployhart (2004) discovered that both openness to new experiences and agreeableness were not positively related to transformational leadership but found a positive relationship for extroversion and transformational leadership. This finding for the importance of the trait of extroversion was supported in Leung and Bozionelos (2004), who highlighted that extroversion was positively linked to prototypical notions of effective leaders.

A more recent application of trait leadership has been the contribution of Daniel Goleman in the area of emotional intelligence. In their book on *Primal Leadership*, Goleman et al. (2004) found that emotional intelligence was linked to superior business performance. Goleman (1998: 82) defined emotional intelligence as 'The capacity for understanding our own feelings and those of others, for motivating others and ourselves whilst using leadership, empathy and integrity' and identified the four characteristics of emotional intelligence as self-awareness, self-management, social awareness and relationship management. One of the key findings of Goleman's work (Goleman, 1995) is that emotional intelligence was found to be twice as important as intelligence in producing effective leaders. For their part, Sosik and Megerian (1999) found that managers with high levels of self-awareness were considered to be more effective leaders than those who were not self-aware. An empirical study by Dulewicz and Higgs (2004) proved that the emotional intelligence components of self-awareness, sensitivity and influence can be successfully developed through training interventions, while conscientiousness and intuitiveness were less amenable to training.

There is evidence to suggest that many traits linked to superior leadership performance can be successfully developed. Allio (2005) maintains that there is a strong need to design experiments that establish a causal relationship between training initiatives and improvements in leadership and such evidence is beginning to emerge. There is considerable consensus among leadership experts (Doh, 2003) that certain leadership traits (but not all) can be acquired and developed through leadership development programmes. There is also agreement that some leadership skills can be more easily acquired and that some individuals will acquire leadership skills more quickly than others. Doh (2003) argues that leadership programmes should adopt a holistic approach and include mentoring, coaching and trial-and-error experiences to help individuals acquire particular traits and skills.

Behavioural leadership

Arising out of the criticisms levelled at trait leadership, researchers began to turn their focus to looking at the behaviours displayed by leaders. Behavioural leadership research focuses on the actions taken by leaders and believes that leadership is a set of behaviours that can be learned and perfected. As such, leadership is viewed as an observable process with leaders using different leadership styles to bring about desired results in given situations (Jacques et al., 2008). As Ehigie and Akpan (2004) point out, discussion on leadership styles is often presented as on a continuum and in this section we will examine three dimensions: relation-oriented versus task-oriented (Likert, 1961); autocratic versus democratic versus laissez-faire (Lippitt, 1969); and transactional versus transformational (Bass, 1985).

Relation-oriented versus task-oriented

The University of Iowa studies were followed by a series of studies conducted at University of Ohio which examined leadership style in terms of initiating structure and consideration (Stogdill, 1974). Initiating structure explores the extent to which a leader organises and defines employee roles and work and structures the roles of the leader and team members, whereas consideration examines the leader's commitment to building trust, respect and rapport with employees and listening to their ideas and opinions (Robbins et al., 1997). The University of Ohio studies were followed by leadership research carried out at the University of Michigan which classified leaders as being production-oriented or employee-oriented. Leaders who were production-oriented focused on the technical aspects of work, emphasising high performance levels and output, whereas employee-oriented leaders looked to identify and fulfil employee welfare needs in the workplace and developing interpersonal relations. The Ohio and Michigan studies were popularised with the publication of the Blake and Mouton (1964) Managerial Grid, which identified five leadership styles along two axes labelled concern for production and concern for people (see Figure 12.1). The authors argued that the most effective leadership style was the 9.9 team style.

Autocratic versus democratic versus laissez-faire

This leadership style dimension originated from studies carried out at the University of Iowa in the 1930s. According to Kustin and Jones (1995), an autocratic leadership style is characterised by high levels of managerial direction and low levels of employee involvement. This style is very directive and results-focused and typified by one-way communication, centralised power and an expectation of obedience and loyalty on behalf of employees. In contrast, Kustin and Jones (1995) explain that a democratic leadership style embraces a more supportive form of leadership with higher levels of employee input, autonomy, involvement and self-direction. Finally, a laissez-faire style describes a situation where the leader allows the followers to make the decisions. The leader takes little action to influence the group and generally allows the group total freedom in relation to its activities.

Transactional versus transformational

With the transactional/transformational dimension, Bass (1985) focused on the exchanges that take place between leader and followers. Transactional leadership was characterised

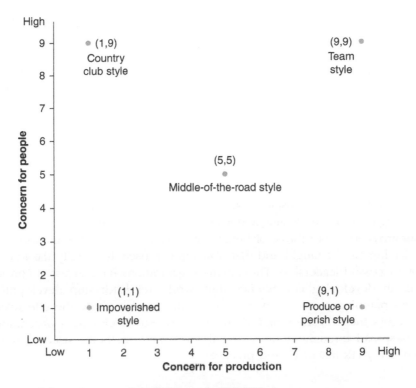

Figure 12.1 Blake and Mouton's (1964) managerial grid

as a form of leadership where the follower was motivated by the rewards provided by the leader in fulfilment of particular tasks or activities. Cardona (2000) describes transactional leadership as a zero sum where the form of exchange is either economic or social. In contrast, transformational leaders succeed in moving followers beyond a zero-sum scenario in getting them to transcend their own self-interests and bring about significant change for the benefit of the organisation or society as a whole. Further details on transformational leadership can be found in a later section of this chapter.

Since the early 1980s, behavioural leadership research has increasingly focused on the possession of so-called behavioural competencies. As defined by Boyatzis (1982: 21), a competency is 'an underlying characteristic of a person, which results in effective and/or superior performance in a job'. In essence, Boyatzis began by identifying the key characteristics of effective performance and leadership and positioning such competencies on a scale between threshold level and superior performance level. Competencies are thus increasingly used by organisations for a variety of purposes: as performance standards and norms; as developmental tools to further employee skills; as measures from which to award bonuses and incentives; to identify candidates in the succession planning process; and to assess key qualities during the recruitment process. In the UK, a competency-based approach is used by many national certification bodies and forms the basis for the National Vocational Qualifications (NVQ) and Scottish Vocational Qualifications (SVQ) systems.

In terms of research studies, authors have attempted to define leadership competencies in a variety of situations and contexts. For example, Mussig (2003) focuses on isolating the characteristics of values-driven leadership in an increasingly value-driven world. He identifies honesty, sustainability, commitment and understanding/supportiveness as key emotional and relationship competencies required for this form of leadership. McKenna (1998) examines cross-cultural understandings of leadership and the components of leadership. He found that leadership cannot be singularly defined but varies according to the national and cultural context. Finally, Boak and Coolican (2001) highlight six competencies – acting strategically; influencing and inspiring others; taking action; developing a high-performance team; making decisions; evaluating and learning – as critical to effective retail leadership.

In summary, the core thrust of behavioural leadership revolves around the belief that leadership can be taught and that research can usefully identify the key components of successful leadership. Thus, many organisations have invested considerable resources in developing competency frameworks for leadership development and succession planning purposes in order to identify and increase the effectiveness of leaders across their organisations. Competency-based development programmes are now widespread throughout most organisations and are being used to frame and underpin many HR initiatives and practices.

Talking point   Profile of an entrepreneur – Michael Dell

As chairman of the board of directors and chief executive officer of the company he founded at the age of 19, Michael Dell is considered to be one of the leading figures within the global IT community. Michael Dell's life story is one of an aspiring entrepreneur. At the age of 12, he was assistant Maitre D at a Chinese restaurant in his hometown of Houston, Texas, with a sideline of selling stamps. At 16, he was selling subscriptions to the *Houston Post* newspaper and was earning more money than his high-school economics teachers. Two years later he started building his own computers in his college dorm room and selling them directly to the public. In his own words, he says:

> I became very interested in computers when I was young, and my interest soon evolved from a hobby into a business opportunity. I wanted to learn as much as I could about PCs, so I would take them apart and then rebuild them with enhanced components. At that time a PC sold in a store for about $3,000, but I noticed the components could be purchased for $700. I also noticed that the people operating computer stores didn't know much about PCs and couldn't offer much in the way of support. I figured that if I could build my own

machines, I could compete with the computer stores – not just on price, but on quality and service. I didn't know, at age eighteen, how big the opportunity would become, but I knew that was what I wanted to do.

In his first year of sales, he made over $6 million and by the age of 24 he was named as Ernst & Young's first US National Entrepreneur of the Year and three years later, in 1992, he became the youngest CEO ever to earn a ranking on the Fortune 500.

In 2012, Michael Dell joined the board of Startup America, an initiative created by the US government to encourage entrepreneurialism and the development of start-ups as a path to economic growth. Dell itself has also been supporting the Dell Global Women's Entrepreneur Network which helps support women achieve their business goals through the use of technology. Michael Dell and his team also hold regular brainstorming sessions at the Dell Education Think Tank forums, which are designed to foster innovation in education, entrepreneurship and civic engagement, and consider such issues as the role of technology in learning.

(Adapted from: McArthur, R. (2012) Perpetual Motion: Michael Dell on Why Standing Still Just Isn't an Option. *Exceptional Magazine*, January–June: 12–16; The Michael Dell Story; http://www.dell.com.)

Questions

How can entrepreneurship be developed effectively? What tools and training interventions might be helpful in fostering entrepreneurial spirit?

Can entrepreneurialism be considered as a trait? Or a behaviour? Or both?

Situational leadership

Situational leadership emphasises the importance of flexibility of leadership approach and situational awareness when a leader is faced with a particular problem or circumstance. It highlights the reality that leaders need to be adaptable in formulating leadership responses and to analyse subordinates, task, organisation and the environment that is facing them. This section will analyse the three most common theories that fall within the category of situational leadership, namely contingency leadership, path-goal theory and situational leadership itself.

Contingency leadership is one of the earliest theories that falls under the category of situational leadership and arises primarily from the work of Fiedler (1964, 1967). Fiedler's original framework (1964) looked at building an understanding of the factors which determine how a leader's personality attributes affect group performance. Adapting the behavioural leadership dimensions of 'task-orientation' and 'relationship-orientation', Fiedler set out to analyse a leader's motivational disposition through the development of the least preferred co-worker scale. The instructions to the least preferred co-worker scale asks respondents (Fiedler, 1964, 1967):

> Think of the one person in your life, with whom you could work least well. This individual may or may not be the person you dislike most. It must be the one person with whom you had the most difficulty getting the job done, the one single individual with whom you would least want to work – a boss, a subordinate or a peer. Describe the person as he or she appears to you by rating them along the following dimensions.

Respondents are then provided with dichotomous sets of dimensions such as 'pleasant–unpleasant', 'boring–interesting', 'nasty–nice' and 'open–closed'. From such ratings, a determination can be made about whether a leader is more task-oriented or relationship-oriented. Through his research, Fiedler (1967, 1971) found that task-oriented leaders were more effective when situations were classified as favourable or unfavourable; whereas relationship-oriented leaders were more effective in moderately favourable environments.

However, to determine the degree of favourability of a particular environment, Fiedler (1964) identified three situational components, namely: leader–member relations, task structure and positional control. Leader–member relations looks at the strength of the relationship bond between the leader and followers and the degree of mutual trust and respect that exists. Task structure examines the nature of the work carried out in terms of clarity and ambiguity (Fiedler, 1964). Finally, positional control is a measure of the leader's ability to influence subordinates (Miller et al., 2004). Once the degree of favourability of a particular environment is established, leaders will be clearer on whether a task-oriented or relationship-oriented leadership style is required.

Northouse (2010) identifies a number of weaknesses with contingency theory. First he argues that the theory does not adequately explain what organisations should do when there is a mismatch between the leader and workplace situation. Second, he identifies a problem with the face validity of the least preferred co-worker scale and argues that it is cumbersome to use in real-world contexts as it requires three separate instruments to test each of the components of the theory. Finally, he suggests that there are problems in relation to the selection of the 'least preferred co-worker' in that respondents are not instructed in how this person should be selected and may confuse 'least preferred co-worker' with 'least liked co-worker'.

Path-goal theory arises out of the research conducted by Robert House in the 1970s. House (1971) viewed one of the primary roles of leadership as enhancing the psychological states of employees such that key outcomes became realisable and attainable and brought satisfaction to employees. House and Mitchell (1974: 84) advance two key propositions for their theory:

- Leader behaviour is acceptable and satisfying insofar as subordinates see such behaviour as an immediate source of satisfaction or instrumental to a future satisfaction.

- Leader behaviour is motivational (increases effort) to the extent that (a) such behaviour makes employee satisfaction contingent upon effective performance by employees and (b) leaders support employees through coaching, guidance and support in order to enable employees to achieve effective performance.

In essence, House identifies an important function of the leader as one of removing obstacles and barriers facing employees and preventing them from achieving effective performance. House (1996) argues that leaders should complement the environment they are working in and make linkages for employees between employee effort and goal attainment and reward. He identifies four types of leader behaviour (directive path-goal clarifying leader behaviour, supportive leader behaviour, participative leader behaviour and achievement leader behaviour) arising out of the 'task-focused' and 'consideration-focused' dimensions of the University of Ohio and Michigan studies. As such, House argues that leaders control the resources that employees value, and need to adopt leader behaviours that make employees respond appropriately to the needs of the organisation.

Situational leadership was developed by Hersey and Blanchard (1969) to recognise that effective leadership depends upon the adoption of an appropriate leadership style and on the development level of employees working for the leader. Four particular leadership styles (telling, selling, participating and delegating) were identified which could be used depending upon the maturity level of employees (Lussier and Achua, 2009). The four leadership styles identified were also broadly based upon the 'task-focused' and 'consideration-focused' dimensions found in the University of Ohio and Michigan studies. A telling leadership style was one characterised by high levels of task-focus with low emphasis on relationship-building and takes the form of the leader issuing instructions for followers. A selling leadership style is one that is high on both task-focus and relationship development. It centres on meeting employee needs as well as task completion and does this through regular communication and feedback as well as coaching, employee involvement and employee recognition. A participating leadership style gives emphasis to supporting employees with less focus on task-related elements. It underlines the importance of team behaviours, cooperation and joint decision-making. The final leadership style, labelled delegating, is low on both task and relationship components and involves the leader handing over decision-making responsibility to employees. It is indicative of a laissez-faire approach to management.

The second aspect to situational leadership looks at the development level of employees and how ready followers are to respond to the instructions of the leader. Hersey and Blanchard (1988) assesses follower readiness along two dimensions: ability (job readiness) and willingness (psychological readiness). They argue that where followers show a high level of self-efficacy, then leaders should adopt a participating or delegating style. However, where employees have a low development level, leaders need to adopt a more directive (i.e. telling or selling) style.

In conclusion, the three theories that fall within the situational leadership paradigm broadly constitute a development of early research on behavioural leadership. They recognise the importance of flexibility in leader approaches to problem-solving and advocate a thorough analysis of environmental factors in advance of adopting a particular leadership style. The development of leaders under the situational leadership paradigm generally involves training leaders to recognise, understand and diagnose the organisational environment; making them more aware of the bonds that exist between leaders and followers and helping leaders assess their own level of control over resources and authority. It also focuses more clearly on leader style, highlighting a clear correlation between leader style, follower responsiveness and overall leadership effectiveness.

Transformational leadership

Transformational leadership refers to the ability of the leader to inspire followers to transcend their own interests and work towards the benefit of all (Nadler and Tushman, 1990). Some of the core tenets of transformational leadership revolve around the ability of the leader to inspire and bring about significant change; articulation of a clear vision; the strong relationship between the leader and followers; and the awareness and fulfilment of follower needs and values. There are four recognised characteristics of transformational leadership (labelled the four I's): idealised influence, inspirational motivation, intellectual stimulation and individualised consideration (Bass, 1990; Burns, 1978; Keegan and Den Hartog, 2004; Posner and Kouzes, 1988).

Idealised influence looks at the ability of the leader to act as a role model to their followers and inspire them through the example of the leader's practice and example. Abu-Tineh et al. (2008) maintain that to set an appropriate standard, transformational leaders need to have a personal philosophy, engage with a set of principles about how people should be treated and ensure consistency between the values they set and the actions they pursue. Both House (1977) and Bass et al. (1987) insist that modelling behaviour has a powerful effect on followers and inspires followers more forcibly towards achieving the vision set out by the leader. As such, modelling behaviour brings with it a stronger level of allegiance and higher bonds of trust between leaders and followers (Coad and Berry, 1998). Through modelling behaviour, leaders communicate important values, a shared sense of purpose, self-sacrifice, persistence and determination, setting them apart and thus winning them the admiration and support of followers (Gillespie and Mann, 2004).

Inspirational motivation involves the ability of the leader to articulate a clear vision of the future that is inclusive, attractive and attainable to followers. Through presenting a compelling vision of the future, leaders engage in a developmental journey with followers, helping them build the skills and resources necessary to realise the vision and connecting with the innermost needs of followers. Kouzes and Posner (1995, 2002) argue that transformational leaders generate much excitement and enthusiasm amongst followers towards the vision through the skilful use of metaphors, imagery, empathy, positive reinforcement and praise. Through the articulation of the vision, the leader must show an awareness of the process and likely road that will need to be travelled towards achieving the desired endpoint. Owen (1999) regards visioning as a critical function of leadership and sees it as the awakening and aligning of the spirit towards achieving a common shared goal.

Intellectual stimulation explores leaders' powers of creativity and critical reasoning and their ability to question old ways of doing things as well as their capacity to formulate new strategies and action plans. The transformational leader must be knowledgeable and be able to project their ideas in a convincing and persuasive manner. Javidan and Waldman (2003) argue that the transformational leader needs to be able to connect the overall vision to the followers' own situation and that the overall vision and message must be solid enough to withstand criticism from vested interests. In this way, the transformational leader needs to help followers overcome individual and collective obstacles to progress. Abu-Tineh et al. (2008) argues that the transformational leader must be willing to learn from their mistakes, test out new ideas, take risks and be prepared to admit their failings. As Sarros and Santora (2001) point out, the notion of intellectual stimulation involves the leader working through problems in an open, egalitarian manner embracing the highest standards of honesty and integrity, yet challenging followers to find and achieve the optimum solutions.

Individualised consideration looks at the close bonds that are formed between the leader and followers and how such relationships are critical in bringing about change. Bass and Avolio (1994) describe individualised consideration as including time spent teaching and coaching others, identification and development of follower strengths and being attentive to follower concerns. This characteristic of transformational leadership recognises that followers need encouragement, motivation and reassurance to achieve the high standards expected of them. In so doing, leaders need to recognise and praise achievement as well as showing tolerance and understanding for mistakes if they occur (Kouzes and Posner, 1995, 2002). Forging a close relationship between leader and follower is critical in realising significant change and helps to elevate followers towards realising their potential.

Developing transformational leaders is not a simple task. While Doh (2003) argues that presentation skills and public speaking are skills that can be taught, there are elements of the leadership process (and particularly the connection/nexus) between leaders and followers that remain something of a 'black box' and mystery to researchers and academics alike. An exploration of transformational leadership practices by Abu-Tineh et al. (2008) indicated that training leaders to develop and communicate a shared vision energises followers and creates a greater sense of meaning and purpose. They argue that the creation of a shared vision creates a bridge between the present and the future fostering long-term commitment to organisational effectiveness. A second study (Gill et al., 2010) found a strong positive relationship between transformational leadership and employee empowerment resulting from the increased level of trust between leader and employee leading the latter to take greater ownership of organisational problems. Finally, a study by Garcia-Morales et al. (2008) identified a positive relationship between transformational leadership and the two variables of organisational innovation and organisational performance. They found that the shared cultures and open supportive structures created by transformational leaders encourage employees to engage creatively with their work and stimulate higher levels of organisational learning.

Talking point   The Gettysburg Address

On 19 November 1863, at the height of the American Civil War, Abraham Lincoln delivered the Gettysburg Address. Read through the text of this short speech and consider the questions that follow:

Four score and seven years ago, our fathers brought forth on this continent a new nation conceived in liberty and dedicated to the proposition that all men are created equal. Now we are engaged in a great civil war testing whether that nation or any nation so conceived and so dedicated can long endure. We are met on a great battlefield of that war. We have come to dedicate a portion of that field as a final resting place for those who here gave their lives that that nation might live. It is altogether fitting and proper that we should do this. But in a larger sense we cannot dedicate, we cannot consecrate, we cannot hallow this ground. The brave men living and dead who struggled here have consecrated it far above our poor power to add or detract. The world will little note nor long remember what we say here, but it can never forget what they did here. It is for us the living rather to be dedicated here to the unfinished work which they who fought here have thus far so nobly advanced. It is rather for us to be here dedicated to the great task remaining before us – that from these honoured dead we take increased devotion to that cause for which they gave the last full measure of devotion – that we here highly resolve that these dead shall not have died in vain, that this nation under God shall have a new birth of freedom, and that government of the people, by the people, for the people shall not perish from the earth.

Questions

What evidence can be found in this speech to support the contention that Abraham Lincoln was a 'transformational leader'?

Speech imagery plays an important role in connecting leaders and followers. What are the most powerful images used in the Gettysburg Address? What makes these images powerful?

Conclusion

Leadership is a composite of multiple aspects and experiences. Consequently, a single leadership theory can never full capture the entirety of the leadership concept, but can facilitate a greater understanding of various facets of leadership. While research has been produced for more than 100 years looking at the characteristics of effective leadership, it appears on the surface that the concept remains as elusive as ever. Indeed, it is arguable that the leadership 'pill' (to use Blanchard and Muchnick's [2005] term) will always retain a secret ingredient that will remain elusive to research.

That said, significant progress has been made in relation to various strands of leadership theory and towards making leaders more effective. Trait-based leadership research has usefully identified various qualities necessary for effective leadership. Indeed, research on emotional intelligence continues to emphasise and prove the importance of emotional intelligence in the make-up of leaders. Research on behavioural leadership has arguably led to the development and adoption of competency frameworks which are used across organisations to frame HR practices and leadership development programmes. Contingency and situational leadership research has made us more aware of the need for leaders to act flexibly according to the circumstances facing them. Finally, transformational leadership has taught us a lot about the bonds that tie leaders and followers and how such relationships can be strengthened and developed.

In conclusion, developing leaders is a complex process and remains something of an art. However, as the research base continues to grow, we can refine this art and improve the effectiveness of our leaders. Good practice leadership development programmes acknowledge the multifaceted nature of leadership and the need to draw across all four strands of leadership theory to produce well-rounded and effective interventions.

CASE STUDY

Google's search to find better bosses

In 2009, statisticians at Google began work on a highly ambitious undertaking code-named Project Oxygen. Using the data-mining and analytical resources at their disposal, their quest was to find the key ingredients of highly effective managers. Through investigation and study of performance reviews, feedback surveys and nominations for top-manager awards (which included over 10,000 observations, 400 pages of interview notes and more than 100 variables), the statisticians at Google were able to determine the eight key habits of effective managers. Such practices included: 'Having a clear vision and strategy for the team', 'Helping your

(Continued)

(Continued)

employees with career development', 'Be a good coach', 'Be a good communicator and listen to your team', 'Express interest in team member's success and well-being', 'Have key technical skills so that you can advise your team', 'Empower your team and don't micro-manage' and 'Be productive and results-oriented'. For a technology-oriented company like Google, Project Oxygen uncovered some unexpected findings. Far from prioritising technical expertise, the research discovered that employees value fair-minded managers who guide and assist people in solving problems through asking questions and taking time for face-to-face meetings. Effective managers also took an interest in their employees' skills and interests and formulated plans for their career development.

The results of Project Oxygen clearly highlight the instrumental role that managers play in both employee retention and employee development. The research found that quality of management was the single biggest factor affecting employee performance and employees' intention to stay with Google. As well as identifying positive managerial attributes, researchers at Google also isolated the reasons why employees leave organisations, namely: they don't feel a connection to the mission of the company, they don't really like or respect their co-workers, or they have a bad boss. The results of Project Oxygen have dramatically helped Google reshape and recast approaches to training and development within the organisation. Through embedding the principles discovered through Project Oxygen in their training and development programmes, Google has experienced a significant improvement in manager quality for 75 per cent of their worst-performing managers. Perhaps key to the overall understanding of Project Oxygen however is the simple message that the core of effective management lies not in the technical expertise and skills of the managers themselves, but in their ability to communicate regularly with employees and provide open, direct and constructive feedback.

(Adapted from: Bryant, A. (2011) Google's Quest to Build a Better Boss. *New York Times*, 12 March. http://www.nytimes.com/2011/03/13/business/13hire.html?pagewanted=all.)

Questions

From the eight principles identified by Google, does the company subscribe to a trait- or behaviour-based approach to leadership?

Based upon your own insights and the evidence of the case study, discuss the view that 'employees don't leave organisations, they leave their managers'.

Discussion questions

Aside from emotional intelligence, how has trait theory contributed to our knowledge of how we develop effective leaders?

'The best predictor of future performance is past performance.' Discuss the view that an effective leader can only be identified through their previous actions.

Does transformational leadership place too much emphasis on oratory and charisma?

Part 3
HRD at the Societal Level

International HRD 13

The objectives of this chapter are to:

- investigate the effect of culture on the character of HRD;
- examine the cultural boundedness of HRD theory and practice;
- present a framework looking at the internationalisation process for organisations;
- identify the HRD opportunities that arise through the internationalisation process.

Introduction

The notion of international human resource development is a relatively new development within the maturing field of HRD (Evarts, 1998; Woodall et al., 2002). In cost-competitive markets, the standardisation of HRD practices across overseas operations has the potential for producing significant financial and human capital savings, improving productivity and streamlining operational procedures (Lunnan et al., 2002). In addition, the increasing use and application of e-learning and computer-based training have resulted in the delivery of HRD solutions that are timely, current and immediately accessible worldwide (Lytras et al. 2002; Russell et al., 2003). However, in spite of technological advances fuelling standardisation of HRD offerings and increasing structural configurations across global organisations, individual behaviour within these organisations continues to manifest nationally culturally based dissimilarities (Adler et al., 1986). Furthermore an outcome of globalisation has been the identification of 'uneven' patterns of economic and social development, making more visible the disparities that exist in education and skill levels (Metcalfe and Rees, 2005). Consequently, HRD has a dual role to play: first, in developing economic and social wellbeing and, second, as a means of leveraging value from human capital (Woodall, 2005).

The lack of emphasis on international HRD stems directly from the origins and early development of the field. Both Jankowicz (1999) and Weinberger (1998) argue that academic research in HRD is primarily western and unicultural in orientation and strongly influenced by the perspectives of US scholars. Indeed, several calls have been made in the literature for academics to move beyond foundational issues, such as defining the boundaries and scope of HRD, towards demonstrating the true value of HRD to the organisation's bottom-line and its applicability in different cultural contexts (McGuire and Cseh, 2006; Ruona et al., 2003). Metcalfe and Rees (2005) argue that current international HRD scholarship that is genuinely international in design and focus remains sparse and fragmented. For their part, Littrell et al. (2006) identify the lack of a unifying theoretical framework as a key factor inhibiting cross-cultural and international HRD endeavours. They advocate the need for greater empirical research to establish the efficacy of current theoretical frameworks. However, Ardichvilli and Kuchinke (2002: 161–162) articulate the importance of exercising care in international HRD research in the following terms:

> Our ability to conduct international HRD research that produces useful results depends not so much on our choice of methodologies, but on our ability to incorporate in our investigation culture as a major influencing factor and to account for culture's influence on phenomena under investigation. And to do this, we need a better understanding of our own and others' centrally conditioned perspectives and assumptions.

As we move towards a view of HRD that is strategically linked to long-term organisational objectives (Garavan et al., 2004) and recognise HRD professionals as 'learning architects' (Harrison and Kessels, 2004: 90), the challenge for HRD is to construct viable international HRD frameworks and demonstrate the capacity of HRD to add value to the organisation across different cultures. As Wang and McLean (2007) argue, the discipline of HRD needs to develop to accommodate the extensive amount of cross-national work being done by transnational corporations, transnational non-government organisations and transnational political entities. In response to the call for greater research into the field of international HRD, this chapter presents a framework describing four phases of internationalisation and outlining the HRD priorities that exist under each phase. It is envisaged that this framework will provide a mechanism for discussing and understanding cross-cultural and international HRD approaches by organisations.

Talking point   Delivering training internationally

With increasing levels of globalisation and organisations trying to save money, stand-ardising courses for global delivery has become popular. Erick Myers gives the follow-ing advice on designing training courses that will be delivered across multiple locations globally:

Understand your audience and their needs

When designing training courses, you need to have an awareness of the profile and characteristics of individuals who will be participating in the training. Answers to the following questions will be helpful to you in designing such training: Who are the participants? What is their educational background? How long have they been at the organisation? Which countries do they live in and what are their cultures? Which lan-guages do they speak natively?

Ensure that your training materials are culturally sensitive

Designing training interventions for overseas delivery requires trainers to display a good insight into the cultures where the programme will be run. You should understand the working norms, cultural values as well as how subsidiaries operate at a practical level.

Ensure your examples are appropriate to the cultural context

Care should be taken to avoid using examples from one culture only. In designing training materials, you can showcase good practice, but ensure that your materials are inclusive and provide examples local to each culture. This will heighten the rele-vance of your training and facilitate training transfer. This principle also applies to the use of video and audio material – ensure appropriate representation from each cultural context where the training will be delivered.

Think cross-culturally

Do not assume that a theory or model is universal. Verify that your materials can be effectively applied cross-culturally.

Ensure legal compliance

When designing materials for overseas delivery, you need to ensure that the con-tent adheres to local laws and regulations.

(Continued)

(Continued)

Create different versions

Consider creating standard and in-depth versions of the programme. In some cultures, focusing on the 'what' and the 'how' of a topic is considered valuable, while in others, the 'why' or underlying reasoning is just as important. The standard version should carry the critical content required for the course to achieve its objectives, while the in-depth version would have additional information for discussion and reflection.

Testing, testing, testing

When designing programmes for international delivery, ensure that the programme contents are tested in each geographic location, prior to accepting actual participants onto the programme. Piloting training programmes can provide very helpful feedback for moulding, shaping and amending the training.

Use local translators

Using professionally qualified translators from the same country or region in which the course is to be delivered is essential to ensuring that the training will be correctly understood. Regional variations in language can sometimes cause training content to be misunderstood – therefore it is helpful to get the content reviewed by someone professionally trained and local to the area where the training will be delivered.

(Adapted from: Myers, E. (2005) How to ... Design a Course for Global Delivery. *People Management*, 10 February.)

Questions

What additional advice might you offer trainers and HRD professionals in designing and delivering training courses in overseas locations?

Should all training courses be designed locally? Or is it acceptable for them to be designed globally, but approved locally?

Constructing a comprehensive international HRD framework

Cross-cultural issues in HRD have to date focused almost exclusively on the training of individuals without consideration of the larger issue of the applicability and transferability of actual HRD practices across national boundaries (Bartlett et al., 2002; Wexley and Latham, 2002: 310). The importance of developing a strong research stream in this area is clear. Cultural differences and national contexts have important implications for our thinking about HRD (Marquardt, 1999; Marquardt and Engel, 1993). Weiss (1996), for example, argues that effective communication with culturally diverse individuals and groups requires an understanding of both cultural assumptions and differences. In a review of the state of HRD internationally, McLean and McLean (2001) argue that cultural and value systems, the nature of the economy, government and legislative influences, educational system influences and the role of professional organisations represent underresearched dimensions of HRD.

Within the broader management literature, much attention has been devoted to the training provided to expatriates and those pursuing short-term overseas assignments as well as the long-standing convergence/divergence debate on management practices (Forster, 2000; Leiba-O'Sullivan, 1999; McGuire et al., 2001). Advocates of a culture-free thesis include Edwards and Ferner (2002), who identify a 'country of origin' effect as one of the major influence on HRM practices in multinational companies. Similarly, Noble (1997) signals that institutional isomorphic tendencies may be at work amongst nation-states in the adoption of training policies. In contrast, both McGaughey and DeCieri (1999) and Huo and Von Glinow (1995) hold strongly to the view that the form and content of functional specialisation that develops with growth will vary according to culture. Such dichotomies ignore the reality that multinationals will decide upon their overseas approach taking into account factors such as strategic importance of the subsidiary, degree of experience in international management and long-term objectives. In addition, several studies have pointed to the natural progression of companies from country of origin practices to host country practices over time as companies become more experienced and comfortable with the host country environment (Jackson, 2002: 57; Walker, 2001: 72). Arvidsson (1997) points to the notion of certainty as being highly influential in determining an organisation's internationalisation strategy. He argues that in cases of high uncertainty regarding an overseas market, the organisation will adopt a gradual internationalisation approach, making incremental investments over time. Such views acknowledge the accepted reality that the internationalisation process is a multi-stage evolving process and characterising the organisation's approach as fitting the convergence or divergence thesis may only reflect the organisation's approach at one particular point in time. While Nadkarni and Perez (2007) refer to several studies showing that firms new to internationalisation start with low commitment activities and gradually increase their commitments to international markets, their own research challenges these findings and shows many firms are not adverse to making high international commitments from the outset and that domestic resources and competitive action propensity affect early international commitments.

Iles and Yolles (2003) identify international HRD alliances as an increasingly popular resource-efficient means of securing knowledge transfer and diffusion across national boundaries. They argue that alliances may provide organisations with rapid market entry and access to academic and technological resources in the host country. They maintain that alliances offer significant opportunities for organisational learning, particularly in relation to the transfer of culturally embedded knowledge; provided issues of control, trust and conflict are properly managed.

Acknowledging the complexity of the internationalisation process, the framework in Table 13.1 examines the provision of international HRD under four separate stages of the internationalisation process. The framework builds upon Adler and Ghadar's (1990) typology which identifies the four internationalisation phases as multi-domestic, international, multinational and transnational. The multi-domestic strategy refers to a country-by-country configuration with each national operation having complete autonomy. Walton (1999) describes this structure as a decentralised federation and posits that this structure ensures the organisation is response to social, cultural and political issues. The international strategy is often viewed as an organisation's first major step in overseas expansion. It sees the organisation retaining a large measure of control over the subsidiary through the use of expatriate assignments and retention of key decision-making by headquarters. The multinational strategy has as its principal objectives price competitiveness and product standardisation and consequently adopts a centralised approach to maximise organisational efficiencies. It establishes regional hubs for product dissemination and utilises modern technologies for intensive communications (Walton, 1999). The transnational strategy involves complete adaption to local markets of global products. It emphasises cultural diversity and advocates concepts of knowledge management and experiential learning (Jackson, 2002: 47).

The multi-domestic organisation

The multi-domestic organisation is characterised by a local approach to business and employee issues. Each subsidiary is treated as a distinct autonomous entity and possesses a high degree of flexibility enabling it to respond quickly to changing market conditions and national requirements. Adler and Ghadar (1990) characterise this approach as indicative of a product orientation.

Structural issues

Firms operating within a multi-domestic structure are equipped to respond flexibly and quickly to changing local conditions. Consequently, the firm is highly exposed to local cultural, political and economic factors. Berggren (1996) describes the principal advantage of a multi-domestic approach as one of being local worldwide, allowing for increased decentralisation, local accountability and increased transparency. He argues that such approaches enable organisations to claim they have 'many home countries' and sensitise managers to local cultural standards. In agreement, Allred and Steensma (2005) maintain that organisations operating a multi-domestic approach to internationalisation tend to cater to the specific needs of the local customer and tailor their product offerings to the different countries they serve. In this regard, Ghoshal and

Table 13.1 International HRD framework

	Multi-domestic	International	Multinational	Transnational
STRUCTURAL ISSUES				
Type of structure envisaged	Organisation in each country will be influenced by cultural, social and political factors. Structure will be unique to host country.	Overseas subsidiary is largely developed and controlled by home-country management to support overseas objectives.	A standardised structure exists across international markets. It makes use of centralised hub and distribution outlets.	No overriding organisational dimensions. Equal power held by each of the subsidiaries within the group.
Nature of structural relationship	Organisation in each country is completely independent, with no linkages to organisation in other countries.	Overseas subsidiary is dependent on home-country management to provide strategic direction, but decides on mechanisms for local implementation.	Overseas subsidiary is integrated within a global system with other subsidiaries in order to increase productivity and effectiveness.	Subsidiary may be organised by division or country and integrated through normative control.
Level of strategic input	Strategy is determined at national level taking into account local factors.	Overseas subsidiary has little, if any strategic input. Strategic objectives will be determined by home-country management.	Strategy is determined on a global basis with input from all subsidiaries.	All subsidiaries have an equally important role in strategy formulation.
Autonomy	Organisation in each country is completely independent and free to determine policy and strategy.	A dependency relationship exists between subsidiary and home organisation; however, some discretion is given to the subsidiary in the method of implementation.	Overseas subsidiary has very limited autonomy due to standardised products and processes.	Subsidiaries are highly autonomous and successful practices are disseminated to other subsidiaries within the organisation.
Technology	Level of technology is dependent on standards and general practices of a particular country.	Modern technology provides the mechanism for maintaining control of overseas subsidiaries and providing the strategic direction required.	Technology is an integral component in a system designed to satisfy price competitiveness and customer satisfaction.	Technology is used to promote learning and knowledge transfer for the benefit of the group as a whole.
Competitive advantage	Determined by local factors and will vary considerably according to the country.	Competitive advantage of home-country organisation and overseas subsidiary will be determined by home-country management.	Competitive advantage in one country is significantly influenced by its position in other countries.	Competitive advantage can be derived in many different countries and regions simultaneously.

(Continued)

Table 13.1 (Continued)

	Multi-domestic	International	Multinational	Transnational
CULTURAL ISSUES				
Value of cultural experience	No emphasis placed on cultural experience. Nationals of the particular country are mostly employed.	Overseas subsidiary will recruit from the host country for lower-level managerial functions.	Due to standardisation and global integration, culture becomes a less important variable.	Culture is regarded as very important in ensuring customer needs are identified and satisfied.
Benchmarking/ evaluation	Measurement against particular country standards with no reference to international standards.	Performance of overseas subsidiary will be evaluated and benchmarked against home-country standards.	Subsidiary performance is measured over time and across regions.	Widespread use of evaluation and benchmarking across a large number of dimensions.
Adaption of HRD provision to local norms and values	HRD will be closely matched to accord with local norms and values.	Overseas subsidiary will seek to adapt to local cultural norms.	A standardised HRD model is used with room for local cultural customisation.	HRD is adapted to local norms and customs. Cultural sensitivity is a critical issue.
Long-term orientation	Due to its independence, the organisation is free to determine long- or short-term objectives.	Very much a 'wait and see' approach adopted. Use of long-term expatriates to provide continuity and ensure subsidiary is on a secure financial footing.	Competitive advantage of organisation in one country is significantly influenced by its position in other countries.	Long-term orientation is very much prevalent. Subsidiaries are focused on future development.
HRD ISSUES				
HRD priorities	HRD priorities will be determined through analysis of individual and organisational needs and with reference to skill standards.	HRD priorities will be determined by home-country management exclusively.	HRD will be derived from global strategy and relative performance of overseas subsidiary.	HRD priorities will be determined locally. Experiential learning and knowledge management are key organisational issues.
Competency/ skill development	Emphasis on skill development to respond to local organisational needs.	Skill development will respond to strategic needs identified by host-country management.	Overseas subsidiary will follow global competency model of organisation and skill gaps will be identified on a regional basis.	Customer satisfaction, global mindset, strategic capabilities, learning on the fly and thinking outside the box are critical competencies.

	Multi-domestic	International	Multinational	Transnational
Responsibility for HRD activities	Local management will take responsibility for HRD activities.	While local facilitators may be involved in HRD delivery, home-country management will assume overall responsibility.	Each subsidiary is responsible for HRD activities in conjunction with overall strategy of home-country management.	Subsidiary has complete responsibility for its own HRD activities.
Team development	Teams will consist entirely of nationals of the particular country and objectives will be local.	Teams will be comprised of host-country nationals, but objectives will be determined by home-country management.	Regional teams with some inter-liaison to establish best-practice models.	Multifunctional teams, multinational teams are adopted to exploit organisational synergies.
Cost of HRD provision	HRD will be funded completely from organisation profits.	HRD will be funded from profits of overseas subsidiaries. Resources will also be provided by home-country management.	Cost of HRD will be borne by the particular subsidiary.	HRD is regarded as critical to organisational development. Cost of HRD provision is regarded as an investment.
Key actors in the HRD process	Local management are key decision-makers.	Home-country managers are key decision-makers.	Home-country management are interested in strategic issues and devolve operational issues to subsidiary.	Local subsidiaries are key decision-makers.
HRD outcomes	HRD will help organisation to achieve locally set goals.	HRD provides home-country management with means for upskilling overseas employees to home-country standards.	HRD will allow organisation to meet price competitiveness and product standardisation objectives through formation of regional teams and global competency frameworks.	HRD contributes to the enhancement of individual, organisation and society at large. Push to make learning more transferable across organisation.
Career development	Individuals develop within the local organisation in a stepwise hierarchical manner.	Individual develops within the local organisation. Some possibilities exist for expatriate assignment, especially if individual is a member of home-country management.	Career development opportunities exist within the company. High probability of working on regional teams. Expatriate assignment is likely for management.	Large number of career development options. Possibilities exist for vertical and horizontal career development, as well as international assignment. High degree of internal career mobility exists.
Status of the individual	'Colleague' working for local company servicing locally identified market needs.	'Employee' working for overseas firm adopting an expansionist international agenda.	'Member of global team' servicing regional market through the provision of standardised quality products.	'Partner of global, locally sensitive team' servicing local market through the provision of customised quality products.

Adapted from: Adler and Ghadar (1990).

Reprinted with permission from Walter de Gruyter GmbH,. Adler, N.J. & Ghadar, E. (1990). 'Strategic Human Resource Management: A Global Perspective'. In R. Pieper (ed.) *Human Resource Management in International Comparison*. Berlin: de Gruyter.

Nohria (1993) characterise the multi-domestic approach as having weak forces for global integration and strong forces for local responsiveness. Allred and Steensma (2005) argue that a multi-domestic approach leads to a localised value chain where a 'let a thousand flowers bloom' orientation may lead to greater innovation and success.

Cultural issues

A multi-domestic approach embraces local values and customs, and operates according to nationally recognised rules and procedures. Experience in other cultures is not valued as firms adopting this strategy emphasise local knowledge and standards. By adopting a multi-domestic approach, organisations avoid the reality that many firms face in that failure in overseas business settings most frequently results from an inability to understand and adapt to 'host country' ways of thinking (Ferraro, 1990; Hays, 1974; Tung, 1981). However, deferring to local values and norms does not necessarily result in an asynchronous culture. Peterson (1997) argues that cultural frames that affect business are multidimensional in that employees are shaped by not only national-societal values, but also organisational affiliation and occupational alliances.

HRD issues

An examination of HRD issues highlights a country-specific approach to HRD. Firms operating multi-domestic approaches compete in independent domestic markets and consequently this requires an indigenous workforce that understands and is responsive to local market conditions (Adler, 1994). This suggests that there may be considerable geographic differentiation of HRD practices and activities. Connelly et al. (2007) describe the role of HRD under a multi-domestic approach as one of developing managers and employees in sensing and exploiting local opportunities using region-specific and non-transferable knowledge. Social networks perform an important role in providing access to tacit knowledge and attuning product and service offerings to local norms and standards. For these reason, Belis-Bergouignan et al. (2000) argue that under a multi-domestic approach, subsidiaries are not deemed to possess any specific set of competences, especially in terms of technology and know-how, which could be transferred to the centre. Consequently, they maintain a one-way relationship of domination subsists, and there is no reciprocity between the areas in which the company's subsidiaries are located.

The international organisation

The international organisation adopts a market orientation and is characterised by a drive for increased growth, efficiency and market penetration (Adler and Ghadar, 1990). The international organisation operates under a headquarters and multiple subsidiary model with a high level of centralised control.

Structural issues

Operating a number of subsidiaries allows an organisation to have a presence in a number of international markets and gain from cost benefits derived through standardised learning and development programmes and the harmonisation of organisational processes and procedures. Connelly et al. (2007) argue that the international firm creates value by the transfer and leveraging of core competencies and resources from headquarters to the subsidiary. They argue that some degree of local customisation is permitted, but that this is often limited in scope. Likewise, Bartlett and Ghoshal (1998: 50) identify the dependence of the subsidiary on the parent as a key aspect of an international firm and highlight the high level of control retained by headquarters through sophisticated management systems and specialist staff. Bartlett et al. (2004) maintain that with an internationalisation strategy, products are developed for the home market and only subsequently sold abroad. They maintain that in the early stages of internationalisation, many managers tend to view the overseas subsidiary as a distant outpost whose role is to support the domestic parent company through contributing incremental sales and upholding the company's revenue stream.

Cultural issues

In examining the reasons why firms seek to internationalise their operations, Bartlett and Ghoshal (1998: 98) identify the search for new markets, resources and cheap labour as key factors motivating overseas and international expansion. However, Armagan and Ferreira (2005) argue that the political culture of the firm's home country will exercise a strong effect on the firm's internationalisation strategy. For this reason, it is arguable that international organisations will recruit lower-level managers who they can mould to fit with the dominant home-country ethos and standards. Nonetheless, the subsidiary is likely to adapt to local cultural norms and is likely to hire long-term expatriates who are familiar with and capable of negotiating both cultures.

HRD issues

Due to the emphasis on centralised control by headquarters, the overseas subsidiary will have limited autonomy in relation to HRD matters. Responsibility for HRD matters will normally be devolved for operational matters but most strategic decisions will be taken by management in the home country. Håkanson (1990) identifies the key reasons for the strengthening of central control on subsidiary operations as stagnating global demand, increasing competitive pressure to boost efficiency and the need for specialisation. While HRD may be cited as important to growth prospects, HRD is likely to be funded by subsidiary profits with resources being managed by home-country management. Opportunities will probably exist for overseas placements and expatriate assignments but subsidiary operations are likely to be regarded as secondary and individuals will see their development as primarily within the home-country organisation.

Talking point   International career competencies

Working as an expatriate can often be an exciting challenge, positioning managers on the fast-track to career success. However, living and working as an expatriate means adjusting to an unfamiliar culture and becoming accustomed to local norms, traditions, climate, clothing, food and way of life. Research by Suutari and Mäkelä (2007) and Dickmann and Mills (2010) collected data on expatriate experiences and discussed the relocation decisions of expatriates (and the motives why expatriates accepted overseas assignments) within the context of the three career competencies of knowing-how, knowing-why and knowing-whom. We summarise each of the three competencies below and include some quotes from expatriates from the work of Suutari and Mäkelä (2007) and Dickmann and Mills (2010).

Knowing-how career competencies

Knowing-how career competencies comprise the broad range of knowledge and skills that the expatriate expects to accumulate as a result of the international assignment. Working on international assignments allows expatriates to build up their stock of cultural capital, including cross-cultural skills as well as an awareness of problems that may exist across the headquarters–subsidiary divide. Some quotes from expatriate managers in relation to know-how career competencies follow:

> International experience has developed my management skills. In different kinds of problems and situations you have to think about how you manage these situations. You learn how to lead a team and what your leadership philosophy is: how you learn to be a leader in an international community.

> I felt that by going to London I would gain wider perspectives and, through these, learn so much more than in Barcelona.

Knowing-why career competencies

Partaking in international assignments can often have the beneficial effect of improving managers' levels of self-awareness and self-confidence as well as giving them a greater appreciation of their own values, beliefs, working preferences and career strengths and weaknesses. Some quotes from expatriate managers describe the development of knowing-why career competencies in the following terms:

> You need to learn to deal with so many different issues, and that's when you start to find your strengths and weaknesses ... I've started to think about this

from my own point of view: what areas I'm good at, and in which ones I need to get help from others.

London is famous for being competitive. So, I felt challenged and, as a result, motivated.

Knowing-whom career competencies

International assignment provides expatriates with valuable opportunities to build international contacts and develop overseas professional and social connections. Networking and social capital are crucial instruments in the toolkits of international managers. Some quotes from expatriate managers in relation to know-whom career competencies follow:

> The contact network I have developed is of very high importance. When there are problems or questions, I can call directly to quite a number of people because I know them in person.

> London has probably the best experts in making television ... and it was quite a driver for me. I had seen that I simply cannot get the quality in Hamburg or Berlin ... Over time, this has not just made my films better but also more valuable.

(Adapted from: Dickmann, M. and Mills, T. (2010) The Importance of Intelligent Career and Location Considerations: Exploring the Decision to go to London. *Personnel Review*, 39(1), 116–134; Suutari, V. and Mäkelä, K. (2007) The Career Capital of Managers with Global Careers. *Journal of Managerial Psychology*, 22(7), 628–648.)

Questions

What are the downsides to working as an expatriate and undertaking international assignments?

How can expatriates overcome the mindset of 'out of sight, out of mind' that may exist in company headquarters?

The multinational organisation

The multinational organisation has a significant presence in overseas environments and leverages opportunities from different geographical markets. For his part, Dunning

(1993) defines the multinational organisation as one which engages in foreign direct investment and owns or controls value-adding activities in more than one country. Overseas subsidiaries possess a high degree of flexibility and are sensitive and responsive to changes in local conditions.

Structural issues

There are many variables which can affect the structure adopted by the multinational organisation. Miroshnik (2002) maintains that a multinational organisation is a complex organisational form which usually has fully autonomous units operating in a number of countries which possess a great deal of independence to address local issues such as consumer preferences, political pressures and economic trends. The nature of the structural relationship between headquarters and the subsidiary organisation has received attention in the literature. Malnight (2001) argues that internally differentiated structures are associated with a strategic shift in the focus of organisations to outside a company's home market. He argues that the benefits of a multinational framework result not only from the strength of dispersed units, but also from the nature and management of linkages between them. More recent contributions view the multinational as a network of affiliates capable of sustaining knowledge and information flows through a series of common systems (McGraw, 2004).

One of the criticisms of the multinational form of overseas management is the lack of coordination and control exercised by head office. Chang and Taylor (1999) emphasise this point and maintain that as multinationals expand their operations, the level of uncertainty associated with overseas investment will increase and complex issues of organisational control will need to be addressed to ensure that different parts of the organisation are contributing to the overall goals.

Cultural issues

Negotiating common cultural meanings is a difficult challenge for multinational organisations. Garabaldi de Hilal (2006) maintains that the complexity of multinational organisations increases the probability that their culture tends to differentiation and that different systems of meanings or subcultures can greatly affect the operations of those organisations. For this reason, multinational organisations will often advocate standardised processes and systems with some room for local cultural customisation. Subsidiary performance is likely to be measured over time and across regions. Some research indicates that the multinational's country of origin may exert considerable influence on organisational strategy. McGuire et al. (2002) argue that while cultural characteristics may shape managerial attitudes, beliefs and values, it is the nationality of subsidiary ownership that is a strong determinant of corporate strategy. Hennart and Larimo (1998) suggest that multinational companies based in countries where the dominant cultural traits are high power distance and low uncertainty avoidance may have an inherent preference for full ownership of their foreign subsidiary and consequently may be more likely to assimilate parent and subsidiary cultures.

HRD issues

The responsibility for HRD issues is a contentious one with a lack of consensus in the literature. On the one hand, De Pablos (2004) argues that human resource management systems are likely to be transferred to the overseas affiliate for two reasons: first, multinational organisations will seek to reduce their level of uncertainty when operating internationally by using the nearest management practices that have worked in the country of origin; and second, if the management system of the country of origin offers a distinctive advantage, then this advantage may be duplicated when transferred to the overseas affiliate. However, there exists evidence from empirical studies of local autonomy in relation to HRD practices. In examining the impact of global and local influences on HRD practice, Collings (2003) found that the subsidiary possessed considerable autonomy in relation to HRD content issues while headquarters were concerned with budgetary issues. This supports earlier research by Tregaskis (1998), who revealed considerable support for local national context as a determinant of HRD practice over the country of origin of the multinational.

The transnational organisation

The transnational organisation has been recognised as the highest form of business internationalisation. However, despite achieving much coverage in textbooks, it remains relatively rare in practice. Rugman (2005) argues that of the world's largest 500 multinationals, only a handful – nine – operate a truly global or transnational strategy. Iles and Hayers (1997) define transnational organisations as ones which successfully transcend cultural, geographic and managerial barriers in achieving organisational effectiveness. By working beyond borders, transnational organisations hope to achieve a global presence and harvest regional and geographic synergies.

Structural issues

Transnational organisations are structured to provide autonomy and flexibility to subsidiaries to allow them to respond to local opportunities. Coakes (2006) maintains that transnational organisations are pluri-located, integrated communities that focus on a network of competencies across the world. The potency of transnational organisations lies in the speed by which subsidiaries in the network can react to changing market conditions. Bartlett et al. (2004) maintain that transnational organisations recognise the demands to be responsive to local market and political needs and the pressures to develop global-scale competitive efficiency, and consequently can react well to political and economic volatility. The dispersed, yet specialised nature of resources and activities of subsidiaries requires intensive coordination and shared decision-making. In identifying the three goals of transnational organisations as the achievement of global efficiencies of scale/standardisation, flexibility to local conditions/differentiation and worldwide learning or global diffusion of innovation, Bartlett and Ghoshal (1998) recognise that transnational organisations fluctuate between a centralised and decentralised organisational structure.

Cultural issues

Transnational organisations operate in multicultural environments, but seek to move beyond cultural boundaries in their business activities. Iles and Hayers (1997) argue that developing and managing the transnational organisation requires individuals to move beyond the embeddedness of organisational systems, processes and cultures towards thinking, leading and acting from a global perspective. They point to the existence of three separate cultures within transnational organisations – national culture, corporate culture and professional culture – and that cultural differences need to be recognised, valued and used to the organisation's advantage. MacLean (2006) maintains that it is the flows of communication, information and knowledge that are a critical component of the competitive capabilities possessed by transnational corporations and ensuring that these flows are not distorted, diverted or blocked is essential to the development and maintenance of core competencies.

HRD issues

The management and coordination of HR activities across the transnational organisation is decidedly complex and involves balancing a series of competing priorities (geographic, business and functional). Kidger (2002) argues that the transnational organisation requires geographic managers who are accountable for local responsiveness; business managers who are responsible for global efficiency and integration; and functional managers who are accountable for knowledge transfer and learning. Operating within such a dynamic structure requires a flexible approach to HR issues. Engle et al. (2001) argue that traditional, structurally embedded job-based HR processes are inadequate to address the complexity created by the need to balance an in-depth local understanding with the coordination of global capabilities and resources required by transnational organisations. Consequently, Choy (2007) argues that within transnational organisations there is a strong need for HR structures that are culturally responsive in order to enhance interactions among staff from different cultures and nationalities. Likewise, Stedham and Engle (1999) argue that international

HRM and HRD systems can act as repositories and levers to support cultural change through first changing individual attitudes and mindsets, then interpersonal relationships and processes, and finally formal structures and responsibilities.

Conclusion

The framework established by this chapter clearly confirms that an organisation's international HRD approach is contingent on the stage that the organisation has reached in the internationalisation process. It indicates that the more international experience an organisation attains, the greater the devolvement of control to management of the overseas subsidiary. In later stages of the internationalisation process, overseas subsidiaries are empowered to provide greater strategic input and stronger linkages are forged between subsidiaries. This is particularly significant in the area of HRD as the further an organisation progresses in the internationalisation process, the greater the flexibility of the subsidiary to determine and respond to locally identified needs through targeted HRD interventions. In such cases, the subsidiary is also able to draw upon the experiences and best practices of other subsidiaries and may be involved in multinational teams focused on organisational development.

The type of structure adopted by the organisation during the internationalisation process will affect the product and service delivery as well as the degree of autonomy exercised by the subsidiary. Such matters are often dictated by the overall objectives decided upon for the subsidiary. For the multi-domestic and international organisation, the overseas subsidiary is an offshoot of the main organisation and exists on a dependency basis. Multinational and transnational organisations exercise greater levels of independence and relations with headquarters are dictated by a need to maximise operational efficiencies.

The chapter identifies opportunities for particular groups depending on the stage of internationalisation reached by the organisation. For instance, an international organisation typically seeks continuity and stability, characteristics which can be met by long-term expatriates. Likewise, individuals with high mobility and language skills will be valued by transnational organisations as they are adaptable to change and can be located in various geographic environments. Consequently, internationalisation provides openings to individuals who are not geographically restricted and who enjoy working in a diverse cultural environment.

Finally, responsibility for HRD activities operates on a continuum from full ownership by headquarters to complete devolvement to the subsidiary organisation. The framework shows that the decentralisation of HRD takes place on a gradual strategic basis until the subsidiary achieves full autonomy. Complete ownership of HRD activities allows the subsidiary to achieve a greater level of customisation in line with the ideal of local responsiveness. However, in such instances, it is likely that subsidiaries will be provided with templates for provision of interventions in order to maximise organisational efficiency.

Colgate-Palmolive's global HR strategy

Imagine calling the world your home. Not just your home as in your country, state, city and ultimately your address, but more precisely where you hang your hat. For Colgate-Palmolive Co., the world is where the company hangs its hat, its coat and all its belongings. Because although the household and personal-care products conglomerate has an official corporate headquarters in New York City, it has businesses and people all over the world – and has for more than half a century. The company's product line is immense, so extensive, in fact, that at one point the parent company began to lose track of where all of its 'children', or businesses producing its myriad products, were. So, in 1989 Colgate remodelled its home so as to contain its products in five 'rooms': oral care, personal care, hard-surface care, fabric care and pet nutrition. With the remodelling came new business strategies. But as these strategies began to roll out, one fact became painfully clear – there was a gap between the business strategies and the company's current people strategies. For the businesses to succeed, the company would need to better align its human resources with its business objectives.

It has done so by creating a true partnership between senior line management and human resources leaders. The alignment has resulted in a human resources strategy tied to business needs, and a strong link between Colgate's 35,000 people throughout the world.

HR and business leaders strategise together. The partnership effort began with the creation of a Global Human Resources Strategy Team. 'The objective of the team was to work in partnership with management to build organizational excellence', says Brian Smith, director of global HR strategy. 'We define organizational excellence as the continuous alignment of Colgate people, business processes and the organization in general with our vision, values and strategies, to become the best.'

The team itself constituted a partnership. Approximately half of its 25 members were human resources leaders, the other half senior line managers. Among the members were the president of the Far East division, the president of the pet nutrition business and the global leader of the oral care business, as well as senior staff such as general managers. 'We wanted to ensure that our major HR activities were helping the business achieve its primary objectives', says Douglas M. Reid, senior vice-president, global HR for Colgate-Palmolive.

Colgate-Palmolive has over 200 expatriates who make a career of going from one country to another throughout their work tenure with the company. All of these factors make Colgate-Palmolive a truly global company with an ability to deal with issues, markets and customers on a worldwide basis. Considerable attention is paid to personal, financial and logistical concerns to help expatriates adjust to local environmental conditions. However, with the rise of dual-careers, Colgate-Palmolive faced a problem in the mid-1990s in how they looked after the spouses of expatriate managers. Colgate responded by introducing the spouse assistance programme, which aimed to help spouses source employment in overseas locations, support spouses who wished to undertake educational programmes and provide networking assistance to spouses helping them meet with professionals in overseas locations.

To reinforce its global approach to business, Colgate-Palmolive incorporated three fundamental values: caring, global teamwork and continuous improvement. These values commit Colgate-Palmolive to working with employees, customers and business partners to attain a more sustainable future, support employees across various geographical locations and develop more innovative products. Expatriates are provided with training and development programmes, targeted at developing leadership and technical competencies. Considerable efforts are made to assess the effectiveness of this training and maximise learning that promotes career development and business productivity.

Employees at Colgate-Palmolive express a high degree of satisfaction with the company. A purported 25 per cent of its workers have been with the company for over 20 years and cite great benefits, employee development programmes, a positive work–life balance and flexible hours as among the advantages of working at Colgate-Palmolive.

(Adapted from: Anfuso, D. (1995) Colgate's Global HR Unites Under One Strategy. *Personnel Journal*, 74(10), 44–44; Berry, P. (2008) ROI and HR? The Colgate Palmolive Example. *Global HR News*, 24 December; Burke, R.J. and Cooper, C.L. (2005) *Reinventing Human Resources Management: Challenges and New Directions.* Abingdon: Routledge; Colgate-Palmolive website: http://www.colgate.co.uk, accessed 28 February 2013.)

Questions

How successful has Colgate-Palmolive been in operating on a global basis and transcending cultural boundaries?

How can organisations successfully develop managers that are globally aware and locally responsive?

Discussion questions

What are the key obstacles faced by the HRD function in 'exporting' HRD programmes to overseas subsidiaries?

Should organisations be seeking to impose a single culture across all these global business units?

What types of cost-efficiencies can be derived from cross-cultural standardisation?

What key facets should an internationalisation strategy possess?

HRD and the Environment 14

The objectives of this chapter are to:

- explore the importance of environmental issues and their relevance to the field of HRD;
- examine the business case for going green;
- discuss in depth the six R's of sustainable environmental activity;
- consider a model of green HRD and the tools HRD possesses to respond to the climate crisis.

Introduction

In 2006, Nobel Prize winner and former US Vice-President Al Gore released an Oscar-winning documentary titled *An Inconvenient Truth*. In the documentary, Gore reported on a series of significant claims made by leading scientists about climate change and fluctuations witnessed over time to the earth's atmosphere. Chief among the claims made were the following (Gore, 2006):

- Almost all of the mountain glaciers in the world are now melting, many of them quite rapidly.

- If you look at the 21 hottest years measured on a global scale, 20 of the 21 have occurred within the last 25 years.
- At no point in the last 650,000 years before the pre-industrial age did the CO_2 concentration go above 300 parts per million. It is currently estimated that CO_2 concentration in the earth's atmosphere stands at 381 parts per million.
- Major storms spinning in both the Atlantic and the Pacific since the 1970s have increased in duration and intensity by about 50 per cent.
- The amount of precipitation globally has increased in the last century by almost 20 per cent.
- In 2004, the all-time record for tornadoes in the United States was broken.
- There is a strong emerging consensus that global warming is indeed linked to a significant increase in both the duration and intensity of hurricanes.
- Rising seas levels have resulted in many residents of low-lying Pacific island nations already having to evacuate their homes.
- The number of days each year that the tundra in Alaska is frozen solidly enough to drive on has fallen from over 200 to fewer than 80 days per year.
- Current global population estimates stand at 6.5 billion inhabitants. This figure is projected to rise to 9.1 billion in 2050.
- Almost 30 per cent of the CO_2 released into the atmosphere each year results from deforestation and the burning of woodland and brushland for subsistence agriculture and wood fires for cooking.

The stark, cumulative nature of the claims made in the documentary led to the clear, unavoidable conclusion that human activity is having a profound and deeply damaging effect on the earth's fragile climate and ecosystem. Moreover, it emphasised the need for individuals and organisations to take steps to create more sustainable, eco-friendly systems of production to mitigate against the worst effects of climate change and to enable individuals to live more in harmony with their environment. It argued that the accelerating release of greenhouse gases is having a profound, devastating effect on the earth's climate, leading to a dramatic increase in the frequency of extreme natural disasters, thus stressing the need to proactively change behaviours and the adoption of environmental solutions that bring about a green sustainable future for individuals, organisations and society.

For too long, climate science and the broad disciplines of business and management have been viewed as separate, non-connected entities with few crossovers and interlinkages. Many business and management scholars and practitioners do not possess the requisite scientific training and education to make sense of the reports published by climate scientists and more importantly, they lack an awareness of the practical steps to be taken to ensure their organisational practices and systems accord with good environmental practice. However, Russ-Eft (2009) reminds HRD practitioners of their professional responsibilities to communities, the societies in which they live and the planet. In doing so, it is clear that the field of HRD, and practitioners that work within it, possesses the knowledge, skills and tools necessary to help organisations and societies craft their own unique response to the threats posed by climate change.

In the field of HRD, with some notable exceptions (Haddock et al., 2010; Lee, 2007; McGuire, 2010; Sadler-Smith, 2013; Valentin, 2012), little has been written to date which explores HRD's response to this planetary emergency or provides guidance and direction to practitioners on what steps they should be taking to create a more sustainable future. This chapter provides some initial thinking and concepts which may help the field begin to address this important research gap. It first outlines the business case for going green. The remainder of the chapter is structured around a model of green HRD in organisations. It examines the four R's of sustainable environmental activity (reduce, reuse, recycle and renew). It then looks at HRD's toolkit for fostering greener organisations and society through the use of interventions including the Green Redesign, Green Scorecard and Green Contract. The chapter includes some useful case examples of organisational practices that have been implemented which accord with sustainable environmental practice.

The business case for going green

Since the emergence of *An Inconvenient Truth* and other documentaries that followed in its wake, environmental issues have begun to play a significant role in shaping how organisations conduct business. Awareness of the adverse effects of planetary climate change is increasing and evidence is appearing that consumers are starting to take such issues into account in both their online and face-to-face transactions with organisations. Pickett-Baker and Ozaki (2008) identify a generational shift towards pro-environmental behaviour and consumption. Empirically, they discovered that consumers will likely purchase more from organisations that are seen to be pro-environmental. Similarly, Flatters and Wilmott (2009) argue that environmentalism is now deeply rooted in the consumer mindset and they are looking to express their concern for climate change and the environment through consumption and other forms of behaviour.

In response to changing consumer values, many organisations are looking for ways to create more sustainable processes and systems. Sustainability has been defined as 'the impact of products or operations on human rights, labor, health, safety, regional development and other community concerns' (Katsoulakos and Katsoulacos, 2007: 361) and is often concerned about the triple bottom-line of profits, planet and people. In organisational terms, the interaction of people and planet opens up a role for HRD practitioners to ensure green-value alignment and that environmentalism is claimed as a core organisational priority. For his part, Ardichvili (2012) advances the need to move away from a fixation on constant economic and organisational growth and an obsession with quarterly results towards a more sustainable, longer-term holistic view of organisations and society. He argues that a perpetual obsession with ever-expanding bottom-lines leads to a depletion of natural resources and the loss of collective wisdom, decline in moral standards and the persistence of inequality and oppression. He advocates that

HRD practitioners need to be developed as well-rounded, well-informed, critically reflective individuals capable of balancing economic, performance-driven goals against the need to operate in a environmentally sustainable and responsible manner.

Three key benefits are cited by Rimanoczy and Pearson (2010) as reasons for going green. First, as consumers are demanding higher levels of corporate responsibility, organisations need to demonstrate more sustainable ways of working and enhance their public reputation. Second, implementing green initiatives and engaging in crisis planning is beneficial to organisations as preparedness for an environmental catastrophe should it arise. Finally, going green is helpful in marking an employer out as both responsible and caring, which can help recruitment and retention efforts. For his part, Friedman (2008) argues that there exists a strong economic rationale for going green. Producing products and services in a more energy-efficient manner saves organisations money, reduces waste, cuts costs and boosts profits. He cites the example of Walmart, who pushed manufacturers from producing incandescent bulbs into making compact fluorescent bulbs which last 10 times longer than incandescent bulbs and require only a quarter of their energy to emit the same level of light. Such a move helped consumers save money but also enhanced Walmart's environmental credentials as well as helping it meet the growing environmental expectations of its consumers.

Talking point   The Alaskan village set to disappear under water in a decade

Have you ever heard of the Alaskan village of Kivalina? I'm guessing you probably haven't. It sits on a narrow spit of sand on the edge of the Bering Sea and is home to 400 indigenous Inuit people who live in small single-storey cabins and make their living hunting and fishing.

Well, it looks possible that Kivalina may earn the unwanted distinction of becoming the birthplace of America's first climate change refugees. For within a decade, due to the effects of global warming, Kivalina may be under water.

With the ever-increasing rise in global temperature, the future of this small Alaskan village looks bleak. Research from climate scientists has shown that temperatures in the Arctic are warming twice as fast as in the rest of the United States, leaving the shoreline of Kivalina increasingly vulnerable to coastal erosions. Whereas in the past, thick sea ice protected this tiny village from the destructive power of autumn and winter storms, rising seas levels are threatening settlements and livelihoods along this narrow strip of land.

The Kivalina Council leader, Colleen Swan, says that local inhabitants are paying the price for a problem they did not create. She says: 'If we're still here in 10 years' time, we will either wait for the flood and die, or just walk away and go somewhere else.'

So, just as Kivalina residents contemplate their future, elsewhere in Alaska, beneath the North Slope lies America's largest oil field containing an estimated 50 billion as-yet untapped barrels of oil. Oil revenues make up 90 per cent of the state budget of Alaska and the Trans Alaska pipeline is an important source of carbon-based fossil fuels, which are critical to the growth of the US economy.

Shell, one of the world's largest oil companies, has even recently applied to begin offshore Arctic drilling, despite objections and protests from environmental groups. They point to a growing demand from a still carbon-fuelled US economy and the need to tap untouched-as-yet Alaskan oil reserves.

Alaskans have benefited greatly from the oil economy and booming oil prices. Apart from jobs and employment, oil money means no income tax and an annual handout to every Alaskan resident.

In summary, Alaska stands at a cross-road. It must in some way balance the need to protect a fragile environment and ecosystem, yet satisfy the demands of a carbon-based economy with growing energy needs.

(Adapted from: Sackur, S. (2013) The Alaskan Village Set to Disappear Under Water in a Decade. *BBC News Magazine*, 30 July. http://www.bbc.co.uk/news/magazine-23346370?print=true.)

Questions

Calculate your carbon and ecological footprint using the WWF Footprint Calculator at the following link: http://footprint.wwf.org.uk/

What steps can you take to reduce your personal carbon and ecological footprint?

How can organisations be encouraged to reduce their carbon and ecological footprint?

A model of green HRD

In order to achieve the goal of becoming sustainable, organisations are required to take a more holistic approach to their activities and operate in a responsible, ethical and resource-efficient manner. This requires organisations to move to a triple bottom-line approach (people, profit and planet) ensuring the organisation takes a balanced approach and is conscious of the social, economic and environmental impact of its activities. For their part, Haddock et al. (2010: 3) define green HRD as 'a cyclic process of continuous development and transformation of self, others and the organisation, as prudent users of natural and man-made resources, aligning economic, environmental and social growth for present and future generations'.

Figure 14.1 presents a model of green HRD. Inspired by Heraty's (2004) work on organisational-led learning, it argues that for green HRD approaches to succeed there is a need for strong green leadership. As leaders sit atop the organisation, they set appropriate behaviours and values which employees are expected to follow. Leaders have an important role in setting, embedding and transmitting organisational culture. Through their actions and behaviour, leaders communicate to employees an organisation's key priorities and expectations. Leaders act as role models to employees and their direction is crucial in fostering a positive approach to embedding green principles across the organisation. For his part, Schein (2010) argues that the most powerful mechanism that leaders possess for communicating what they believe in or care about is what they systematically pay attention to. This underscores the importance of the two external pillars in the green HRD model, namely, shared environmental vision and communications.

For green sustainable principles to be embedded across the organisation, its importance must be accentuated in key organisational documentation such as mission and vision statements. Galpin and Whittington (2012) argue that the inclusion or exclusion of a statement about sustainability in an organisation's mission statement is indicative of a firm's commitment towards a green sustainable future. Moreover, it sets an example to staff and customers regarding corporate sustainability and ethical principles at work. Similarly, a vision statement is described by Nanus (1992: 8) as a 'realistic, credible and attractive future for your organisation'. He argues that vision statements act as signposts, pointing the way to employees who need to understand what the organisation is and where it intends to go. In this regard, vision statements can have an energising, jump-start effect on organisations, helping employees to work together collaboratively towards a desired future state.

Regular and consistent communication is critical to embedding a culture of environmentalism across organisations. As Nanus (1992) points out, leaders are carefully and closely watched, referred to and emulated, so that whatever they do and say communicates volumes to others. Communication about green issues should therefore take the form of a two-way dialogue that engages both staff and management in creating a more sustainable future. Grant (2007) maintains that the goal of sustainability can only be achieved through adherence to the following four principles:

- Engagement in social progress which recognises the needs of everyone
- The effective protection of the environment
- The prudent use of natural resources
- The maintenance of high and stable levels of economic growth and employment

The need for regular and frequent communication is also required given the regular scientific advances being made in tackling climate change. It is critical that scientific breakthroughs are effectively translated into operational terms and embedded within the systems and structures of the organisation.

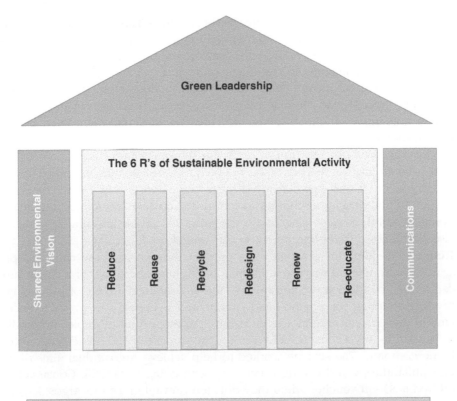

Figure 14.1 **A model for green HRD**

The six R's of sustainable environmental activity

The six R's of sustainable environmental activity refer to the internal structures of the green HRD model that facilitate and assist an organisation in achieving its goal of becoming sustainable.

- **Reduce:** Reducing an organisation's carbon footprint as well as lowering waste and energy consumption are critical steps towards becoming more sustainable. Initiatives such as teleworking, teleconferencing, the replacement of lighting with light-emitting diodes and the adoption of smart energy-saving devices are being advanced to help the transition to a low carbon society (Lee et al., 2013). The goal for many companies of becoming carbon-neutral is often linked to the ambition of instilling a culture of environmental sustainability. This often leads to the nomination and appointment of environmental champions in the organisation that monitor, educate and promote environmental good practice. In the case of the UK company Innocent Smoothies, an audit was undertaken to calculate the organisation's carbon footprint and to take steps to lessen its impact on the environment. Three key initiatives taken were to lower its carbon footprint (Innocent, 2012): first, Innocent decided not to use airfreight for its products and raw materials, but rather to use ships (as first preference) or road transport as an alternative. Second, Innocent opted to squeeze, pulp and puree fruit in the country where it was grown to avoid waste being transported. Finally, Innocent use oxygen-free packaging technology to reduce the cooling requirements during transportation. All three steps have had a significant impact on lowering food miles, but also have helped lower transportation and overall product costs.

- **Reuse:** Extending the shelf-life of a product through its reuse can help protect scarce environmental resources. Finding multiple applications for a single product can reduce cost and waste and reduces the environmental costs of producing new products. Opting for second-hand or donated materials can avoid unnecessary landfill and lessens greenhouse emissions. An interesting example of recycling in action is the Toy Exchange scheme run by Argos, the UK home retail and catalogue company. The scheme worked to help achieve Argos's dual aims of corporate philanthropy and cutting down on waste going to landfill. Consumers were offered a £5 gift voucher when they donated unwanted toys to Argos. Argos then presented such toys to Barnardo's, the UK children's charity. Argos benefited significantly from the goodwill and reputation value of the scheme, whilst the charity received toy donations worth over £700,000 (Fisher, 2012).

- **Recycle:** Recycling is the process whereby materials are collected and broken down into usable forms which then become the raw ingredients for new products. Ho and Choi (2012) distinguish between two forms of used or discarded materials: post-industrial waste and post-consumer waste. They argue that the recycling process for post-industrial waste is usually more straightforward than with post-consumer waste, as the content and composition of the waste is known and relatively uniform. According to Kassaye (2001), a large number of US companies are relearning the reusing and recycling processes that they abandoned many years ago. In particular, he cites soft drinks bottlers, dairy farms, breweries and tyre companies as industries that have readopted recycling systems as part of their core business. A large growth area in relation to recycling lies in the garment and textile sector. Eco-fashion has become an established movement aimed at minimising adverse environmental impacts through the use of recycled and biodegradable materials. Alongside responsible production processes, eco-fashion is designed to appeal to environmentally conscious consumers who hold high ethical and environmental values which they apply to consumption decisions (Chan and Wong, 2012). An innovative example of the reuse of natural resources is the living roof at Ford Motor Company's Rouge Complex in Dearborn,

Michigan. This vegetated roof, measuring 454,000 square foot (or 10.4 acres) collects, filters and recycles rainwater helping moderate the temperature of the complex, which manufacturers pick-up trucks for the US and overseas market. Recovered filtered rainwater from the roof is also used in restroom and sanitary facilities on the site. Aside from acting as a natural habitat for birds, butterflies and insects, the living roof is expected to last twice as long as a conventional roof and reduces heating and cooling costs by about 5 per cent annually. It also helps absorb CO_2 and release oxygen back into the atmosphere, improving overall air quality (The Living Roof, 2013).

- **Redesign:** Improving the ecological and environmental properties of products and services is an important step that organisations can take towards a more sustainable future. The process of green product redesign requires organisations to reflect and take action in the areas of raw material sourcing, product manufacture, waste disposal and product packaging. Working with suppliers to make products more environmentally friendly can help cut overall product costs, improve the recycling and biodegradable qualities of the product, reduce the life-cycle impact of the product and lead to the reduction in the use of toxic chemicals in the manufacturing of the product (Sanborn and Sheehan, 2009). Two examples of green product redesign include: the replacement of plastic with cardboard in the production of Easter eggs by Nestlé, leading to a 25 per cent reduction in waste and 700 ton saving in packaging costs (Vidal, 2009) and the introduction of the eco-refill pack by coffee manufacturer Kenco, resulting in 97 per cent less packaging weight, dramatically lowering transportation and logistics costs (Alarcon, 2009). Redesign also involves the improvement and modification of organisational processes to prevent pollution and create more sustainable production processes. The Environmental Protection Agency (EPA, 2010) defines pollution prevention in the following words: 'Reducing or eliminating waste at the source by modifying production processes, promoting the use of non-toxic or less-toxic substances, implementing conservation techniques, and re-using materials rather than putting them into the waste stream.' Pollution prevention and cleaner production can help minimise the organisational impact on the environment, whilst reducing costs and improving productivity.

- **Renew:** The use of renewable energy sources is critical to building sustainable organisations and societies. Friedman (2008) argues that clean power and the use of renewable energy is going to be the global standard within the next decade derived from sources such as wind, solar, geothermal, solar thermal, hydrogen and cellulosic ethanol. He argues that roughly 40 per cent of America's total CO_2 emissions come from the production of electricity for homes, offices and workplaces with another 30 per cent of emissions arising from the transportation sector, predominantly cars, trains, aeroplanes and trucks. However, valuable examples exist of where the use of renewable energy is helping organisations save money and produce products in a more innovative way. In 2008, the US crisps/chips manufacturer Frito-Lay installed a 5 acre solar panel field at its plant in Modesto, California to help in the production of its Sunchips products. The solar energy generated from the solar panels was used to generate steam to heat the cooking oil used in the Sunchips manufacturing process.

Currently, over 400,000 packets of Sunchips are produced daily at the Modesto plant using energy derived from the solar panels (Pepsi Climate Change, 2013).

- **Re-educate:** Delivering a sustainable environmental future will require ensuring that both employees and customers are aware of the environmental consequences of their actions. In this regard, the last decade has seen organisations transition from implementing regulatory and technological approaches to environmental management towards recognising the importance of human behaviour in reducing pollution through making employees more aware of environmental issues (Boiral, 2009). Rimanoczy and Pearson (2010) argue that HRD practitioners can play an important role in educating and providing relevant information to employees and customers on green issues. They argue that a central activity in this regard is to help employees and customers understand what sustainability means for each functional area within the business. To this end, both the CIPD (2008b) and Renwick et al. (2008) recommend that job descriptions are altered to ensure that employees are aware of their responsibilities towards pollution-reduction and building individual and organisational effectiveness in the sustainable use of resources. Indeed, the leading Japanese information and communications technology company Fujitsu (2013) has been carrying out environmental education and enlightenment training of employees since 1995. Every employee in the company is expected to undertake environmental e-learning once every three years covering environmental protection and environmental issues pertaining to the specific area of the business they work in.

Talking point   Environmentalism and competitive advantage

In 1990, renowned Harvard University Professor Michael Porter made the following prediction:

> Appropriately planned environmental regulations will stimulate technological innovation, leading to reductions in expenses and improvements in quality. As a result, businesses may attain a superior competitive position in the international marketplace and industrial productivity may improve as well.

Questions

Can environmental regulation help reduce business costs?

Do environmental regulations help businesses compete more effectively in international markets?

Can environmental regulation help the growth and advancement of businesses and societies?

HRD's toolkit to promote sustainable environmental activity

In this section, we will provide a brief summary of each of the nine interventions that form the HRD toolkit aimed to help organisations promote sustainable environmental activity.

- **Organisational learning:** As a powerful change management tool, organisational learning can help organisations manage, share, utilise and transfer knowledge related to environmental and sustainability issues leading to greater overall awareness and ownership of these issues. Blake-Scontrino and Schafer (2012) assert that organisational learning allows for the transformation of process and technological competence, so that organisations can build expertise and competitive advantage in environmental and sustainability issues. For their part, Oncica-Sanislav and Candea (2010) view sustainability as an ideal state that owners and managers should attempt to achieve through the deployment of organisational learning tools. They argue that organisational learning will allow for the identification of learning gaps leading to better strategic planning and more focused learning interventions.
- **Societal HRD:** Increasingly, it is recognised that HRD possesses the tools and capabilities to operate at a societal level. Hatcher (2003: 53) argues that the field of HRD has a moral responsibility to work 'beyond short sighted economic gain, behaviourally oriented psychological fulfilment or bounded or limited world-views'. In so doing, Kim (2012) argues HRD can perform an important role at a societal level as a change agent and can be deployed to address global concerns requiring international cooperation and collaboration. McLean et al. (2012) identify action research approaches as an obvious example of how HRD can be deployed to address issues at an international and societal level.
- **Environmental labelling:** As consumers become more environmentally conscious and pressure is placed on companies to highlight their green credentials, the issue of environmental labelling becomes increasingly important. Environmental labels have become an important vehicle for organisations to communicate their values and commitment to safeguarding the environment. Many companies use labels such as the German Blue Angel (Blue Angel, 2013), CO_2 Measurement Label (Carbon Trust, 2013) or Cradle-to-Cradle Certification (Cradle-to-Cradle Products Innovation Institute, 2013) to showcase their environmental credentials. Such labels attest to either the independent auditing or evaluation of the organisation's environmental standards, claims regarding the environmental or recycling properties of the product or an investigation of the product life-cycle process with regard to waste generation, pollution or resource utilisation.
- **Green scorecard:** Based upon the balanced scorecard (Kaplan and Norton, 1996), the green scorecard is a useful framework or monitoring index for helping organisations assess progress in achieving their environmental goals. As DeBusk et al. (2003) explain, the scorecard operates as a dashboard through which organisational leaders and managers can receive real-time data on a range of environmental performance

indicators. As such, the scorecard allows organisations to more accurately record and demonstrate improvements in the achievement of short- and long-term goals. For their part, Phillips and Phillips (2010) argue that a green scorecard allows organisations to track progression on metrics such as:

○ Green energy
○ Water conservation
○ Air pollution
○ Green meetings and events
○ Waste management
○ Green marketing
○ Recycling
○ Green training
○ Sustainable food

● **Corporate consciousness:** Building greater awareness of environmental issues across both management and staff requires significant investment in learning and communication. In order for organisational environment goals to be accepted and effectively implemented, staff need to understand the rationale underpinning such goals and take ownership for their operational implementation. Research by Azzone and Noci (1998) has established that training staff in relation to green issues is a necessary requirement for fostering environmental innovation. They suggest that training courses can help organisations build core competence in environmental issues and promote a culture of shared ownership of environmental issues.

● **Environmental outreach:** Outreach often forms an important part of an organisation's corporate social responsibility (CSR) activities, demonstrating how businesses are active partners in the local community. Being a good corporate citizen and working together with local communities and neighbourhoods are increasingly being regarded as a worthwhile organisational venture. Outreach also helps organisations establish a strong identity and makes individuals more aware of an organisation's culture and values. Environmental outreach is an opportunity for organisations to showcase their commitment to green issues and to educate consumers on the organisational initiatives they are taking to protect the environment as well as actions that consumers can take themselves to improve overall quality of life. Environmental outreach can also involve organisations working closely with special interest groups to accomplish valued environmental goals or improve regulatory frameworks and standards.

● **Green management:** Identified and chosen as the theme for the 2009 Academy of Management Conference, green management acknowledges a seismic shift in how organisations manage and leverage the resources at their disposal. It recognises that management has social responsibilities, beyond narrow shareholder perspectives. The term 'green management' provides a useful vehicle for integrating discussions of environmental issues and their impacts into business curricula and helping build student awareness that organisations need to consider the environmental impact of their business across all organisational functions – such as marketing, operations, logistics and change management. Green management acknowledges that whilst there may exist 'green champions' – i.e. individuals who may act as environmental ambassadors across organisations – every line manager and employee needs to take responsibility for environmental issues within their respective departments and business areas.

- **Green contract:** As described in McGuire (2010), the green contract acknowledges that there exists a reciprocal set of environmental expectations that affect the relationship between organisations and customers. It argues that customers will expect and support organisations to act in an environmentally responsible manner and in return, such organisations will benefit from higher customer loyalty and commitment. Evidence for the green contract is still emerging; however, growing consumer consciousness regarding environmental issues is forcing organisations to adapt their practices to meet higher environmental standards. Indeed, it is suggested that consumers are increasingly looking to express their concern for the environment through the act of consumption and that organisations need to pay attention to the sustainable qualities of their product and associated production processes.

- **Scenario planning:** Drawing up contingency plans and preparing for the possibility of an environmental disaster are actions befitting prudent and responsible organisations. Scenario planning is defined by Chermack and Lynham (2002: 376) as 'a process of positing several informed, plausible and imagined alternative future environments in which decisions about the future may be played out, for the purpose of changing current thinking, improving decision making, enhancing human and organisation learning and improving performance'. Planning organisational responses to a range of environmental scenarios is appropriate and necessary as in the last decade epidemics such as SARS, Avian flu, mad cow disease and the foot-and-mouth crisis have severely affected global business. Early preparation for such eventualities can lead to more decisive and informed decision-making and ensures a coordinated response with clear lines of responsibility and accountability.

Conclusion

The environment is playing an increasingly important role in how businesses operate in both domestic and international markets. Organisations can no longer afford to ignore environmental issues and concerns and must ensure that they address the expectations and needs of employees and customers in how businesses are run and operated. There is a clear case that climate change is having a profound effect on the livelihoods and well-being of individuals across the planet – thus environmental issues possess important ethical and moral overtones and cannot be ignored. With many scientists and commentators including Ellis (2012) recognising that 'the current rate and intensity of human alteration of the Earth system has no precedent', the planetary crisis has provided a wake-up call to organisations, communities and society as a whole to renew values, motivations and capabilities towards a more sustainable future. Increasingly, organisations are moving towards a triple bottom-line, looking to evaluate their activities in terms of impacts on people, profits and planet.

Becoming a sustainable organisation requires strong leadership, a shared vision and regular communication from senior management. Strong leadership is helping organisations reconsider how to configure value chains to fulfil stakeholder needs, whilst delivering more sustainable products and services. Moreover, the core of sustainable development lies in its key principle of 'development, which meets the needs of the present without compromising the ability of future generations to meet their own needs' (Report of the World Commission on Environment and Development [WCED], 1987). Leadership must be provided by both organisational leaders and government figures to ensure that a genuine commitment exists to reduce carbon emissions as well as sharing responsibility for environmental issues across society. With the greening of the global economy, opportunities will arise for organisations willing to invest in new technologies if they are capable of effectively operationalising stability and harnessing the resources and talent that exist within the organisation.

Operationalising sustainability will mean signing up organisations to the six R's of sustainable environmental change. The six R's provide a platform for organisations to take firm steps to making their processes and systems more environmentally sound. It forces organisations to refocus and re-examine their procedures for supplying products and services and ensuring that these fit the values and expectations of employees and customers. Underpinning the six R's is an HRD toolkit designed to showcase the role that HRD can play in promoting responsible environmental activity in organisations. While this toolkit in its present form is not exhaustive, it provides some guidance and suggestions for how HRD practitioners can actively contribute to organisational initiatives. Whilst it is increasingly recognised that the adoption of green technologies and standards can provide organisations with new sources of competitive advantage, it is contended that HRD can be at the forefront of this new advancement and through learning, education and training make significant improvements to the safeguarding of the global environment.

CASE STUDY

Marks & Spencer's Plan A – because there is no Plan B

Since its launch in 2007, Marks & Spencer's 'Plan A' green strategy has been viewed as a pioneering initiative in the area of environmental responsibility, strengthening the M&S brand and boosting perceptions of M&S in the eyes of the public. Hailed by Al Gore, leading environmental campaigner as a global inspiration, the example of M&S has shown that it is possible to establish a strong business case for being sustainable and carbon-positive.

Marks & Spencer's Plan A with its focus on cutting waste, saving energy, trading ethically, sourcing sustainable raw materials, and human and animal welfare has been widely regarded as integral to the rebirth of M&S. With 180 ethical and environmental commitments, the aim of Plan A is to help M&S become the world's most sustainable major retailer.

Whilst consumers of other retailers have worried about food sourcing and labour issues (due to the horsemeat controversy and the collapse of the Bangladeshi clothing factory), such scandals have not touched the M&S brand due to the company's strong sourcing policies and ethical values. Chief executive of M&S, Marc Bolland, says: 'Plan A has given us an additional strength and trust in our business and brands and helped us improve and protect the provenance of our sourcing. In the economic times of today, interest in sustainability is under pressure and it shouldn't be because it is more critical now.'

To date, M&S says that it has met 138 of the 180 environmental and ethical commitments contained within Plan A. It reports that through Plan A, it saved £135 million in 2012 and £105 million in 2011, through installing low energy lighting and changing the refrigerators in its stores, amongst other initiatives. Plan A has helped the company cut its carbon emissions by 23 per cent since 2006.

Usage of plastic bags by M&S customers has fallen by 1.7 million in the last five years and the charges that customers pay for plastic bags are handed over to environmental organisations. The company has also devoted over half a million hours to training and educating suppliers to ensure brand standards are adhered to.

A new initiative launched by M&S is to make 5 per cent of its product range 'cradle-to-cradle' certified in the next five years. Cradle-to-cradle certification is an approach which evaluates products across five categories: social fairness, materials health, renewable energy, water stewardship and material reutilisation. Such an approach inevitably involves considerable adjustments to the M&S supply chain and amongst M&S suppliers.

M&S has also recommitted itself to engaging with customers and helping them adjust their lifestyles and behaviours towards becoming more ethically and environmentally aware.

(Adapted from: Butler S (2013) Plan A Integral to the Rebirth of Marks & Spencer's. *Guardian*, 7 July. http://www.theguardian.com/business/2013/jul/07/plan-a-integral-rebirth-marks-spencer.)

(Continued)

(Continued)

Questions

Is there a valid business case for an organisation cutting back on its environmental ambitions during times of recession, when consumers are looking for cheaper products and services?

Much is beginning to be written about 'cradle-to-cradle' environmental approaches. What do we mean by 'cradle-to-cradle' approaches and why are they considered an advancement from the three R's of 'reduce, reuse and recycle'?

Marks & Spencer is considered to operate at the more affluent end of the grocery/food retail market. Can the adoption of environmental initiatives be equally as successful amongst low-price food retailers?

Discussion questions

How can the field of HRD assist organisations in translating scientific environmental advancements into operational improvements?

What are the risks of HRD extending its boundaries to look at environmental issues?

How can the field of HRD itself become more environmentally sound?

15 HRD at the Community and Societal Level

The objectives of this chapter are to:

- examine the social responsibilities of organisations and how HRD can contribute to corporate social responsibility approaches;
- outline ethical principles affecting the field of HRD and how HRD practitioners act and behave;
- examine the role of HRD in developing communities and society.

Introduction

It is increasingly recognised that HRD performs an important role at the community and societal level. Beyond narrow organisational interests, HRD embraces a broader agenda of building and growing the capacity of individuals, groups and communities. As Kim (2012) points out, the traditional focus of HRD on organisations as the primary context for HRD is slowly shifting, with the realisation that HRD possesses the tools and capabilities to make a real difference to local communities, nations and at an international level.

HRD at the community and societal level stresses the importance of acting responsibly and in an ethical manner and in doing so embraces a social justice agenda. HRD practitioners have a professional duty to act in an ethical manner – to act in a fair and honest fashion and observe the rights, dignity and welfare of others. Such behaviours are critical for the orderly development of the profession and to ensure that HRD's reputation is upheld in the eyes of the public. Organisations too have clear responsibilities to communities and society. The field of corporate social responsibility (CSR) recognises that there are economic, legal, ethical and discretionary expectations impinging on how businesses act and behave. Indeed, organisations need to consider the broad implications of their actions and how their activities affect the welfare and wellbeing not only of employees and shareholders, but also of local communities, the environment and the world at large.

A learning and growth focus is the key driver for HRD at the community and societal level. As many developing countries have recognised, education and training provide the vehicles through which inward investment can be attracted, boosting the value of their human capital. As Paprock (2006) points out, the mission of HRD at a national level is to develop a nation's human wealth in order to increase economic productivity and output. In so doing, McLean (2004) argues that HRD investments can help bring about greater national and local stability, end cycles of poverty, violence, unemployment and illiteracy, and improve overall quality of life.

In this chapter, we look at how HRD's role in human development and how HRD through human capital formation can positively impact on the economic and social outlook of communities and society. It first examines the CSR obligations of organisations bringing companies and corporations in closer contact with local communities and reframing organisations as good corporate citizens interested in the growth and development of local districts and neighbourhoods. It then proceeds to delineate the ethical responsibilities of HRD professionals, taking a close look at the set of ethical standards produced by the Academy of Human Resource Development. The final section of the chapter explores the importance of vocational education and training programmes and the shape of HRD at the community and national level.

HRD and corporate social responsibility

Just as organisations are realising that adherence to sustainability principles and working in an environmentally responsible manner are necessary to fulfil changing societal values, so too are organisations expected to positively contribute to the communities and society in which they operate. In addition to their annual sets of accounts, most large organisations now produce annual reports documenting their social and philanthropic activities. One of the first definitions of corporate social responsibility was provided by Archie Carroll (1979: 500) when he defined the concept as:

> The social responsibility of business encompasses the economic, legal, ethical and discretionary expectations that society has of organisations at a given point in time.

This hierarchy of expectations requires organisations to make a profit (economic), act lawfully (legal), behave ethically (ethical) and be a good corporate citizen (philanthropic/ discretionary). Imbuing organisations with a social conscience extends organisational responsibility beyond mere profit-and-loss accounts and looks at how the actions and values of the organisation are aligned with those of society. By definition, Carroll (1999) extends the notion of accountability beyond narrow economic and technical interests of organisations towards considering the needs and welfare of the wider social community. Garavan et al. (2010) assert that such an ethos may require organisations to reconsider issues such as organisational culture, reward systems and hierarchies to ensure both values and systems enable the effective implementation of CSR approaches.

In the field of human resource development, increasing emphasis is being placed on reconciling the resource-based view of the firm with a more humanistic value-based approach to human development. Bierema and D'Abundo (2004) argue that HRD needs to be more concerned about socially conscious practice and engaged with both the democratisation of the workplace and the creation of more sustainable communities and environments. As McGuire et al. (2005) point out, humanistic approaches to HRD call for taking into account human needs, motivations and well-being in fostering egalitarian and supportive work settings. Whilst the field of HRD has expressed increasing levels of interest in ethics, integrity and sustainability, allied with a growth in critical HRD literature (Fenwick and Bierema, 2008), a narrow profit-performance paradigm still pervades much research and thinking in HRD.

For her part, Wilcox (2006: 187) articulates a view of corporations as 'moral communities' based upon the cooperative relationships of its members. She uses this view to argue that the global economic system, through the actions of individual corporations, has been responsible for unequal wealth distribution and social injustice, leading to the marginalisation and exploitation of developing countries by more advanced nations. From this vantage point, she imposes a moral duty and obligation on organisations to consider the wider global consequences of their actions and respect the humanity and welfare of all peoples.

Barriers to implementing CSR in organisations are identified by both Garavan et al. (2010) and Fenwick and Bierema (2008). Both sets of authors found that within organisations, there was often a lack of knowledge and awareness about CSR issues and the underpinning rationale for engaging in these activities. Often, a disconnect was observed by employees between CSR principles and approaches (which were sometimes viewed as mere altruistic gestures) and the values and strategies of the organisation. Both sets of authors also found resistance by employees to CSR initiatives fuelled by a view that these initiatives are either too costly, time-consuming or divorced from core business goals. Finally, both sets of authors acknowledge that CSR initiatives can often be at odds with shareholder priorities and values.

In outlining HRD's role in advancing corporate social responsibility, Wilcox (2006) adopts a macro perspective, seeing access to education and training as critical factors in advancing social cohesion and economic prosperity. She outlines a number of

HRD initiatives that will help create a more favourable work environment, including: family-friendly policies, workforce flexibility, access to lifelong learning and professional development, and equality, access and affirmative action programmes. At the organisational level, Garavan et al. (2010) argue that HRD can design ethical awareness and leadership programmes, engage in more frequent communication regarding CSR initiatives and build stronger organisational CSR values and norms.

Talking point   Rebuilding the brand – RBS and corporate social responsibility

In 2008, the Royal Bank of Scotland (RBS) almost collapsed after posting the biggest loss in UK corporate history. At its peak in 2007, RBS became one of the world's top five banks through the aggressive acquisition of competitors including NatWest, Coutts, Direct Line, Ulster Bank, Churchill and Citizens Bank in the US. Its huge balance sheet boasted loans and investments worth £2 trillion – a sum considerably larger than the UK annual output or gross domestic product (GDP). Whilst the takeover of NatWest was lauded as a huge success, its acquisition of Dutch bank ABN Amro proved a step too far. Purchased for a price of £49 billion at the height of the financial crisis, many commentators now argue that RBS paid too much for the bank, which severely affected RBS's liquidity position. Initially, RBS issued a massive rights issue to shore up its reserves and raise new capital. However, in October 2008, RBS received its first tranche of bailout and to date has received £45.5 billion of UK public money.

For the 10 years from 1998 to 2008, RBS was led by its charismatic and abrasive CEO Fred Goodwin. Knighted in 2004 for his services to banking, Fred Goodwin was given the nickname 'Fred the Shred' due to his reputation for ruthlessly generating cost savings and efficiencies. His assertive and robust style of management led to morning meeting conference calls between executives being referred to as 'morning beatings'. His passion for vintage cars, massive salary (£4.2 million in 2007, which included a £2.86 million bonus) and a pension pot of £16 million led to a huge public outcry following the bank's collapse in 2008, and the revoking of his knighthood.

With the government bailout in 2008, efforts commenced to rebuild RBS's reputation as a safe, strong and sustainable financial institution. Its new CEO, Stephen Hester, set out his vision to remake RBS into one of the world's most admired, valuable and stable universal banks. The 2009 annual report identifies community involvement as a key mechanism for rebuilding RBS's reputation. It states that 'community involvement activities complement the day-to-day activities of our businesses, but enable us to go further and rebuild the reputation of the Group as a responsible business that has a sustainable impact upon the communities in which we operate'.

In terms of charitable endeavours, RBS operates four separate initiatives. First, they match all employee donations to charity helping benefit a range of different causes. Second, RBS directly supports through grants and fundraising around 3,800 charities and good causes around the world. Third, they encourage volunteering amongst their staff through their employee volunteering programme. UK retail staff are allocated at least one day off annually to volunteer in their communities, amassing to approximately 9,500 volunteer days. Finally, RBS encourages its customers to donate to charity. Customers can give directly to charity through the bank's ATM network, helping a range of charities including Age UK, Barnardo's, Oxfam, Cancer Research UK, Children in Need and the Disaster Emergency Committee.

Alongside charitable initiatives, RBS operates its MoneySense financial education programme. This programme works with secondary schools in the UK and Ireland to increase knowledge and awareness of financial matters and help young people manage their money more effectively. In 2009, over 700 RBS employees participated in the MoneySense programme delivering lessons on financial matters to over 330,000 students. The MoneySense for Adults initiative provides guidance on money matters through the RBS website to adults globally and receives over 60,000 visitors a month. RBS has received a number of community awards due to the success of the MoneySense programme.

In the United States, the Citizens Bank (a subsidiary of RBS) invested over $14 million in charitable donations and community grants supporting over 1,000 non-profit organisations combating hunger, providing shelter, strengthening communities and instructing citizens in money matters. A further $1 million was raised through an employee contribution matching programme to help more than 1,100 non-profit organisations. US employees also logged over 60,000 hours of volunteer time in helping local communities, charities and good causes.

(Adapted from: RBS Annual Reports and Accounts, 2009 and 2012.)

Questions

Do the initiatives outlined in the case study represent a genuine commitment by RBS to the principles and practices of CSR, or do they represent a cynical attempt to rebrand RBS in the eyes of the public after the near collapse of the bank?

In 2009, the late Anita Roddick (founder of the Body Shop) announced that 'Corporate Social Responsibility isn't working' arguing that 'Social Responsibility in business has been hijacked by Corporate Social Responsibility'. She maintained that the corporate agenda of profit and productivity takes precedence over genuine commitments to social responsibility and employee and community welfare. She argued that corporations have become obsessed with the measurement of CSR effects and publicising their good works. Do you agree?

HRD and ethics

The issue of ethics is an important one as it dictates the range of behaviours that individuals and organisations can morally engage in. In an era characterised by the collapse of Enron and Worldcom due to corporate fraud and wrongdoing, Doran (2005: 36) argues that 'more than any time in history, HRD professionals have a responsibility and an opportunity to make a positive contribution to ethical practice in business'. For his part, Hatcher (2002) asserts that HRD professionals have a responsibility for leading and managing ethics in organisations. While some might argue that this represents a further broadening of the HRD practitioner's role, acting ethically and in a socially responsible manner is critical to the long-term sustainable future of organisations. Moreover, Foote and Ruona (2008) argue that HRD professionals possess many of the necessary skills needed to promote ethical behaviour in organisations: namely, the ability to facilitate formal and informal meetings; the ability to build consensus; the ability to provide educational and training experiences; the ability to listen and communicate well; and the ability to assess the ethical implications of different situations.

In 1999, the Academy of Human Resource Development (AHRD) produced a set of standards on ethics and integrity applicable to practitioners working in the field of HRD. These standards articulate six general principles or values through which the field encourages ethical behaviour and expects its members to act in a socially responsible manner. These six general principles are as follows:

- **Competence:** HRD professionals should seek to achieve personal mastery in their work, whilst recognising the boundaries and limitations of their own individual expertise and experience. It argues that HRD professionals should exercise caution and due care both in their work and their dealings with others, so that the welfare of others is not harmed. It also advocates that HRD interventions are grounded in evidence-based research and are resourced appropriately for the task being undertaken.
- **Integrity:** This standard expects HRD professionals to act fairly, honestly and respectfully in their dealings with others. HRD professionals are expected to be truthful in communicating their knowledge, skills and relevant experience. They are also required to avoid conflicts of interest in their work where possible.
- **Professional responsibility:** HRD practitioners are expected to take professional responsibility for their behaviour and adapt their methods and techniques to suit the needs of different groups of participants. They must also not act in a manner which is likely to reduce trust and confidence in the field as a whole.
- **Respect for people's rights and dignity:** HRD professionals must fully observe and accord individuals their rights and dignity. Confidentiality, privacy, anonymity and autonomy must be adhered to and unfair discriminatory practices must not be engaged in.
- **Concern for others' welfare:** HRD practitioners must be sensitive in their dealings with others and act in a responsible manner that avoids injury and harm to

others. They must not mislead or exploit others in their dealings and their conduct should be above reproach.

- **Social responsibility:** HRD practitioners have a responsibility to the community, society and planet in which we live. As such, they must be committed to delivering a more sustainable future and working in the best interests of their client, the public and society at large.

Talking point   Ethical issues in HRD

In their research, Russ-Eft and Hatcher (2003) identified three key ethical areas affecting the field of HRD:

Striving to create humane workplaces

We (HRD practitioners) serve as the conscience of the organisation. We advocate and model organisational practices that respect the individual and support a humane workplace in times of stability and change. We also value multidimensional learning experiences that facilitate the development of both emotional and spiritual intelligence as well as knowledge skills. We believe that an enjoyable learning experience can enhance an otherwise meaningful learning experience.

Developing a sense of social responsibility

We expect every individual and organisation to be socially and ethically responsible, and we value the role of HRD in creating systems and processes to support individual, organisational, community, national and global well-being.

Embracing globalisation

To foster increased creativity, productivity and learning, and for sustained results in organisational settings, we will promote the following, through research and organisational change:

- Moving from a tolerance of differing cultures in the workplace to embracing synergistic advantage for increased productivity;
- Utilising appropriate communication approaches, processes and systems to improve both distant and face-to-face communications;
- Connecting global organisations to local communities to provide mutual advantage.

(Continued)

(Continued)

Questions

Is it truly HRD's role to act as the conscience of the organisation?

The renowned management guru Peter Drucker once said that 'Leaders in every single institution and in every single sector ... have two responsibilities. They are responsible and accountable for the performance of their institutions, and that requires them and their institutions to be concentrated, focused, limited. They are responsible also, however, for the community as a whole.' How can these sometimes conflicting responsibilities be reconciled?

Vocational education and training and national HRD policy

To achieve competitive advantage at a national level, countries need to recognise the importance of investing in and developing a strong educational infrastructure. Human capital development is critical in achieving a range of community and societal goals, including reducing poverty and injustice and improving social mobility, health and human rights (Kim, 2012). Critically a society's vocational education and training (VET) system can enhance overall competence and employability levels helping build more cohesive and inclusive communities. Stewart and Rigg (2011: 42) define VET as 'referring primarily to public policy aimed at improving international, national, organisational and individual skills as a means of improving economic performance at those same levels'. In this sense, VET can often be considered as education and training directly linked to specific occupations or employment opportunities. The critical importance of VET is articulated well by Thurow (1994: 52) when he states:

> Show me a skilled individual, a skilled company or a skilled country and I will show you an individual, a company or a country that has a chance to be successful. Show me an unskilled individual, company or country and I will show you a failure in the 21st Century. In the economy ahead, there is only one source of competitive advantage: skills. Everything else is available to everyone on a more or less equal access basis.

For their part, Griffiths and Koukpaki (2012) argue that knowledge has overtaken skills as the primary mechanism for the achievement of societal competitive advantage. They maintain that educational institutions have a duty to act as incubators for future competitive advantage through being a source of knowledge production and innovation and building a knowledge workforce. In this way, VET arrangements can have a strong effect on industrial and economic policy, influencing levels of foreign direct investment and the attraction of knowledge-intensive firms to specific geographic locations. Cooke and Noble (1998) found evidence that a country's education and skills base is by far the most critical factor in the location decision of large multinational firms. This often leads to the creation of a knowledge cluster or knowledge regions due to the mimetic tendencies of firms to locate in regions perceived to offer a high-quality workforce, low levels of regulation and labour cost, and a low corporate tax rate (Gunnigle and McGuire, 2001).

From an HRD outlook, research is emerging that focuses on the importance of 'human development'. Kuchinke (2010) argues that the four values of human development, namely humanitarianism, utilitarianism, equity and human rights, hold particular relevance for engaging with the notion of increasing individuals' capability for good health and productive work through development. He argues that if the ideal of human flourishing is to be achieved, then the field of HRD will need to take a more all-embracing, holistic view of development, where well-being embraces social, political and spiritual dimensions. To this end, HRD at the community and societal levels focuses on rediscovering the human factor in HRD and addresses economic, social and environmental challenges involving employer associations, community groups, religious institutions, special interest groups and government agencies (Kim, 2012).

A focus on HRD at a national level has particular relevance for a number of reasons. As McLean (2004) argues, for many countries starved of natural resources, human resources are their primary resource. Investment in the development of its citizens can be vital in improving productivity and gross domestic product (GDP) as well as helping organisations compete and collaborate globally and adjust to technological advances. With greater levels of mobility and an uncertain, imperfect and unpredictable labour market, Cho and McLean (2004) argue that HRD at the national level will require careful and integrated planning at the central, regional and local level. They assert the need for dynamic (rather than mandatory) approaches that attract students and citizens to needed fields of study and for the provision of incentives where necessary to make this happen. In this regard, they highlight the need for a close relationship between education and industry and proactive boundary-scanning in order to identify new growth areas within the international economy.

Both Cho and McLean (2004) and Lynham and Cunningham (2006) identify five key models of national human resource development. The *centralised model* advances a top-down, state-driven approach to education, where formulation, planning, implementation and assessment take place through the actions of central government. Strong collectivist controlling values are often at the core of the centralised model alongside a concern for social and equitable values. The *transitional model* embraces a social partnership approach whereby government, employers and trade unions agree a coordinated approach to educational, economic and social development. This often results in three- or five-year plans framed through the participation and involvement of multiple government departments and agencies. The *government-initiated model* adopts a stakeholder approach, and educational policy is decided through representation from employers, community groups, educational bodies, employee representatives, large corporations and interest groups. A standardised national framework such as Investors in People in the UK is often the outcome from such an approach. The *decentralised/ free-market model* pushes responsibility for development to the private sector with the state providing indirect financial support. This encourages competition and individuals are driven to take greater ownership. The *small-nation model* is driven by the need to achieve regional competitiveness and involves collaboration of small communities and nations in pooling resources to achieve benefits for all. Intergovernmental organisations often play an important role in identifying, planning for and meeting the educational needs of individual nations.

A recent OECD report (OECD, 2013) examined the impact of the recession (2008–2011) on employment and posited that educational attainment has a significant impact on employability and that a good education provides valuable insurance against the prospect of unemployment. It argued that countries need to do a lot more to facilitate the transition between education and work and advocates the creation of strong part-nerships between education and enterprise. The report also found strong evidence of a link between educational attainment and earnings – such that individuals with higher education benefited from an income premium compared to individuals not possessing such education. They concluded that educational attainment has long-lasting and positive mutually reinforcing effects over the course of a lifetime and that investing in young people's education can dramatically improve their overall life chances. On a policy level, they argue that national governments need to continually ensure that educational experiences remain efficient and relevant and that individuals receive a good level of foundation 'hard' skills as well as 'soft' skills such as teamwork, communication and negotiation.

Conclusion

Beyond the individual and organisational levels of analysis, HRD has an important role to play in shaping the well-being and vitality of communities and nations. The values and philosophy of HRD at the community and societal level are distinctive from organisational imperatives of profitability and productivity and emphasises human flourishing, whilst taking into account the economic, social and cultural context for development. Organisations through corporate social responsibility initiatives are increasingly recognising the need to contribute to the enrichment of local communi-ties and the prospect of 'giving back' is fast becoming an expected business norm. Being a 'good corporate citizen' is useful in boosting an organisation's reputation and helping it become an employer of choice in local communities.

For HRD to be sustainable in the long term, it is critical that HRD practitioners act and behave in an ethical manner. In an era marked with financial scandals, such as

Worldcom and Enron, some commentators have argued that HRD must act as the moral conscience of the organisation, standing up to hegemonic power displays in organisations and upholding the interests of employees and stakeholder groups. It is clear that in upholding the highest ethical standards, HRD practitioners must act with integrity, display competence in their work, respect the rights and dignity of others, take professional responsibility for their behaviour, show concern for the welfare of others and behave in a socially responsible manner.

HRD has an important role in human capital formation at the community and societal level. Framed traditionally within the concepts of vocational education and training (VET) and lifelong learning, national HRD plans and policies articulate the educational and training structures through which individuals acquire knowledge and skills, upon which to build their careers. The prioritisation of education and training at the national level significantly affects the overall competitiveness of an economy and the attraction of foreign direct investment. In this regard, HRD has an important responsibility not only in human development terms, but also in respect of economic and social development.

CASE STUDY

The democratic workplace – the experience of working at Valve

Established in 1996, video games maker Valve likes to do things differently. For starters, the company operates under a flat organisational structure, where all employees are equal and managers don't exist. 'We're a flat organisation, so I don't report to anybody and people don't report to me', explained one employee, D.J. Powers. A core value underpinning Valve's philosophy is that talent needs to be unleashed by setting employees free to pursue their interests without unnecessary organisational barriers. Employees are free to participate in and take responsibility for seeing projects through from cradle to grave, liberating employees from hierarchical structures and allowing employees to self-organise with emergent project leaders. Dialogue, collaboration and collective engagement are critical to the process and employees are tasked with directly interacting with customers to find out their needs and then developing solutions to meet those needs.

Valve's handbook for new employees issues the following direction to its staff: 'We do have a founder/president, but even he isn't your manager. This company is yours to steer – towards opportunities and away from risks. You have the power to

(Continued)

(Continued)

green-light projects. You have the power to ship products.' Decision-making takes place in groups based upon a democratic process, where each employee has an equal say in how the company is run. Typically, projects that have a high, measurable, predictable return for the company gain the highest priority alongside working on perceived problems and threats to the organisation.

Even the internal configuration of Valve's offices is unconventional. Staff sit at desks which have wheels – a symbolic message to employees that they are free to move and join groups where they feel they can add the most value. In that sense, individuals are encouraged to move their desks to sit alongside project collaborators creating a dynamic vibrant workplace. T-shaped employees are particularly valued and prized. These individuals tend to be both broad-range specialists (horizontal axis of the T) as well as possessing deep expertise in one area (vertical axis of the T). A key perk to working a Valve is that the company takes its 300-plus workforce on a week-long tropical vacation once a year. This experience helps the organisation build teamwork and a family atmosphere amongst employees – also giving them time to socialise and build bonds of trust and friendship outside of a formal work environment.

Employee performance at Valve is measured through two primary mechanisms: peer reviews and stack ranking. Peer reviews allow constructive feedback to be collected, collated, anonymised and delivered to each employee indicating areas for improvement and developmental opportunities. Valve makes it clear that the key purpose of peer review is to provide employees with information that helps them grow. Stack ranking is a system whereby employees are annually ranked against each other to gain an insight or perspective on which individuals are adding the most value to the organisation. In this way, overall salary and compensation are determined – so in essence salary over time gets adjusted to fit an employee's internal, peer-driven valuation. The stack ranking is based upon four metrics: skill and technical ability; productivity and output; group contribution; and product contribution.

(Adapted from: Valve (2012) *Valve: Handbook for New Employees.* Seattle: Valve Press.)

Questions

What are the key challenges of working in a flat organisation without a lot of top-down direction?

Is the concept of a 'democratic organisation' a romanticised ideal?

Discussion questions

How can organisations be convinced of the virtues of CSR beyond mere charitable giving?

Should ethics be included as a compulsory module on HRD programmes?

Are HRD practitioners the moral conscience of the organisation?

Comment on the statement made by Harbison and Myers (1964: 13) that 'if a country is unable to develop its human resources, it cannot develop much else'.

Conclusion

Introduction

Human resource development lives in a constant state of becoming. It lives in the boundaries and interfaces of organisations, questioning assumptions, proposing alternatives and making organisations more relevant to the environments in which they operate. Through a broad interdisciplinary base, HRD embraces the concept of development and moves the field beyond a narrow training focus, giving it a strategic remit and a commission to advance innovative structures and models for organising and engaging employees in a more effective manner. In so doing, HRD becomes not only change-ready, but a change leader moving organisations towards dynamic, proactive, sustainable solutions and giving organisations an appetite for continuous learning and transformation.

At the individual level, HRD works with the individual to develop their potential, bringing meaning and satisfaction to work. It equips employees with the knowledge and skills necessary to adequately fulfil job tasks, but should also make employees future-ready in preparing them for challenges that lie ahead. Career planning and development should be essential elements in the employees' continuing formation and should represent the nexus by which individuals and organisations prepare their common futures. In this way, HRD should foster greater self-esteem and motivation amongst individuals and should contribute to a higher quality of working life and sense of accomplishment.

At the organisational level, HRD is linked to the overarching objectives of innovation, efficiency and effectiveness. First, HRD is a critical approach to preparing organisations for tomorrow's challenges. Through creating a trained, flexible, adaptable workforce, organisations can meet and lead environmental change. Second, HRD can deliver real and substantial improvements to organisational systems. The knowledge economy demands more integrative, cross-functional approaches that draw upon unique competency sets and leverages tacit understandings (or the knowledge that exists between and behind individuals). Third, in today's competitive age, HRD encourages a spirit of entrepreneurialism and innovation across all employee groups. Employees are encouraged to be autonomous and work smarter – indeed, it is arguable that the dual concepts of devolvement and empowerment serve to heighten pressure particularly amongst middle and senior managers for more innovative strategic solutions. Finally, with the pervasive, all-consuming nature of technology, HRD has a distinct role in ensuring fit-for-purpose, ease of user-interface and client customisation.

At the societal level, HRD is associated with the community, environmental and CSR agendas. HRD is tasked with developing appropriate structures for delivering knowledge and skills training to individuals and communities. HRD is linked to the environmental agenda whereby organisations are increasingly recognising the importance of building products and services in a more sustainable manner. At the community and societal level, a key concern is the alignment of industrial development policy with educational resources and community-based support. As Porter (1990) indicates, the competitive advantage of regions and attractiveness of regions to inward investment often depend upon specialist investment in education and training.

In this final chapter, we offer a vision for the future of human resource development with some suggestions for advancing the field.

A vision of HRD

HRD is not new. While some may argue that HRD is a maturing field (Evarts, 1998) or reaching adolescence (Lee and Stead, 1998), the reality is that HRD in a holistic form has been with us for a very long time. The seeds of HRD were sown long before Harbison and Myers (1964) formally defined the concept of human resource development. For generations, progressive organisations and managers have realised the importance of developing their people. They understood that upskilling, engaging with and motivating employees were crucial tasks in building a successful, profitable organisation and satisfied, committed workforce. They recognised the reality and necessity of building mutuality between the interests of employees and those of the organisation. In such matters, HRD is not new. So, what is new?

Each year, much is written about HRD with claims of original insights and revolutionary thinking. New models are presented to supplant previously accepted paradigms and to fit changing organisational and societal contexts. Researchers compete to develop better and more advanced solutions to age-old problems. In many cases, the problems haven't changed, but the remedies have become much more effective. And in other cases, the problems haven't changed and only small incremental improvements have occurred.

As an interdisciplinary field, one of the great merits associated with HRD is that it offers space for competing paradigms and alternative views on how individuals and organisations can be developed more effectively. Throughout this book, we have attempted to present a series of ideas, concepts, theories and practices on how HRD can be deployed more effectively. Such discussions have as much as possible avoided prescriptive recipes as we have tried to engage the reader in a deeper, research-based, critical understanding of the assumptions underpinning particular approaches.

So, with all of this new thinking and the greater volume and dissemination of ideas, which theories and practices should be followed? Which applications are universal and which are context-specific? How do we distinguish the effective from the ineffective? The answer to these questions lies in the relativity of the HRD concept. The fact that agreement cannot still be reached on a consensual definition of HRD some 40 years after its original formulation points to an evolving, shifting field in tune with the transitions of organisations and society. It acknowledges that there can be no one true HRD, but multiple variants of HRD fitting particular contexts and situations. The universal becomes local and adjusted to fit particular factors and circumstances. Effectiveness depends upon best fit and close alignment of HRD solutions with problem characteristics.

In short, there is a need to develop the evidence base for HRD. To be truly innovative and effective, HRD solutions must work well. Innovation rarely occurs in a vacuum. Notwithstanding some exceptional cases, innovation builds upon existing contexts and problems, but frames solutions in a ground-breaking and creative way. In some cases, innovation occurs through reclaiming lost insights and revisiting long-forgotten research studies. In this regard, new perspectives often involve presenting old wine in new bottles. They entail communicating old accepted truths in a manner that connects with modern realities and contexts. This may require employing new technology and tools to deliver practical applications more efficiently and with greater effectiveness.

So, where is the value in repackaging old theories and concepts? Like management, HRD is an art as well as a science. Just as there is no single best artistic masterpiece, HRD recognises the value of Tayloristic 'one best way' approaches, but strongly acknowledges their limitations. The myriad circumstances and contexts that exist at organisational and societal levels demands a plethora of tools that are timely and appropriate to contemporary realities. The development of new approaches needs to be an ongoing iterative process. In so being, it need to be attuned to the changing economic, social, political and environmental realities facing organisations and society.

New perspectives on HRD challenge stasis and foster a progressive dynamism about the HRD concept, its value and purpose. They promote diversity of thought and generate conflict through forcing HRD practitioners to move beyond their narrow comfort zones towards critical reflexivity and deeper thinking about HRD's purpose and functions (Garavan et al., 2007). The shifting character of HRD has recently been identified by Sambrook (2008) when she discusses HRD stretch – the development of multiple collaborative relationships pulling the field along horizontal and vertical dimensions.

To my mind, relationships lie at the core of HRD. Through HRD, individuals become more connected to each other, to their work, to their organisations, to communities and to society. That HRD creates multiple relationships means that it must reconcile conflicting needs and agendas. In this regard, the HRD discipline and profession are formed around a tension in values (McGuire et al., 2007). Viewing HRD through a multiperspectival lens allows greater appreciation and understanding of individual interests, motivations and priorities. As Torraco (2004) points out, acknowledging different perspectives creates flux, where differences may initially appear wider than they are in reality. However, it is only through exposing difference and questioning assumptions that HRD can truly progress and remain relevant as a field of study.

Appendix
Preparing for HRD Examinations

Appendix objectives

The objectives of this appendix are to:

- provide advice on how to prepare for HRD examinations;
- showcase examples of examination answers (high, medium and low);
- identify hallmarks of effective examination answers.

Introduction

Examinations can be stressful, nerve-wracking occasions. For many students, they are all-consuming, holding a central position in their thoughts, dreams and preoccupations in the days and weeks before the main event. While academics sometimes tell students that examinations are valuable opportunities to showcase their knowledge and learning, the pressure induced by examinations can cause students to freeze and clam up. Careful preparation and good technique can help mitigate the tensions caused by examinations. The purpose of this short appendix is to provide guidance and advice on how best to prepare for HRD examinations. It provides examples of examination questions and answers to help you clearly distinguish the key hallmarks of effective examination answers.

Advice on preparing for HRD examinations

The following six key pointers are worth careful consideration when getting ready to sit HRD examinations:

Answer the question you are asked, not the question you'd like to be asked

Many students have preprepared answers to expected examination questions and really do not engage with the question posed. Some key advice would be to start your answer by addressing the question directly. When you have answered the question, only then tell us everything else you know about the wider topic.

An examination answer is not a summary of a particular lecture

Many students in answering examination questions adopt a very linear approach. They feel that they need to start an answer by defining key terms and giving a history of a particular topic before addressing the question posed. While in some cases definitions and a history of the topic may be required by the examination question, this is not always the case. Structuring your answer as a summary of a particular lecture misses the point. The purpose of a lecture is most often to introduce the student to a particular topic and lecturers will often cover many aspects of the topic within their lecture. An examination question is likely to focus on only one or two specific aspects of the topic – not the whole topic itself.

Make a plan

This may sound obvious, but formulating a plan will keep you structured and will ensure you stay on track. It helps the readability of your answer and ensures that key components/models or theories are included as part of your answer. Making a plan helps you signpost the reader by including an introduction, middle section and conclusion. You may also decide to incorporate case examples or practical illustrations of models and theories.

Watch your timing

Good examination practice requires you to keep an eye on your time and make sure you devote enough time to each exam question that you attempt. At the start of the exam, decide how much time you will allocate to each question – and once the time expires, move onto the next question.

Showcase your knowledge of the research literature

The best examination answers always make reference to key research contributions and leading thinkers within a particular field. Being able to quote and critique key authors helps show the examiners that you understand the topic and can apply relevant knowledge to a case problem or examination topic. Citing key contributions means that you will need to be able to recall such contributions and understand the academic and practical implications of models, theories and frameworks.

Develop a critical writing style

As a student, your role in an examination is not just to reproduce or describe key models, theories or frameworks, but to critique these contributions and identify strengths and weaknesses. You should be able to demonstrate the relevance and utility of theories and models and how a discipline has developed over time. In developing a critical writing style, you need to recognise that authors' contributions can and should be validly critiqued. It is only through valid critique that a discipline grows and develops.

Examples of examination questions and sample answers

In this section, two sample HRD examination questions are provided, along with three sample (high pass, mid-range pass and borderline pass) solutions for each question. The purpose of providing sample answers is to help you distinguish the higher order learning required to achieve top grades. The key objective of this section is to help you prepare more completely for written examinations. Students should, however, be aware that academic standards and expectations can differ across academic institutions, so please check with your own professors, lecturers and tutors in relation to what they are looking for in any examination. The sample solutions provided are based upon real examination answers provided by students at a UK university under normal examination conditions.

Question 1

With the advent of boundaryless careers and staff mobility and turnover, critically examine why organisations should engage in employee career development?

Answer 1

A career can be described as a 'succession of related jobs arranged in a hierarchy of prestige, through which persons moved in an ordered (more or less) predictable sequence' (Wilensky, 1964), which is a definition which may have been appropriate at the time it was written, but is something that is almost unrecognisable in today's organisations.

Due to a number of factors, including the recession, causing companies to downsize and make redundancies or the creation of flatter organisational structures, the pattern of careers described by Wilensky is very rare today. There is a great deal of lateral career moves as there are fewer opportunities of rising up the hierarchical pyramid of the organisation. Indeed, increasingly common is backward movement due to high unemployment and increasing competition for jobs. A job for life has become very rare with many employees only staying with a company a few years before moving on. With this thought, it would be understandable why organisations may choose not to engage in career development.

Notions of career are also changing. The traditional notion of career development took a very paternalistic approach in that the company took a lot of responsibility for its employees' career development. This echoes back to the idea of a job for life where employees could expect to stay with the same company and as a reward for their loyalty would be promoted up the ranks. However, this is less common now and is something which is more likely to be seen in the public sector.

More common is the notion of a boundaryless career where employees can move freely between employers. This is a notion which was encouraged by Thatcher when she was in power as it would spread skills and knowledge between companies. The UK as a country is no longer seen as a boundary either due to globalisation and improved technology. Employment can be sought all over the world. This can benefit employers and employees as it allows knowledge and skills to be developed which can then be transferred.

However, an employer may be reluctant to engage in career development due to this as they would be investing in an employee who may at any time decide to leave the organisation, taking with them all the skills and knowledge they have learned. Despite this, there are still a number of reasons why employers should participate in their employees' career development.

By engaging in an employee's career development, the company shows that they are willing to invest in that employee, thus showing their loyalty and trust in that individual. This will enhance the employee's psychological contract with the company resulting in them feeling more engaged and possibly increasing their loyalty. Also, if they feel that the employer is buying into their career development, it could make them feel more secure in their position. So, by showing an interest in an employee's career, the employer may be able to encourage the employee to continue their employment and be more engaged.

A company who actively is involved in their employees' career development will also be more appealing to potential new employees which could make it easier to recruit high quality employees. Therefore, bringing in new knowledge and skills which could help enhance the overall organisation.

(Continued)

(Continued)

The processes which are used in career development can also be considered. Hirsch's (2003) model shows:

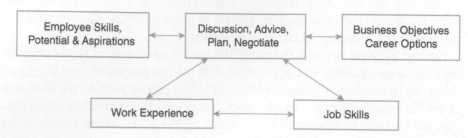

Figure A1

By considering each of these things, it is possible to put a plan in place, which employees are involved with, so they can see what they need to do to achieve their goal. Getting the employee to take responsibility for their career, but ensuring that the employer will support them will again make the employee feel more secure and should increase their performance.

From this career plan, the organisation will be able to take part in succession planning and talent management. By doing this, the organisation can ensure that they have employees lined up with skills to take over when other employees leave the organisation.

Succession planning as part of career development allows the organisation to prepare other employees to have the necessary skills to be able to fill key roles within the organisation. This can prevent any large holes being created when an employee leaves. However, this in itself may cause problems as employees may feel pushed out if they think another employee is being trained to take their position or if an employee is given the skills to be able to take on a role but never promoted to believe it, they may leave.

Talent management will allow the company to see employees which they think are going to have the skills which will benefit the organisation to be identified. They can then encourage that employee to stay with the company by showing they are willing to invest in them by participating in their career development. If they are able to show a talented individual what they could achieve with the company and put things in place to allow them to reach that, it should keep them engaged.

However, there could be an issue with this if employers do get involved with their career development. They must ensure they can fulfil their promises, otherwise they risk breaking the trust between employer and employee as well as the psychological contract. So from that respect, it could be considered that career development should be left as the responsibility of the individual employee.

Career development is something which employers should consider; the notion of boundaryless careers should not prevent them and may help retain and attract talent. It does not have to be at a huge financial cost to the company, but one which could help increase employee engagement and better performance. The boundaryless career can also be seen as an advantage for companies as new employees will bring with them a wealth of knowledge and experience from previous employers which can be used in their new employment.

Examiner's comments

Satisfactory but underwhelming answer. Greater detail could be provided on the boundaryless career. Many of the concepts are discussed in general terms and you need to show a greater degree of depth in your discussion. In particular, you also could cite more research. Some adequate arguments made in relation to reasons why organisations should engage in career development, but cite more examples and research!

Grade

Borderline Pass

Answer 2

Traditionally, careers saw people move through the hierarchy for extrinsic rewards (Rosenbaum, 1978), however careers no longer move in a linear trajectory (Sullivan and Baruch, 2009). Career development was a key element of a traditional career, where progression was predictable (McDonald et al., 2009), long service was rewarded and the workplace was more focused on staff loyalty rewarded by job security. Careers have changed with the emergence of boundaryless (where careers transcend more than one organisation), protean (where employees drive their careers due to their desire for self-fulfilment), portfolio (where individuals contract their skills and services to different organisations giving them mobility and freedom, while the onus is on them to ensure that their knowledge and skills are marketable) (Arnold, 2001) and hybrid careers (where employees want self-fulfilment, the ability to move organisations and job security). Because of these changes, it is important for organisations to determine if they should still offer career development to employees.

(Continued)

(Continued)

Careers have changed for many reasons. Due to the recession, the labour market is more buoyant allowing organisations to buy in skills instead of developing them internally. Some organisations would argue that buying in pre-trained workers is ideal (Hall, 2005). The recession has led to an increase in redundancies which breaks the traditional promise of job security offered by organisations. Technological advances have allowed for outsourcing and offshoring to become more prevalent due to the reduction in cost this provides organisations. Another phenomenon altering careers is the increase of women in work, dual earning couples and single parents. Current employees have different priorities and needs than the traditional male workforce. Finally, changes to legislation removing the age of retirement means that older workers are staying in their roles for longer, acting as a block to younger workers who will therefore go externally to another organisation to progress up the career ladder and get the job they want. These changes demonstrate that careers are not just about the job itself, but external factors (Sullivan and Baruch, 2009) and the complexities show why Edgar (1995) found over 30 different terms for the word career.

It is clear that changes have led to a more transactional exchange between employees and employers (Hall, 2004) with career development not being as evident. Despite the fear of organisations that investing money in developing employees' careers could be fruitless due to their likelihood of leaving the organisation, it is still important they do so. Career development is often viewed as part of the psychological contract. Despite employees moving organisations, they still expect their skills and knowledge to be developed and recognised. Where this isn't done, employees can become disengaged and less productive. Career development can also be offered as part of an organisation's employee value proposition. When recruiting, organisations want the best talent; therefore, offering career development can attract high performers. During times of recession, career development can be offered to current employees instead of financial rewards, incentivising them with the ability to improve their employability. Further, in times of a recession, where redundancies occur, it is important for organisations to lose their poor performers to retain their leading potential. Offering career development is a way to do this. It can be argued that people and their knowledge are an organisation's competitive advantage (Boud and Garrick, 1999) and are the key to organisational wealth (Sveiby, 1997). By utilising career development, organisations can entice employees to stay. Finally, employees are often the glue in an organisation, ensuring that the culture and values are demonstrated and spread. Career development is a way to ensure talent is retained and progressed in an organisation, ensuring that this isn't lost.

There are arguments against career development, including the cost; the fact that it doesn't focus enough on blue collar workers (Sullivan and Baruch, 2009) and the fact those not on a talent programme or who haven't been picked out for career development may become disengaged. However, there are many examples of where career development has been beneficial to organisations. Michelin have seen low turnover and relate it to their rigorous career development (although this is done in a very paternalistic, traditional way). Standard Life reflect Hirsch's (2003) model for career development through corporate managed initiatives (i.e. talent programmes, executive coaching, women's development networks, women in leadership programmes), core HR offerings (appraisals carried out between all managers and employees at least biannually) and support for self-managed careers (e-learning opportunities, self-study options at the bespoke learning zone, CIPD workshops). Because of this, Standard Life have recognised low turnover compared to the financial services norm and the engagement survey positively reflects the career commitment of its people.

In conclusion, despite boundaryless careers becoming more common, organisations must invest in career development as it can help retain talent, reduce dis-engagement and help organisations use their people to give them a key competitive advantage.

Examiner's comments

Well-focused solid answer which draws well upon the research to support key arguments. Good attempt made in the answer to describe the context for contemporary careers and the rationale for investing in career development. Overall, the answer needs a more critical focus and some of the arguments could be sharper and more developed. That said, some useful arguments are made and advanced.

Grade

Mid-range Pass

Answer 3

Due to changing social, political and economic environment, notions of career have moved away from traditional paternalistic notions to new ones that reflect the changed environment. Boundaryless careers are one of these new notions and with its focus on independence from, rather than dependence on one organisation for a career would suggest that organisations may no longer be required to engage in career development. This view is challenged as looking at the environment and the

(Continued)

(Continued)

different notions of careers this develops shows there is still a requirement to engage in employee career development to ensure engagement with the organisation, to attract employees and to achieve competitive advantage.

Traditional notions of career were based upon economic growth and stability and job security. However, changes in the economic environment (recession, redundancies, technological advancement, globalisation and outsourcing) have resulted in undermining the basis of this concept. No longer are employees expected to have a job for life, but instead there are greater expectations of staff mobility and turnover. This has led to new notions of careers. Sullivan and Baruch (2009) however challenge whether this has really led to the end of traditional careers as little research has been done on populations such as immigrant and blue collar workers.

Michelin, for example, continues to take a paternalistic, traditional approach to careers despite globalisation and expansion. Therefore, some organisations may be required to still engage in career development. Egan et al. (2006) in highlighting that career development is context and outcome based effectively highlight the need for organisations to be clear of their individual context and outcomes to understand to what level they need to engage in employee career development.

However, much of the research has focused on the decline of traditional notions of career and as a result, new notions have arisen that take into account the changing environment. Boundaryless careers (Arthur and Rousseau, 1996) are one of these. Boundaryless careers are not dependent on one organisation (as in traditional notions of career) as employees are responsible for their own career development as a result of not being physically or psychologically tied to one organisation. This results in greater mobility (internal and external) and greater turnover. However, this is not the only career notion to develop. Others such as the protean career (Hall, 1996) where employees develop skills, capabilities to make them marketable to other employers also challenge the need for career development as organisations are faced with a more mobile, turnover-prone workforce who seek self-fulfilment from their career as well as other aspects of life.

Investment in employee career development in these circumstances may therefore be ineffective as organisations are less likely to have long serving employees and therefore reap the rewards of the investment. This highlights the conflict of career development as employers want to retain employees and therefore may limit development whilst employees require/want under new notions of careers employability to ensure they are marketable.

Fundamentally, whilst there are new notions of careers, these are restricted by challenges for employees such as not having the skills and capabilities to work for another employer and for not being able to quickly adapt to new work environments in order to perform (Sullivan and Baruch, 2009). This may limit staff mobility and turnover therefore putting the onus back on the organisation to engage in career development of employees so that their skills remain relevant and useful to the organisation.

Although the economic environment has changed and challenged notions of career development for organisations, there are some factors that mean career development is still important. These are lessons from the 1990s recession, achieving competitive advantage and meeting changing employee expectations. Harrison (2009) highlights how a lesson that was learnt in the 1990s recession was that it was an organisation's cost not to invest in employee development during the tougher economic times (despite learning and development budgets often being the first to be cut for example as seen in the public sector – as competitors who invest will get ahead when the economy changes). This suggests that organisations should engage in career development even in tough economic times. Harrison also highlights the need for a flexible and adaptive workforce who are skilled and trained to ensure effectiveness of the organisation in turbulent economic times. Again, despite the potential for mobility and turnover, this highlights the need for employee career development.

Rainbird (1995) states how competitive advantage be achieved through ensuring that employees have unique skills and capabilities that are difficult for competitors to replicate. As a result, organisations often focus on talent management (i.e. focus career development on high performing employees) such as in the case of Barclays who expanded their talent management programme to have a global focus. However, Harrison (2009) is critical of this approach stating that unless effectively integrated with career development of all employees, it can result in the effective disengagement of other employees. Moreover, this traditional approach to career development (for a select few in the organisation) highlights the conflict between employer and employee mentioned earlier. The employer invests in the employee, however this makes the employee more marketable outside the organisation and for the employee, depending on their individual notion of career, they may not be loyal to the organisation – i.e. boundaryless career.

This motivation of individuals demonstrates how employee expectations of careers may have changed. This is due to many factors such as cost restricted organisations offering career development as an incentive for attraction and retention rather than pay and bonuses – as shown in Tesco's 'Grow with us' recruitment campaign. Also, the changing nature of the workforce (ageing workforce, dual-earning households, more women in the workforce) also provides a role for career development as whilst employees aren't tied to one organisation, their expectations of career

(Continued)

(Continued)

development to achieve employability result in career development being a part of the psychological contract.

An example of this is in the area of self-development. Boundaryless careers put the onus on the employee for self-development of their careers – however as shown in Hirsch's (2003) model, organisations still have a role to play in providing resources for self-development. For example, Nike (Harrison, 2009) have moved away from classroom based learning to self-development and Standard Life provides a learning zone which is a dedicated physical and online area for employee self-development. However, the effectiveness in the psychological contract is determined not only by the organisation providing resources, but also the time, commitment and support of this alternative form of employee career development.

In summary, even with the advent of boundaryless careers and staff mobility and turnover, organisations as a result of a changing social, cultural and economic environment still engage in employee career development. In highlighting the hybrid career model (Sullivan and Baruch, 2009) show that there is, for some employees and organisations a rationale for achieving the upward mobility and development of traditional career notions, whilst also allowing for elements of boundaryless and protean careers.

Examiner's comments

This is an excellent answer. A very focused response to the question is given from start to finish. The student builds a series of strong arguments and demonstrates an excellent knowledge of the literature as well as a capability to explore tensions and debates. Some good examples of key concepts in practice are provided.

Grade

High Pass

Question 2

Ulrich (1998) argues that to deliver organisational excellence, the HRD function must:

Act as *partners* with senior and line management in strategy execution
Act as *experts* in the way work is organised and executed
Act as *champions* for employees
Act as *agents* of continuous organisational transformation

Critically examine the strategic contributions being made by the HRD function in contemporary organisations through reference to Strategic HRD models and frameworks.

Answer 1

Garavan (1991) defines strategic human resource development as 'the long term learning of employees, cultural complexity and strategic alignment'. With the new public reforms (NPM) of the 1980s, human resources (HR) as well as other administrative functions were to fundamentally change in the way in which they functioned. They now had to be seen as a service which would have to show their worth and value. But with the changes that evolved from the emergence of NPM, this completely shifted the traditional role of HRD to the line manager (Harrison, 2005). The convergence of the European Union (1980s) had an adverse effect as well as the impact of globalisation and technological advances.

Globalisation and technology

With the NPM and administrative reform, Information technology (IT) led at the forefront some would say. It moved at almost an alarming rate. Apple, Microsoft and other IT companies lead the way on innovation. Many forms of communication are now available 24 hours a day (e.g. Skype, Twitter and other social networks). HRD have moved away from its traditional role and the way in which it delivered it due to electronic changes. This meant a much more strategic approach was required. They now had to align their HRM strategy both vertically and horizontally, with other business strategies. With the strategic approach being now sought, a number of strategic human resource development (SHRD) models emerged.

Models

Garavan's (1991) model of nine SHRD characteristics covered the likes of culture, values, ethicism partnership etc. but was criticised as complicated. Nine years later, McCracken and Wallace (2000) introduced a replica of the model first introduced by Garavan in 1991. Well, what does that tell you? Either Garavan 'nailed it' or not much progress has been evidenced in the way in which the HRD delivery model functions.

Peterson (2008) also introduced a SHRD model. Her model focused on partnership – a critical area with the shift of some of the traditional HRD functions to line managers emphasising the partnership approach now required. The most recognised model in modern business today is Ulrich's first introduced

(Continued)

(Continued)

in 1997. Ulrich argued that to deliver organisational excellence, the GRD function must:

Act as <u>partners</u> with senior and line management in strategy formulation and execution. Both HRD and line managers have a dual responsibility – therefore, they need to work together further emphasising partnership. This gives HRD people a real opportunity to work at the front line in the business and understand their needs. Learning is at the heart of the organisation that wants to enhance the employees' capabilities and performance. However, line managers are questioning the need for HRD if they need to take on this function (Peterson, 2008).

Act as <u>experts</u> in the way work is organised and executed. Unlike those staff in HRD classed as business partners, Ulrich has also recognised a need for certain skills that would still be necessary. He classed these as 'centres of excellence' – e.g. employment law, reward and recognition etc. Yet, these can be dependent on the size of the business. Relatively small companies don't have large HRD teams to enable this to be managed separately (Garavan, 2001). However, some companies may look to outsource these functions.

Act as <u>champions</u> for employees. HRD can work alongside employees now, quite often hotdesking in the same area. They have the opportunity to build relationships and give them a 'voice' with management (Harrison, 2005). But it can sometimes be a fine line, almost like being devil's advocate. HR staff need to be careful in finding a balance that works for both employees and line managers.

Act as agents of continuous organisational transformation. This is probably no different for HRD staff than any other part of the organisation. The world in which we now live in is one of globalisation, technology and innovation.

Most organisations today will recognise Ulrich's three-legged stool. But it is not without criticism. It has been said it's time-consuming and only works in mid-to-large organisations (CIPD, 2012). Ulrich (2001) defends this through saying that 'strategic changes take time'.

HRD needs to provide its need, value and worth. By evaluation and measurement and perhaps through adopting a balanced scorecard approach (Kaplan and Norton, 2001), as this is recognised in organisations today and has a 'people' section. If they can prove their value, then maybe, just maybe they can achieve that much sought after recognition as a true business partner.

Examiner's comments

Quite a confused answer. The student muddles a number of areas (SHRD, HRM) as well as confusing the contributions of some authors. The student needs to be clearer on the importance contributions of SHRD models. NPM stands for New Public Management, rather than new public reforms. By focusing on new public management, you appear to be confining strategic HRD to the public sector and fail to fully recognise its important role in the private sector. Strategic HRD initiatives apply to both public and private sectors. The context for change (European Union, Technology, Globalisation) is briefly described. Similarly, there is insufficient detail on Peterson's contribution and no mention is made of Garavan's most recent (2007) HRD model.

Grade

Borderline Pass

Answer 2

In order to critically examine the contributions being made by the HRD function through reference to Strategic Human Resource Development models, it is first important to understand what strategic HRD is, why it is considered important and why it has evolved.

Peterson (2008) outlines that strategic HRD is the long-term, proactive approach to HRM initiatives at both the individual and organisational level which impacts on bottom-line organisational goals and competitive advantage. It is considered that employee knowledge is what gives an organisation its competitive advantage, therefore learning and development departments have been criticised as being too short-term focused and not preparing employees for the changing global context in which we are now operating. Friedman's (2007) 11 global flatteners have identified the environment in which organisations now operate as a global one in which there is much competition due to the free movement of people, increased power of communities and the ability of organisations to work 24 hours a day around the world. HRD has responded to this with the rise of strategic HRD (SHRD) in which the goals of HRD help shape the strategy of an organisation to prepare for its internal and external environment.

Garavan (1991) proposed 9 characteristics of SHRD. McCracken and Wallace (2000) were critical of this model as not being strategic enough in order to have real impact on the organisation. They proposed an advance of these 9 characteristics. We will consider these models now. In order for SHRD to be strategic, Garavan (1991) proposed that an organisation would need HRD plans and policies. McCracken and Wallace (2000) argued that these were required to be HRD strategies similar to Ulrich's model of Centres of Excellence/Experts. Peterson (2008) however critiques this and argues that we are in danger of role overload in HR/HRD asking what HRD

(Continued)

(Continued)

superhuman can take on this level of work, pulling HRD specialists in too many ways, both operationally and strategically. Therefore, is it possible for a strategic contribution by the HRD function in light of such heavy operational requirements? Garavan (1991) felt that SHRD should expand the trainer role to be more than it is currently. McCracken and Wallace felt that the role of the trainer should be an organisational change agent. Similar to Ulrich's model (1997) in which he proposes that HRD perform an important role as agents of continuous organisational transformation. Such agents should work within the organisation in order to facilitate change in the organisation to adapt to its changing environment internally and externally, readying the organisation with knowledge and competitive advantage. Peterson (2008) however was critical of this arguing that change is often not strategic and is in fact operational and therefore argues that a more holistic approach must be taken to change. Therefore, it could be argued that SHRD is not able to make a strategic contribution to change through the role of change agents.

Ulrich (1998) argues that in order to deliver organisational excellence, the HRD function must act as partners with senior and line management devolving some of HRD's activities to line management in order for it to be delivered throughout the organisation. Garavan (1999) also argued that line management should be involved in SHRD with McCracken and Wallace (2000) proposing that HRD should forge strategic partnerships with line management in order for the HRD function to make strategic contributions. Peterson (2008) is critical of this however arguing that this devolution to line management fragments the model and in order for the HRD function to add a strategic contribution, these roles need to be clearly outlined.

In order to understand the strategic contribution being made by the HRD function in contemporary organisations, it is necessary to measure the 'added value'. Garavan (2007) outlines that it is important to understand the contribution that SHRD has on the bottom line of the organisation, however Peterson (2008) is critical that this is possible. Ulrich (2007) outlines that value is perceived in the view of the receiver and not the giver. He argues that a multi-stakeholder approach is one which is best in order to assess the added value and therefore, the contribution of the HRD function to contemporary organisations. Peterson (2008) however argues that the models of SHRD only address two of these multi-stakeholders: employees and line management and that external stakeholders are not considered (shareholders and customers in particular). Therefore, it is not possible to measure the added value of SHRD accurately and therefore difficult to examine the strategic contribution being made by HRD.

Westpac Bank is a case study in which you can see an example of SHRD which uses the Ulrich model. Through a centre of expertise in learning and development, they have changed the culture of learning away from classroom style to one in which learning is inherent with the employees' everyday job. Through working with line managers, learning and development have managed to bring learning into everyday roles shaping the culture of the organisation and forming the strategic direction of the organisation through the learning of employees. SHRD is integrated both horizontally and vertically working across a number of departments to lead the strategy of the organisation. Lee (2006) proposed a 6-point scale of SHRD maturity within organisations, with 1 being strategy led and informed by SHRD and 6 being no systemic approach to HRD. This is an example of how SHRD can make a strategic contribution to an organisation through HRD, using SHRD frameworks and models.

Garavan (2007) states that in order for the HRD function to make a strategic contribution within contemporary organisations, there must be 5 underlying assumptions: firstly, its goals must be aligned with that of the organisations and the HRM strategy – this is seen in the Westpac case study. Second, it must be involved in environmental scanning both internally and externally. Third, it must be integrated with HRM policies. Fourth, it must be owned by a number of areas in the organisation – for example, not just HRD, but also line managers and senior leadership in order for it to add real value: this is seen in Ulrich's model of business partners. Fifth, it must add real value to the organisation and must be measurable.

In conclusion, in order for the HRD function to make a strategic contribution in contemporary organisations, it is important to consider Garavan's (2007) five underlying assumptions as well as the context in which the organisation operates. Through the use of various models (Garavan, 1991; McCracken and Wallace, 2000; Ulrich, 1998), it is possible to consider the role that HRD can play in adding a strategic contribution. Peterson (2008) however is critical of this and argues that with many complex models, it is still difficult to define what contributions SHRD can make.

Examiner's comments

Very solid answer that produces a good synthesis of the contributions of the models and criticisms of them. You conduct a good comparison across the three models (Garavan, 1991; McCracken and Wallace, 2000; Peterson, 2008) albeit, you could elaborate further on Garavan's (2007) contribution. That said, you have a good working knowledge of how each of the Strategic HRD models arose as well as the

(Continued)

(Continued)

criticisms levelled at these models. Good case example provided (Westpac Bank), with solid examination of strategic HRD in practice.

Grade

Mid-range Pass

Answer 3

Due to changes in the working environment, including globalisation, advances in technology and fragmented markets, companies need to keep their competitive advantage in order to survive. This has led to a call for HRD to add more value to the business. This is in line with HRM adding more value as more and more companies convert to Ulrich's business partner model to structure their HR departments. As the move to HR becoming more strategic in nature, HRD now also needs to do the same. This has given rise to the concept of strategic HRD (SHRD), which views learning and development as an investment in people rather than a cost to the business. Various authors have written on this topic and introduced SHRD models and frameworks. However, it is important to look closely at these models in order to understand what is happening in practice. This essay will explain some of the key SHRD models and what they are trying to achieve. This will then be critically analysed with what is happening in reality, in order to assess whether SHRD is delivering excellence through Ulrich's framework.

SHRD was brought to organisations' attention in 1991 when Garavan introduced the 9 characteristics a company should possess in order to work in a SHRD nature. The key agenda of SHRD is to add value to the business by investing in the core competencies of employees to ensure their talent is unique and cannot be mimicked by competitors. This will give a company the competitive advantage it needs to have an impact on the bottom line. In order to do this, Garavan (1991) states that HRD must be integrated into the company's overall strategy, be supported by senior management and there must be a correlation with HRM. Furthermore, it is essential that environmental scanning takes place with HRD being the focus. These are some of the characteristics that Garavan introduced in 1991. However, almost a decade later, McCracken and Wallace (2000) refined these 9 characteristics in order to demonstrate how HRD can truly become strategic in nature. For example, instead of HRD being integrated with strategy, they suggest that it should shape the strategy, through focusing on the skills and competencies of their employees. They refine all 9 characteristics in a similar way, for example instead of senior management support, they suggest it should be senior management leadership and that the environmental scanning should be carried out by senior management with HRD being at the centre. McCracken and Wallace (2000) refining of what SHRD is, ensures that HRD is a key stakeholder in strategy implementation and therefore sitting high on Lee's (1996) scale of SHRD maturity. The characteristics of McCracken and Wallace's refinement of SHRD form the basis of their model which puts their characteristics in the SHRD section, whereas Garavan (1991) is described as HRD. This would suggest that Garavan's (1991) model now sits much lower on Lee's (1996) scale – with HRD being placed at level 3, i.e. integrated with strategy but in a reactive nature. Learning and development is called into question after the strategy has been implemented instead of being at the formation stage.

In 2007, Garavan extended his work on SHRD in response to the literature that was presented after 1991. Not only did McCracken and Wallace (2000) introduce a new view of the topic, but various other SHRD models were introduced, for example Harrison's six critical factors and Grieves' work. All of the models are very similar, with true SHRD being place at the level where it can shape organisational strategy. Garavan's (2007) new model describes SHRD as the 'coherent, vertically aligned and horizontally integrated set of learning and development practices that contribute to the organisation's strategy'. The new model is based on four levels of context, both external and internal. It then suggests how HRD needs to react to the context in order to contribute strategically to the organisation. The focus on alignment is essential to Garavan's (2007) model as this is how HRD interacts with key stakeholders in strategy formulation. The horizontal nature of integration is also important as it suggests that the relationships between HRD and line managers are crucial to working in a strategic manner.

Garavan's (2007) model takes account of Ulrich's (1998) framework for delivering excellence and adding value. This is part of the 'SHRD orientation' phase in the model. HRD can position itself in a traditional or employee-focused role, however Ulrich points out that this is operational in nature and will unlikely result in working strategically. However, if HRD takes the strategic partner or change agent orientation, then it will add value to the business by focusing on the strategic aspects of learning and development, such as talent management and succession planning. This also ties in with Lepak et al.'s (2005) domains of HRD – transactional, traditional and transformational. It is argued that transactional learning and development will never add value to the business and strategic HRD operates on the spectrum between traditional to transformational learning and development practices. By working towards transformational HRD, then Ulrich's (1998) framework will succeed and HRD will become strategic in nature and have an impact on the bottom line.

(Continued)

(Continued)

However, although the models presented explain what HRD needs to do in order to become strategic and add value, there are criticisms that must be addressed. Peterson (2008) criticises Garavan's (2007) model. It is suggested that although Garavan has tried to make the model exhaustive, the external and internal influences could render the model too complex to operationalise or test. It is further argued that despite the numerous models introduced, it is still unclear what SHRD actually is or how it can be achieved. Furthermore, it is not addressed as to whether or not HRD is strategic or not actually matters. It is also worth noting that although 'alignment' is a key feature in the SHRD models, there is little empirical evidence that the SHRD models that have been introduced are great in theory, but with little substance in reality. McCracken and Wallace (2000) undertook some further research in order to understand the reality of SHRD. During a study of various organisations from various sectors, it was found that Garavan's (1991) characteristics of SHRD were prominent; however, very little of McCracken and Wallace's refined characteristics were present in companies. The main issue being line management support, which struggled to exist in Garavan's terms, let alone a strategic relationship with line managers as McCracken and Wallace suggested. It was also interesting to see that within the companies that rated themselves as high on the HRD maturity scale (Lee, 1996), the evidence in reality suggested that they were much lower. Furthermore, the CIPD (2007) survey found that only a third of training and learning managers felt that learning and development implications were considered at strategy formation level and of half of the organisations surveyed, HRD was not seen as a key stakeholder in strategy formation. This has further emphasised in recent years due to the economic climate, training budgets have been slashed, which would suggest that HRD is still seen as a 'cost' to the business, rather than an investment.

In conclusion, Ulrich's framework of how HRD can add value is backed with various SHRD models, which puts HRD in the strategy formation stage and a key stakeholder within the business. By achieving this, companies can invest in their current core competencies, giving them a competitive advantage and thus having an impact on the bottom line. However, the models presented have been criticised for being overly complex and not in line with what is happening in reality. It seems that in theory the models presented are the way forward for businesses, however it appears that HRD is still fighting for its position to shape the business strategy and the recent economic downturn has only highlighted HRD as still being viewed as a cost to the business, rather than an investment. Although the CIPD (2012) survey suggests an increase in focus on talent management, etc., the numbers are still low, so HRD has a long journey before becoming truly strategic in nature.

Examiner's comments

Excellent answer. Focused, clear, lucid and well executed. Opening paragraph provides an excellent synthesis of the background to strategic HRD. You show an excellent awareness of criticisms of the SHRD models and how these relate to Ulrich's framework. You also display a good understanding of how SHRD works in practice with reference to some good sources. The answer presented is well framed and takes a high-level overview of the SHRD landscape charting developments in this area of HRD and explaining why these developments took place.

Grade

High Pass

Conclusion

Performing well in HRD examinations requires careful planning and an ability to produce thoughtful, critical answers under time-restrictive conditions. Students should ensure that they construct an outline structure to their answer beforehand, ensuring that key arguments are built comprehensively and supported with reference to both research contributions and practice-based examples. It also helps to keep the student focused in their work and less likely to drift down interesting, but largely irrelevant cul-de-sacs. At its core, students are expected to demonstrate a good awareness and understanding of the key theories and concepts and a capability to critically assess the continued relevance of these concepts to organisational practice.

It is worth remembering that good examination technique is something that can be practised and perfected over time. Recalling particular authors and research contributions will require detailed reading and an ability to trace the development of an area of HRD over time. Students should not be afraid to critique the contributions of key authors, provided that they can substantiate their arguments through reference to other research and/or practice. Finally, on a personal level, I wish you every success in your HRD examination and hope this appendix has been helpful to you in your examination preparation.

References

Abu-Tineh, A.M., Khasawneh, S.A. and Al-Omari, A.A. (2008) Kouzes and Posner's Transformational Leadership Model in Practice: The Case of Jordanian Schools. *Leadership and Organization Development Journal*, 29(8), 648–660.

Ackah, C. and Heaton, N. (2004) The Reality of 'New' Careers for Men and for Women. *Journal of European Industrial Training*, 28(2/3/4), 141–158.

Addesso, P.J. (1996) *Management Would be Easy – If it Weren't for the People*. New York: AMACOM.

Adler, N.J. (1994) Competitive Frontiers: Women Managing Across Borders. *Journal of Management Development*, 13(2), 24–41.

Adler, N.J. and Ghadar, E. (1990) Strategic Human Resource Management: A Global Perspective. In R. Pieper (ed.), *Human Resource Management in International Comparison*. Berlin: de Gruyter.

Adler, N.J., Doktor, R. and Redding, G. (1986) From the Atlantic to the Pacific Century: Cross-cultural Management Reviewed. *Journal of Management*, 12(2), 295–318.

Aguilar, J.L. (1981) Insider Research: An Ethnography of a Debate. In D.A. Messerschmidt (ed.), *Anthropologists at Home in North America*. Cambridge: Cambridge University Press.

Aik, C. and Tway, D.C. (2003) Cognitivism, Constructivism and Work Performance. *Academic Exchange*, 7(3), 274–278.

Alagaraja, M. and Dooley, L.M. (2003) Origins and Historical Influences on Human Resource Development: A Global Perspective. *Human Resource Development Review*, 2(1), 82–96.

Alarcon, C. (2009) Kenco Launches Reduced Packaging Initiative. *Marketing Week*. http://www.marketingweek.co.uk/kenco-launches-reduced-packaging-initiative/3004971.article

Alavi, M and Denford, J.S. (2012) Knowledge Management: Process, Practice and Web 2.0. In M. Easterby-Smith (ed.), *Handbook of Organisational Learning and Knowledge Management*. London: Wiley.

Allred, B.B. and Steensma, H.K. (2005) The Influence of Industry and Home Country Characteristics on Firms' Pursuit of Innovation. *Management International Review*, 45(4), 383–412.

Allen, N.J. and Meyer, I.P. (1990) The Measurement and Antecedents of Affective, Continuance, and Normative Commitment to the Organization, *Journal of Occupational Psychology*, 63(1), 1–18.

Allio, R.J. (2005) Leadership Development: Teaching Versus Learning. *Management Decision*, 43(7/8), 1071–1077.

Alvesson, M. and Deetz, S. (1996) Critical Theory and Postmodernism Approaches to Organizational Studies. In S.R. Clegg, C. Hardy and W.R. Nord (eds), *Handbook of Organization Studies*. London: Sage.

Alvesson, M. and Skoldberg, K. (2000) *Reflexive Methodology*. London: Sage.

Alvesson, M. and Wilmott, H. (1992) Critical Theory and Management Studies: An Introduction. In M. Alvesson and H. Wilmott (eds), *Critical Management Studies*. London: Sage.

Amabile, T.M. (1983) *The Social Psychology of Creativity*. New York: Springer-Verlag.

Amabile, T.M. (1996) *Creativity in Context*. Boulder, CO: Westview Press.

Amabile, T.M. (1998) How to Kill Creativity. *Harvard Business Review*, 76(5), 77–87.

Amabile, T.M. and Conti, R. (1999) Changes in the World Environment for Creativity during Downsizing. *Academy of Management Journal*, 42(6), 630–640.

Amabile, T.M., Barsade, S.G., Mueller, J.S. and Staw, B.M. (2005) Affect and Creativity at Work. *Administrative Science Quarterly*, 50(3), 367–403.

Amabile, T.M., Conti, R., Coon, H., Lazenby, J. and Herron, M. (1996) Assessing the Work Environment for Creativity. *Academy of Management Journal*, 39(5), 1154–1185.

Amabile, T.M., Goldfarb, P. and Brackfield, S.C. (1990) Social Influences on Creativity: Evaluation, Coaction and Surveillance. *Creativity Research Journal*, 3(1), 231–253.

Amabile, T.M., Schatzel, E.A., Moneta, G.B. and Kramer, S.J. (2004) Leader Behaviors and the Work Environment for Creativity: Perceived Leader Support. *The Leadership Quarterly*, 15(1), 5–32.

Anacona, D.G. and Caldwell, D.F. (1992) Demography and Design: Predictors of New Product Team Performance. *Organization Science*, 3(3), 321–341.

Analoui, F. and Karami, A. (2002) How Chief Executives' Perception of the Environment Impacts on Company Performance. *Journal of Management Development*, 21(4), 290–305.

Anand, R. and Winters, M.F. (2008) A Retrospective View of Corporate Diversity Training from 1964 to Present. *Academy of Management Learning and Education*, 7(3), 356–372.

Anderson, B. (1999) Industrial Benchmarking for Competitive Advantage. *Human Systems Management*, 18(3/4), 287–296.

Anderson, J.R. (1993) Problem Solving and Learning. *American Psychologist*, 48(1), 35–44.

Anderson, J.R. (2000) *Cognitive Psychology and its Implications*. New York: Worth Publishers.

Anderson, V. (2007) Desperately Seeking Alignment: Reflections of Senior Line Managers and HRD Executives. *Human Resource Development International*, 12(3), 263–277.

An Inconvenient Truth (2006) Directed by Guggenheim, D. [DVD]. Los Angeles: Paramount Home Entertainment.

Andresen, M. (2007) Diversity Learning, Knowledge Diversity and Inclusion: Theory and Practice as Exemplified by Corporate Universities. *Equal Opportunities International*, 26(8), 743–760.

Andrews, F.M. and Farris, G.F. (1967) *Supervisory Practices and Innovation of Scientific Teams*. Paper presented at the Proceedings of the American Psychological Association.

Ardichvili, A. (2012) Sustainability or Limitless Expansion: Paradigm Shift in HRD Practice and Teaching. *European Journal of Training and Development*, 36(9), 873–887.

Ardichvili, A. and Kuchinke, K.P. (2002) The Concept of Culture in International and Comparative HRD Research: Methodological Problems and Possible Solutions. *Human Resource Development Review*, 1(2), 145–166.

Ardichvili, A., Page, V. and Wentling, T. (2003) Motivation and Barriers to Participation in Virtual Knowledge-sharing Communities of Practice. *Journal of Knowledge Management*, 7(1), 64–77.

Argyris, C. (1996) Prologue: Toward a Comprehensive Theory of Management. In B. Moingeon and A. Edmondson (eds), *Organizational Learning and Competitive Advantage*. London: Sage.

Argyris, C. (1999) *On Organizational Learning*, 2nd edn. Oxford: Blackwell.

Argyris, C. and Schon, D.A. (1974) *Theory in Practice: Increasing Professional Effectiveness*. San Francisco, CA: Jossey-Bass.

Argyris, C. and Schon, D.A. (1978) *Organisational Learning*. Reading, MA: Addison-Wesley.

Armagan, S. and Ferreira, M.P. (2005) The Impact of Political Culture on Firms' Choice of Exploitation-Exploration: Internationalization Strategy. *International Journal of Cross Cultural Management*, 5(3), 275–292.

Armstrong, M. (1999) *A Handbook of Human Resource Management Practice*. London: Kogan Page.

Arnold, J. (1997) *Managing Careers into the 21st Century*. London: Paul Chapman.

Arthur, M.B. and Rousseau, D.M. (eds) (1996) *The Boundaryless Career: A New Employment Principle for a New Organizational Era*. Oxford: Oxford University Press.

Arthur, M.B., Hall, D.T. and Lawrence, B.S. (1989) Generating New Directions in Career Theory: The Case for a Transdisciplinary Approach. In M.B. Arthur, D.T. Hall and B.S. Lawrence (eds), *The Handbook of Career Theory*. Cambridge: Cambridge University Press.

Arthur, M.B., Khapova, S.N. and Wilderom, C.P.M. (2005) Career Success in a Boundaryless Career World. *Journal of Organizational Behavior*, 26(2), 177–202.

Arvidsson, N. (1997) Internationalisation of Service Firms: Strategic Considerations. In G. Chryssochoidis, C. Millar and J. Clegg (eds), *Internationalisation Strategies*. London: Macmillan.

Atkinson, H. (2006) Strategy Implementation: A Role for the Balanced Scorecard? *Management Decision*, 44(10), 144–160.

Avolio, B.J. (2007) Promoting more Integrative Strategies for Leadership Theory-building. *American Psychologist*, 62(1), 25–33.

Azzone, G. and Noci, G. (1998) Seeing Ecology and 'Green' Innovations as a Source of Change. *Journal of Organizational Change Management*, 11(2), 94–112.

Bachkirova, T., Cox, E. and Clutterbuck, D. (2013) Introduction. In E. Cox, T. Bachkirova and D. Clutterbuck (eds), *The Complete Handbook of Coaching*. London: Sage.

Baer, M., Oldham, G.R. and Cummings, A. (2003) Rewarding Creativity: When Does it Really Matter? *The Leadership Quarterly*, 14(4), 569–586.

Bairstow, S. and Skinner, H. (2007) Internal Marketing and the Enactment of Sexual Identity. *Equal Opportunities International*, 26(7), 653–664.

Baldwin, T.T. and Ford, J.K. (1988) Transfer of Training: A Review and Directions for Future Research. *Personnel Review*, 26(3), 201–213.

Bandura, A. (1977) *Social Learning Theory*. Englewood Cliffs, NJ: Prentice Hall.

Bandura, A. (2002) Social Cognitive Theory in Cultural Context. *Applied Psychology: An International Review*, 51, 269–290.

Barbosa, I. and Cabral-Cardoso, C. (2007) Managing Diversity in Academic Organisations: A Challenge to Organisational Culture. *Women in Management Review*, 22(4), 274–288.

Barrett, I.C., Cervero, R.M. and Johnson-Bailey, J. (2004) The Career Development of Black Human Resource Developers in the United States. *Human Resource Development International*, 7(1), 85–100.

Barrie, J. and Pace, R.W. (1998) Learning for Organisational Effectiveness: Philosophy of Education and Human Resource Development. *Human Resource Development Quarterly*, 9(1), 39–54.

Barron, F. and Harrington, D.M. (1981) Creativity, Intelligence and Personality. *Annual Review of Psychology*, 32, 439–476.

Bartlett, C.A. and Ghoshal, S. (1998) *Managing across Borders: The Transnational Solution*, 2nd edn. Boston, MA: Harvard Business School Press.

Bartlett, C.A., Ghoshal, S. and Birkinshaw, J. (2004) *Transnational Management: Text, Cases and Readings in Cross-border Management*. Boston, MA: McGraw-Hill.

Bartlett, K.R., Lawler, J.J., Bae, J., Chen, S. and Wan, D. (2002) Differences in International Human Resource Development among Indigenous Firms and Multinational Affiliates in East and Southeast Asia. *Human Resource Development Quarterly*, 13(4), 383–405.

Baruch, Y. (2004) *Managing Careers: Theory and Practice*. Harlow: Pearson.

Bass, B.M. (1985) *Leadership and Performance Beyond Expectations*. New York: Free Press.

Bass, B.M. (1990) *Bass and Stogdill's Handbook of Leadership*, 3rd edn. New York: Free Press.

Bass, B.M. and Avolio, B.J. (1994) *Improving Organizational Effectiveness Through Transformational Leadership*. London: Sage.

Bass, B.M., Avolio, B.J. and Goodheim, L. (1987) Biography and the Assessment of Transformational Leadership at the World-class Level. *Journal of Management*, 13(1), 7–19.

Bassi, L.J and Van Buren, M.E. (1999) The 1999 ASTD State of the Industry Report. *Training and Development*, 53(1), 23–33.

Bates, R. (2004) A Critical Analysis of Evaluation Practice: The Kirkpatrick Model and the Principle of Beneficence. *Evaluation and Program Planning*, 27(3), 341–348.

Baumard, P. (1999) *Tacit Knowledge in Organisations*. London: Sage.

Bazerman, M.H. (1994) *Judgment in Decision-making*. New York: Wiley.

Beattie, R.S. (2006) Line Managers and Workplace Learning: Learning from the Voluntary Sector. *Human Resource Development International*, 9(1), 99–119.

Beaver, G. and Hutchings, K. (2004) The Big Business of Strategic Human Resource Management in Small Business. In J. Stewart and G. Beaver (eds), *HRD in Small Organizations: Research and Practice*. London: Routledge.

Bednar, A.K., Cunningham, D., Duffy, T.M. and Perry, J.D. (1991) Theory into Practice: How Do We Link? Instructional Technology: Past, Present and Future. In G. Anglin (ed.), *Instructional Technology*. Englewood, CO: Libraries Unlimited.

Belis-Bergouignan, M.C., Bordenave, G. and Lung, Y. (2000) Global Strategies in the Automobile Industry. *Regional Studies*, 34(1), 41–54.

Benjamin, A. (1994) Affordable Restructured Education: A Solution through Information Technology. *RSA Journal*, (May), 45–49.

Berge, Z., de Verneil, M., Berge, N., Davis, L. and Smith, D. (2002) The Increasing Scope of Training and Development Competency. *Benchmarking*, 9(1), 43–61.

Bergenhenegouwen, G.J. (1990) The Management and Effectiveness of Corporate Training Programmes. *British Journal of Educational Technology*, 21(3), 196–202.

Berggren, C. (1996) Building a Truly Global Organisation? ABB and the Problems of Integrating a Multi-domestic Enterprise. *Journal of Management*, 12(2), 123–137.

Bernard, L.L. (1926) *An Introduction to Social Psychology*. New York: Holt.

Beyer, L.E. (2001) The Value of Critical Perspectives in Teacher Education. *Journal of Teacher Education*, 52(2), 151–163.

Bhutta, K.S. and Huq, F. (1999) Benchmarking – Best Practices: An Integrated Approach. *Benchmarking: An International Journal*, 6(3), 254–268.

Bibby, P.A. and Payne, S.J. (1996) Instruction and Practice in Learning to Use a Device. *Cognitive Science*, 20(4), 539–578.

Bierema, L.L. (1997) Development of the Individual Leads to a More Productive Workplace. In R. Rowden (ed.), *Workplace Learning: Debating Five Critical Questions of Theory and Practice*. San Francisco, CA: Jossey-Bass.

Bierema, L.L. (2009) Critiquing Human Resource Development's Dominant Masculine Rationality and Evaluating its Impact. *Human Resource Development Review*, 8(1), 68–96.

Bierema, L.L. and Cseh, M. (2003) Evaluating AHRD Research Using a Feminist Research Framework. *Human Resource Development Quarterly*, 14(1), 5–26.

Bierema, L.L. and D'Abundo, M.L. (2004) HRD with a Conscience: Practising Socially Responsible HRD. *International Journal of Lifelong Education*, 23(5), 443–458.

Biggs, J. (2003) *Teaching for Quality Learning at University*. London: Open University Press and Society for Research into Higher Education.

Billet, S. (1999) Guided Learning at Work. In D. Boud and J. Garrick (eds), *Understanding Learning at Work*. London: Routledge.

Bing, J.W., Kehrhahn, M.T. and Short, D.C. (2003) Challenges to the Field of Human Resource Development. *Advances in Developing Human Resources*, 5(3), 342–351.

Blackler, F. (1995) Knowledge, Knowledge Work and Organisations: An Overview and Interpretation. *Organisation Studies,* 16(6), 1021–1049.

Blackman, D. and Henderson, S. (2005) Why Learning Organisations Do Not Transform. *The Learning Organisation*, 12(1), 42–56.

Blake, M.K. and Hanson, S. (2005) Rethinking Innovation: Context and Gender. *Environment and Planning*, 37(4), 681–701.

Blake, R.R. (1995) Memories of HRD. *Training and Development*, 49 (March), 22–28.

Blake, R.R. and McCanse, A.A. (1991) *Leadership Dilemmas: Grid Solutions*. Houston, TX: Gulf Publishing Co.

Blake, R.R. and Mouton, J.S. (1964) *The Managerial Grid: The Key to Leadership Excellence*. Houston, TX: Gulf Publishing Co.

Blake-Scontrino, P. and Schafer, M. (2012) *HRD Practitioners as Change Agents within the Sustainability Strategic Domain*. Paper presented at the Academy of Human Resource Development Conference in the Americas, Denver, Colorado, 29 February–3 March.

Blankenship, S.S. and Ruona, W.E.A. (2009) Exploring Knowledge Sharing in Social Structures: Potential Contributions to an Overall Knowledge Management Strategy. *Advances in Developing Human Resources*, 11(3), 290–306.

Blanton, B.B. (1998) The Application of the Cognitive Learning Theory to Instructional Design. *International Journal of Instructional Media*, 25(2), 171–177.

Bligh, M.C., Pearce, C.L. and Kohles, J.C. (2006) The Importance of Self and Shared Leadership in Team Based Knowledge Work: A Meso Level Model of Leadership Dynamics. *Journal of Managerial Psychology*, 21(4), 296–318.

Bluckert, P. (2005) Critical Factors in Executive Coaching: The Coaching Relationship. *Industrial and Commercial Training*, 37(7), 336–340.

Blue Angel (2013) The Blue Angel: Active in Climate Protection. http://www.blauer-engel.de/en/index.php

Boaden, R.J. (2006) Leadership Development: Does it Make a Difference? *Leadership and Organization Development Journal*, 27(1), 5–27.

Boak, G. and Coolican, D. (2001) Competencies for Retail Leadership: Accurate, Acceptable, Affordable. *Leadership and Organisational Development Journal*, 22(5), 212–220.

Boiral, O. (2009) Greening the Corporation through Organisational Citizenship Behaviours. *Journal of Business Ethics*, 87(2), 221–236.

Bokeno, R.M. (2003) Introduction: Appraisals of Organisational Learning as Emancipatory Change. *Journal of Organizational Change Management*, 16(3), 603–618.

Boud, D. and Garrick, J. (1999) *Understanding Learning at Work*. London: Routledge.

Boulaksil, Y. and Fransoo, J.C. (2010) Implications of Outsourcing on Operations Planning: Findings from the Pharmaceutical Industry. *International Journal of Operations and Production Management*, 30(10), 1059–1079.

Boyatzis, R.E. (1982) *The Competent Manager: A Guide for Effective Management*. New York: Wiley.

Boyatzis, R.E. and Kolb, D.N. (1995) From Learning Styles to Learning Skills: The Executive Skills Profile. *Journal of Managerial Psychology*, 10(5), 24–27.

Bramley, P. (1996) *Evaluating Training Effectiveness*. Maidenhead: McGraw-Hill.

Bramming, P. (2004) *The One and the Many: Contemplating Conceptions of Individual and Organisation in Relation to Human Resource Practices*. Paper presented at Fifth European Conference on Human Resource Development Theory and Practice, University of Limerick, Ireland.

Brim, O.G. and Wheeler, S. (1966) *Socialisation after Childhood: Two Essays*. New York: Wiley.

Brinkerhoff, R.O. (2003) *The Success Case Method: Find Out Quickly What's Working and What's Not*. San Francisco, CA: Berrett-Koehler.

Brinkerhoff, R.O. (2006a) Increasing Impact of Training Investments: An Evaluation Strategy for Building Organisational Learning Capability. *Industrial and Commercial Training*, 38(6), 302–307.

Brinkerhoff, R.O. (2006b) Using Evaluation to Measure and Improve the Effectiveness of Human Performance Technology Initiatives. In J.A. Pershing (ed.), *Handbook of Human Performance Technology*. San Francisco, CA: Wiley.

Brinkerhoff, R. and Montesino, M. (1995) Partnerships for Transfer of Training: Lessons from a Corporate Study. *Human Resource Development Quarterly*, 6(3), 263–274.

Brookfield, S.D. (2003) *The Concept of Critically Reflective Practice*. San Francisco, CA: Jossey-Bass.

Brosnan, K. and Burgess, R.C. (2003) Web-based Continuing Professional Development: A Learning Architecture Approach. *Journal of Workplace Learning*, 15(1), 24–33.

Brown, J.S. and Duguid, P. (2001) Knowledge and Organization: A Social-practice Perspective. *Organization Science*, 12(2), 198–213.

Brown, T.C. and McCracken, M. (2004) *The Relationship between Managerial Barriers to Learning and Transfer of Training: Preliminary Results*. Paper presented at Fifth European Conference on Human Resource Development Theory and Practice, University of Limerick, Ireland.

Brown, T.C. and Morrissey L. (2004) The Effectiveness of Verbal Self-guidance as a Transfer of Training. *Innovations in Education and Teaching International*, 41(3), 255–271.

Browne, I. and Misra, J. (2003) The Intersection of Gender and Race in the Labor Market. *Annual Review of Sociology*, 29, 487–513.

Bruce, R.W. (1933) Conditions of Transfer of Training. *Journal of Experiential Psychology*, 6, 343–361.

Bryans, P. and Smith, R. (2000) Beyond Training: Reconceptualising Learning at Work. *Journal of Workplace Learning*, 12(6), 228–235.

Burkitt, I. (1991) *Social Selves: Theories of the Social Formation of Personality*. London: Sage.

Burns, J.M. (1978) *Leadership*. New York: Harper & Row.

Burrow, J. and Berardinelli, P. (2003) Systematic Performance Improvement: Refining the Space Between Learning and Results. *Journal of Workplace Learning*, 15(1), 6–14.

Business in the Community (2009) *2009 Benchmarking Report: Transparency at the Heart of Diversity*. London: Business in the Community.

Cabrera, E.F. (2009) Protean Organizations: Reshaping Work and Careers to Retain Female Talent. *Career Development International*, 14(2), 186–201.

Callahan, J.L. (2007) Gazing into the Crystal Ball: Critical HRD as a Future of Research in the Field. *Human Resource Development International*, 10(1), 77–82.

Callahan, J. and Dunne de Davila, T. (2004) An Impressionistic Framework for Theorizing Human Resource Development. *Human Resource Development Review*, 3(1), 75–95.

Campbell, C.P. (1994) A Primer on Determining the Cost Effectiveness of Training – Part 1. *Industrial and Commercial Training*, 26(11), 32–38.

Campbell, C.P. (1998) Training Course/Program Evaluation: Principles and Practice. *Journal of European Industrial Training*, 22(8), 323–344.

Cappelli, P. and Singh, H. (1992) Integrating Strategic Human Resources and Strategic Management. In D. Lewin, O. Mitchell and P. Shewer (eds), *Research Frontiers in Industrial Relations and Human Resources*. Madison: Industrial Relations Association, University of Wisconsin.

Carbon Trust (2013) Carbon Footprint Labels from the Carbon Trust. http://www.carbontrust.com/client-services/footprinting/footprint-certification/carbon-footprint-label

Cardona, P. (2000) Transcendental Leadership. *Leadership and Organisational Development Journal*, 21(4), 201–207.

Carroll, A.B. (1979) A Three-dimensional Conceptual Model of Corporate Performance. *Academy of Management Review*, 4(4), 497–505.

Carroll, A.B. (1999) Corporate Social Responsibility: Evolution of a Definitional Construct. *Business and Society*, 38(3), 268–296.

Carter, S.D. (2002) Matching Training Methods and Factors of Cognitive Ability: A Means to Improve Training Outcomes. *Human Resource Development Quarterly*, 13(1), 71–87.

Cavanagh, J.M. (2004) Head Games: Introducing Tomorrow's Business Elites to Institutionalised Inequality. In C. Grey and E. Antonacopoulou (eds), *Essential Readings in Management Learning*. London: Sage.

Chakravarthy, B.S. (1985) Measuring Strategic Performance. *Strategic Management Journal*, 7(5), 437–457.

Chalofsky, N. (1992) A Unifying Definition for the Human Resource Development Profession. *Human Resource Development Quarterly*, 3(2), 175–182.

Chalofsky, N. (2004) *Human and Organization Studies: The Discipline of HRD*. Paper presented at the Academy of Human Resource Development Conference, Austin, Texas.

Chalofsky, N. and Lincoln, C. (1983) *Up the HRD Ladder*. Reading, MA: Addison-Wesley.

Chan, T.Y. and Wong, C.W.Y. (2012) The Consumption Side of Sustainable Fashion Supply Chain: Understanding Fashion Consumer Eco-fashion Consumption Decision. *Journal of Fashion Marketing and Management*, 16(2), 193–215.

Chang, E. and Taylor, M.S. (1999) Control in Multinational Corporations (MNCs): The Case of Korean Manufacturing Subsidiaries. *Journal of Management*, 25(4), 541–553.

Chang, L.C. (2007) The NHS Performance Assessment Framework as a Balanced Scorecard Approach: Limitations and Implications. *International Journal of Public Sector Management*, 20(2), 101–117.

Chen, C. (1998) Understanding Career Development: A Convergence of Perspectives. *Journal of Vocational Education and Training*, 50(3), 437–461.

Cheng, E.W.L. and Ho, D.C.K. (2001) A Review of Transfer of Training Studies in the Past Decade. *Personnel Review*, 30(1), 102–118.

Chermack, T.J. and Lynham, S.A. (2002) Definitions and Outcome Variables of Scenario Planning. *Human Resource Development Review*, 1(1), 366–383.

Childs, M. (2005) Beyond Training: New Firefighters and Critical Reflection. *Disaster Prevention and Management*, 14(4), 558–566.

Chimombo, M.P. and Roseberry, R.L. (1998) *The Power of Discourse*. Mahwah, NJ: Lawrence Erlbaum.

Cho, D.Y. and Kwon, D.B. (2005) Self-directed Learning Readiness as an Antecedent of Organisational Commitment: A Korean Study. *International Journal of Training and Development*, 9(2), 140–152.

Cho, E. and McLean, G.N. (2004) What We Discovered about NHRD and What it Means for HRD. *Advances in Developing Human Resources*, 6(3), 382–391.

Choo, C.W. (1996) The Knowing Organisation: How Organisations Can Use Information to Construct Meaning, Create Knowledge and Make Decisions. *International Journal of Information Management*, 16(5), 329–340.

Choy, W.K.W. (2007) Globalisation and Workforce Diversity: HRM Implications for Multinational Corporations in Singapore. *Singapore Management Review*, 29(2), 1–20.

CIPD (Chartered Institute of Personnel and Development) (2007a) *The Changing HR Function: Survey Report*. London: CIPD.

CIPD (Chartered Institute of Personnel and Development) (2007b) *The Value of Learning: A New Model of Value and Evaluation*. London: CIPD.

CIPD (Chartered Institute of Personnel and Development) (2008a) *Annual Survey Report: Learning and Development*. London: CIPD.

CIPD (Chartered Institute of Personnel and Development) (2008b) *The Environment and People Management*. London: CIPD.

CIPD (Chartered Institute of Personnel and Development) (2013a) Evaluating Learning and Talent Development. http://www.cipd.co.uk/hr-resources/factsheets/evaluating-learning-tal-ent-development.aspx#link_cipd_view

CIPD (Chartered Institute of Personnel and Development) (2013b) CIPD 'RAM' Approach to Evaluation. http://www.cipd.co.uk/hr-resources/factsheets/identifying-learning-talent-development-needs.aspx

Clark, C.S., Dobbins, G.H. and Ladd, R.T. (1993) Exploratory Field Study of Training Motivation: Influence of Involvement, Credibility and Transfer Climate. *Group and Organisation Management*, 18(3), 292–307.

Clark, R.E., Blake, S.B., Tennyson, R.D., Schott, F., Seel, N. and Dijkstra, S. (1997) Designing Training for Novel Problem Solving Transfer. In R.D. Tennyson, F. Schott, N. Seel and S. Dijkstra (eds), *Instructional Design: International Perspectives*. Mahwah, NJ: Lawrence Erlbaum.

Clarke, N. (2005) Workplace Learning Environment and Its Relationship with Learning Outcomes in Healthcare Organisations. *Human Resource Development International*, 8(2), 185–206.

Clutterbuck, D. (2004) *Everybody Needs a Mentor*, 4th edn. London: CIPD.

Clutterbuck, D. (2008) What's Happening in Coaching and Mentoring? And What is the Difference between Them. *Development and Learning in Organizations*, 22(4), 8–10.

Coad, F.C. and Berry, A.J. (1998) Transformational Leadership and Learning Organization. *Leadership and Organization Development Journal*, 19(3), 164–172.

Coakes, E. (2006) Storing and Sharing Knowledge: Supporting the Management of Knowledge Made Explicit in Transnational Organisations. *The Learning Organisation*, 13(6), 579–593.

Cohen, E. and Tichy, N. (1997) How Leaders Develop Leaders. *Training and Development*, 51(5), 58–73.

Colgan, F., Creegan, C., McKearney, A. and Wright, T. (2007) Equality and Diversity Policies and Practices at Work: Lesbian, Gay and Bisexual Workers. *Equal Opportunities International*, 26(6), 590–609.

Collings, D.G. (2003) HRD and Labour Market Practices in a US Multinational Subsidiary: The Impact of Global and Local Influences. *Journal of European Industrial Training*, 27(2/3/4), 188–200.

Collins, D. (2002) Performance-level Evaluation Methods Used in Management Development Studies from 1986 to 2000. *Human Resource Development Review*, 1(1), 91–110.

Communications, B. (2001) How Frequently Will You Use These Training Delivery Methods This Year? *Training*, 38(1), 118.

Competitiveness (1996) *Creating the Enterprise Centre of Europe*. London: DTI Publications.

Conley, C.A. and Zheng, W. (2009) Factors Critical to Knowledge Management Success. *Advances in Developing Human Resources*, 11(3), 290–306.

Conlon, T.J. (2004) A Review of Informal Learning Literature: Theory and Implications for Practice in Developing Global Professional Competence. *Journal of European Industrial Training*, 28(2/3/4), 283–295.

Connelly, B., Hitt, M.A., DeNisi, A.S. and Ireland, R.D. (2007) Expatriates and Corporate-level International Strategy: Governing with the Knowledge Contract. *Management Decision*, 45(3), 564–581.

Cooke, W. and Noble, D. (1998) Industrial Relations Systems and U.S. Foreign Direct Investment Abroad. *British Journal of Industrial Relations*, 36(4), 581–598.

Cooley, C.H. (1909) *Social Organisation: A Study of the Larger Mind*. New York: Charles Scribner's Sons.

Cooley, C.H. (1922) *Human Nature and the Social Order*. New York: Charles Scribner's Sons.

Cooper, L., Orrell, J. and Bowden, M. (2010) *Work Integrated Learning: A Guide to Effective Practice*. London: Routledge.

Coren, S. (2003) Sensation and Perception. In D.K. Freedheim, W.F. Velicer, J.A. Schinka and R.M. Lerner (eds), *Handbook of Psychology* (Vol. 1, *History of Psychology*). Hoboken, NJ: Wiley & Sons.

Costa, P.T. and McCrae, R.R. (1992) *Revised NEO Personality Inventory (NEO-PI-R) and NEO Five-factor Inventory (NEO-FFI) Manual*. Odessa, FL: Psychological Assessment Resources.

Cox, T.H. and Blake, S. (1991) Managing Cultural Diversity: Implications for Organisational Competitiveness. *Academy of Management Executive*, 5(3), 45–57.

Craddock, M. (2004) *The Authentic Career: Following the Path of Self-discovery to Professional Fulfillment*. Novato, CA: New World Library.

Cradle-to-Cradle Products Innovation Institute (2013) Cradle to Cradle Certification. http://www.c2ccertified.org/product_certification

Craig, R. (1976) *Training and Development Handbook*, 2nd edn. New York: McGraw-Hill.

Cseh, M., Watkins, K. and Marsick, V. (1999) *Reconceptualising Marsick and Watkins Model of Informal and Incidental Learning in the Workplace*. Paper presented at the Proceedings of the Academy of Human Resource Development Conference, Baton Rouge, Louisiana.

Csikszentmihalyi, M. (1988) Society, Culture and Person: A Systems View of Creativity. In R.J. Sternberg (ed.), *The Nature of Creativity*. Cambridge: Cambridge University Press.

Csikszentmihalyi, M. (1996) *Creativity: Flow and the Psychology of Discovery and Invention*. New York: HarperCollins.

Csikszentmihalyi, M. (1999) Implications of a System Perspective for the Study of Creativity. In R.J. Sternberg (ed.), *Handbook of Creativity*. Cambridge: Cambridge University Press.

Cummings, T.G. and Worley, C.G. (2001) *Essentials of Organisational Development and Change*. New York: South Western College Publishing.

Cunningham, I. and Hyman, J. (1995) Transforming the HR Vision into Reality: The Role of Line Managers and Supervisors in Implementing Change. *Employee Relations*, 17(8), 5–20.

D'Abate, C.P., Eddy, E.R. and Tannenbaum, S.I. (2003) What's in a Name: A Literature-based Approach to Understanding Mentoring, Coaching and Other Constructs that Describe Developmental Interactions. *Human Resource Development Review*, 2(4), 360–385.

Daniels, K., De Chernatony, L. and Johnson, G. (1995) Validating a Method of Mapping Managers' Mental Models of Competitive Industry Structures. *Human Relations*, 48(8), 975–991.

Davenport, T. and Prusak, L. (1998) *Working Knowledge: How Organisations Manage What They Know*. Cambridge, MA: Harvard Business School Press.

Davies, A.J. and Kochhar, A.K. (2002) Manufacturing Best Practice and Performance Studies: A Critique. *International Journal of Operations and Production Management*, 22(3), 289–305.

Day, S.X. and Rounds, J. (1998) Universality of Vocational Interest Structure among Racial and Ethnic Minorities. *American Psychologist*, 53(7), 728–736.

DeBusk, G.K., Brown, R.M. and Killough, L.N. (2003) Components and Relative Weights in Utilisation of Dashboard Measurement Systems like the Balanced Scorecard. *British Accounting Review*, 35(3), 215–231.

Deci, E.L. and Ryan, R.M. (1985) *Intrinsic Motivation and Self-determination in Human Behavior*. New York: Plenum.

De Dreu, C.K.W. and West, M.A. (2001) Minority Dissent and Team Innovation: The Importance of Participation in Decision Making. *Journal of Applied Psychology*, 86(6), 1191–1201.

Dehler, G.E., Welsh, A. and Lewis, M.W. (2001) Critical Pedagogy in the 'New Paradigm'. *Management Learning*, 32(4), 493–511.

Delpachitra, S. and Beal, D. (2002) Process Benchmarking: An Application to Lending Products. *Benchmarking: An International Journal*, 9(4), 409–420.

Demarest, M. (1997) Understanding Knowledge Management. *Long Range Planning*, 30(3), 374–384.

Densten, I.L. and Gray, J.H. (2001) Leadership Development and Reflection: What is the Connection. *International Journal of Educational Management*, 15(3), 119–124.

De Pablos, P.O. (2004) Knowledge Flow Transfers in Multinational Corporations: Knowledge Properties and Implications for Management. *Journal of Knowledge Management*, 8(6), 105–116.

Dewey, J. (1916) *Democracy and Education: An Introduction to the Philosophy of Education*. New York: Free Press.

Dewey, J. (1933) *How We Think*. Boston, MA: Heath.

Dick, P. and Cassell, C. (2002) Barriers to Managing Diversity in the UK Constabulary: The Role of Discourse. *Journal of Management Studies*, 39(7), 953–976.

Dick, W., Carey, L. and Carey, J.O. (2001) *The Systematic Design of Instruction*. New York: Addison-Wesley.

Dilworth, L. (2003) Searching for the Future of HRD. *Advances in Developing Human Resources*, 5(3), 241–244.

Dionne, P. (1996) The Evaluation of Training Activities: A Complex Issues Involving Different Stakes. *Human Resource Development Quarterly*, 7(3), 279–299.

Dixon, N.M. (1999) *The Organisational Learning Cycle: How Can We Learn Collectively*, 2nd edn. Aldershot: Gower.

Doh, J. (2003) Can Leadership be Taught? Perspectives from Management Educators. *Academy of Management Learning and Education*, 2(1), 54–67.

Donelan, H., Herman, C., Kear, K. and Kirkup, G. (2009) Patterns of Online Networking for Women's Career Development. *Gender in Management: An International Journal*, 24(2), 92–111.

Donnellon, A. (1986) Language and Communication within Organisations: Building Cognition and Behaviour. In H.P. Sims and D.A. Gioia (eds), *The Thinking Organisation*. San Francisco, CA: Jossey-Bass.

Donovan, L.L. and Marsick, V.J. (2000) *Trends in Literature: A Comparative Analysis of 1998 HRD Research*. Paper presented at the Annual Academy of Human Resource Development (AHRD), Baton Rouge, Louisiana.

Doran, M. (2005) HRD and Business Ethics. http://www.ahrd.org/conference

Dougherty, D. and Hardy, C. (1996) Sustained Product Innovation in Large, Mature Organizations: Overcoming Innovation-to-Organization Problems. *Academy of Management Journal*, 39(5), 1120–1153.

Douglas, M. (1986) *How Institutions Think*. Syracuse, NY: Syracuse University Press.

Dulewicz, V. and Higgs, M. (2004) Can Emotional Intelligence be Developed? *International Journal of Human Resource Management*, 15(1), 95–111.

Duncan, S.J. (1972) Some Signals and Rules for Taking Speaking Turns in Conversation. *Journal of Personality and Social Psychology*, 23(2), 283–292.

Duncan, W.J. (1984) Planning and Evaluating Management Education and Development: Why So Little Attention to Such Basic Concerns? *Journal of Management Development*, 2(4), 57–68.

Dunning, J.H. (1993) *The Globalisation of Business*. London: Routledge.

Durkheim, E. (1954) *The Elementary Forms of Religious Life*. Chicago: The Free Press.

Dye, R.W. (2003) Keeping Score. *CMA Management*, (December/January), 18–23.

Easterby-Smith, M. (1986) *Evaluation of Management Education, Training and Development*. Aldershot: Gower.

Edmondson, A. and Moingeon, B. (1996) When to Learn How and When to Learn Why: Appropriate Organizational Learning Processes as a Source of Competitive Advantage. In B. Moingeon and A. Edmondson (eds), *Organizational Learning and Competitive Advantage*. London: Sage.

Edvinsson, L. (1997) Measuring Intellectual Capital at Skandia. *Long Range Planning*, 30(3), 266–273.

Edvinsson, L. and Malone, M.S. (1997) *Intellectual Capital: Realizing Your Company's True Value by Finding its Hidden Brainpower*. New York: Harper Business.

Edwards, T. and Ferner, A. (2002) The Renewed American Challenge: A Review of Employment Practices in US Multinationals. *Industrial Relations Journal*, 33(2), 94–111.

Egan, T.M. (2005) Factors Influencing Individual Creativity in the Workplace: An Examination of Quantitative Empirical Research. *Advances in Developing Human Resources*, 7(2), 160–182.

Ehigie, B.O. and Akpan, R.C. (2004) Roles of Perceived Leadership Styles and Rewards in the Practice of Total Quality Management. *Leadership and Organisation Development Journal*, 25(1), 24–41.

Ehrich, L.C. (2008) Mentoring and Women Managers: Another Look at the Field. *Gender in Management: An International Journal*, 23(7), 469–483.

Eisenberger, R., Fasolo, P. and Davis-LaMastro, V. (1990) Perceived Organisational Support and Employee Diligence, Commitment and Innovation. *Journal of Applied Psychology*, 75(1), 51–59.

Elangovan, A.R. and Karakowsky, L. (1999) The Role of Trainee and Environmental Factors in Transfer of Training: An Exploratory Framework. *Leadership and Organisation Development Journal*, 20(5), 268–275.

Ellinger, A.D., Ellinger, A.E., Yang, B. and Howton, S.W. (2002) The Relationship between the Learning Organization Concept and Firms' Financial Performance: An Empirical Assessment. *Human Resource Development Quarterly*, 13(1), 23–29.

Elliot, R. (1996) Discourse Analysis: Exploring Action, Function and Conflict in Social Texts. *Marketing Intelligence and Planning*, 14(6), 12–26.

Elliott, C. (2003) Representations of the Intellectual: Insights from Gramsci on Management Education. *Management Learning*, 34(4), 411–427.

Ellis, E. (2012) Environments are Not Constraints. http://www.thisisafricaonline.com/Comment/Environments-are-not-constraints?ct=true

Elsbach, K.D. and Kramer, R.M. (2003) Assessing Creativity in Hollywood Pitch Meetings: Evidence for a Dual-process Model of Creativity Judgments. *Academy of Management Journal*, 46(3), 283–301.

Engle, A.D., Mendenhall, M.D., Powers, R.L. and Stedham, Y. (2001) Conceptualising the Global Competency Cube: A Transnational Model of Human Resources. *Journal of European Industrial Training*, 25(7), 346–353.

Environmental Protection Agency (EPA) (2010) Pollution Prevention (P2). http://www.epa.gov/p2/index.htm

Eraut, M. (2004) Transfer of Knowledge between Education and Workplace Settings. In H. Rainbird, A. Fuller and A. Munro (eds), *Workplace Learning in Context*. London: Routledge.

Eraut, M., Alderton, J., Cole, G. and Senker, P. (1998) *Development of Knowledge and Skills in Employment*. Final report of a research project funded by 'The Learning Society' Programme of the Economic and Social Research Council. Institute of Education, University of Essex.

Etherington, K. (2004) *Becoming a Reflective Researcher*. London: Jessica Kingsley.

Evarts, T.M. (1998) Human Resource Development as a Maturing Field of Study. *Human Resource Development Quarterly*, 9(4), 385–391.

Faifua, D. (2008) Democratic Reason and Practice: Repositioning Community Aspirations. *Journal of Organisational Change Management*, 21(4), 511–518.

Farmer, S.M., Tierney, P. and McIntyre, K.K. (2003) Employee Creativity in Taiwan: An Application of Role Identity Theory. *Academy of Management Journal*, 46(5), 618–630.

Feldman, D.C. and Bolino, M.C. (1996) Careers within Careers: Reconceptualizing the Nature of Career Anchors and Their Consequences. *Human Resource Management Review*, 6(2), 89–112.

Feldman, D.H. (1999) The Development of Creativity. In R.J. Sternberg (ed.), *Handbook of Creativity*. Cambridge: Cambridge University Press.

Fenwick, T.J. (2003) Professional Growth Plans: Possibilities and Limitations of an Organizationwide Employee Development Strategy. *Human Resource Development Quarterly*, 14(1), 59–79.

Fenwick, T. (2004) Towards a Critical HRD in Theory and Practice. *Adult Education Quarterly*, 54(3), 193–209.

Fenwick, T. (2007) Rethinking Processes of Adult Learning. In *Understanding Adult Education and Training*, 3rd edn. Sydney: Allen & Unwin.

Fenwick, T. and Bierema, L.L. (2008) Corporate Social Responsibility: Issues for Human Resource Development Professionals. *International Journal of Training and Development*, 12(1), 24–35.

Ferraro, G.P. (1990) *The Cultural Dimension of International Business*. Englewood Cliffs, NJ: Prentice Hall.

Fiedler, F.E. (1964) A Contingency Model of Leadership Effectiveness. In L. Berkowitz (ed.), *Advances in Experimental Social Psychology* (Vol. 1). New York: Academic Press.

Fiedler, F.E. (1967) *A Theory of Leadership Effectiveness*. New York: McGraw-Hill.

Fiedler, F.E. (1971) Validation and Extension of the Contingency Model of Leadership Effectiveness: A Review of Empirical Findings. *Psychological Bulletin*, 76(2), 128–148.

Fiedler, F.E. (1996) Research on Leadership Selection and Training: One View of the Future. *Administrative Science Quarterly*, 41(2), 241–250.

Financial Express (2010) What Apple Says about Innovation. *Financial Express*, 22 April.

Fiol, M.C. and Lyles, M.A. (1985) Organisational Learning. *Academy of Management Review*, 10(4), 803–813.

Fisher, J. (2012) Barnardo's Gains £700,000 from Argos Toy Exchange. *Retail Gazette*. http://www.retailgazette.co.uk/articles/31134-barnardos-gains-700000-from-argos-toy-exchange

Flatters, P. and Wilmott, M. (2009) Understanding the Post-recession Consumer. *Harvard Business Review*, 87(7/8), 106–112.

Fleishman, E.A., Harris, E.F. and Burtt, H.E. (1955) *Leadership and Supervision in Industry*. Columbus, OH: Bureau of Educational Research, Ohio State University.

Foote, M.F. and Ruona, W.E.A. (2008) Institutionalizing Ethics: A Synthesis of Frameworks and the Implications for HRD. *Human Resource Development Review*, 7(3), 292–308.

Forbes, B.J. and Domm, D.R. (2004) Creativity and Productivity: Resolving the Conflict. *S.A.M. Advanced Management Journal*, 69(2), 4–11.

Forster, N. (2000) Expatriates and the Impact of Cross-cultural Training. *Human Resource Management Journal*, 10(3), 63–78.

Fournier, V. and Grey, C. (2000) At the Critical Moment: Conditions and Prospects for Critical Management Studies. *Human Relations*, 53(1), 7–32.

Fraser, N. (1994) Rethinking the Public Sphere: A Contribution to the Critique of Actually Existing Democracy. In P. McLaren (ed.), *Between Borders: Pedagogy and the Politics of Cultural Studies*. New York: Routledge.

Freire, P. (1970) *Pedagogy of the Oppressed*. New York: Seabury.

Friedman, T. (2005) *The World is Flat: A Brief History of the 21st Century*. New York: Farrar, Straus and Giroux.

Friedman, T.L. (2006) *The World is Flat: The Globalized World in the Twenty-first Century*. London: Penguin.

Friedman, T.L. (2008) *Hot, Flat and Crowded: Why the World Needs a Green Revolution – and How We Can Renew Our Global Future*, 1st edn. London: Penguin.

Froiland, P. (1993) Industry Report. *Training*, (October), 49–59.

Fujitsu (2013) In-house Educational and Enlightenment Activities. http://www.fujitsu.com/global/about/environment/management/education/

Fulmer, R.M., Stumpf, S.A. and Bleak, J. (2009) The Strategic Development of High Potential Leaders. *Strategy and Leadership*, 37(3), 17–22.

Gagne, M. (2009) A Model of Knowledge-sharing Motivation. *Human Resource Management*, 48(4), 571–589.

Galagan, P. (1986) HRD is . . . *Training and Development Journal*, 40(3), 4.

Galpin, T. and Whittington, J.L. (2012) Sustainability Leadership: From Strategy to Results. *Journal of Business Strategy*, 33(4), 40–48.

Gammelgaard, J. and Ritter, T. (2005) The Knowledge Retrieval Matrix: Codification and Personification as Separate Strategies. *Journal of Knowledge Management*, 9(4), 133–143.

Gandz, J. (2006) Talent Development: The Architecture of a Talent Pipeline that Works. *Ivey Business Journal Online* (January/February), 1–4.

Garabaldi de Hilal, A.V. (2006) Brazilian National Culture, Organizational Culture and Cultural Agreement: Findings from a Multinational Company. *International Journal of Cross Cultural Management*, 6(2), 139–168.

Garavan, T.N. (1991) Strategic Human Resource Development. *Journal of European Industrial Training*, 15(1), 21–34.

Garavan, T.N. (1997) The Learning Organisation: A Review and Evaluation. *The Learning Organisation*, 4(1), 1–16.

Garavan, T.N. (2007) A Strategic Perspective on HRD. *Advances in Developing Human Resources*, 9(1), 11–30.

Garavan, T.N. and McCarthy, A. (2008) Collective Learning Processes and Human Resource Development. *Advances in Developing Human Resources*, 10(4), 451–472.

Garavan, T.N. and McGuire D. (2001) Competencies and Workplace Learning: Some Reflections on the Rhetoric and the Reality. *Journal of Workplace Learning*, 13(4), 144–164.

Garavan, T.N., Carbery, R. and Rock, A. (2012) Mapping Talent Development: Definition, Scope and Architecture. *European Journal of Training and Development*, 36(1), 5–24.

Garavan, T.N., Heraty, N., Rock, A. and Dalton, E. (2010) Conceptualising the Behavioural Barriers to CSR and CR in Organisations: A Typology of HRD Interventions. *Advances in Developing Human Resources*, 12(5), 587–613.

Garavan, T.N., McGuire, D. and O'Donnell, D. (2004) Exploring Human Resource Development: A Level of Analysis Approach. *Human Resource Development Review*, 3(4), 417–441.

Garavan, T.N., O'Donnell, D., McGuire, D. and Watson, S. (2007) Exploring Perspectives on Human Resource Development: An Introduction. *Advances in Developing Human Resources*, 9(1), 3–11.

Garcia-Morales, V.J., Matias-Reche, F. and Hurtado-Torres, N. (2008) Influence of Transformational Leadership on Organizational Innovation and Performance Depending on the Level of Organizational Learning in the Pharmaceutical Sector. *Journal of Organizational Change Management*, 21(2), 188–212.

Gardner, H. (1993) *Creating Minds: An Anatomy of Creativity Seen through the Livers of Freud, Einstein, Picasso, Stravinsky, Eliot, Graham and Gandhi*. New York: Basic Books.

Garrick, J. (1998) *Informal Learning in the Workplace*. London: Routledge.

Garvey, B. (2004) The Mentoring/Counseling/Coaching Debate: Call a Rose by any Other Name and Perhaps it's a Bramble? *Development and Learning in Organizations*, 18(2), 6–8.

Garvey, B. (2013) Mentoring in a Coaching World. In E. Cox, T. Bachkirova and D. Clutterbuck (eds), *The Complete Handbook of Coaching*. London: Sage.

Garvey, B. and Williamson, B. (2002) *Beyond Knowledge Management: Dialogue, Creativity and the Corporate Curriculum*. London: Financial Times Prentice Hall.

Gedro, J.A. (2010) Lesbian Presentations and Representations of Leadership, and the Implications for HRD. *Journal of European Industrial Training*, 34(6), 552–564.

Gedro, J.A., Cervero, R.M. and Johnson-Bailey, J. (2004) How Lesbians Learn to Negotiate the Heterosexism of Corporate America. *Human Resource Development International*, 7(2), 181–195.

Georgenson, D.L. (1982) The Problem of Transfer Calls for Partnership. *Training and Development Journal*, 36(10), 75–78.

Gergen, K. (1985) The Social Constructionist Movement in Modern Psychology. *American Psychology*, 40(3), 266–275.

Gerstman, R.L (1998) *Multiple Career Identities: The Key to Career Development and Career Transitions of Second Advanced Degree Seekers*. Dissertation presented to the Faculty of the Graduate School of the University of Texas at Austin.

Ghoshal, S. and Nohria, N. (1993) Horses for Courses: Organizational Forms for Multinational Corporations. *Sloan Management Review*, 34, 23–35.

Gibb, S. (2008) *Human Resource Development. Process, Practices and Perspectives*. Basingstoke: Macmillan.

Gibelman, M. (2000) The Nonprofit Sector and Gender Discrimination. *Nonprofit Management and Leadership*, 10(3), 251–269.

Gibson, E.J. (1941) Retroactive Inhibition as a Function of the Degree of Generalisation and Differentiation to Verbal Learning. *Psychology Review*, 28, 93–115.

Gibson, R. (1986) *Critical Theory and Education*. London: Hodder & Stoughton.

Gibson, S.K. (2004) Social Learning (Cognitive) Theory and its Implications for Human Resource Development. *Advances in Developing Human Resources*, 6(2), 193–210.

Gilgeous, V. and Parveen, K. (2001) Core Competency Requirements for Manufacturing Effectiveness. *Integrated Manufacturing Systems*, 12(3), 217–227.

Gill, A., Fitzgerald, S.P., Bhutani, S., Mand, H.S. and Sharma, S.P. (2010) The Relationship between Transformational Leadership and Employee-desire for Empowerment. *International Journal of Contemporary Hospitality Management*, 22(2), 1–19.

Gillespie, N.A. and Mann, L. (2004) Transformational Leadership and Shared Values: The Building Blocks of Trust. *Journal of Managerial Psychology*, 19(6), 588–607.

Gilley, J. and Eggland, S. (1989) *Principles of Human Resource Development*. Reading, MA: Addison-Wesley.

Ginzburg, S. and Dar-El, E.M. (2000) Skill Retention and Relearning: A Proposed Cyclical Model. *Journal of Workplace Learning*, 12(8), 327–332.

Giroux, H.A. (1997) *Pedagogy and the Politics of Hope: Theory, Culture and Schooling*. Boulder, CO: Westview Press.

Githens, R.P. (2007) *Critical Action Research in Human Resource Development*. Paper presented at the Academy of Human Resource Development Conference, Indianapolis, IN, 28 February–4 March.

Godshalk, V.M. and Sosik, J.J. (2003) Aiming for Career Success: The Role of Learning Goal Orientation in Mentoring Relationships. *Journal of Vocational Behavior*, 63(3), 417–437.

Goffee, R. and Jones, G. (2008) Bright Sparks. *People Management*, 14(3), 28–31.

Goh, S.C. (1998) Toward a Learning Organization: The Strategic Building Blocks. *SAM Advanced Management Journal*, 63(2), 15–22.

Gold, J. and Smith, V. (2003) Advances Towards a Learning Movement: Translations at Work. *Human Resource Development International*, 6(2), 139–154.

Gold, J., Holden, R., Iles, P., Stewart, J. and Beardwell, J. (2010) *Human Resource Development: Theory and Practice*. Basingstoke: Palgrave Macmillan.

Goldberg, L.R. (1990) An Alternative Description of Personality: The Big-Five Factor Structure. *Journal of Personality and Social Psychology*, 59(6), 1216–1229.

Goleman, D. (1995) *Emotional Intelligence: Why It Can Matter More Than IQ*. New York: Bantam Books.

Goleman, D. (1998) *Working with Emotional Intelligence*. London: Bloomsbury.

Goleman, D., Boyatzis, R. and McKee, A. (2004) *Primal Leadership: Learning to Lead with Emotional Intelligence*. Boston, MA: Harvard Business Press.

Good, T.L. and Brophy, J.E. (1990) *Educational Psychology: A Realistic Approach*. White Plains, NY: Longman.

Gore, A. (2006) *An Inconvenient Truth: The Planetary Emergency of Global Warming and What We Can Do About It*. London: Bloomsbury.

Gourlay, S. (2000) *Knowledge Management and HRD*. Paper presented at the First Conference on HRD Research and Practice across Europe, Kingston upon Thames, UK, 15 January 2000.

Granovetter, M.S. (1973) The Strength of Weak Ties. *American Journal of Sociology*, 78(6), 1360–1380.

Grant, A.M. (2007) Enhancing Coaching Skills and Emotional Intelligence through Training. *Industrial and Commercial Training*, 39(5), 257–266.

Grant, J. (2007) *The Green Marketing Manifesto*. Chichester: Wiley.

Greenhaus, J., Callanan, G. and DiRenzo, M. (2008) A Boundaryless Perspective on Careers. In J. Barling and C. Cooper (eds), *Sage Handbook of Organisational Behaviour*. Thousand Oaks, CA: Sage.

Greenhaus, J.H., Callanan, G.A. and Godshalk, V.M. (2010) *Career Management*, 4th edn. Thousand Oaks, CA: Sage.

Grey, C. and Mitev, N. (1995) Management Education: A Polemic. *Management Learning*, 26(1), 73–90.

Grieves, J. (2003) *Strategic Human Resource Development*. London: Sage.

Grieves, J. and Redman, T. (1999) Living in the Shadow of OD: HRD and the Search for Identity. *Human Resource Development International*, 2(2), 81–102.

Griffiths, D.A. and Koukpaki, S. (2012) Societal HRD and Societal Competitive Advantage. *Advances in Developing Human Resources*, 14(3), 318–332.

Grimes, D. (2001) Putting Your Own House in Order: Whiteness, Change and Organization Studies. *Journal of Organisational Change Management*, 14(2), 132–150.

Groves, K.S. (2007) Integrating Leadership Development and Succession Planning Best Practices. *Journal of Management Development*, 26(3), 239–260.

Groves, K.S., McEnrue, M.P. and Shen, W. (2008) Developing and Measuring the Emotional Intelligence of Leaders. *Journal of Management Development*, 27(2), 225–250.

Guest, D. (1987) Human Resource Management and Industrial Relations. *Journal of Management Studies*, 24(5), 503–521.

Gunnarsson, B.L. (1997) *The Construction of Professional Discourse*. New York: Longman.

Gunnarsson, B.L., Linell, P. and Nordberg, B. (1997) *The Construction of Professional Discourse*. New York: Longman.

Gunnigle, P. and McGuire, D. (2001) Why Ireland?: A Qualitative Review of the Factors Influencing the Location of US Multinationals in Ireland with Particular Reference to the Impact of Labour Issues. *Economic and Social Review*, 32(1), 43–67.

Habermas, J. (1987) *The Theory of Communicative Action, Volume 2, Lifeworld and System: A Critique of Functionalist Reason*. Boston, MA: Beacon Press.

Habermas, J. (2001) *On the Pragmatics of Social Interaction: Preliminary Studies in the Theory of Communicative Action*. Cambridge, MA: MIT Press.

Haddock, J., Jeffrey, J., Miles, D., Muller-Carmen, M. and Hartog, M. (2010) *Green HRD: The Potential Contribution of HRD Concepts and Theories to Environmental Management*. Paper presented at the 11th UFHRD Conference on HRD Theory and Practice across Europe, Pecs, Hungary, 2–4 June.

Hafeez, K. and Essmail, E.A. (2007) Evaluating Organisation Core Competences and Associated Personal Competencies Using Analytical Hierarchy Process. *Management Research News*, 30(8), 530–547.

Håkanson, J. (1990) International Decentralization of R&D – The Organizational Challenges. In C.A. Bartlett, Y. Doz and G. Hedlund (eds), *Managing the Global Firm*. London: Routledge.

Hales, C. (2005) Rooted in Supervision, Branching into Management: Continuity and Change in the Role of First-line Manager. *Journal of Management Studies*, 42(3), 471–506.

Hall, D.T. (1975) Pressures from Work, Self and Home in the Life Stages of Married Women. *Journal of Vocational Behaviour*, 6(1), 121–132.

Hall, D.T. (2002) *Careers in and out of Organizations*. Thousand Oaks, CA: Sage.

Hall, D. and Mirvis, P. (1995) The New Career Contract: Developing the Whole Person at Midlife and Beyond. *Journal of Vocational Behavior*, 47(3), 269–289.

Hamblin, A.C. (1974) *Evaluation and Control of Training*. London: McGraw-Hill.

Hamel, G. and Prahalad, C. (1994) *Competing for the Future*. Boston, MA: Harvard Business School Press.

Hamlin, B. (2002) Towards Evidence-based HRD Practice. In J. McGoldrick, J. Stewart and S. Watson (eds), *Understanding Human Resource Development: A Research Based Approach*. London: Routledge.

Handy, C. (1994) *The Empty Raincoat: Making Sense of the Future*. London: Hutchinson.

Harbison, F. and Myers, C.A. (1964) *Education, Manpower and Economic Growth*. New York: McGraw-Hill.

Harris, L., Doughty, D. and Kirk, S. (2002) The Devolution of HR Responsibilities – Perspectives from the UK's Public Sector. *Journal of European Industrial Training*, 26(5), 218–229.

Harrison, R. (2000) Learning, Knowledge, Productivity and Strategic Progress. *International Journal of Training and Development*, 4(4), 244–258.

Harrison, R. (2002) *Learning and Development*. London: CIPD.

Harrison, R. and Kessels, J. (2004) *Human Resource Development in a Knowledge Society: An Organisation View*. London: Palgrave Macmillan.

Hassan, A. (2007) Human Resource Development and Organizational Values. *Journal of European Industrial Training*, 31(6), 435–448.

Hatcher, T.G. (2002) *Ethics in HRD*. Cambridge, MA: Perseus.

Hatcher, T.G. (2003) Worldviews that Inhibit HRD's Social Responsibility. In M. Lee (ed.), *HRD in a Complex World*. London: Routledge.

Hatcher, T.G. (2006) An Editor's Challenge to Human Resource Development. *Human Resource Development Quarterly*, 17(1), 1–4.

Hawkins, P. (1991) The Spiritual Dimension of the Learning Organisation. *Management Education and Development*, 22(3), 166–181.

Hayes, J. and Allinson, C.W. (1996) The Implications of Learning Styles for Training and Development: A Discussion of the Matching Hypothesis. *British Journal of Management*, 7(1), 63–73.

Hays, R.D. (1974) Expatriate Selection: Insuring Success and Avoiding Failure. *Journal of International Business Studies*, 5(1), 25–37.

Hedberg, B. (1981) How Organisations Learn and Unlearn? In P.C. Nystrom and W.H. Starbuck (eds), *Handbook of Organisational Design*. London: Oxford University Press.

Henderson, J. (2001) *Transformative Learning in the Executive Suite: CEOs and the Role of Context in Mezirow's Theory*. Unpublished Doctoral Dissertation, George Washington University, Washington, DC.

Hennart, J.F. and Larimo, J. (1998) The Impact of Culture on the Strategy of Multinational Enterprises: Does National Origin Affect Ownership Decisions? *Journal of International Business Studies*, 29(3), 515–538.

Henriques, D.B. (1991) Piercing Wall Street's Lucite Ceiling. *New York Times*, 11 August.

Heraty, N. (2004) Towards an Architecture of Organisation-led Learning. *Human Resource Management Review*, 14(4), 449–472.

Heraty, N. and Morley, M. (2008) Dimensioning the Architecture of Organization-led Learning: A Framework for Collective Practice. *Advances in Developing Human Resources*, 10(4), 451–472.

Hersey, P. and Blanchard, K.H. (1969) Life Cycle Theory of Leadership. *Training and Development Journal*, 23(2), 26–34.

Hersey, P. and Blanchard, K.H. (1988) *Management of Organizational Behaviour: Utilizing Human Resources*. Englewood Cliffs, NJ: Prentice-Hall.

Higgins, M.C. (2000) The More the Merrier? Multiple Developmental Relationships and Work Satisfaction. *Journal of Management Development*, 19(4), 277–296.

Hill, J. and McGowan, P. (1999) Small Business and Enterprise Development: Questions about Research Methodology. *International Journal of Entrepreneurial Behaviour and Research*, 5(1), 5–18.

Hill, R.C. and Levenhagen, M. (1995) Metaphors and Mental Models: Sensemaking and Sensegiving in Innovative and Entrepreneurial Activities. *Journal of Management*, 21(6), 1057–1074.

Hillman, D.C., Willis, D.J. and Gunawardena, C.N. (1994) Learner Interface Interaction in Distance Education: An Extension of Contemporary Models and Strategies for Practitioners. *American Journal of Distance Education*, 8(2), 30–42.

Hilton, B. and McLean, G.N. (1997) *The Status of Human Resource Development in French Companies* Paper presented at the Academy of Human Resource Development 1997 Conference Proceedings, Baton Rouge, Louisiana.

Hinton, M., Francis, G. and Holloway, J. (2000) Best Practice Benchmarking in the UK. *Benchmarking: An International Journal*, 7(1), 52–61.

Hirsh, W. and Jackson, C. (2004) *Managing Careers in Large Organisations*. London: The Work Foundation.

Hite, L.M. (1996) Black Women Managers and Administrators: Experiences and Implications. *Women in Management Review*, 11(6), 11–17.

Hite, L.M. (2007) Hispanic Women Managers and Professionals: Reflections on Life and Work. *Gender, Work and Organisation*, 14(1), 20–38.

Hite, L.M. and McDonald, K.S. (2006) Diversity Training Pitfalls and Possibilities: An Exploration of Small and Mid-size US Organisations. *Human Resource Development International*, 9(1), 365–377.

Ho, H.P.Y. and Choi, T.M. (2012) A Five-R Analysis for Sustainable Fashion Supply Chain Management in Hong Kong: A Case Analysis. *Journal of Fashion Marketing and Management*, 16(2), 161–175.

Hodgkinson, M. (2002) A Shared Strategic Vision: Dream or Reality? *The Learning Organisation*, 9(2), 89–95.

Hogan, R. and Blake, R. (1999) John Holland's Vocational Typology and Personality Theory. *Journal of Vocational Behavior*, 55(1), 41–56.

Holbeche, L. (2008) Performance Management. In CIPD (ed.), *CIPD Recipe for Success*. London: CIPD.

Holladay, C.L. and Quinones, M.A. (2008) The Influence of Training Focus and Trainer Characteristics on Diversity Training Effectiveness. *Academy of Management Learning and Education*, 7(3), 343–354.

Holland, J.L. (1966) *The Psychology of Vocational Choice*. Waltham, MA: Blaisdell.

Holland, J.L. (1985) *Making Vocational Choices: A Theory of Vocational Personalities and Work Environments*. Englewood Cliffs, NJ: Prentice Hall.

Holland, J.L. (1997) *Making Vocational Choices: A Theory of Vocational Personalities and Work Environments*, 2nd edn. Odessa, FL: Psychological Assessment Resources.

Holman, D. (2000) Contemporary Models of Management Education in the UK. *Management Learning*, 31(2), 197–217.

Holman, D., Pavlica, K. and Thorpe, R. (1997) Rethinking Kolb's Theory of Experiential Learning in Management Education: The Contribution of Social Constructionism and Activity Theory. *Management Learning*, 28(2), 135–148.

Holmes, L. (2004) Challenging the Learning Turn in Education and Training. *Journal of European Industrial Training*, 28(8/9), 625–638.

Holton, E.F. (1996) The Flawed Four-level Evaluation Model. *Human Resource Development Quarterly*, 7(1), 5–21.

Holton, E.F. (2002) Theoretical Assumptions Underlying the Performance Paradigm of Human Resource Development. *Human Resource Development International*, 5(2), 199–215.

Holton, E.F. and Bates, R.A. (2000) Development of a Learning Transfer System Inventory. *Human Resource Development Quarterly*, 11(4), 333–360.

Holton, V., Voller, S., Schofield, C. and Devine, M. (2010) *Improving Learning Transfer: A Pilot Study with Three Ashridge Client Organisations*. Ashridge, Herts: Ashridge Business School.

Honey, P. (1998) The Debate Starts Here. *People Management*, (October), 28–29.

Horkheimer, M. (1972) *Critical Theory*. New York: Herder & Herder.

Horkheimer, M. and Adorno, T. (1979) *The Dialectic of Enlightenment*. London: Verso.

Horwitz, F.M., Bowmaker-Falconer, A. and Searll, P. (1996) Human Resource Development and Managing Diversity in South Africa. *International Journal of Manpower*, 4/5, 134–151.

House, R.J. (1971) A Path-goal Theory of Leadership Effectiveness. *Administrative Science Quarterly*, 16, 321–338.

House, R.J. (1977) Theory of Charismatic Leadership. In J.G. Hunts and L.L. Larson (eds), *Leadership: The Cutting Edge*. Carbondale, IL: Southern Illinois University Press.

House, R.J. (1996) Path-goal Theory of Leadership: Lessons, Legacy, and a Reformulated Theory. *The Leadership Quarterly*, 7(3), 323–352.

House, R.J. and Mitchell, T.R. (1974) Path-goal Theory of Leadership. *Journal of Contemporary Business*, 3, 81–97.

Houseman, K. (2007) *The Effects of Mandated Standardized Testing on Teachers' Perceptions on the Formation and Development of Professional Learning Communities in the Schools of the Rock Valley Conference*. Proquest: UMI Dissertation Publishing.

Howard, A. (2012) The Thinking Organisation. *Journal of Management Development*, 31(6), 620–632.

Howe, M.J. (1980) *The Psychology of Human Learning*. New York: Harper & Row.

Humphreys, L.G. (1979) The Construct of General Intelligence. *Intelligence*, 3, 105–120.

Huo, Y.P. and Von Glinow, M.A. (1995) On Transplanting Human Resource Practices to China: A Culture-driven Approach. *International Journal of Manpower*, 16(9), 3–15.

Hwang, A. (1996) Positivist and Constructivist Persuasions in Instructional Development. *Instructional Science*, 24, 343–356.

Hymowitz. C. and Schellhardt, T. (1986) The Glass Ceiling: Why Women Can't Seem to Break the Invisible Barrier that Blocks them from Top Jobs. *Wall Street Journal* (A Special Report: The Corporate Woman), 24 March: 1, 4–5.

Hytti, U. (2010) Contextualizing Entrepreneurship in the Boundaryless Career. *Gender in Management: An International Journal*, 25(1), 64–81.

Iles, P. and Hayers, P.K. (1997) Managing Diversity in Transnational Project Teams: A Tentative Model and Case Study. *Journal of Managerial Psychology*, 12(2), 95–117.

Iles, P. and Yolles, M. (2003) International HRD Alliances in Viable Knowledge Migration and Development: The Czech Academic Link Project. *Human Resource Development International*, 6(3), 301–325.

Infosys (2012) *Infosys Annual Report 2011–2012*. Pune, India: Infosys.

Innocent (2012) *Sustainability Report*. London: Innocent Smoothies.

Isen, A.M. (1999) On the Relationship between Affect and Creative Problem Solving. In S. Russ (ed.), *Affect, Creative Experience and Psychological Adjustment*. Philadelphia: Brumner/Mazel.

Itami, H. (1987) *Mobilizing Invisible Assets*. Cambridge, MA: Harvard University Press.

ITD (Institute of Training and Development) (1992) *Human Resource Development: Diploma in Training Management – Syllabus Regulations and Approved Centres*. Marlow: ITD.

Jackson, T. (2002) *International HRM: A Cross-cultural Approach*. London: Sage.

Jacques, P.H., Garger, J. and Thomas, M. (2008) Assessing Leader Behaviours in Project Managers. *Management Research News*, 31(1), 4–12.

James, C. and Roffe, I. (2000) The Evaluation of Goal and Goal-free Training Innovation. *Journal of European Industrial Training*, 24(1), 12–20.

James, W. (1880) Great Men and their Environment, *Atlantic Monthly*, 276, 441–459.

Jankowicz, D. (1999) Editorial: Putting the 'I' into HRD … Why Do We Do It? *Human Resource Development International*, 2(3), 171–174.

Jaussi, K.S. and Dionne, S.D. (2003) Leading for Creativity: The Role of Unconventional Leader Behavior. *The Leadership Quarterly*, 14, 475–498.

Javidan, M. and Waldman, D.A. (2003) Exploring Charismatic Leadership in the Public Sector: Measurement and Consequences. *Public Administration Review*, 63(2), 229–242.

Jones, H. (1998) *Making it Happen*. London: Fontana.

Jones, J. (1981) The Organizational Universe. In J. Jones and J. Pfeiffer (eds), *The 1981 Annual Handbook for Group Facilitators*. San Diego: University Associates.

Jones, N.B., Herschel, R.T. and Moesel, D.D. (2003) Using 'Knowledge Champions' to Facilitate Knowledge Management. *Journal of Knowledge Management*, 7(1), 49–63.

Jones, R. and Kriflik, G. (2005) Strategies for Managerial Self-change in a Cleaned-up Bureaucracy: A Qualitative Study. *Journal of Managerial Psychology*, 20(5), 397–416.

Jones, R.A., Rafferty, A.E. and Griffin, M.A. (2006) The Executive Coaching Trend: Towards More Flexible Executives. *Leadership and Organization Development Journal*, 27(7), 584–596.

Judge T.A. and Bono J.E. (2000) Five Factor Model of Personality and Transformational Leadership. *Journal of Applied Psychology*, 85(5), 751–765.

Judge, T.A., Ilies, R., Bono, J.E. and Gerhardt, M.W. (2002) Personality and Leadership: A Qualitative and Quantitative Review. *Journal of Applied Psychology*, 87(4), 765–780.

Kang, J. (2007) Testing Impact of Knowledge Characteristics and Relationship Ties on Project Performance. *Journal of Knowledge Management*, 11(3), 126–144.

Kannan, G. and Aulbur, W.G. (2004) Intellectual Capital: Measurement Effectiveness. *Journal of Intellectual Capital*, 5(3), 389–413.

Kaplan, R.S. and Norton, D. P. (1996) *Translating Strategy into Action: The Balanced Scorecard*. Boston, MA: Harvard Business School.

Karp, H.B. and Sutton, N. (1993) Where Diversity Training Goes Wrong. *Training*, 30(7), 30–34.

Kassaye, W.W. (2001) Green Dilemma. *Marketing Intelligence and Planning*, 19(6), 444–455.

Katsoulakos, T. and Katsoulacos, Y. (2007) Integrating Corporate Responsibility Principles and Stakeholder Approaches into Mainstream Strategy: A Stakeholder-oriented and Integrative Strategic Management Framework. *Corporate Governance*, 7(4), 355–369.

Kaufman, R., Keller, J. and Watkins, R. (1995) What Works and What Doesn't: Evaluation Beyond Kirkpatrick. *Performance and Improvement* (November/December), 8–13.

Kaye, L. (2012) Time to Start Valuing Human Capital as an Asset on the Balance Sheet. *Guardian*. http://www.guardian.co.uk/sustainable-business/valuing-human-capital-asset-balance-sheet

Keegan, A.E. and Den Hartog, D.N. (2004) Transformational Leadership in a Project-based Environment: A Comparative Study of the Leadership Styles of Project Managers and Line Managers. *International Journal of Project Management*, 22(8), 609–617.

Kelliher, F. and Reinl, L. (2009) A Resource-based View of Micro-firm Management Practice. *Journal of Small Business and Enterprise Development*, 16(3), 521–532.

Kelly, H.K. (1982) A Primer on Transfer of Training. *Training and Development Journal*, 36(11), 102–106.

Kerka, S. (1999) *Self-directed Learning: Myths and Realities*. Columbus, OH: ERIC Clearinghouse on Adult Career and Vocational Education.

Kerr, S. (1975) On the Folly of Rewarding A, while Hoping for B. *Academy of Management Journal*, 18(4), 769–783.

Kessels, J. (2007) HRD Research in a Diversified Field. *Human Resource Development International*, 10(1), 83–89.

Kessels, J. and Harrison, R. (2004) *Reaching Knowledge Productivity*. Paper presented at the Fifth European Conference on Human Resource Development Theory and Practice, University of Limerick, Ireland.

Kidd, J.M. (2006) *Understanding Career Counselling: Theory, Research and Practice*. London: Sage.

Kidger, P.J. (2002) Management Structure in Multinational Enterprises: Responding to Globalisation. *Employee Relations*, 24(1), 69–85.

Kim, J.H. and Lee C. (2001) Implications of Near and Far Transfer of Training on Structured On-the-Job Training. *Advances in Developing Human Resources*, 3(4), 442–452.

Kim, N. (2012) Societal Development through Human Resource Development: Contexts and Key Change Agents. *Advances in Developing Human Resources*, 14(3), 239–250.

King, I.W. (1995) Learning? I've Got No Time for That? *Management Learning*, 26(2), 249–257.

Kipp, P.H., Artiles, A.J. and Lopez-Torres, L. (2003) Beyond Reflection: Teacher Learning as Praxis. *Theory into Practice*, 42(3), 248–264.

Kirby, S. (2006) American Gay and Lesbian Student Leaders' Perceptions of Job Discrimination. *Equal Opportunities International*, 25(2), 126–140.

Kirkpatrick, S.A. and Locke, E.A. (1991) Leadership: Do Traits Matter? *Academy of Management Executive*, 5(2), 48–60.

Kline, S. and Harris, K. (2008) ROI is MIA: Why are Hoteliers Failing to Demand the ROI of Training? *International Journal of Contemporary Hospitality Management*, 20(1), 45–59.

Knowles, M.S. (1998) *The Adult Learner: The Definitive Classic in Adult Education and Human Resource Development*. Houston, TX: Gulf Publishing Co.

Knowles, M.S., Holton, E.F. and Swanson, R.S. (2005) *The Adult Learner*. New York: Butterworth-Heinemann.

Kondrat, M.E. (1999) Who is the Self in Self-aware: Professional Self-awareness from a Critical Theory Perspective. *Social Service Review*, 73(4), 451–475.

Kouzes, J.M. and Posner, B.Z. (1995) *The Leadership Challenge: How to Keep Getting Extraordinary Things Done in Organizations*, San Francisco, CA: Jossey-Bass.

Kouzes, J.M. and Posner, B.Z. (2002) *The Leadership Challenge*, 3rd edn. San Francisco, CA: Jossey-Bass.

Kram, K.E. (1985) *Mentoring at Work: Developmental Relationships in Organizational Life*. Glenview, IL: Scott Foresman.

Kramlinger, T. and Huberty, T. (1990) Behaviorism versus Humanism. *Training and Development Journal*, 44(12), 41–46.

Krinks, P. and Stack, R. (2008) The Talent Crunch. *People Management*, 14(13), 30–31.

Kroth, S.J. (2000) Single and Double Loop Learning: Exploring Potential Influence of Cognitive Style. *Organization Development Journal*, 18(3), 87–98.

Kucherov, D. and Zavyalova, E. (2012) HRD Practices and Talent Management in the Companies with the Employer Brand. *European Journal of Training and Development*, 36(1), 86–104.

Kuchinke, K.P. (1998) Moving Beyond the Dualism of Performance and Learning: A Response to Barrie and Pace. *Human Resource Development Quarterly*, 9(4), 377–384.

Kuchinke, K.P. (2004) Theorising and Practising HRD: Extending the Dialogue over the Roles of Scholarship and Practice in the Field. *Human Resource Development International*, 7(4), 535–540.

Kuchinke, K.P. (2007) Kaleidoscopes and Multiplicity of Perspectives in Human Resource Development. *Human Resource Development International*, 10(2), 117–121.

Kuchinke, K.P. (2010) Human Development as a Central Goal for Human Resource Development. *Human Resource Development International*, 13(5), 575–585.

Kumar, S. and Chandra, C. (2001) Enhancing the Effectiveness of Benchmarking in Manufacturing Organizations. *Industrial Management and Data Systems*, 101(2), 80–89.

Kunnanatt, J.T. (2004) Emotional Intelligence: The New Science of Interpersonal Effectiveness. *Human Resource Development Quarterly*, 15(4), 489–495.

Kur, E. and Bunning, R. (2002) Assuring Corporate Leadership for the Future. *Journal of Management Development*, 21(9), 761–779.

Kustin, R. and Jones, R. (1995) The Influence of Corporate Headquarters on Leadership Styles in Japanese and US Subsidiary Companies. *Leadership and Organisational Development Journal*, 16(5), 11–15.

Lahteenmaki, G., Toivonen, J. and Mattila, M. (2001) Critical Aspects of Organisational Learning Research and Proposals for its Measurement. *British Journal of Management*, 12(2), 113–129.

Lam, A. (2000) Tacit Knowledge, Organisational Learning and Societal Institutions: An Integrated Framework. *Organisation Studies*, 21(3), 487–513.

Lammintakanen, J. and Kivinen, T. (2012) Continuing Professional Development in Nursing: Does Age Matter? *Journal of Workplace Learning*, 24(1), 34–47.

Lanigan, M.L. and Bentley, J. (2006) Collecting Sophisticated Evaluations Even When Corporate Culture is Resistant. *Performance Improvement*, 45(1), 32–38.

Larsen, H.H. and Brewster, C. (2003) Line Management Responsibility for HRM: What is Happening in Europe? *Employee Relations*, 25(3), 228–244.

Learning Unlimited (2006) *Fostering Creativity: A Hard Look at Soft Thinking*. Edinburgh: The Stationery Office.

Lee, M. (1996) Holistic Learning in the New Central Europe. In M. Lee, H. Letiche, R. Crawshaw and N. Thomas (eds), *Management Education in the New Europe: Boundaries and Complexity*. London: Routledge.

Lee, M. (1998) Creating Clover. *Human Resource Development International*, 1(3), 259–262.

Lee, M. (2001) A Refusal to Define HRD. *Human Resource Development International*, 4(3), 327–341.

Lee, M. (2007) Human Resource Development from a Holistic Perspective. *Advances in Developing Human Resources*, 9(1), 97–110.

Lee, M. and Smith, A. (2004) *The National Agenda, Incidental Learning and Television as a Learning Medium: The Case of the Professional Development Channel*. Paper presented at the Proceedings of the Fifth UFHRD/AHRD Conference, University of Limerick, Ireland, 27–28 May.

Lee, M. and Stead, V. (1998) Human Resource Development in the United Kingdom. *Human Resource Development Quarterly*, 9(3), 297–308.

Lee, S.M., Park, S.H. and Trimi, S. (2013) Greening with IT: Practices of Leading Countries and Strategies of Followers. *Management Decision*, 51(3), 629–642.

Lee-Kelley, L., Blackman, D.A. and Hurst, J.P. (2007) An Exploration of the Relationship between Learning Organisations and the Retention of Knowledge Workers. *The Learning Organisation*, 14(3), 204–221.

Lefrancois, G. (1999) *The Lifespan*, 6th edn. Belmont, CA: Wadsworth.

Leiba-O'Sullivan, S. (1999) The Distinction between Stable and Dynamic Cross-cultural Competencies: Implications for Expatriate Trainability. *Journal of International Business Studies*, 30(4), 709–725.

Lenaghan, J.A. and Seirup, H.J. (2007) Transition and Transparency in the Employment Contract. *Journal of Management Development*, 26(5), 459–467.

Leonard-Barton, D. (1992) The Factory as a Learning Laboratory. *Sloan Management Review*, 34(1), 23–38.

Leont'ev, A.N. (1981) The Problem of Activity in Psychology. In J.V. Wertsh (ed.), *The Concept of Activity in Soviet Psychology*. New York: Sharpe.

Leskiw, S.L. and Singh, P. (2007) Leadership Development: Learning from Best Practices. *Leadership and Organization Development Journal*, 28(5), 444–464.

Leung, S.L. and Bozionelos, N. (2004) Five-factor Model Traits and the Prototypical Image of the Effective Leader in the Confucian Culture. *Employee Relations*, 26(1), 62–71.

Lewis, P. and Thornhill, A. (1994) The Evaluation of Training: An Organisational Culture Approach. *Journal of European Industrial Training*, 18(8), 25–32.

Lievens, F. (2007) Employer Branding in the Belgian Army: The Importance of Instrumental and Symbolic Beliefs for Potential Applicants and Military Employees. *Human Resource Management*, 46(1), 51–69.

Likert, R. (1961) *New Patterns of Management*. New York: McGraw-Hill.

Lim, B.C. and Ployhart, R.E. (2004) Transformational Leadership: Relations to the Five-factor Model and Team Performance in Typical and Maximum Contexts. *Journal of Applied Psychology*, 89(4), 610–621.

Lincoln, Y.S. and Lynham, S.A. (2007) *Criteria for Assessing Good Theory in Human Resource Development and Other Applied Disciplines from an Interpretive Perspective*. Paper presented at the Annual Conference of the Academy of Human Resource Development, Bowling Green, Ohio.

Lindsay, C. (1994) Things that Go Wrong in Diversity Training: Conceptualization and Change with Ethnic Identity Models. *Journal of Organisational Change Management*, 7(6), 18–34.

Linstead, S., Folup, L. and Lilley, S. (2004) *Management and Organisation: A Critical Text*. London: Palgrave Macmillan.

Lippitt, G. (1969) *Organizational Renewal*. New York: Appleton Century Crofts.

Littrell, L.N., Salas, E., Hess, K.P., Paley, M. and Riedel, S. (2006) Expatriate Preparation: A Critical Review of 25 Years of Cross-cultural Training Research. *Human Resource Development Review*, 5(3), 355–388.

Loan-Clarke, J., Boocock, G., Smith, A. and Whittaker, J. (1999) Investment in Training and Development by Small Businesses. *Employee Relations*, 21(3), 296–310.

Longenecker, C.O. and Fink, L.S. (2006) Closing the Management Skills Gap: A Call for Action. *Development and Learning in Organisations*, 20(1), 16–19.

Losert, A. (2008) Coping with Workplace Heteronormativity among Lesbian Employees: A German Study. *Journal of Lesbian Studies*, 12(1), 47–58.

Lundberg, C.C. (1995) Learning in and by Organisations: Three Conceptual Issues. *International Journal of Organizational Analysis*, 3(1), 353–360.

Lunnan, R., Amdam, R.P., Hennestad, B., Lervik, J.E. and Nilsen, S. (2002) Standardised Leadership Tools in MNEs: Critical Reflections for the Conditions for Successful Implementations. *Journal of European Industrial Training*, 26(6/7), 274–283.

Lussier, R.N. and Achua, C.F. (2009) *Leadership: Theory, Application and Skill Development.* Mason, OH: Cengage Learning.

Lynham, S. (2000) *Leadership Development: A Review of the Theory and Literature.* Paper presented at the Academy of Human Resource Development Conference. Raleigh-Durham, North Carolina, 8–12 March.

Lynham, S.A. and Cunningham, P.W. (2006) National Human Resource Development in Transitioning Societies in the Developing World: Concept and Challenges. *Advances in Developing Human Resources*, 8(1), 116–135.

Lytras, M.D., Pouloudi, A. and Poulymanakou, A. (2002) Knowledge Management Convergence: Expanding Learning Frontiers. *Journal of Knowledge Management*, 6(1), 40–52.

Mabey, C. and Finch-Lees, T. (2008) *Management and Leadership Development.* London: Sage.

MacLean, D. (2006) Beyond English: Transnational Corporations and the Strategic Management of Language in a Complex Multilingual Business Environment. *Management Decision*, 44(10), 1377–1390.

MacNeil, C. (2004) *The First-line Supervisor as a Facilitator of Knowledge Sharing in Teams.* Paper presented at the Fifth European Conference on Human Resource Development Theory and Practice, University of Limerick, Ireland.

Madden, C.A. and Mitchell, V.A. (1993) *Professions, Standards and Competence: A Survey of Continuing Education for the Professions.* Bristol: University of Bristol.

Madjar, N. (2005) The Contributions of Different Groups of Individuals to Employee Creativity. *Advances in Developing Human Resources*, 7(2), 182–206.

Maher, F.A. and Tetreault, M.K.T. (2001) *The Feminist Classroom: Dynamics of Gender, Race, and Privilege.* Lanham, MD: Rowman & Littlefield.

Mainiero, L.A. and Sullivan, S.E. (2006) *The Opt-out Revolt: Why People are Leaving Companies to Create Kaleidoscope Careers.* Palo Alto, CA: Davies-Black Publishing.

Majaro, S. (1988) *The Creative Gap: Managing Ideas for Profit.* London: Longman.

Malmi, T. (2001) Balanced Scorecards in Finnish Companies: A Research Note. *Management Accounting Research*, 12, 207–220.

Malnight, T.W. (2001) Emerging Structural Patterns within Multinational Corporations: Toward Process Based Structures. *Academy of Management Journal*, 44(6), 1187–1210.

Maltz, A.C., Shenhar, A.J. and Reilly, R.R. (2003) Beyond the Balanced Scorecard: Refining the Search for Organisational Success Measures. *Long Range Planning*, 36, 187–204.

Manikoth, N.N. and Cseh, M. (2011) *Career Behaviour Patterns of Professional Women: A Study of Protean Careers.* Paper presented at the 2011 AHRD International Research Conference in the Americas, Schaumberg, Chicago, 23–26 February.

Mankin, D.P. (2001) A Model for Human Resource Development. *Human Resource Development International*, 4(1), 65–85.

Mann, R.D. (1959) A Review of the Relationships between Personality and Performance in Small Groups. *Psychological Bulletin*, 56, 241–270.

Marcus, M. (2004) Preparing High-potential Staff for the Step Up to Leadership. *Canadian HR Reporter*, 17(18), 11–12.

Marquardt, M.J. (1999) The Global Age and Global Economy. *Advances in Developing Human Resources*, 1(4), v–viii.

Marquardt, M.J. and Engle, D.W. (1993) *Global Human Resource Development.* Englewood Cliffs, NJ: Prentice Hall.

Marsick, V. (1988) Learning in the Workplace: The Case for Reflectivity and Critical Reflectivity. *Adult Education Quarterly*, 38(4), 187–198.

Marsick, V. and Watkins, K. (1990) *Informal and Incidental Learning in the Workplace.* London: Routledge.

Marsick, V. and Watkins, K. (1999) Envisioning New Organisations of Learning. In D. Boud and J. Garrick (eds), *Understanding Learning at Work*. London: Routledge.

Marx, R.D. and Frost, P.J. (1998) Toward Optimal Use of Video in Management Education: Examining the Evidence. *Journal of Management Development*, 17(4), 243–250.

Matheson, B. (2006) A Culture of Creativity: Design Education and the Creative Industries. *Journal of Management Development*, 25(1), 55–64.

Mavin, S. (2008) Queen Bees, Wannabees and Afraid to Bees: No More 'Best Enemies' for Women in Management? *British Journal of Management*, 19 (Suppl.). 75–84.

Mavin, S., Wilding, P., Stalker, B., Simmonds, D., Rees, C. and Winch, F. (2007) Developing 'New Commons' between HRD Research and Practice: Case Studies of UK Universities. *Journal of European Industrial Training*, 31(1), 4–18.

Maxwell, G., Watson, S. and Quail S. (2004) Quality Service in the International Hotel Sector: A Catalyst for Strategic Human Resource Development? *Journal of European Industrial Training*, 28(2/3/4), 159–182.

McCauley, C.D. and Douglas, C.A. (1998) Developmental Relationships. In C.D. McCauley, R.S. Moxley and E. Van Velsor (eds), *The Center for Creative Leadership Handbook of Leadership Development*. San Francisco, CA: Jossey-Bass.

McClelland, D. (1973) Testing for Competence rather than Intelligence. *American Psychologist*, 28(1), 1–14.

McCracken, M. (2005) Towards a Typology of Managerial Barriers to Learning. *Journal of Management Development*, 24(6), 559–575.

McCracken, M. and Wallace, M. (2000a) Towards a Redefinition of Strategic HRD. *Journal of European Industrial Training*, 24(5), 281–290.

McCracken, M. and Wallace, M. (2000b) Exploring Strategic Maturity in HRD: Rhetoric, Aspiration or Reality? *Journal of European Industrial Training*, 24(8), 425–437.

McFadzean, E. (2001) Supporting Virtual Learning Groups. Part 1: A Pedagogical Perspective. *Team Performance Management: An International Journal*, 7(3/4), 53–62.

McGaughey, S. and DeCieri, H. (1999) Reassessment of Convergence and Divergence Dynamics: Implications for International HRM. *International Journal of Human Resource Management*, 10(2), 235–250.

McGoldrick, J., Stewart, J. and Watson, S. (2001) Theorizing Human Resource Development. *Human Resource Development International*, 4(3), 343–356.

McGoldrick, J., Stewart, J. and Watson, S. (2002a) Researching HRD: Philosophy, Process and Practice. In J. McGoldrick, J. Stewart and S. Watson (eds), *Understanding Human Resource Development: A Research Based Approach*. London: Routledge.

McGoldrick, J., Stewart, J. and Watson, S. (2002b) Understanding HRD: A Research Approach. *International Journal of Human Resources Development and Management*, 1/2, 17–30.

McGraw, P. (2004) Influences on HRM Practices in MNCs: A Qualitative Study in the Australian Context. *International Journal of Manpower*, 25(6), 525–546.

McGuire, D. (2010) Engaging Organizations in Environmental Change: A Greenprint for Action. *Advances in Developing Human Resources*, 12(5), 508–523.

McGuire, D. and Cseh, M. (2006) The Development of the Field of HRD: A Delphi Study. *Journal of European Industrial Training*, 30(8), 653–667.

McGuire, D., Garavan, T.N., O'Donnell, D. and Watson, S. (2007) Metaperspectives and HRD: Lessons for Research and Practice, *Advances in Developing Human Resources*, 9(1), 120–139.

McGuire, D., O'Donnell, D. and Cross, C. (2005) Why Humanistic Practices in HRD Won't Work. *Human Resource Development Quarterly*, 16(1), 131–137.

McGuire, D., O'Donnell, D., Garavan, T.N., Saha, S.K. and Murphy, J. (2001) *The Cultural Boundedness of Theory and Practice in HRD*. Paper presented at the Global Human Resource Management Conference, Barcelona, June.

McGuire, D., O'Donnell, D., Garavan, T.N., Saha, S.K. and Murphy, J. (2002) The Cultural Boundedness of Theory and Practice in HRD? *Cross Cultural Management*, 9(2), 25–44.

McGuire, D., Stoner, L. and Mylona, S. (2008) The Role of Line Managers as Human Resource Agents in Fostering Organisational Change in Public Services. *Journal of Change Management*, 8(1), 73–84.

McIntosh, P. (1988) White Privilege and Male Privilege: A Personal Account of Coming to See Correspondences Through Work in Women's Studies. In M.L. Andersen and P.H. Collins (eds), *Race, Class and Gender: An Anthology*. Belmont, CA: Wadsworth.

McIntosh, P. (1993) White Privilege and Male Privilege: A Personal Account of Coming to See Correspondences through Work in Women's Studies. In A. Minas (ed.), *Gender Basics: Feminist Perspectives on Women and Men*. Belmont, CA: Wadsworth.

McIntosh, P. (1998) White Privilege and Male Privilege: A Personal Account of Coming to See Correspondences through Work in Women's Studies. In M.L. Andersen and P.H. Collins (eds), *Race, Class and Gender: An Anthology*. Belmont, CA: Wadsworth.

McIntosh, P. (2002) White Privilege and Male Privilege: A Personal Account of Coming to See Correspondences through Work in Women's Studies. In C. Harvey and M. Allard (eds), *Understanding and Managing Diversity: Readings, Cases, and Exercises*, 2nd edn. Upper Saddle River, NJ: Prentice-Hall.

McKenna, S. (1998) Cross-cultural Attitudes towards Leadership Dimensions. *Leadership and Organisation Development Journal*, 19(2), 106–112.

McKinney, F. (1933) Quantitative and Qualitative Essential Elements of Transfer. *Journal of Experiential Psychology*, 16, 854–864.

McLagan, P. (1989) *Models for HRD Practice*. Alexandria, VA: ASTD Press.

McLean, G.N. (1998) HRD: A Three Legged Stool, an Octopus, or a Centipede? *Human Resource Development International*, 1(4), 375–387.

McLean, G.N. (2004) National Human Resource Development: What in the World Is It? *Advances in Developing Human Resources*, 6(3), 269–275.

McLean, L. (2005) Organizational Culture's Influence on Creativity and Innovation: A Review of the Literature and Implications for Human Resource Development. *Advances in Developing Human Resources*, 7(2), 226–246.

McLean, G.N. and McLean, L. (2001) If We Can't Define HRD in One Country, How Can We Define it in an International Context? *Human Resource Development International*, 4(3), 313–326.

McLean, G.N. and Wang, X. (2007) *Defining International Human Resource Development: A Proposal*. Paper presented at the Annual Conference of the Academy of Human Resource Development, Bowling Green, Ohio.

McLean, G., Kuo, M.-H., Budhwani, N.N., Yamnill, S. and Virakul, B. (2012) Capacity Building for Societal Development: Case Studies in Human Resource Development. *Advances in Developing Human Resources*, 14(3), 251–263.

Megginson, D., Joy-Matthews, J. and Banfield, P. (1993) *Human Resource Development*. London: Kogan Page.

Mele, D. (2003) The Challenge of Humanistic Management. *Journal of Business Ethics*, 44(1), 77–88.

Merriam, S.B. (2001) Andragogy and Self-directed Learning: Pillars of Adult Learning Theory. In S.B. Merriam (ed.), *New Directions for Adult and Continuing Education* (Vol. 89). San Francisco, CA: Jossey-Bass.

Merriam, S.B., Johnson-Bailey, J., Lee, M., Kee, Y., Niseane, G. and Mazanah, M. (2001) Power and Positionality: Negotiating Insider/Outsider Status within and across Cultures. *International Journal of Lifelong Education*, 20(5), 405–416.

Merx-Chermin, M. and Nijhof, W. (2004) *Factors Influencing Knowledge Creation and Innovation in an Organisation*. Paper presented at the Fifth European Conference on Human Resource Development Theory and Practice, University of Limerick, Ireland.

Messick, S. (1984) The Nature of Cognitive Styles: Problems and Promises in Educational Research. *Educational Psychologist*, 19, 59–74.

Metcalfe, B.D. and Rees, C.J. (2005) Theorizing Advances in International Human Resource Development. *Human Resource Development International*, 8(4), 449–466.

Michalski, G.V. and Cousins, J.B. (2001) Multiple Perspectives on Training Evaluation: Probing Stakeholder Perceptions in a Global Network Development Firm. *American Journal of Evaluation*, 22(1), 37–53.

Miles, R. (1988) *The Women's History of the World*. London: HarperCollins.

Miller, R.L., Butler, J. and Cosentino, C.J. (2004) Followership Effectiveness: An Extension of Fiedler's Contingency Model. *Leadership and Organisation Development Journal*, 25(4), 362–369.

Minton, A. (2010) Supporting Learners Through Mentoring in the Workplace. In J. Mumford and S. Roodhouse (eds), *Understanding Work-based Learning*. London: Gower.

Mintzberg, H (1994) The Fall and Rise of Strategic Planning. *Harvard Business Review*, 72(1), 107–114.

Mintzberg, H. (2004) *Managers not MBAs*. San Francisco, CA: Berrett-Koehler.

Miroshnik, V. (2002) Culture and International Management: A Review. *Journal of Management Development*, 21(7), 521–544.

Mitchell, R. and Boyle, B. (2010) Knowledge Creation Measurement Methods. *Journal of Knowledge Management*, 14(1), 67–82.

Monserrat, S.I., Duffy, J.A., Olivas-Lujan, M.R., Miller, J.M., Gregory, A., Fox, S., Lituchy, T.R. and Punnett, B.J. (2009) Mentoring Experiences of Successful Women across the Americas. *Gender in Management: An International Journal*, 24(6), 455–476.

Mooraj, S., Oyon, D. and Hostettler, D. (1999) The Balanced Scorecard: A Necessary Good or an Unnecessary Evil? *European Management Journal*, 17(5), 481–491.

Morgan, G.A. and Smircich, L. (1980) The Case for Qualitative Research. *Academy of Management Review*, 5(4), 491–500.

Morrison, M. (2009) *Leadership and Learning: Matters of Social Justice*. New York: Information Age Publishing.

Mostovicz, E.I., Kakabadse, N.K. and Kakabadse, A.P. (2009) A Dynamic Theory of Leadership Development. *Leadership and Organisation Development Journal*, 30(6), 563–576.

Mumford, M.D., Scott, G.M., Gaddis, B. and Strange, J.M. (2002) Leading Creative People: Orchestrating Expertise and Relationships. *The Leadership Quarterly*, 13(6), 705–750.

Murphy, C., Cross, C. and McGuire, D. (2006) The Motivation of Nurses to Participate in Continuing Professional Education in Ireland. *Journal of European Industrial Training*, 30(5), 365–384.

Mussig, D.J. (2003) A Research and Skills Training Framework for Values-driven Leadership. *Journal of European Industrial Training*, 27(2/3/4), 73–79.

Myers, I.B. and McCauley, M.H. (1986) *Manual: A Guide to the Development and Use of the Myers-Briggs Type Indicator*. Palo Alto, CA: Consulting Psychologists Press.

Nadkarni, S. and Perez, P.D. (2007) Prior Conditions and Early International Commitment: The Mediating Role of Domestic Mindset. *Journal of International Business Studies*, 38 (1), 160–176.

Nadler, D.A. and Tushman, M.L. (1990) Beyond the Charismatic Leader: Leadership and Organizational Change. *California Management Review*, 32(2), 77–97.

Nadler, L. (1970) *Developing Human Resources*. Houston, TX: Gulf Publishing Co.

Nagy, G., Trautwein, U. and Ludtwe, O. (2010) The Structure of Vocational Interests in Germany: Different Methodologies, Different Conclusions. *Journal of Vocational Behavior*, 76(2), 153–169.

Nair, P.K., Ke, J., Al-Emadi, M.A.S., Conser, J., Cornachione, E. and Devassy, S.M. (2007) *National Human Resource Development: A Multi-level Perspective*. Paper presented at the Annual Conference of the Academy of Human Resource Development, Bowling Green, Ohio.

Nam Cam Trau, R. and Hartel, C.E.J. (2004) One Career, Two Identities: An Assessment of Gay Men's Career Trajectory. *Career Development International*, 9(7), 627–637.

Nanus, B. (1992) *Visionary Leadership*. San Francisco, CA: Jossey-Bass.

Nathan, R. and Hill, L. (2006) *Career Counselling*, 2nd edn. London: Sage.

National Skills Task Force (2000) *Third Report of the National Skills Taskforce: Tackling the Adult Skills Gap: Upskilling Adults and the Role of Workplace Learning*. London: DfEE.

Neely, A., Gregory, M. and Platts, K. (1995) Performance Measurement System Design: A Literature Review and Research Agenda. *International Journal of Operations and Production Management*, 15(4), 80–116.

Nelson, R.R. and Winter, S.G. (1982) *An Evolutionary Theory of Economic Change*. Cambridge, MA: Harvard University Press.

Newall, A., Shaw, J.C. and Simon, H.A. (1979) The Processes of Creative Thinking. In H.A. Simon (ed.), *Models of Thought*. New Haven, CT: Yale University Press.

Newby, T. (1992) *Training Evaluation Handbook*. Aldershot: Gower.

Nickerson, R.S. (1999) Enhancing Creativity. In R.J. Sternberg (ed.), *Handbook of Creativity*. Cambridge: Cambridge University Press.

Nijman, D.J., Nijhof, W.J, Wognum, A.A.M. and Veldkamp, B.P. (2006) Exploring Differential Effects of Supervisor Support on Transfer of Training. *Journal of European Industrial Training*, 30(7), 529–549.

Nilsson, S. and Ellstrom, P.E. (2012) Employability and Talent Management: Challenges for HRD Practices. *European Journal of Training and Development*, 36(1), 26–45.

Nitsch, K.E. (1977) *Structuring Decontextualised forms of Knowledge*. Unpublished doctoral dissertation, Vanderbilt University, Nashville, Texas.

Noble, C. (1997) International Comparisons of Training Policies. *Human Resource Management Journal*, 7(1), 5–18.

Nonaka, I. (1991) The Knowledge-creating Company. *Harvard Business Review*, 69(6), 96–104.

Nonaka, I. and Konno, N. (1998) The Concept of the 'Ba': Building a Foundation for Knowledge Creation. *California Management Review*, 40(3), 40–54.

Nonaka, I. and Takeuchi, H. (1995) *The Knowledge-creating Company: How Japanese Companies Create the Dynamics of Innovation*. New York: Oxford University Press.

Nonaka, I., Toyama, R. and Nagata, A. (2000) A Firm as a Knowledge-creating Entity: A New Perspective on the Theory of the Firm. *Industrial and Corporate Change*, 9(1), 1–20.

Northouse, P.G. (2010): *Leadership: Theory and Practice*, Thousand Oaks, CA: Sage.

Nyhan, B. (2002) *Human Resource Development in Europe – at the Crossroads*. Paper presented at Third Annual UFHRD Conference of HRD Theory and Practice Across Europe, Napier University, Edinburgh.

Oakes, D.W., Ferris, G.R., Martocchio, J.J., Buckley, M.R. and Broach, D (2001) Cognitive Ability and Personality Predictors of Training Program Skill Acquisition and Job Performance. *Journal of Business and Psychology*, 15(4), 523–548.

O'Connell, G. (2008) Crystal Clear. *People Management*, 14(5), 40–41.

O'Donnell, D., McGuire, D. and Cross, C. (2006) Critically Challenging Some Assumptions in HRD. *International Journal of Training and Development*, 10(1), 4–16.

O'Donnell, D., Porter, G., McGuire, D., Garavan, T.N., Heffernan, M. and Cleary, P. (2003) Creating Intellectual Capital: A Habermasian Community of Practice (CoP) Introduction. *Journal of European Industrial Training*, 27(2/3/4), 80–87.

OECD (2013) *Education at a Glance 2013*. Paris: OECD.

Office for National Statistics (2008) *Annual Survey of Hours and Earnings*. London: Office for National Statistics.

Office for National Statistics (2009) *Labour Market Statistics*. London: Office for National Statistics.

Oldham, G.R. and Cummings, A. (1996) Employee Creativity: Personal and Contextual Factors at Work. *Academy of Management Journal*, 39(3), 607–634.

Olivares, O.J., Peterson, G. and Hess, K.P. (2007) An Existential-phenomenological Framework for Understanding Leadership Development Experiences. *Leadership and Organizational Development Journal*, 28(1), 76–91.

Olve, N., Roy, J. and Wetter, M. (1999) *Performance Drivers: A Practical Guide to Using the Balanced Scorecard*. Chichester: Wiley.

Oncica-Sanislav, D. and Candea, D. (2010) The Learning Organization: A Strategic Dimension of the Sustainable Enterprise. *Proceedings of the European Conference on Management, Leadership and Governance*, 263–270.

O'Neil, D.A. and Bilimoria, D. (2005) Women's Career Development Phases: Idealism, Endurance and Reinvention. *Career Development International*, 10(3), 168–189.

Ormond, J.E. (1999) *Human Learning*. Upper Saddle River, NJ: Prentice Hall.

Othman, R. (2006) Balanced Scorecard and Causal Model Development: Preliminary Findings. *Management Decision*, 44(5), 690–702.

Othman, R. (2008) Enhancing the Effectiveness of the Balanced Scorecard with Scenario Planning. *International Journal of Productivity and Performance Management*, 57(3), 259–266.

Owen, G. (2004) Mind the Gap: The Critical Role of Continuing Professional Development. *Development and Learning in Organisations*, 18(3), 7–9.

Owen, H. (1999) *The Spirit of Leadership: Liberating the Leader in Each of Us*. San Francisco, CA: Berrett-Koehler.

Palmer, J. and Smith, P. (1999) Turning to Learning. *Canadian Underwriter*, (August), 62.

Pangarkar, A.M. and Kirkwood, T. (2008) Strategic Alignment: Linking your Learning Strategy to the Balanced Scorecard. *Industrial and Commercial Training*, 40(2), 95–101.

Paprock, K.E. (2006) National Human Resource Development in Transitioning Societies in the Developing World: Introductory Overview. *Advances in Developing Human Resources*, 8(1), 12–27.

Parker, S.K. and Axtell, C.M. (2001) Seeing Another Viewpoint: Antecedents and Outcomes of Employee Perspective Taking. *Academy of Management Journal*, 44(6), 1085–1102.

Parker-Gore, S. (1996) Perception is Reality: Using 360-degree Appraisal against Behavioural Competences to Effect Organizational Change and Improve Management Performance. *Career Development International*, 1(3), 24–27.

Passmore, J. and Velez, M. (2012) SOAP-M: A Training Evaluation Model for HR. *Industrial and Commercial Training*, 44(5), 315–325.

Patel, N.V. (2003) A Holistic Approach to Learning and Teaching Interaction: Factors in the Development of Critical Learners. *International Journal of Educational Management*, 17(6), 272–284.

Patriotta, G. (2003) On Studying Organizational Knowledge. *Knowledge Management Research and Practice*, 2, 3–12.

Pearce, C.L. and Conger, J.A. (2003) All Those Years Ago: The Historical Underpinnings of Shared Leadership. In C.L. Pearce and J.A. Conger (eds), *Shared Leadership: Reframing the Hows and Whys of Leadership*. Thousand Oaks, CA: Sage.

Pedler, M., Burgoyne, J. and Boydell, T. (1997) *The Learning Organisation: A Strategy for Sustainable Development*, 2nd edn. Maidenhead: McGraw-Hill.

Pendry, L.F., Driscoll, D.M. and Field, S.C.T. (2007) Diversity Training: Putting Theory into Practice. *Journal of Occupational and Organizational Psychology*, 80(1), 27–50.

Pepsi Climate Change (2013) Solar Solutions. http://www.pepsico.com/Purpose/Environmental-Sustainability/Climate-Change.html

Perry, E.L. and Kulik, C.T. (2008) The Devolution of HR to the Line: Implications for Perceptions of People Management Effectiveness. *International Journal of Human Resource Management*, 19(2), 262–273.

Perry-Smith, J.E. (2006) Social Yet Creative: The Role of Social Relationships in Facilitating Individual Creativity. *Academy of Management Journal*, 49(1), 85–101.

Pershing, J.A. and Pershing, J.L. (2001) Ineffective Reaction Evaluation. *Human Resource Development Quarterly*, 12(1), 73–90.

Perunovic, Z., Christoffersen, M. and Mefford, R.N. (2012) Deployment of Vendor Capabilities and Competences throughout the Outsourcing Process. *International Journal of Operations and Production Management*, 32(3), 351–374.

Peterson, L.A. (1997) International HRD: What We Know and Don't Know. *Human Resource Development Quarterly*, 8(1), 63–79.

Peterson, S.L. (2008) Creating and Sustaining a Strategic Partnership: A Model for Human Resource Development. *Journal of Leadership Studies*, 2(2), 83–97.

Pettigrew, A.M. (1979) On Studying Organisational Culture. *Administrative Science Quarterly*, 24, 570–581.

Phillips, J. (1991) *Handbook of Training and Evaluation and Measurement Methods*, 2nd edn. Houston, TX: Gulf Publishing Co.

Phillips, P.P. and Phillips, J.J. (2010) *The Green Scorecard: Measuring the Return on Investment in Sustainability Initiatives*. Boston, MA: Nicholas Beasley Publishing.

Phillips, T. (2009) *Stephen Lawrence Speech: Institutions Must Catch Up with Public on Race Issues*. Delivered on the 10th anniversary of the Stephen Lawrence Inquiry, 19 January.

Piaget, J. (1952) *The Origins of Intelligence in Children*. New York: International University Press.

Piaget, J. (1970) *Structuralism*. New York: Basic Books.

Pickett-Baker, J. and Ozaki, R. (2008) Pro-environmental Products: Marketing Influence on Consumer Purchase Decision. *Journal of Consumer Marketing*, 25(5), 281–293.

Pierce, J.L. and Newstrom, J.W. (2008) *Leaders and the Leadership Process: Readings, Self-assessments and Applications*. Boston, MA: McGraw-Hill.

Platman, K. (2003) The Self-designed Career in Later Life: A Study of Older Portfolio Workers in the United Kingdom. *Ageing and Society*, 23(3), 281–302.

Ployhart, R.E., Lim, B.C. and Chan, K.Y. (2001) Exploring Relations between Typical and Maximum Performance Ratings and the Five Factor Model of Personality. *Personnel Psychology*, 54(4), 809–843.

Poell, R.F. and Van der Krogt, F.J. (2003) Learning-program Creation in Work Organisations. *Human Resource Development Review*, 2(3), 252–272.

Pondy, L.R., Frost, P.J., Morgan, G. and Dandridge, T.C. (1983) *Organisational Symbolism*. Greenwich, CT: JAI Press.

Porter, M.E. (1990) *The Competitive Advantage of Nations*. London: Macmillan.

Posner, B.Z. and Kouzes, J.M. (1988) Relating Leadership and Credibility. *Psychological Reports*, 63, 527–530.

Post, H.A. (1997) Building a Strategy on Competences. *Long Range Planning*, 30(5), 733–740.

Power, W.T. (1973) *Behavior, the Control of Perception*. Chicago: Aldine.

Preskill, H. (2007) *Building an Organization's Evaluation System: A Case Example of using Appreciative Inquiry*. Paper presented at the Academy of Human Resource Development Conference, Indianapolis, IN, 28 February–4 March.

Preskill, H. and Russ-Eft, D. (2005) *Building Evaluation Capacity: 72 Activities for Teaching and Training*. Thousand Oaks, CA: Sage.

Preskill, H. and Torres, R.T. (1999) *Evaluative Inquiry for Learning in Organizations*. Thousand Oaks, CA: Sage.

Purdy, M. (1997) Humanist Ideology and Nurse Education. 2. Limitations of Humanist Education Theory in Nurse Education. *Nurse Education Today*, 17, 196–202.

Rainbird, H. (1995) The Changing Role of the Training Function: A Test for Integration of Human Resources and Business Strategy. *Human Resource Management Journal*, 5(1), 72–90.

Rajan, A. and Martin, B. (2001) *Harnessing Creativity to Improve the Bottom Line*. London: CIMA Publishing.

Ralston, D., Wright, A. and Kumar, J. (2001) Process Benchmarking as a Market Research Tool for Strategic Planning. *Market Intelligence and Planning*, 19(4), 273–281.

Rappe, C. and Zwink, T. (2007) Developing Leadership Competence of Production Unit Managers. *Journal of Management Development*, 26(4), 312–330.

Reber, A.S. (1993) *Implicit Learning and Tacit Knowledge: An Essay on the Cognitive Unconscious*. Oxford: Oxford University Press.

Reilly, P. and Williams, T. (2006) *Strategic HR: Building the Capability to Deliver*. London: Gower.

Renwick, D., Redman, T. and Maguire, S. (2008) *Green HRM: A Review, Process Model and Research Agenda*. Discussion Paper. 2008,01, University of Sheffield Business School.

Reynolds, M. (1998) Reflection and Critical Reflection in Management Learning. *Management Learning*, 29(2), 183–200.

Reynolds, M. (1999) Critical Reflection and Management Education: Rehabilitating Less Hierarchical Approaches. *Journal of Management Education*, 23(5), 537–553.

Reynolds, M. and Trehan, K. (2003) Learning from Difference. *Management Learning*, 34(2), 163–180.

Riege, A. (2005) Three-dozen Knowledge Sharing Barriers Managers Must Consider. *Journal of Knowledge Management*, 9(3), 18–35.

Rimanoczy, I. and Pearson, T. (2010) Role of HR in the New World of Sustainability. *Industrial and Commercial Training*, 42(1), 11–17.

Robbins, S.P., Bergman, R. and Stagg, I. (1997) *Management*. Sydney: Prentice Hall.

Robinson, A. and Stern, S. (1997) *Corporate Creativity: How Innovation and Improvement Actually Happen*. San Francisco, CA: Berrett-Koehler.

Robotham, D. (2003) Learning and Training: Developing the Competent Learner. *Journal of European Industrial Training*, 27(9), 473–480.

Rock, A. and Garavan, T. (2006) Reconceptualising Developmental Relationships. *Human Resource Development Review*, 5(3), 330–355.

Rodgers, W.M. III (2006) Male White–Black Wage Gaps, 1979–1994: A Distributional Analysis. *Southern Economic Journal*, 72(4), 773–786.

Roffe, I. (1999) Innovation and Creativity in Organisations: A Review of the Implications for Training and Development. *Journal of European Industrial Training*, 23(4/5), 224–241.

Rogers, J. (2008) *Coaching Skills: A Handbook*. New York: McGraw-Hill International.

Rojek, C. (2003) *Stuart Hall*. Cambridge: Polity Press.

Romme, A.G.L. and Van Witteloostuijn, A. (1999) Circular Organizing and Triple Loop Learning. *Journal of Organisational Change Management*, 12(5), 439–453.

Rosinski, P. (2004) *Coaching across Cultures*. London: Nicholas Brealey.

Ross, D.J. (2007) Mentoring. http://login.learningthroughwork.org/ufiresources/mentoring/intro/p1.html

Rothwell, W. (2002) Putting Success into Your Succession Planning. *Journal of Business Strategy*, 23(3), 32–42.

Rounds, J. and Tracey, T.J. (1996) Cross-cultural Structural Equivalence of RIASEC Models and Measures. *Journal of Counseling Psychology*, 43(3), 310–329.

Rugman, A. (2005) *The Regional Multinationals: MNEs and Global Strategic Management*. Cambridge: Cambridge University Press.

Rummler, G. and Brache, A. (1995) *Improving Performance,* San Francisco, CA: Jossey-Bass.

Ruona, W.E.A. (2000) Core Beliefs in Human Resource Development: A Journey for its Profession and its Professionals. *Advances in Developing Human Resources*, 2(3), 1–27.

Ruona, W.E.A. (2001a) The Foundational Impact of Training Within Industry Project on the Human Resource Development Profession. *Advances in Developing Human Resources*, 3(2), 119–126.

Ruona, W.E.A. (2001b) Systems Theory as a Foundation for HRD. In R.A. Swanson and E.F. Holton (eds), *Foundations of Human Resource Development*. San Francisco, CA: Berrett-Koehler.

Ruona, W.E.A., Lynham, S.A. and Chermack, T.J. (2003) Insights on Emerging Trends and the Future of Human Resource Development. *Advances in Developing Human Resources*, 5(3), 272–282.

Rusaw, A.C. (2000) Uncovering Training Resistance: A Critical Theory Perspective. *Journal of Organizational Change Management*, 13(3), 40–51.

Russ-Eft, D.F. (2009) Human Resource Development (HRD) Evaluation and Principles Related to the Public Interest. *American Journal of Evaluation*, 30(2), 225–231.

Russ-Eft, D. and Hatcher, T. (2003) The Issue of International Values and Beliefs: The Debate for a Global HRD Code of Ethics. *Advances in Developing Human Resources*, 5(3), 296–307.

Russ-Eft, D. and Preskill, H. (2001) *Evaluation in Organisations: A Systematic Approach to Enhancing Learning, Performance and Change*. New York: Perseus.

Russ-Eft, D. and Preskill, H. (2005) In Search of the Holy Grail: Return on Investment Evaluation in Human Resource Development. *Advances in Developing Human Resources*, 7(1), 71–85.

Russell, C. and Parsons, E. (1996) Putting Theory to the Test at the OU. *People Management*, 2(1), 30–32.

Russell, D., Calvey, D. and Banks, M. (2003) Creating New Learning Communities: Towards Effective E-learning Production. *Journal of Workplace Learning*, 15(1), 34–45.

Ryan, M.K. and Haslam, S. A. (2004) Introducing the Glass Cliff. http://news.bbc.co.uk/1/hi/magazine/3755031.stm

Ryan, M.K. and Haslam, S.A. (2007) The Glass Cliff: Exploring the Dynamics Surrounding the Appointment of Women to Precarious Leadership Positions. *Academy of Management Review*, 32(2), 549–572.

Sacks, H., Schegloff, E.A. and Jefferson, G. (1974) A Simplest Systematics for the Organisation of Turn-taking for Conversation. *Language*, 50(4), 696–735.

Sadler-Smith, E. (2006) *Learning and Development for Managers: Perspectives from Research and Practice*. Malden, MA: Blackwell.

Sadler-Smith, E. (2013) *Making Sense of Global Warming: Designing a Human Resource Development Response?* Paper presented at the 14th UFHRD Conference on HRD Theory and Practice Across Europe, Brighton Business School, 5–7 June.

Sadler-Smith, E., Allinson, C.W. and Hayes, J. (2000) Learning Preferences and Cognitive Style: Some Implications for Continuing Professional Development. *Management Learning*, 31(2), 239–256.

Salaman, G. and Butler, J. (1994) Why Managers Won't Learn. In C. Mabey and P. Iles (eds), *Managing Learning*. London: Routledge.

Sambrook, S. (2004) A Critical Time for HRD? *Journal of European Industrial Training*, 28(8/9), 611–624.

Sambrook, S. (2008) People, Organisations and Development: Is HRD Being Stretched? *Human Resource Development International*, 11(3), 219–223.

Sambrook, S. and Stewart, J. (2000) Factors Influencing Learning in European Learning Oriented Organisations: Issues for Management. *Journal of European Industrial Training*, 24(2/3/4), 209–219.

Sambrook, S. and Stewart, J. (2002) Reflections and Discussion. In S. Trepkema, J. Stewart, S. Sambrook, M. Mulder, H. ter Horst and J. Scheerens (eds), *HRD and Learning Organisations*. London: Routledge.

Sambrook, S. and Stewart, J. (2005) A Critical Review of Researching Human Resource Development. In C. Elliott and S. Turnbull (eds), *Critical Thinking in Human Resource Development*. London: Routledge.

Sanborn, H. and Sheehan, B. (2009) *Evaluating End-of-Life Beverage Container Management Systems for California*. Sacramento, CA: California Conservation Division of Recycling.

Sanchez, J.I. and Medkik, N. (2004) The Effects of Diversity Awareness Training on Differential Treatment. *Group and Organization Management*, 29, 517–536.

Sandhawalia, B.S. and Dalcher, D. (2011) Developing Knowledge Management Capabilities: A Structured Approach. *Journal of Knowledge Management*, 15(2), 313–328.

Santos, A. and Stuart, M. (2003) Employee Perceptions and their Influence on Training Effectiveness. *Human Resource Management Journal*, 13(1), 27–45.

Sarros, J.C. and Santora, J.C. (2001) The Transformational-Transactional Leadership Model in Practice. *Leadership and Organization Development Journal*, 22(8), 383–394.

Saunders, M.N.K., Skinner, D. and Beresford, R. (2005) Mismatched Perceptions and Expectations: An Exploration of Stakeholders' Views of Key and Technical Skills in Vocational Education and Training. *Industrial and Commercial Training*, 29(5), 369–382.

Schein, E.H. (1996) Career Anchors Revisited: Implications for Career Development in the 21st Century. *Academy of Management Executive*, 10(4), 80–88.

Schein, E.H. (2010) *Organisational Culture and Leadership*, 4th edn. San Francisco, CA: Jossey-Bass.

Schein, E. (2013) Career Anchors. http://www.careeranchorsonline.com

Schmidt, C.K. and Nilsson, J.E. (2006) The Effects of Simultaneous Developmental Processes: Factors Relating to the Career Development of Lesbian, Gay and Bisexual Youth. *Career Development Quarterly*, 55(1), 22–37.

Schmidt, F.L. and Hunter, J.E. (1992) Development of a Causal Model of Processes Determining Job Performance. *Current Directions in Psychological Science*, 1, 89–92.

Schon, D.A. (1983) *The Reflective Practitioner*. New York: Basic Books.

Schulz, K.P. (2005) Learning in Complex Organisations as Practicing and Reflecting: A Model Development and Application from a Theory of Practice Perspective. *Journal of Workplace Learning*, 17(8), 493–507.

Schwartz Driver, S. (2010) *Economic Literacy: A Complete Guide*. London: Marshall Cavendish.

Scott, S.G. and Bruce, R.A. (1994) Determinants of Innovative Behaviour: A Path Model of Individual Innovation in the Workplace. *Academy of Management Journal*, 37(3), 580–607.

Selvarajah, C. (2006) Dimensions that Relate to Cross-cultural Counselling: Perceptions of Mental Health Professionals in Auckland, New Zealand. *Cross Cultural Management*, 13(1), 54–68.

Semler, S.W. (1997) Systematic Agreement: A Theory of Organisational Alignment. *Human Resource Development Quarterly*, 8(1), 23–40.

Senge, P. (1990) *The Fifth Discipline: The Act and Practice of the Learning Organisation*. New York: Random House.

Seufert, A., Von Krogh, G. and Bach, A. (1999) Towards Knowledge Networking. *Journal of Knowledge Management*, 3(3), 180–190.

Shalley, C.E. and Gilson, L.L. (2004) What Leaders Need to Know: A Review of Social and Contextual Factors that can Foster or Hinder Creativity. *The Leadership Quarterly*, 15(1), 33–53.

Shalley, C.E., Gilson, L.L. and Blum, T.C. (2000) Matching Creativity Requirements and the Work Environment: Effects on Satisfaction and Intentions to Leave. *Academy of Management Journal*, 43(2), 215–223.

Shalley, C.E., Zhou, J. and Oldham, G.R. (2004) The Effects of Personal and Contextual Characteristics on Creativity: Where Should We Go from Here? *Journal of Management*, 30(6), 933–958.

Sheppard, E. (2002) The Spaces and Times of Globalisation: Place, Scale, Networks and Positionality. *Economic Geography*, 78(3), 307–331.

Shore, L.M. and Wayne, S.J. (1993) Commitment and Employee Behaviour: Comparison of Affective Commitment and Continuance Commitment with Perceived Organizational Support. *Journal of Applied Psychology*, 78(5), 774–780.

Short, D.C., Bing, J.W. and Kehrhahn, M.T. (2003) Will Human Resource Development Survive? *Human Resource Development Quarterly*, 14(3), 239–244.

Shuell, T.J. (1990) Phases of Meaningful Learning. *Review of Educational Research*, 60(4), 531–547.

Silber, K.H. (2002) Using the Cognitive Approach to Improve Problem-solving Training. *Performance Improvement*, 41(3), 28–36.

Simmonds, D. and Pedersen, C. (2006) HRD: The Shape and Things to Come. *Journal of Workplace Learning*, 18(2), 122–135.

Sippola, A. (2007) Developing Culturally Diverse Organisations: A Participative and Empowerment-based Method. *Women in Management Review*, 22(4), 253–273.

Sirotnik, K.A. (1983) What You See is What you Get: Consistency, Persistency and Mediocrity in Classrooms. *Harvard Educational Review*, 53, 16–31.

Skinner, B.F. (1953) *Science and Human Behaviour*. New York: Macmillan.

Slotte, V., Tynjala, P. and Hytonen, T. (2004) How do HRD Practitioners Describe Learning at Work? *Human Resource Development International*, 7(4), 541–544.

Smith, E.A. (2001) The Role of Tacit and Explicit Knowledge in the Workplace. *Journal of Knowledge Management*, 5(4), 311–321.

Smith, I.W. (2004) Continuing Professional Development and Workplace Learning 9: Human Resource Development – Measuring Return on Investment. *Library Management*, 25(6/7), 318–320.

Smith, I. (2005) *Different in Similar Ways: Making Sense of Learning Styles*. Paisley: Learning Unlimited.

Smith, P.J. (2000) Flexible Delivery and Apprentice Training: Preferences, Problems and Challenges, *Journal of Vocational Education and Training*, 52(3), 483–502.

Smith, R. (1988) *Human Resource Development: An Overview*. Washington, DC: Office of Educational Research and Improvement.

Sodano, S.M. (2011) Integrating Vocational Interests, Competencies, and Interpersonal Dispositions in Middle School Children. *Journal of Vocational Behaviour*, 79(1), 110–120.

Sommerlund, J. and Boutaiba, S. (2007) Borders of 'The Boundaryless Career'. *Journal of Organizational Change Management*, 20(4), 525–538.

Sosik, J. and Megerian, L. (1999) Understanding Leader Emotional Intelligence and Performance: The Role of Self–Other Agreement on Transformational Leadership Perceptions. *Group and Organization Management*, 24(3), 367–390.

Souder, W. (1983) Planning a Career Path from Engineering to Management. *Engineering Management International*, 1(4), 249–258.

Sparrow, P. (2000) Strategic Management in a World Turned Upside Down: The Role of Cognition, Intuition and Emotional Intelligence. In P.C. Flood, T. Dromgoole, S.J. Carroll and L. Gorman (eds), *Managing Strategy Implementation*. Oxford: Blackwell.

Spender, J.C. (1996a) Making Knowledge the Basis of a Dynamic Theory of the Firm. *Strategic Management Journal*, 17(1), 45–62.

Spender, J.C. (1996b) Organisational Knowledge, Learning and Memory: Three Concepts in Search of a Theory. *Journal of Organisational Change Management*, 9(1), 63–78.

Stead, V. and Lee, M. (1996) Inter-cultural Perspectives on HRD. In J. Stewart and J. McGoldrick (eds), *HRD Perspectives, Strategies and Practices*. London: Pitman.

Stedham, Y. and Engle, A. (1999) *Multinational and Transnational Strategies: Implications for Human Resource Management*. Paper presented at the Eighth Biennial Research Symposium of the Human Resource Planning Society, Ithaca, NY, June.

Stein, D.S. (2000) *Teaching Critical Reflection: Myths and Realities No. 7*. Columbus, OH: Eric Clearinghouse on Vocational Education and Training.

Stein, D.S. (2001) Situated Learning and Planned Training on the Job. *Advances in Developing Human Resources*, 3(4), 415–425.

Stern, L.R. (2008) *Executive Coaching: Building and Managing Your Professional Practice*. London: Wiley.

Sternberg, R.J. (1997) *Successful Intelligence*. New York: Penguin.

Sternberg, R.J. and Lubart, T.I. (1999) The Concept of Creativity: Prospects and Paradigms. In R.J. Sternberg (ed.), *Handbook of Creativity*. Cambridge: Cambridge University Press.

Stewart, J. (1999) *Employee Development Practice*. London: Financial Times Management.

Stewart, J. (2002) Individual Learning. In J. Leopold (ed.), *Human Resources in Organisations*. Upper Saddle River, NJ: Prentice Hall.

Stewart, J. (2007) The Future of HRD Research: Strengths, Weaknesses, Opportunities and Threats. *Human Resource Development International*, 10(1), 93–99.

Stewart, J. and McGoldrick, J. (1996) *Human Resource Development: Perspectives, Strategies and Practice*. London: Pitman.

Stewart, J. and Rigg, C. (2011) *Learning and Talent Development*. London: CIPD.

Stewart, M.M., Crary, M. and Humberd, B.K. (2008) Teaching Value in Diversity: On the Folly of Espousing Inclusion, while Practicing Exclusion. *Academy of Management Learning and Education*, 7(3), 374–386.

Stogdill, R.M. (1948) Personal Factors Associated with Leadership: A Survey of the Literature. *Journal of Psychology*, 25, 35–71.

Stogdill, R.M. (1974) *Handbook of Leadership: A Survey of the Literature*, 2nd edn. New York: Free Press.

Stoll, L., Bolam, R., McMahon, A., Wallace, M. and Thomas, S. (2006) Professional Learning Communities: A Review of the Literature. *Journal of Educational Change*, 7(4), 221–258.

Streibel, M.J. (1991) Instructional Plans and Situated Learning: The Challenge of Suchman's Theory of Situated Action for Instructional Designers and Instructional Systems. In G. Anglin (ed.), *Instructional Technologies: Past, Present and Future*. Denver, CO: Libraries Unlimited.

Sturges, J., Conway, N., Guest, D. and Liefooghe, A. (2005) Managing the Career Deal: The Psychological Contract as a Framework for Understanding Career Management, Organizational Commitment and Work Behaviour. *Journal of Organisational Behaviour*, 26(7), 821–838.

Sturges, J., Guest, D., Conway, N. and Mackenzie Davey, K. (2002) A Longitudinal Study of the Relationship between Career Management and Organizational Commitment among Graduates in the First Ten Years at Work. *Journal of Organisational Behaviour*, 23(6), 731–748.

Sullivan, S.E. and Baruch, B. (2009) Advances in Career Theory and Research: A Critical Review and Agenda for Future Exploration. *Journal of Management*, 35(6), 1542–1571.

Sullivan, S.E. and Mainiero, L.A. (2007) The Changing Nature of Gender Roles, Alpha/Beta Careers and Work–Life Issues: Theory-driven Implications for Human Resource Management. *Career Development International*, 12(3), 238–263.

Suutari, V. and Taka, M. (2004) Career Anchors of Managers with Global Careers. *Journal of Management Development*, 23(9), 833–847.

Svejenova, S. (2005) 'The Path with the Heart': Creating the Authentic Career. *Journal of Management Studies*, 42(5), 947–974.

Svensson, L., Ellstrom, P.E. and Äberg, C. (2004) Integrating Formal and Informal Learning at Work. *Journal of Workplace Learning*, 16(8), 479–491.

Swan, J., Newell, S., Scarbrough, H. and Hislop, D. (1999) Knowledge Management and Innovation: Networks and Networking. *Journal of Knowledge Management*, 3(4), 262–275.

Swanson, R.A. (1995) Human Resource Development: Performance is the Key. *Human Resource Development Quarterly*, 6(2), 207–213.

Swanson, R.A. (1999) HRD Theory, Real or Imagined? *Human Resource Development International*, 2(1), 6–8.

Swanson, R.A. (2005) Evaluation: A State of Mind. *Advances in Developing Human Resources*, 7(1), 16–22.

Swanson, R.A. and Arnold, D.E. (1997) The Purpose of HRD is to Improve Performance. In R Rowden (ed.), *Workplace Learning: Debating Five Critical Questions of Theory and Practice*. San Francisco, CA: Jossey-Bass.

Swanson, R.A. and Holton, E.F. (2001) *Foundations of Human Resource Development*. San Francisco, CA: Berrett-Koehler.

Swart, J., Mann, C., Brown, S. and Price, A. (2005) *Human Resource Development: Strategy and Tactics*. Oxford: Elsevier Butterworth-Heinemann.

Swieringa, J. and Wierdsma, A. (1992) *Becoming a Learning Organisation*. Wokingham: Addison-Wesley.

Taggar, S. (2002) Individual Creativity and Group Ability to Utilise Individual Creative Resources: A Multi-level Model. *Academy of Management Journal*, 45(2), 315–330.

Tajfel, H. (1982) Instrumentality, Identity, and Social Comparisons. In H. Tajfel (ed.), *Social Identity and Intergroup Relations*. Cambridge: Cambridge University Press.

Takacs, D. (2002) Positionality, Epistemology, and Social Justice in the Classroom. *Social Justice*, 29(4), 168–182.

Tamkin, P., Reilly, P. and Strebler, M. (2006) *Change Agenda: The Changing HR Function – The Key Questions*. London: CIPD.

Tan, H. and Tan, C.S. (2000) Toward the Differentiation of Trust in Supervisor and Trust in Organization. *Genetic, Social, and General Psychology Monographs*, 126(2), 241–260.

Tannenbaum, R. and Schmidt, W.H. (1958) How to Choose a Leadership Pattern. *Harvard Business Review*, 36(2), 95–101.

Templar, A.J. and Cawsey, T.F. (1999) Rethinking Career Development in an Era of Portfolio Careers. *Career Development International*, 4(2), 70–76.

Terry, R.W. (1993) *Authentic Leadership*. San Francisco, CA: Jossey-Bass.

Tesluk, P.E., Farr, J.L. and Klein, S.R. (1997) Influences on Organizational Behavior and Climate on Individual Creativity. *Journal of Creative Behavior*, 31(1), 27–41.

Thagard, P. (1996) *Mind: Introduction to Cognitive Sciences*. Cambridge, MA: MIT Press.

The Living Roof (2013) The Living Roof at Ford Factory Rouge. http://www.thehenryford.org/rouge/leedlivingroof.aspx

Thite, M. (2004) *Managing People in the New Economy*. Thousand Oaks, CA: Sage.

Thomas, D.A. (2001) The Truth about Mentoring Minorities: Race Matters. *Harvard Business Review*, 79(4), 98–107.

Thomas, K.M., Willis, L.A. and Davis, J. (2007) Mentoring Minority Graduate Students: Issues and Strategies for Institutions, Faculties and Students. *Equal Opportunities International*, 26(3), 178–192.

Thompson, D.E. and Thompson, C. (2004) *Students' Perceptions of Human Resource Development Classes Presented by Distance Education*. Paper presented at Fifth European Conference on Human Resource Development Theory and Practice, University of Limerick, Ireland.

Thompson, L. (2003) Improving the Creativity of Organizational Work Groups. *Academy of Management Executive*, 17(1), 96–111.

Thomson, A., Mabey, C., Storey, J., Gray, C. and Iles P. (2001) *Changing Patterns of Management Development*. Oxford: Blackwell.

Thurow, L. (1994) New Game, New Rules, New Strategies. *RSA Journal*, 142(5454; November), 1056.

Tichy, N.M. and Devanna, M.A. (1990) *The Transformational Leader*. New York: Wiley.

Tierney, P. and Farmer, S.M. (2002) Creative Self-efficacy: Potential Antecedents and Relationship to Creative Performance. *Academy of Management Journal*, 45(6), 1137–1148.

Tonge, J. (2008) Barriers to Networking for Women in a UK Professional Service. *Gender in Management: An International Journal*, 23(7), 484–505.

Torraco, R. (2004) Challenges and Choices for Theoretical Research in Human Resource Development. *Human Resource Development Quarterly*, 15(2), 171–188.

Tosey, P., Visser, M. and Saunders, M.N.K. (2011) The Origins and Conceptualizations of 'Triple-loop' Learning: A Critical Review. *Management Learning*, 43(3), 291–307.

Toulouse, E.S.C. (2002) *Call for Papers*. Call for Papers Issued at the Third Annual UFHRD Conference of HRD Theory and Practice Across Europe, Napier University, Edinburgh.

Tracey, T.J. and Rounds, J. (1993) Evaluating Holland's and Gati's Vocational Interest Models: A Structural Meta-analysis. *Psychological Bulletin*, 113, 229–246.

Tregaskis, O. (1998) HRD in Foreign MNEs. *International Studies of Management and Organisation*, 28(1), 136–163.

Trehan, K. (2004) Who is Not Sleeping with Whom? What's Not Being Talked about in HRD? *Journal of European Industrial Training*, 28(1), 23–38.

Tschannen-Moran, B. (2013) Skills and Performance Coaching. In E. Cox, T. Bachkirova and D. Clutterbuck (eds), *The Complete Handbook of Coaching*. London: Sage.

Tung, R.L. (1981) Selection and Training of Personnel for Overseas Assignments. *Columbia Journal of World Business*, 26(4), 68–78.

Ty, R. (2007) *Performance, Learning and Social Justice: Theorising HRD Practices in the International Training Office, Yesterday, Today and Tomorrow*. Paper presented at the Academy of Human Resource Development Conference, Indianapolis, Indiana, 28 February–4 March.

Tziner, A. and Haccoun, R.R. (1991) Personal and Situational Characteristics Influencing the Effectiveness of Transfer of Training Improvement Strategies. *Journal of Occupational Psychology*, 64(2), 167–177.

Ulrich, D. (1998) A New Mandate for Human Resources. *Harvard Business Review*, 76(1): 124–34.

Ulrich, D. (2007) Dreams: Where Human Resource Development is Headed to Deliver Value. *Human Resource Development Quarterly*, 18(1), 1–8.

Unsworth, K. (2001) Unpacking Creativity. *Academy of Management Journal*, 26(2), 289–297.

Utman, C.H. (1997) Performance Effects of Motivation State: A Meta-analysis. *Personality and Social Psychology Review*, 1, 170–182.

Valentin, C. (2006) Researching Human Resource Development: Evidence of a Critical Approach to HRD Enquiry. *International Journal of Training and Development*, 10(1), 17–29.

Valentin, C. (2012) *Greening HRD: Discourses of Sustainability and Corporate Social Responsibility*. Paper presented at the 13th UFHRD Conference on HRD Theory and Practice Across Europe, Portugal, 4–6 June.

Van der Veen, R. (2006) Human Resource Development: Irreversible Trend or Temporary Fad? *Human Resource Development Review*, 5(1), 3–7.

Van Vianen, A.E.M. and Fischer, A.H. (2002) Illuminating the Glass Ceiling: The Role of Organizational Culture Preferences. *Journal of Occupational and Organizational Psychology*, 75(3), 315–337.

Van Woerkom, M. (2004) *The Value of Critically Reflective Work Behaviour*. Paper presented at the Academy of Human Resource Development Conference, Austin, Texas.

Velada, R. and Caetano, A. (2007) Training Transfer: The Mediating Role of Perception of Learning. *Journal of European Industrial Training*, 31(4), 283–296.

Verdonschot, S. and Kwakman, K. (2004) *Borderless Learning Experiences – The Development of Design Guidelines for Collaborative Distance Learning Environments*. Paper presented at Fifth European Conference on Human Resource Development Theory and Practice, University of Limerick, Ireland.

Vermeulen, R.C.M. (2002) Narrowing the Transfer Gap: The Advantages of 'As If' Situations in Training. *Journal of European Industrial Training*, 26(8), 366–374.

Vidal, J. (2009) Lighter, Thinner—Easter Egg Packaging Goes on a Diet. *Guardian*, 9 April. http://www.guardian.co.uk/environment/2009/apr/09/easter-eggs-packagingreduced

Vince, R. (2003) The Future Practice of HRD. *Human Resource Development International*, 6(4), 559–563.

Von Krogh, G. (1988) Care in Knowledge Creation. *California Management Review*, 40(3), 133–153.

Von Krogh, G., Roos, J. and Slocum, K. (1994) An Essay on Corporate Epistemology. *Strategic Management Journal*, 15 (Summer Special Issue), 53–71.

Von Oech, R. (1990) *A Whack on the Side of the Head*. New York: Business Plus Imports.

Vrasidas, C. and Zembylas, M. (2003) The Nature of Technology-mediated Interaction in Globalised Education. *International Journal of Training and Development*, 7(4), 271–286.

Waldersee, R. and Eagleson, G. (2002) Shared Leadership in the Implementation of Re-orientations. *Leadership and Organization Development Journal*, 23(7), 400–407.

Walker, J.W. (2001) Are We Global Yet? In M.H. Albrecht (ed.), *International HRM: Managing Diversity in the Workplace*. Oxford: Blackwell.

Walton, J. (1999) *Strategic Human Resource Development*. London: Financial Times/Prentice Hall.

Walton, J.S. (2003) *All the World's a Stage – HRD as Theatre*. Paper presented at Academy of Human Resource Development Conference Proceedings, Minneapolis, MN, 23–26 February.

Wang, X. and McLean, G.N. (2007) The Dilemma of Defining International Human Resource Development. *Human Resource Development Review*, 6(1), 96–108.

Ward, J. and Winstanley, D. (2005) Coming out at Work: Performativity and the Recognition and Renegotiation of Identity. *Sociological Review*, 53(3), 447–474.

Ward, T.B. (1995) What's Old about New Ideas? In S.M. Smith, T.B. Ward and R.A. Finke (eds), *The Creative Cognition Approach*. Cambridge, MA: MIT Press.

Warr, P., Bird, M. and Rackham, N. (1976) *Evaluation of Management Training*. London: Gower Press.

Watkins, K. (1989) Five Metaphors: Alternative Theories for Human Resource Development. In D.B. Gradeous (ed.), *Systems Theory Applied to Human Resource Development*. Alexandria, VA: ASTD.

Watkins, K. and Marsick, V. (1994) *Sculpting the Learning Organisation: Lessons in the Art and Science of Systematic Change*. San Francisco, CA: Jossey-Bass.

Watkins, K.E. and Marsick, V.J. (1997) Building the Learning Organisation: A New Role for Human Resource Developers. In D. Russ-Eft, H. Preskill and C. Sleezer (eds), *HRD Review, Research and Implications*. Thousand Oaks, CA: Sage.

Watson, E. (2007) Who or What Creates? A Conceptual Framework for Social Creativity. *Human Resource Development Review*, 6, 419–441.

Watts, A. (2010) *The Relationship between Professional Learning Communities and School Based Change*. PhD dissertation submitted to the Graduate School of Education and Human Development of the George Washington University.

Wayne, S.J., Shore, L.M. and Liden, R.C. (1997) Perceived Organisational Support and Leader Member Exchange: A Social Exchange Perspective. *Academy of Management Journal*, 40(1), 82–111.

WCED (1987) *Our Common Future. World Commission on Environment and. Development*. New York: Oxford University Press.

Weeks, K., Weeks, M. and Frost, L. (2007) The Role of Race and Social Class in Compensation Decisions. *Journal of Managerial Psychology*, 22(7), 701–718.

Weick, K.E. (1995) *Sensemaking in Organisations*. Thousand Oaks, CA: Sage.

Weick, K.E. (1996) Enactment and the Boundaryless Career: Organizing as We Work. In M.B. Arthur and D. Rousseau (eds), *The Boundaryless Career*. New York: Oxford University Press.

Weick, K.E. and Westley, F. (1996) Organisational Learning: Affirming an Oxymoron. In S.R. Clegg, C. Hardy and W.R. Nord (eds), *Handbook of Organisation Studies*. London: Sage.

Weinberger, L. (1998) Commonly Held Theories of Human Resource Development. *Human Resource Development International*, 1(1), 75–93.

Weiss, C.H. (1987) *Evaluating Action Programs*. New York: Sage.

Weiss, J.W. (1996) *Organisation Behaviour and Change: Managing Diversity, Cross Cultural Dynamics and Ethics*. New York: West.

Wenger, E.C. and Snyder, W.M. (2000) Communities of Practice: The Organisational Frontier. *Harvard Business Review*, 78(1), 139–145.

Wever, R., Boks, C., Marinelli, T. and Stevels, A. (2007) Increasing the Benefits of Product-level Benchmarking for Strategic Eco-efficient Decision-making. *Benchmarking: An International Journal*, 14(6), 711–727.

Wexley, K.N. and Latham, G.P. (1991) *Developing and Training Human Resources in Organisations*. New York: Harper & Row.

Wexley, K. and Latham, L. (2002) *Developing and Training Human Resources in Organisations*, 2nd edn. London: Pearson.

Wexley, K.N. and Nemeroff, W. (1975) Effectiveness of Positive Reinforcement and Goal Setting as Methods of Management Development. *Journal of Applied Psychology*, 64, 239–246.

Wilcox, T. (2006) Human Resource Development as an Element of Corporate Social Responsibility. *Asia Pacific Journal of Human Resources*, 44(2), 184–198.

Wilensky, H.L. (1964) The Professionalization of Everyone? *American Journal of Sociology*, 137–158.

Wilkesmann, U., Fischer, H. and Wilkesmann, M. (2009) Cultural Characteristics of Knowledge Transfer. *Journal of Knowledge Management*, 13(6), 464–477.

Williams, C.L. (1992) The Glass Escalator: Hidden Advantages for Men in the 'Female' Professions. *Social Problems*, 39(3), 253–267.

Willis, V.J. (1997) *HRD as Evolutionary System: From Pyramid-building to Space-walking and Beyond*. Paper presented at Proceedings of the Academy of Human Resource Development Conference, Atlanta, 20–22 February.

Wilson, C. (2012) Retaining Good People through a Focus on Talent and Purpose: Proper Inductions make Employees Feel as Though They Truly Belong. *Human Resource Management International Digest*, 20(2), 29–31.

Wilson, J.P. and Beard, C. (2002) *Experiential Learning: Linking Theory and Practice*. Paper presented at the Third Conference on Human Resource Development: Research and Practice across Europe: Creativity and Innovation in Learning, Edinburgh, 25–26 January.

Wilson, J.P. and Beard, C. (2003) The Learning Combination Lock: An Experiential Approach to Learning Design. *Journal of European Industrial Training*, 27(2/3/4), 87–97.

Wiltsher, C. (2005) Fundamentals of Adult Learning. In J.P. Wilson (ed.), *Human Resource Development: Learning and Training for Individuals and Groups*. London: Kogan Page.

Winterton, J. (2004) A Conceptual Model of Labour Turnover and Retention. *Human Resource Development International*, 7(4), 371–390.

Woodall, J. (2003) The Common Underlying Assumptions of HRD? *Human Resource Development International*, 6(3), 281–283.

Woodall, J. (2005) Theoretical Frameworks for Comparing HRD in an International Context. *Human Resource Development International*, 8(4), 399–402.

Woodall, J., Alker, A., McNeil, C. and Shaw, S. (2002) Convergence and Divergence in HRD: Research and Practice across Europe. In J. McGoldrick, J. Stewart and S. Watson (eds), *Understanding Human Resource Development: A Research-based Approach*. London: Routledge.

Woolcock, M. (1998) Social Capital and Economic Development: Toward a Theoretical Synthesis and Policy Framework. *Theory and Society*, 27(2), 151–208.

Wright, P.C. and Belcourt, M. (1995) Costing Training Activity: A Decision-Maker's Dilemma. *Management Decision*, 33(2), 5–15.

Yang, B. (2003) Towards a Holistic Theory of Knowledge and Adult Learning. *Human Resource Development Review*, 2(2), 106–129.

Yasin, M.M. (2002) The Theory and Practice of Benchmarking: Then and Now. *Benchmarking: An International Journal*, 9(3), 217–243.

Yeo, R. (2002) From Individual to Team Learning: Practical Perspectives on the Learning Organisation. *Team Performance Management*, 8(7/8), 157–170.

Zaccaro, S.J. and Klimoski, R.J. (2001) *The Nature of Organizational Leadership: Understanding the Performance Imperatives Confronting Today's Leaders*. San Francisco, CA: Jossey-Bass.

Zboralski, K. (2009) Antecedents of Knowledge Sharing in Communities of Practice. *Journal of Knowledge Management*, 13(3), 90–101.

Zhou, J. (2003) When the Presence of Creative Co-workers is Related to Creativity: Role of Supervisor Close Monitoring, Developmental Feedback and Creative Personality. *Journal of Applied Psychology*, 88(3), 413–422.

Zuriff, G.E. (1985) *Behaviourism: A Conceptual Reconstruction*. New York: Columbia University Press.

Index

N.B. Page numbers in italic indicate figures; numbers in bold indicate tables.